Male and Female Homosexuality

THE SERIES IN CLINICAL AND COMMUNITY PSYCHOLOGY

Male and Female Homosexuality

Psychological Approaches

Edited by
Louis Diamant
University of North Carolina at Charlotte

HEMISPHERE PUBLISHING CORPORATION, Washington
A subsidiary of Harper & Row, Publishers, Inc.

Cambridge   New York   Philadelphia   San Francisco
London   Mexico City   São Paulo   Singapore   Sydney

MALE AND FEMALE HOMOSEXUALITY: Psychological Approaches

1 2 3 4 5 6 7 8 9 0   B C B C   8 9 8 7

This book was set in Press roman by Hemisphere Publishing Corporation. The editors were Christine Flint Lowry and Eleana Cornejo-de-Villanueva; the production supervisor was Miriam Gonzalez; and the typesetter was Sandi Stancil.
BookCrafters, Inc. was printer and binder.

Library of Congress Cataloging in Publication Data

Male and female homosexuality.

  (The Series in clinical and community psychology)
  Includes bibliographies and index.
  1. Homosexuality–Psychological aspects.
2. Homosexuality–Social aspects. I. Diamant,
Louis, date. II. Series. [DNLM: 1. Homosexuality.
2. Psychological Theory. WM 615 M245]
RC558.M35 1987   616.85'834   86-25816
ISBN 0-89116-449-9
ISSN 0146-0846

CONTENTS

Contributors   *ix*
Foreword   *xi*
Preface   *xv*

I
TOWARD A PSYCHOLOGICAL APPROACH

1   **Introduction**   *Louis Diamant*   3

   Conclusions   16
   References   17

2   **The First Clinicians**   *Vern L. Bullough*   21

   References   29

II
THEORY AND RESEARCH

3   **Kinsey and Others: Empirical Input**   *Marvin Siegelman*   33

   Pre-Kinsey: A Historical Note   34
   Kinsey   35
   Post-Kinsey   36

Research Strategies and Theoretical Considerations   59
References   67

4   **Psychoanalytic Theory**   *Reuben Fine*   81

Introduction   81
Treatability   84
Is Homosexuality Per Se a "Neurosis"?   86
The Psychodynamics of Homosexuality   90
References   93

5   **The Neo-Freudians**   *Manny Sternlicht*   97

References   106

6   **A Behavioristic Approach**   *Joel Greenspoon and P. A. Lamal*   109

The Ethical Issue   109
Origins of Homosexuality   113
Therapy   120
References   127

7   **Psychobiological Contributions**   *Brian A. Gladue*   129

Biological Approaches toward Understanding Sexual Orientation   130
Hormone-Brain Interactions: The Prenatal Hormone Theory   134
Other Psychobiological Factors Related to Sexual Orientation   143
Summary: Is Sexual Orientation Biologically Determined   144
References   146
Notes Added in Proof   153

8   **Gender Role**   *Ihsan Al-Issa*   155

The Gender Role Reversal Hypothesis in Homosexuality   156
Gender Role Reversal and Homosexual Relationship   157
Gender Role Reversal and Attitudes toward Homosexuality   160
Gender Role Reversal and Parent-Child Relationship   162
Gender Role Reversal, Psychopathology, and Other Behavior   164
Summary   165
References   166

III
CLINICAL CONCERNS

9   **The Relationship of Homosexuality to Mental Disorders**
     Louis Diamant and Ronald B. Simono   171

Introduction   171

Homosexuality and Diagnostic Classifications 172
Alcohol Abuse and Homosexuality 174
Homosexuality and Paranoia 178
Homosexuality and Phobic Reaction 182
References 185

10 **Ego-Dystonic Homosexuality and Treatment Alternatives**
Faye E. Sultan, Denise M. Elsner, and Jaime Smith 187

Psychiatric Nosology 187
Evolution of a Diagnosis: The DSM Story 188
The Development of the Ego-Dystonic Homosexual 192
Clinical Implications and Considerations 194
References 196

11 **The Therapies** *Louis Diamant* 199

The Clinical Approach: Trick or Treatment? 199
The Medical Beginning 202
Psychodynamic Treatment, Theory, Research, Case Studies 203
Behaviorists and Their Treatments 207
Beyond Aversive Reinforcement 208
Conversion without Pathology; Satisfaction without Change 210
Toward Ego Syntonic Homosexuality 211
Conclusions 213
References 215

IV
SOCIETY AND THE HOMOSEXUAL INDIVIDUAL

12 **Contributions from Social Psychology** *Gary T. Long
and Faye E. Sultan* 221

Introduction 221
Social Perception of the Homosexual 222
Homosexuality in Prison 228
Social Problems for the Homosexual Individual Caused by
Social Attitudes 231
References 235

13 **A Theory of Normal Homosexuality** *Michael W. Ross* 237

Introduction 237
The Essentialist-Gender Based Paradigm 238
Meaning of Sexuality as a Determinant of Partner Choice 241
Possible Alternative Paradigms 243

Homosexuality and Normality: Cross-Cultural Issues   247
References   257

14   **The Humanistic Outlook**   *Josef E. Garai*   261

References   268

15   **On Morals and Ethics**   *C. A. Tripp*   271

Historical Perspectives   279
References   282

Index   283

CONTRIBUTORS

IHSAN AL-ISSA, University of Calgary, Alberta, Canada

VERN L. BULLOUGH, State University of New York College at Buffalo, Buffalo, New York, USA

LOUIS DIAMANT, University of North Carolina at Charlotte, Charlotte, North Carolina, USA

DENISE M. ELSNER, University of North Carolina at Charlotte, Charlotte, North Carolina, USA

REUBEN FINE, Adelphi University, Garden City, New York, USA

JOSEF E. GARAI, Pratt Institute; The New School for Social Research; Psychotherapist, Private Practice, New York, USA

BRIAN A. GLADUE, North Dakota State University, Fargo, North Dakota, USA

JOEL GREENSPOON, University of Texas at the Permian Basin, Odessa, Texas, USA

P. A. LAMAL, University of North Carolina at Charlotte, Charlotte, North Carolina, USA

GARY T. LONG, University of North Carolina at Charlotte, Charlotte, North Carolina, USA

JOHN MONEY, The Johns Hopkins University and Hospital, Baltimore, Maryland, USA

MICHAEL W. ROSS, Flinders University of South Australia, Australia

MARVIN SIEGELMAN, City College of New York, New York, USA

RONALD B. SIMONO, University of North Carolina at Charlotte, Charlotte, North Carolina, USA

JAIME SMITH, St. Paul's Hospital and the University of British Columbia, Vancouver, Canada

MANNY STERNLICHT, Yeshiva University, New York City, New York, USA

FAYE E. SULTAN, University of North Carolina at Charlotte, North Carolina, USA

C. A. TRIPP, Psychological Research Associates, New York, USA

FOREWORD

The simple definition of homosexuality is that it is an erotic, sexual, and usually genital relationship between two people who have the same genital morphology. Under scrutiny, however, this simplicity becomes complex. Some people who have all the bodily morphology of a man, including a penis and scrotum but no testicles, were born with two ovaries and a uterus, internally, and also have, in all the cells of the body, the 46,XX chromosomes that are regularly found in the female. Such a person marries as a man, has the sex life of a man, and a family by donor insemination of his wife. His friends and family unhesitatingly regard him and his wife as heterosexual. Nonetheless, both of them are chromosomally female, and both were born with the reproductive organs of a female. Moreover, with a different clinical history as a newborn, this same person could have been surgically, hormonally, and socially habilitated to have the body morphology of a female, and to carry a normal pregnancy.

Having received feminizing treatment and grown up as a girl, however, there is a nearly 50 percent possibility that she (not he) in adolescence or adulthood would have fallen in love as a female with another female. Friends and relatives would then have regarded the two women as lesbians, because they both had been born with the same 46,XX chromosomal status as females, with internal female reproductive organs, and both would have female body morphology. In the one partner, the body would have feminized at puberty, normally, without medical intervention. In the other, feminization would have been the end result of surgical feminization of the external sex organs, together with prepubertal and pubertal regulation of the adrenocortical hormonal error that caused the condition in the first place. The condition is the syndrome of virilizing adrenal hyperplasia (CVAH).

This example does, indeed, demonstrate that homosexuality is defined on the criterion of the morphology of the sex organs of the two partners. It also demonstrates the great psychobiological complexity, behind the scenes, of what determines that two people with the same genital morphology will be erotosexually attracted to one another, and possibly will have the experience of falling in love. Is the determinant genetic? Prenatal hormonal? Neuro-hormonal? Genital anatomical? Pubertal hormonal? Or is it in the rearing and socialization? If not only one of the foregoing, then how many, and at what stage of development?

These same questions apply to homosexual attraction between people born with normal sexual anatomy. As a matter of fact, they also apply to heterosexual attraction, and to bisexual attraction. When answers are available, they will explain, ipso facto, heterosexuality and bisexuality, as well as homosexuality. In the meantime, the answers are fragmentary and incomplete, as the chapters of this book amply demonstrate. One must accommodate to living with scholarly uncertainty!

Uncertainty is difficult to live with, but it is preferable to false certainty. It was the false certainty of a former era that endorsed the self-righteousness of conceptualizing homosexuality as a sin and then, subsequently, in the nineteenth century, as a sickness. It remained conceptualized as a sickness until well into the twentieth century. Then, like left-handedness, it metamorphosed from a sickness into a social option—not the social norm, but tolerated within the body politic as an alternative mode of existence, sexually. This metamorphosis was catalyzed, in part, by political activists of the gay liberation movement, and endorsed by scholars of the history and comparative ethnology of homosexology.

Historical and ethnographic studies have made it abundantly clear that same-sex and other-sex relationships, either sequentially or concurrently, may be socially prescribed as an integral component of, respectively, manhood or womanhood. Our own society's categorization of homosexuality as a deviation from allosexuality is relativistic, not absolute. The chapters of this book amply demonstrate this principle, together with the principle of etiological uncertainty.

Eventually, of course, this book will become a document in the history of sexological scholarship. As history, it may well be viewed as marking the end of an era—the era of scholarly feuding as to whether homosexuality belongs to psychology or biology. In large part this is a territorial feud between those who have a vested interest in psychological versus biological treatments—or no treatments at all.

As a historical document, this book will also be recognized as harboring the sociopsychobiological seeds of a homosexology yet to come. Today, no one can conjecture, even as science fiction, what new knowledge the application of neuroscience to sexology will have produced by the turn of the century.

One of the great new specialties that will surely be developed will be that of homosexual paraphilias. Homosexuality, per se, does not qualify as a paraphilia any more than does heterosexuality. Paraphilias are syndromes that do not discriminate between homosexuals and heterosexuals. They warp and distort the developing "lovemaps" (Money, 1986) of growing children, irrespective of whether their future erotosexual status will be hetero- bi- or homosexual.

Today's scholarship neglects to differentiate homosexual lovemaps from paraphilic homosexual ones. The difference is of great theoretical and applied importance politically, legally, socially, and therapeutically. Homosexual paraphilia, just like heterosexual paraphilia, needs treatment, whereas ordinary homosexuality, like ordinary heterosexuality, does not. Not every author in this book agrees with this statement about treatment. There is a rationale behind each position, which allows readers to become their own Sherlock Holmes. Very interesting reading, you will find. Read on!

John Money, Ph.D.
The Johns Hopkins University and Hospital

REFERENCE

Money, J. (1986). *Lovemaps: Clinical concepts of sexual erotic health and pathology, paraphilia, and gender transposition in childhood, adolescence, and maturity.* New York: Irvington.

PREFACE

At this point in time, little elaboration is needed to explain the importance of a serious study of homosexuality. University curricula give testimony to both social and scientific concern given human sexual variance. During the 1970s, Americans were exposed to many thought-provoking books, articles, television programs, and films dealing with homosexuality. The media, by closely following the politics of the gay rights movement, has exposed us to conflicting beliefs on the political, social, and sexual freedoms of the homosexual person. The current social and academic attention given to understanding the homosexually oriented person has resulted in a number of books that give the topic the serious treatment it demands. These books have all considered some of the social and psychological aspects of homosexuality.

This book enhances the current literature by providing the student of sexual behavior with a comprehensive organization of topics conceptualized to provide an awareness and understanding of critical issues on the psychology of male and female homosexuality. Since the book was scientifically conceived, the reader will find that the ensuing psychological explanations are presented within appropriately theoretical and empirical frameworks. In addition, the book offers an essential socioclinical ground for understanding the development of the psychology of male and female homosexuality.

This volume is an invaluable source of information and reference for readers whose academic or professional interests include homosexuality, the psychology of sex roles, and the psychology of adjustment. It is also appropriate for advanced undergraduate and graduate students, as well as those professionals who might wish to strengthen their therapeutic and research armamentaria.

The authors discuss events and ideas that have had an important role in creating current social and clinical attitudes toward homosexuality. Each chapter was included on the basis of its theoretical and clinical significance or the influence that the concepts have had in respect to controversy, research, and clinical innovation. Part I, which reviews male and female homosexuality historically, should give the reader a background for current psychological perspectives and controversies, and an understanding of the social vicissitudes involved in the evolution of contemporary social, legal, and clinical attitudes concerning male and female homosexuality. Part II introduces the reader to research designs and studies, the results of which may confirm or refute hypotheses and conjectures on homosexuality as well as the major psychological theoretical positions which have instigated the bulk of studies, experiments, and treatment of male and female homosexuality. These include the psychodynamic views of Freud, Adler, and Sullivan, as well as the behavioral and biological viewpoints of male and female homosexuality. Part III considers the clinical aspects of the male and female homosexual experience. The intent is to examine the clinical phenomenon and still avoid an a priori position on the issue of pathology. This part assays current clinical approaches and deals with (a) the prevalence and nature of male and female homosexuality in patients bearing primary diagnostic labels of major mental disorders; (b) the relatively new Diagnostic and Statistical Manual of Mental Disorders III (DSMIII; American Psychiatric Association, 1980) classification of Ego-Dystonic, which restricts the ascribing of psychopathology to the subject's negative view of homosexuality; and (c) the current treatment of male and female homosexuality as a disorder, or a nondisordered behavior to be strengthened or improved, and the treatment of male and female homosexual persons in which the relief of stress, but not the cessation of homosexuality, is sought. Part IV is concerned with the psychological interaction between the larger heterosexually oriented community and gay and lesbian individuals. The psychology of attitude and attitude change are considered, and the psychological foundations for humanistic and ethical approaches are covered.

I thank my colleagues in relevant disciplines for their help in selecting chapters by proposing topics most suited to their needs and interests, and for their comments on the manuscript. I thank the library staff of the University of North Carolina at Charlotte for help and tolerance above and beyond. I thank those in the gay and lesbian community for invaluable direction and support. I thank the chapter authors for their cooperation and scholarly contributions. Specifically, I thank the Reverend Randy McSpadden for his tutoring in the complexities of homosexuality and the Judeo-Christian ethic; Leif Diamant for sharing insights drawn from his experience as a therapist, sex counselor, and concerned human being; Eleanor Godlewski for her incomparable secretarial skills and personality; and Kate Roach, my editor, for many things. Finally, I express my thanks to John Money who is an inspiration to all those who dare embark on the scientific investigation of human sexuality.

Louis Diamant

I

TOWARD A PSYCHOLOGICAL APPROACH

1

INTRODUCTION

Louis Diamant

Theoretical models and empirical research concerned with an essential definition of homosexuality are a comparatively modern phenomenon. Current attitudes on male and female homosexuality bear the imprint of centuries of medical and cultural vicissitudes from which they have in large measure evolved. It thus appears that an in-depth understanding of the definitions and dimensions of male and female homosexuality requires an examination of the clinical empirical, theoretical, and ethical issues in a matrix involving fundamental psychosocial events.

Freud (1905) referred to homosexuality as inversion, a deviation in which the object of the sexual instinct was a person of the same sex. In later writings he used the term homosexual. Havelock Ellis (1915), another pioneer in the study of human sexual behavior, also used the term inversion in a similar sense. Kinsey, Pomeroy, and Martin (1948) stated that the homosexuality or heterosexuality of any activity is made apparent by determining the sex of the individuals involved in the relationship. They further stated that it would encourage clearer thinking on these matters if persons were not characterized as heterosexual or homosexual but as individuals who have had certain amounts of heterosexual experience and certain amounts of homosexual experience. These researchers believed there was an advantage to be found in describing the nature of a person's overt sexual relationships or the stimuli to which an individual responds erotically, rather than in using the term homosexual or heterosexual. They developed a seven-point rating scale on male sexual behavior to categorize the subjects of their research from exclusive heterosexual (0) to exclusively homosexual (6).

West (1967) described homosexuality as a constant or habitual erotic attraction to a member of the same sex with the degree to which a person acts upon the attraction through sexual stimulation and orgasm with the same-sex partner further describing the practice of homosexuality. However, the more recent literature reflects the importance given to the distinction between homosexual males and females by the frequent use of "lesbian" for females and "gay" for males rather than the single label homosexual (Riddle and Morin, 1978). The terms Gay Activist and Gay Liberation are not, however, gender delimited. Socarides (1965), noting that the law treats male homosexuality in a far more punitive fashion, stated that lesbianism is separated from male homosexuality for legalistic reasons. Wolff (1971) found no valid comparison between male and female homosexuality. She argued that most writers on the subject have not seen the real differences that exist, but have only emphasized superficial similarities between male and female homosexuality. She stated that women possess a greater, more embracing love potential than their male counterparts. According to Wolff, two distinct features characterize and set lesbians apart: the lesbians' reverence for aesthetics and their intense emotionality.

While the effect of psychology and psychotherapy has been essential to the formulation of concepts of male and female homosexuality, this influence is relatively modern. Centuries before the behavioral sciences attempted to define homosexuality within an empirical framework, religious and social views of homosexuality were expressed in the cultures of the ancient Greeks and Hebrews. These views have had a pervasive influence on the development of contemporary social and clinical attitudes and controversy.

According to West (1967) love and sex between two men were celebrated events which were important in Hellenic society. Although homosexual roles were encouraged and developed as part of Greek cultural idealism, laws placed definite restrictions on homosexual relationships. Aspects of homosexuality and evidence of the acceptability as a male function were recorded in the art and literature of ancient Greece (Dover, 1978). According to Dover, homosexuality, with little exception, was described in terms of male behavior.

The main point of reference for discussing female homosexuality in classical Greece is the poet Sappho who lived circa 600 BC. It is from her celebration of female love on the Isle of Lesbos that the term lesbian originates. Dover thought it doubtful that even with Sappho's highly erotic poetry that lesbianism with its current behavioral connotation could have existed under her aegis. It was highly unlikely that the girls of prominent Lesbos families would have been sent to a school in which sexual techniques were practiced.

While the ancient Greeks accepted the homosexual ethos, the Judeo-

Christian ethic was restrictive in its interpretation of permissible sexual behavior. The Old Testament has some of the earliest recorded dictums on homosexuality, but does not use a specific label for the behavior. Pomeroy (1972) stated that the Jews, emphasizing the philosophy of the procreative purpose of sex, placed proscriptions on sexual behavior after their return from Babylon, which bordered on the paranoid. Certain scriptural passages have throughout history been cited to support attitudes antagonistic to homosexuality. Examples include Leviticus 20:13: "If a man lies with a man as with a woman, both have committed an abomination: their blood is upon them."; Genesis 9, where Ham is said to have brought a curse upon himself after having seen Noah lying naked in his tent; and Genesis 19, the account of Sodom and Gomorrah. According to Lovelace (1978) Martin Luther viewed this story as a Biblical admonition against homosexuality. Biblical influence is seen in Augustine's *Confessions;* "Shameful acts against nature as those committed in Sodom, ought everywhere and always to be detested and punished."

The Bible has only one possible reference to female homosexuality and its meaning seems ambiguous. (Romans 1:26, 27):

> *For this cause God gave them up unto vile affections; for even their women did change their natural use for that which is against nature and likewise also the men leaving the natural use of women, burned in their lust toward one another. Men with men wanting that which is unseemly and receiving in themselves that recompense of their error.*

Pomeroy (1972) viewed this as a reference to women assuming a male sexual position in heterosexual intercourse rather than a comment on lesbianism.

Szasz (1970) commented that only male homosexuality is forbidden, because God addresses males only. Thus, there is not a parallel injunction that a woman not lie with a woman as with a man. According to Szaz, the Biblical omission is reflective of the Bible's treatment of women as less than fully human. The legal statutes of modern Western society, which show an indifference to prosecuting lesbians, are rooted in this historical disregard for women.

Boswell (1980) implied that during the eleventh and twelfth centuries a European cultural climate allowed the emergence of a homosexual sub-culture. It is likely that the period was more open in literature—homophile poetry—than in sexual conduct.* His thesis on the church and homosexuality indicated that the oppressive stance on homosexuality was not to be ascribed only to the church but to a repressive political-cultural anti-homosexual bias.

While current controversy regarding homosexuality within some Christian churches has led to a greater acceptance of gay and lesbian worshippers, only

---

*Bullough, V., 1985, personal communication.

in a rare exception has the Christian faith position accepted their ministerial ordination. Separately, theological Judaism has followed the Talmudic anti-homosexual bias which according to Matt (1978) appears to have created a dilemma for both the clergy and the homosexual Jew.

Other societies have also either encouraged or eschewed homosexuality. Ford and Beach (1951), in an investigation of data on seventy-six primitive societies, found homosexuality acceptable in 64%. In the Western United States, the Utes of Colorado viewed homosexuality with antipathy (Opler, 1965); whereas the Southwestern Mohaves institutionalized homosexuality with the practice of berdache. [In berdache, an effeminate boy could be raised in the style of a woman and have definite societal value and acceptance (Devereaux, 1937).] Lesbianism is rarely reported as an institutionalized phenomenon by anthropologists. However, Schaeffer (1965) observed a female Hutenai berdache and Devereaux described an accepted lesbian transvestite of the Mohave. Wolff (1971) saw the historical matriarchal structure evidenced in the remnants of female power in the Ashante as masculine and as having qualities inseparable from female homosexuality.

Karlen (1971) concluded that most societal acceptance of homosexuality is never total but rather situational or variational and that while the rejection of one's sex role can be institutionalized, as among the Mohave, it is not done without cost to the homosexual person.

In the history of Western civilization, governments have traditionally placed sexuality within a restrictive legal framework. Political control of sexual behavior appears for the most part a consequence of the Judeo-Christian ethic. In Europe, ecclesiastical law incorporated the ideas of Jewish tradition, Christian teaching and Roman law as the basis for the punishment of homosexual behavior until the nineteenth century, when a liberalization of attitudes toward homosexuality was brought about by the Napoleonic Code. The prosecution of homosexuals has been historically directed against males. Socarides (1965) found no recorded case of lesbian entrapment by police such as has been common with males. Lesbianism, unlike male homosexuality, has never been a crime in England nor in most other European countries, although Austria retained the proscriptive but unenforced Carolingian law since 1532. Most European governments no longer consider homosexuality in itself a crime, but certain aspects of homosexuality, i.e., sex with minors, coercion, and public indecency, are usually prosecuted as criminal acts (West, 1967). In the United States, most states have criminal laws covering most homosexual acts but lesbians have rarely been tried and sentenced. However, the Louisiana Supreme Court recently affirmed the conviction and sentencing of Mary Young and Dawn de Blanc for unnatural copulation (Legal Citation, 1966).

Homosexuality, long thought of as a crime or sin in Western society, was eventually given a different dimension by Sigmund Freud. While Freud did not see homosexualty in terms of disease, his view of it as a developmental problem supported the study of homosexuality as a clinical syndrome and a psychopathological state. Although Freud was not the only physician of his era to gain recognition from the study of sexuality, he was undoubtedly the most influential. The names Havelock Ellis and Richard von Krafft-Ebing are also associated with the study of sexual variance. Ellis (1915) did not write of homosexuality as either a sin or disease, but he did say that it was congenital and thus constitutional. Krafft-Ebing (1922) believed homosexuality to be a result of physical degeneracy and hereditary defects and therefore both constitutional and a disease. Essentially however, Freud is set apart from his predecessors and contemporaries by the tenets of Psychoanalytic Theory, which was Freud's major innovation and the first set of psychodynamic postulates weaving heterosexuality and homosexuality into the structure of personality theory (Freud, 1905).

The concept of psychological conflict causing a personality disorder or variance in sexual behavior was revolutionary. Freud and later psychological theorists postulated a developmental relationship between infantile sexuality and homosexuality. Otto Fenichel (1945) summarized some of the postulates of Freud and other psychoanalytic theorists. Succinctly, homosexuality occurs when, as an outcome of the Oedipus Complex, the object of the sex instinct is a same-sexed person. According to Psychoanalytic Theory, male homosexuality can be attributed to the fantasy that the female genitalia may be an instrument capable of tearing off the penis, or the son's Oedipal fear of the father because of the child's sexual desire for the mother. Further, most male homosexuals do not easily free themselvs of the biological longing for women. Psychoanalysis revealed that homosexual men do not cease to be sexually aroused by women, but instead repress this interest and displace the excitement to men. Although disappointment with the mother is a major cause of male homosexuality, the homosexual man may identify with the mother and so love men (Fenichel, 1945).

Bieber (1962) emphasized the importance of parental responses to the child's emerging heterosexuality during the Oedipus complex as crucial in determining its outcome. According to Bieber, a poor marital relationship may lead parents to attempt to fulfill frustrated romantic wishes through the son. In a poor marital relationship, the husband is devalued by the wife, which is demasculinizing to both husband and son. The concomitant father-son sex rivalry makes the mother's seductiveness threatening to the son and the intensity of Oedipal castration anxiety may bring about a renunciation of heterosexuality.

Psychoanalytic theory postulates certain complexities in the development of lesbians not found in the etiology of male homosexuality. Although homosexuality in both genders relates to the Oedipus complex and castration anxiety, psychoanalytic theory holds that a woman may cling to the early hope of acquiring a penis and thus her masculinity is related to the fantasy of becoming a man. This masculinity complex may lead to homosexual object choice. Female homosexuality is also considered to result from a woman's early pregenital fixations on the mother and her disappointment with the father which may lead to identification with him and the desire to love the mother as he did (Fenichel, 1945).

Not all the psychodynamic theorists agreed with the Freudian (psychoanalytic) view of sexual development on the origin of mental fixation and disorder. A number of the pioneers in psychodynamic psychology who retained the concept of mental and emotional conflict leading to psychopathology and personality disturbance have been referred to as Neo-Freudians. Some of them were initially disciples of, and close associates of Freud.

Although there emerged other theoretical differences between them, Alfred Adler alienated himself from Freud mainly in emphasizing the role of social forces rather than the instinctual ones in the determination of personality. Adler saw homosexuality as a neurotic type of behavior used to safeguard the individual, and as an attempt at compensation for people with distinct inferiority feelings. To Adler, homosexuality in both males and females was a try for a feeling of superiority. The salient traits in homosexuals are inordinate ambition and fear of life. Adler thought that female homosexuality might be related to such traumatic factors as the brutality of the father, a great personal loss, or a frightening interpretation of the female sex role. In addition, Adler believed that lesbianism could be the result of the masculine protest, and the desire to be like a man, which could thus provide an escape from an inferiority complex that was based on being "only a girl" (Ansbacher, 1956, p. 425). Male homosexuality could result from a feeling of inadequacy for both life and heterosexual performance (Adler, 1971; Ansbacher, 1956).

According to Carl Jung, another early associate and defector from Freud's circle, in homosexuals the persona, rather than the anima or animus, is projected onto the same-sex partner while the homosexual person unconsciously identifies with the anima or animus in playing the role of the opposite sex with his same-sex partner. Jungian psychology describes the anima and animus as the psychical bisexual components in each person. The masculine aspect of the woman is the animus and feminine aspect of the man, the anima. The persona is our role-playing archetype. Oversimplified: archetypes such as the anima, animus, and persona, are our ancestral experiences contained in each generation in the form of imagery. Jung believed such identifications "always involve a defective adaptation" to reality and a lack of relatedness to the object due to the homosexual subject's primary orientation and absorption into inner rather than interpersonal relationships (Jung, 1974).

Harry Stack Sullivan, a figure of some importance in American psychology, saw homosexuality in pre-adolescence in both male and female as having adjustive value. He viewed the development of intimate ties with chums in the juvenile era as facilitative of later socialization and heterosexuality. However, Sullivan designated as one of his syndrome categories of maladjustment, the homosexual syndrome. The term is applicable, with some features being modified by cultural gender roles, to both males and females. The classification is for people whose earlier experiences result in a barrier to persons of the other sex. The homosexual syndrome applies to women (or men) haters and those who preferred in childhood to play with the other sex but who cannot integrate with them sexually. People described by this syndrome in pre-adolescence or later, may have sexual relationships with people of their own sex. Some of the relationships may be loving, stable, and durable. Others could be full of hatred, durable or otherwise. While he avoids a definition of homosexuality as *definitely* pathological, Sullivan does consider it a problem in development (Sullivan, 1953, 1970).

Clara Thompson (1947) also postulated that homosexuality may serve an adjustive purpose. Thompson, a close colleague of Sullivan, examined a multitude of etiological variables and concluded that it is possible for a variety of biological, personal, and interpersonal situations to lead to homosexuality. She saw homosexuality as a symptom in people who are afraid of the opposite sex, of responsibility, and of intimacy, as well as in those who had less opportunity for heterosexual success. Thompson stated that there is a gender differentiation regarding the mental health status of the homosexual person. There is less pathology among female than among male homosexuals because of the woman's socio-cultural limitations in seeking and finding satisfying heterosexual opportunities— age and physical unattractiveness are more of a handicap to women than to men, for example. In addition, male homosexuals must, unlike females, contend with the social disapproval of male-male closeness.

Even while expounding on and receiving acclaim for a system of mental dynamics, Freud nevertheless believed that biochemical processes eventually would explain all mental disturbance, and that the theory of universal bisexuality could account for variance in sexual behavior.

More recently, support for a hormonal-homosexual link in females came from observing the behavior ascribed as masculine in females with androgeno-genital syndrome (Ehrhardt, Epstein, and Money, 1968). Research relevant to male homosexuality reported findings of lower testosterone levels in homosexual males as compared to heterosexual males (Kalodny, Masters, Hendryx, and Toro, 1971). However, replication was not attained by several other researchers (Tourney and Hatfield, 1973; Barlow, Able, and Blanchard, 1974; Pillard, Rose and Sherwood, 1974). Money and Ehrhardt (1972) examined a number of studies in which explanations for male and female homosexuality were sought in terms of hormonal components. They concluded that if hormonal differences exist between the homosexual and heterosexual person, such differences will be found prenatally. They found, however, no systematic data relative to a possible relationship between prenatal hormonal functioning and the subsequent development of homosexuality in adulthood. These researchers prefer an explanation for gender identity which posits that certain dimorphic traits are laid down in the brain before birth. These traits may facilitate homo- or hetero-sexuality, but are too bivalent to be exclusive determinants. Conditions which develop gender identity in late infancy and early childhood are primary determinants of the sexual attitude (Money and Ehrhardt, 1972). A major new study of homosexual men and women at the Alfred C. Kinsey Institute for Sexual Research (Bell, Weinberg, and Hammersmith, 1981) indicated that homosexuality is related to a pattern of feelings and reactions in a child not attributable to a single social or psychological cause. The report considers the possibility that homosexuality may arise from a biological precursor that parents could not control. However, the data from which this assumption was drawn was obtained by an intensive survey unrelated to biochemical evaluations.

The behavioristic model proposes that homosexuality can be understood and treated according to the principles of learning found in the research and writings of Pavlov (1928) and Skinner (1953), whose basic formulations describe classical and operant conditioning. With regard to male-female contingencies for the reinforcement of homosexuality, Lamal (1978) stated that from the radical behavioral viewpoint there are no causal factors unique to the sexual behavior of males or females. Behaviorists postulate that homosexuality depends on contingencies which provide the positive reinforcement of homosexual behavior or the punishment of heterosexual behavior, or both. Thus, homosexual behavior would be most likely to be established when it is followed by events such as orgasm or other physical and social reinforcers, or when heterosexual exploration is followed by threat or punishment. Punitive male behavior, especially in a sexual context, is often cited as a factor in lesbianism. Konopka (1964) reported that delinquent girls who are raped by their fathers frequently turn to women for love. In a survey of raped women, Gundlach (1977) observed that of the 17 lesbians included, 16 had been molested or seduced in childhood by family or friends. However, since clinical experience indicates that a considerable number of exclusively homosexual males are initially molested and raped within the circle of their family and friends and that many persons who have had early orgasmic experience from a same-sex partner before adulthood do eventually choose a heterosexual lifestyle, other variables need to be considered.

The views of Tripp (1975) on male homosexuality have received recent popular and scholarly attention. Tripp is a vigorous opponent of the psychoanalytic hypothesis on the origin and pathology of homosexuality. While he is not considered to be a behaviorist, his theory on the origins of homosexuality includes such behavioral principles (although not in the specific behavioral terminology) as modeling, one-trial reinforced learning, generalization, and the state of the organism (readiness), as determinants of the effect of reinforcement.

A closer analysis of Tripp would suggest that his attitudes toward homosexuality are more existential-humanistic than behavioristic. This is especially true when he considers those clinicians who are psychotherapeutically valuable to homosexual clients. His argument calls for the acceptance of the client's sexual orientation in what can only be described as humanistic-existential terms—for he believes that the client in accepting himself, makes decisions which foster a freedom from external events.

Albert Ellis stated that humanistic psychology "completely accepts people with their human limitations; it particularly focuses upon and employs their experiences and their values; it emphasizes their ability to create and direct their own destinies; and it views them as holistic, goal-directed individuals who are important in their own right, just because they are alive, and who (together with their fellow humans) have the right to continue to exist and to enjoy and fulfill themselves" (Ellis, 1973). Humanistic-existential psychotherapists see homosexuality as authentic when it is based on under-standing and decision. [Authenticity is a term valued by humanistic and existential clinicians (Bugental, 1965)]. The humanistic-existential position does at times appear to be more a state of mind than a school. For example, Davison (1976) a behaviorist and behavioral therapist, is especially humanistic in his belief in a person's right to be of any sexual orientation without undue societal pressures. While Serban (1968) who describes his treatment as "existential," spoke in terms of the neurotic thinking structure (metalogical) of the homosexual.

The medical model provides a postulate of mental disorders which states that unconscious processes cause the symptoms that characterize the disorders. Modern psychiatry has largely been practiced within this framework. Treating the cause of a symptom rather than a symptom itself is an intrinsic consequence of the medical model, as opposed to treatment within a behavioral model which proposes a direct attack upon the symptom. The influences of dynamic psychiatry, psychoanalysis, and the medical model of mental disorder culminated in 1952 with the publication of the first Diagnostic and Statistical Manual of Mental Disorders (DSM I; American Psychiatric Association, 1952).

DSM I classified homosexuality as a mental disorder. Nearly twenty years later, DSM II (American Psychiatric Association, 1968) also categorized homosexuality as a disorder. Homosexuality was thus legitimatized as a psychia-trically treatable mental disorder and had three dimensions: sin, crime, and illness. Although gender differences were not mentioned in DSM they have been noted by some leaders in psychiatry and psychoanalysis (Wolff, 1971; Thompson, 1947). Freud (1920) in an oft cited paper on the psychoanalytic treatment of a lesbian, wrote that female homosexuality had been viewed differently from male homosexuality and that it had largely been ignored by the law and psychoanalysis.

In the spirit of DSM, the mainstream of psychiatry and clinical psychology readily accepted homosexuality as a mental disorder and treatment was routinely directed toward reversing homosexual behavior and attitudes. When the disorder was deemed hopelessly irreversible, the patient might be helped to adjust. Homosexuality was rarely viewed as a non-pathological choice. Kinsey et al. (1948) had however suggested that homosexuality, while mutable, might still be considered a non-pathological variance in human sexual behavior.

The decision by the American Psychiatric Association to classify homosexuality as a mental disorder appeared to have placed psychiatry at odds with the law and the church. This was however, not the case. Although religious institutions did not generally give approval to homosexuality, some have become more accepting. For example, the Catholic Church recently sanctioned Dignity, a national gay organization with chapters in most major cities in the United States.

In contemporary society, the classification of homosexuality as a crime has however proved to be more threatening to homosexual men and women than its classification as a sin. Many states can imprison even consenting adults for homosexuality. In 1976, the United States Supreme Court refused to hear an appeal from a defendant convicted of homosexuality, thus upholding the right of a state to consider homosexuality a crime (Doe v. Commonwealth's Attorney for the City of Richmond, 44 U.S.L. Week 3545, 1976). Judiciary systems probably became liberalized as much by using a mental illness alternative to deal with homosexuality as the eradication of criminal statutes. For many mental health professionals the mental illness concept seemed the soundest framework for the evaluation of homosexuality. If homosexuality was a treatable mental disorder, then mental health professionals were obviously better prepared than jailers to deal with this kind of personality disturbance symptomized by homosexual behavior.

Although there were some humane aspects in a clinically designated homosexuality, the more radical clinicians opposed the diagnosis as did an emerging community of homosexual activists. Szasz (1964) challenged the APA classification system by proposing that the physical disease model had been misapplied with regard to mental and emotional difficulty. Psychiatrist Szasz argued that the goal of curing mental illness was a residue of an outmoded theology. Szasz (1970) used a similar argument against clinically classified homosexuality, noting that during the Inquisition the church considered homosexuality and heresy as the same. He implied that modern psychiatrists approach compliance to heterosexuality with the inquisitor's passion to convert the heretic.

Popular opinion that homosexuals formed a small, socially unacceptable, and unstable group made it easier for institutions to demand compliance to heterosexuality. However the data of Kinsey et al. (1948) bore implications that millions of homosexual men and women were integral to the fabric of American society.

Collective political and social expression which would lead to "Gay Liberation" began with the 1957 formation of the homophile Mattachine

Society (Katz, 1976). However, it is the opinion of Kameny (1971) that Gay Liberation really began in a riot by gay persons in July, 1969, at a gay bar in the Greenwich Village section of New York. Bullough has suggested that the Greenwich Village riots represent the rise to media attention of developments that had been taking place since World War II.* Kameny saw two basic precepts to the Gay Liberation approach to homosexuality: the first is that homosexuals are the equals of heterosexuals; the second, that homosexuality is the equal of heterosexuality. He saw the first precept as raising constitutional and civil rights issues and the second as raising issues related to psychiatry and psychology. Gay activists blamed psychiatric classification for much of their inferior status and lowered self-concept.

In 1973 the American Psychiatric Association discontinued classifying homosexuality as a mental disorder—an action later approved by the American Psychological Association. Coleman, Butcher, and Carson (1980) called the vote an "instant cure" for homosexuality. Psychiatrist Ruth Barnhouse (1977) felt that political activism by the National Gay Task Force ended the illness classification of homosexuality. Ironically, it may have been social and political action which obliterated one diagnostic category and created another—ego dystonic homosexuality—homosexuality unwanted by the patient (DSM III, American Psychiatric Association, 1980). It is possible however, that the last word has not been spoken on this ubiquitous problem of culture and diagnosis. A survey of American psychiatrists (Lief, 1977) indicated that the majority of respondents believed homosexuality was a disorder and a pathological adaptation.

It appears that there is disagreement among those who study, categorize, classify, and treat homosexuality in men and women. Perhaps it should not be too surprising that a behavior which was considered for centuries a sin, a crime, and finally an illness, would not quickly be accepted as a benign and acceptable behavioral variance.

Until the research of Kinsey et al. (1948) described male homosexual incidence in the United States, virtually no systematic and methodologically sound studies had been made. The data of Kinsey et al., collected from 5,300 white American males, demonstrated relationships between homosexuality and such variables as religious beliefs and socio-educational levels. Perhaps most impressively, the research indicated that 37% of those surveyed had some homosexual contact to the point of orgasm, with 4% exclusively homosexual. A later Kinsey project (Kinsey, Pomeroy, Martin, and Gebhard, 1953) studied the reported sexual behavior of 5,914 white American females. This research found, among other results, that 28% of those surveyed had some homosexual response; of these, 20% had actual experience and 13% reported orgasm.

The major works of Kinsey and his collaborators appear to be, spiritually at least, the starting point for a more scientific examination of

*Personal communication, Bullough, V., 1985.

postulates structured to explain male and female homosexuality in terms of etiology, personality, and psychopathology.

"When such homosexual behavior persists in an adult," Hooker (1956) quoted the Group for The Advancement of Psychiatry, "it is then a symptom of a severe emotional disorder." When subjects who were homosexual males were matched with heterosexual males for age, IQ, and education, Hooker (1957) found that on the basis of protocols on the Make A Picture Story, the Thematic Apperception Test, and Rorschach, no discrimination on adjustment could be made between the two groups. Subsequently, the number of studies with results indicating that homosexual males and females have no more psychopathology than heterosexuals when judged by psychological testing and interviewing outnumbered those reporting pathology (Meredith and Riestler, 1980). Doidge and Holtzman (1960) provided some quantified support for the hypothesis that homosexual men are more likely to have a mental disorder than heterosexual men. Using Air Force trainees as subjects, they found that homosexuality related to personality disturbance when the Minnesota Multi-phasic Personality Inventory was used to determine the level of adjustment. While other studies (Evans, 1971; Turner, Pielmaier, James, and Orwin, 1974) have found that there are some relationships between neuroticism and homosexuality, these relationships were believed not necessarily or specifically related to homosexuality. In a study with 63 homosexual male subjects Ross (1978) found maladjustment that was related to the degree of conformity to heterosexual norms, as well as to the subjects' perception of a negative societal reaction to homosexuality.

Thompson, McCandless, and Strickland (1971) while finding some differences between non-clinical homosexual and heterosexual males and females, noted that there were no significant differences in overall psychological well being and adjustment. Siegelman (1972) compared non-clinical homosexual and heterosexual male populations on three dimensions. Within the total group, the homosexual males were more tender-minded, submissive, and anxious, while the heterosexual group was more depressive. However, when the low-feminine homosexual group was compared with the low-feminine heterosexual group, the homosexual subjects were higher on self-acceptance, nurturance, goal directiveness, and sense of self. On a third comparison, high-feminine homosexuals were found to be more submissive, more anxious, more neurotic, and more alienated than low-feminine homosexuals. Siegelman (1972) compared a group of lesbians with a group of heterosexual women for adjustment, and found that the homosexual females were as well adjusted as the heterosexual women, Siegelman's (1979) data supported his earlier findings indicating similarities in the adjustment of homosexual and heterosexual females. Turner, Pielmaier, James, and Orwin (1974) using the Sixteen-Personality Factor Questionnaire, found that when they compared three groups of homosexual males, ascending degrees of adjustment were evident. The highest level of adjustment was found in those volunteers who had never sought treatment, and the lowest level of adjustment was found in those for whom the court had ordered treatment. Clark (1975) studied the relationship between homosexuality and psychopathology in 140 college educated male homosexuals. All were non-patient subjects, grouped in seven groups according to their Kinsey ratings. On the Tennessee Self-Concept Scale the groups did not differ significantly from each other or from established test norms. The author concluded that homosexuality was not a criterion with which to predict psychopathology.

Diamant (1977) found that social rather than clinical factors distinguished a group of college educated female heterosexual women from a matched group of lesbians. There was no difference between the groups on the Neuroticism Scale of the Maudsley Personality inventory, although the lesbians were higher on extrovertism. The lesbians scored significantly higher on civil rights attitudes, had more socialistic political and economic attitudes, were more radical on attitudes toward law and justice, and were more liberal than the heterosexual women on attitudes concerning women's rights.

Saghir and Robbins (1973) and Bell and Weinberg (1978) have collected and analyzed voluminous data in the San Francisco area which, overall, support the assumption that homosexuality does not specifically relate to psychopathology. Saghir and Robbins used the structured psychiatric interview to compare heterosexual and homosexual urban, high socio-economic, male and female populations. When they compared the volunteer non-psychiatric male homosexual group with the heterosexual controls, they generally found no more psychopathology among the male homosexuals than the heterosexuals. In both groups psychotherapy was fairly common, but it was more likely to be sought by the male homosexuals. Although there were more suicide attempts among the homosexual males, the numerical difference was not significant, and the attempts were mild and not completed. Both groups were reported as strikingly similar with regard to psychopathology. Saghir and Robbins found that there was a greater tendency for the lesbian group to drink, to be cross gendered in self-assessment, and to drop out of college. There was a greater prevalence of psychiatric disorders among the lesbians than among the control group, especially in the area of alcohol abuse. However, the degree of functional disability as a result of these disorders did not make them significantly more disabled than the heterosexual women. Saghir and Robbins stated that homosexual women, like homosexual men, show little impairment of function.

Bell and Weinberg (1978) stressed the importance of delineating homosexual types in order to give meaning to data. They concluded that had one overall homosexual category been used instead of delineating homosexual types, they would have been inclined to report that the homosexual men and women were less well adjusted psychologically than their heterosexual counterparts. However, those homosexual men and women who were classified as functional (i.e., single, low regret for homosexuality, high sexual activity and low sexual problems, etc.) and those who were "close-coupled" (i.e., a sexual partner, low cruising, low sexual problems, etc.) were almost indistinguishable from heterosexual men and women on a number of adjustment variables. Beyond that it was reported that functional lesbians appear to be more exuberant than heterosexual women, close-coupled homosexual men were higher on two happiness scores than heterosexual men, and close-coupled lesbians reported less loneliness than heterosexual women.

CONCLUSIONS

The problems that have been historically related to defining homosexuality, in a broad sense, have been reviewed in this section. Problems of definition as well as finding and observing representative homosexual populations recently have been called to attention by others (Bell and Weinberg, 1978; Reiss and Safer, 1979). The difficulty of definition is also complicated by the seeming inevitability of a label itself. This may be understandable in terms of attribution theory (Long, 1978; Karr, 1978). Karr found that when a man was perceived as homosexual there was a general move to devalue him and maintain social distance. Experimental evidence (Snyder and Uranowitz, 1978) indicated that the label lesbian promoted a tendency among perceivers to retain stereotypic impressions.

Studies which relate the etiology of male and female homosexuality to hormonal factors were mentioned. Biochemical studies may however not address themselves to the most pressing issues involving personality, psychopathology, and society.

Behavioral psychologists speculate on the contingencies of reinforcement for homosexuality. They share, surprisingly perhaps, an etiological position of environmental determinism with some psychoanalysts. Bieber et al. (1962) formulated the parental attitudes that result in male homosexuality, and offered suporting data drawn from research involving the diagnoses and psychoanalytic treatment of male homosexuals. His position is quite disparate from the current findings emanating from the Kinsey Institute of Sex Research (Bell, Weinberg, and Hammersmith, 1981) which tend to reduce parental responsibility in homosexuality.

Similarities between Bieber et al.'s position and the behaviorists quickly diminish when the question of psychopathology is disregarded and the issue of behavior change is isolated. Behavior therapy and behavior modification are suited for immediate application in reducing homosexual behavior without demanding certainty of its origin or an in-depth exploration of relationships. Feldman and MacCulloch (1971) have described in detail a method for reducing or eliminating homosexual behavior in male and female subjects through conditioning techniques. However, behavioral therapists not bound by a view that homosexuality is a pathological symptom of intrapsychic conflict may strengthen the behavior. The enhancement of homosexuality as a matter of choice in an adult male pederast (Kohlenberg, 1974) proved a beginning for yet another controversial issue on homosexuality—the ethics of change.

Davison (1974) applauded Kohlenberg as innovative and ethical in his decision to help his client make a homosexual adjustment. Therapy for orientation change and for the improvement of sexual response for homosexual men and women survived the controversy of the Kohlenberg study (Masters and Johnson, 1979). Later, Davison (1976, 1978) repudiated the practice of sex orientation change therapy on moral grounds. Bieber (1976) and Sturgiss and Adams (1978) opposed Davison's position, though from different orientations.

These three positions are characteristic of prevalent clinical attitudes: 1) The psychopathological viewpoint (Bieber) which pressures for change by treatment; 2) The freedom of choice viewpoint of Sturgis and Adams which demands that the unresolved question of psychopathology be decided empirically, and that objectivity be used in considering each case of orientation-change-therapy; 3) The moral and social viewpoint (Davison) which argues that a change in society's prejudice is more at issue than a person's change from homosexuality. Each stand bears relevance to the clinical expectations of homosexual men and women.

REFERENCES

Adler, A. *The practice and theory of individual psychology.* London: Routledge & Kegan Paul, 1971.

American Psychiatric Association. *Diagnostic and statistical manual of mental disorders.* Washington, DC: American Psychiatric Association, 1952, 1968, 1980.

Ansbacher, H. L., & Ansbacher, R. R. *The individual psychology of Alfred Adler.* New York: Basic Books, 1956.

Barlow, D., Abel, G. G., & Blanchard, E. Plasma testosterone levels and male homosexuality: A failure to replicate. *Archives of Sexual Behavior,* 1974, *3,* 571.

Barnhouse, R. T. *Homosexuality: A symbolic confusion.* New York: Seabury Press, 1977.

Bell, A. P., & Weinberg, M. S. *Homosexualities: A study of diversity among men and women.* New York: Simon and Schuster, 1978.

Bell, A. P., Weinberg, M. S., & Hammersmith, S. K. *Sexual preference, its development in men and women.* Bloomington, Ind.: University of Indiana Press, 1981.

Bieber, I., et al. *Homosexuality: A psychoanalytic study of male homosexuals.* New York: Basic Books, 1962.

Bieber, I. A discussion of "Homosexuality: The ethical challenge." *Journal of Consulting and Clinical Psychology,* 1976, *44*(2), 163–166.

Boswell, J. *Christian social tolerance and homosexuality: Gay people in western Europe from the beginning of the Christian era.* Chicago: University of Chicago Press, 1980.

Bugental, James F. T. *The search for authenticity.* New York: Holt, Rinehart and Winston, 1965.

Burton, A. On the nature of loneliness. *American Journal of Psychoanalysis,* 1961, *21,* 34–39.

Clark, T. R. Homosexuality and psychopathology in non-patient males. *American Journal of Psychoanalysis,* 1975, *35,* 163–168.

Coleman, J. C., Butcher, J. N., & Carson, R. C. *Abnormal psychology and modern life.* Glenview, Ill.: Scott, Foresman, 1980.

The confessions of St. Augustine. (J. K. Ryan Ed. and Trans.) Garden City, NY: Image Books, 1960.

Davison, G. C. A message from the president. *Association for Advancement of Behavior Therapy Newsletter,* 1974, *1,* 1–3.

Davison, G. C. Homosexuality: The ethical challenge. *Journal of Consulting and Clinical Psychology,* 1976, *44,* 157–162.

Davison, G. C. Not can but ought: The treatment of homosexuality. *Journal of Consulting and Clinical Psychology,* 1978, *46*(1), 170–172.

Devereaux, G. Institutionalized homosexuality of the Mohave Indian. *Human Biology,* 1937, *9,* 498–527.

Diamant, L. An investigation of a relationship between liberalism and lesbianism. Symposium paper presented at the annual meeting of the American Psychological Association, San Francisco, 1977.

Dover, K. J. *Greek homosexuality.* Cambridge, Mass.: Harvard University Press, 1978.

Ellis, Havelock. *Studies in the psychology of sex.* (3rd. ed.) (Vol. II). *Sexual inversion.* Philadelphia: F. A. Davis, 1915.

Ehrhardt, A., Epstein, R., & Money, J. Fetal androgens and female gender identity in the early treated andrenogenital syndrome. *Johns Hopkins Medical Journal,* 1968, *122,* 160–167.

Feldman, M. P., & MacCulloch, M. J. *Homosexual behavior, therapy, and assessment.* Oxford: Pergamon Press, 1971.

Fenichel, O. *The psychoanalytic theory of neurosis.* New York: W. W. Norton, 1945.

Ford, C. S., & Beach, F. A. *Patterns of sexual behavior.* New York: Harper & Row, 1951.

Freud, S. Three essays on sexuality and other works (1905). In J. Strachey, (Ed.), *The standard edition of the complete psychological works of Sigmund Freud* (Vol. 3). London: Hogarth, 1953.

Freud, S. The psychogenesis of a case of homosexuality in a woman (1920). In J. Strachey (Ed.), *The standard edition of the complete psychological works of Sigmund Freud* (Vol. 18). London: Hogarth, 1955.

Gundlach, R. H. Sexual molestation and rape reported by homosexual and heterosexual women. *Journal of Homosexuality,* 1977, *2*(4), 367–384.

The Holy Bible Revised Standard Version. New York: Thomas Nelson and Sons, 1952.

Hooker, E. A preliminary analysis of group behavior of homosexuals. *Journal of Psychiatry,* 1956, *42,* 217–225.

Kameny, F. E. Gay liberation and psychiatry. *Psychiatric Opinion,* 1971, *7,* 18–27.

Karlen, A. *Sexuality and homosexuality: A new view.* New York: W. W. Norton, 1971.

Karr, R. G. Homosexual labeling and the male role. *Journal of Social Issues,* 1978, *34*(3), 73–83.

Katz, J. *Gay American history: Lesbians and gay men in the USA.* New York: Thomas Y. Crowell, 1976.

Kinsey, A. C., Pomeroy, W. B., & Martin, C. E. *Sexual behavior in the human male.* Philadelphia: W. B. Saunders, 1948.

Kinsey, A. C., Pomeroy, W. B., Martin, C. E., & Gebhard, P. H. *Sexual behavior in the human female.* Philadelphia: W. B. Saunders, 1953.

Klein, M. *Contributions to psychoanalysis.* London: Hogarth, 1948.

Kohlenberg, R. J. Treatment of a homosexual paedophiliac using *in vivo* sensitization: A case study. *Journal of Abnormal Psychology,* 1974, *83,* 192–195.

Kolodney, R. C., Masters, W. H., Hendryx, J., & Toro, G. Plasma testosterone and semen analysis in male homosexuals. *New England Journal of Medicine,* 1971, *285,* 1170.

Konopka, G. Adolescent delinquent girls. *Children,* 1964, *11*(1), 21–26.

Krafft-Ebing, R. von. *Psychopathia sexualis, with especial reference to antipathic sexual instinct.* A medico-forensic study. (F. J. Rebman, Trans.). Brooklyn, NY: Physicians and Surgeons, 1922.

Lamal, P. A behaviorist's view. Symposium paper presented at the annual meeting of the Southeastern Psychological Association, Atlanta, 1978.

Legal Citation: Doe v. Commonwealth's Attorney for the City of Richmond 44 USL Week 3545, 1976.

Legal Citation: State of Louisiana v. Young: 193 2a 243, 1966.

Lief, H. I. Sexual Survey #4: Current thinking on homosexuality. *Medical Aspects of Human Sexuality,* 1977, *11,* 110–111.

Long, G. T. Homosexuality: Mental illness or social role. Symposium paper presented at the annual meeting of the Southeastern Psychological Association, Atlanta, 1978.

Lovelace, R. F. *Homosexuality and the church.* Old Tappan, NJ: Fleming H. Revell, 1978.

Masters, W. H., & Johnson, V. E. *Homosexuality in perspective.* Boston: Little, Brown, 1979.

Matt, H. J. Sin, crime, sickness or alternative life style?: A Jewish approach to homosexuality. *Judaism,* 1978, *27*(1), 13–24.

Meredith, R. L., & Riester, R. W. Psychotherapy, responsibility, and homosexuality: Clinical examination of socially deviant behavior. *Professional Psychology,* 1980, *6,* 174–193.

Michael, R. P., & Zumpe, D. Biological factors in the organization and expression of sexual behavior. In I. Rosen (Ed.), *Sexual deviation,* Oxford: Oxford University Press, 1979.

Money, J., & Ehrhardt, A. *Man and woman, boy and girl: The differentiation and dimorphism of gender identity from conception to maturity.* Baltimore: Johns Hopkins University Press, 1972.

Opler, M. K. Anthropological and cross-cultural aspects of homosexuality. In J. Marmor (Ed.), *Sexual inversion.* New York: Basic Books, 1965.

Pavlov, I. P. *Lectures on conditioned reflexes.* (W. H. Gantt, Trans.). New York: International Publishers, 1928.

Pillard, R., Rose, R. M., & Sherwood, M. Plasma testosterone levels in homosexual men. *Archives of Sexual Behavior,* 1974, *3,* 577.

Pomeroy, W. B. *Dr. Kinsey and the institute for sex research.* New York: Harper & Row, 1972.

Riddle, D. I., & Morin, S. F. (Issue Eds.). Psychology and the gay community. *Journal of Social Issues,* 1978, *34,*(3), 1–142.

Riess, B. F., & Safer, J. M. Homosexuality in females and males. In E. S. Gromberg and V. Franks (Eds.) *Gender and disordered behavior.* New York: Brunner/Mazel, 1979.

Saghir, M. T., & Robins, E. *Male and female homosexuality.* Baltimore: Williams and Wilkins, 1973.

Schaeffer, C. E. The Hutenai female berdache: Courier, guide, prophetess, and warrior. *Ethnohistory,* 1965, *12,*(3), 193–236.

Siegelman, M. Adjustment of homosexual and heterosexual women: A cross-national replication. *Archives of Sexual Behavior,* 1979, *8*(2), 121–125.

Siegelman, M. Adjustment of male homosexuals and heterosexuals. *Archives of Sexual Behavior,* 1972, *2,* 9–25.

Skinner, B. F. *Science and human behavior.* New York: MacMillan, 1953.

Snyder, M., & Uranowitz, S. W. Reconstructing the past: Some cognitive consequences of person perception. *Journal of Personality and Social Psychology,* 1978, *36*(9), 941–950.

Socarides, C. W. Female homosexuality. In R. Slovenko (Ed.) *Sexual behavior and the law.* Springfield, Ill.: C. Thomas, 1965.

Sturgis, E. T., & Adams, H. E. (Comments) The right to treatment: Issues in the treatment of homosexuality. *Journal of Consulting and Clinical Psychology,* 1978, *46*(1), 165–169.

Sullivan, H. S. *Conceptions of modern psychiatry.* New York: W. W. Norton, 1953.

Sullivan, H. S. *The psychiatric interview.* New York: W. W. Norton, 1970.

Szasz, T. *The myth of mental illness.* New York: Holber, 1964.

Thompson, C. Changing concepts of homosexuality in psychoanalysis. *Psychiatry,* 1947, *10,* 183–189.

Thompson, N. L., McCandless, B. R., & Strickland, B. R. Personal adjustment of male and female homosexuals and heterosexuals. *Journal of Abnormal Psychology,* 1971, *78,* 237–240.

Tourney, G., & Hatfield, L. M. Androgen metabolism in schizophrenics, homosexuals, and controls. *Biological Psychiatry,* 1973, *6,* 23.

Tripp, C. A. *The homosexual matrix.* New York: McGraw-Hill, 1975.

Turner, R. K., Pielmaier, H., James, S., & Orwin, A. Personality characteristics of male homosexuals referred for aversion therapy: A comparative study. *British Journal of Psychiatry,* 1974, *125,* 447–449.

West, D. J. *Homosexuality.* Chicago: Aldine Publishing, 1967.

Wolff, C. *Love between women.* New York: St. Martin's Press, 1971.

2

THE FIRST CLINICIANS

Vern L. Bullough

Homosexuality has existed as long as recorded history. Clinicians, however, have only been dealing with homosexuality for a little more than a hundred years. This is not because homosexuality did not appear in the medical literature of the past, it did; rather the entry of the clinician is dependent upon classifying homosexuality as something that can be cured or at least treated. Most of the ancient medical writers regarded homosexuality as a fact of life, something they had observed in their practice. With the advent of Christianity, however, homosexuality came to be classified as a sin, and though medical writers continued to describe the existence of homosexuals, their observations were sometimes uninfluenced by theological assumptions (Bullough, 1978).

In the eighteenth century, there was a growing concern with the "sickness" aspects of sexuality. Reasons for this concern were in part due to the confusion of the effects of venereal disease with sexual activity itself. Third stage syphilis was not fully understood until the end of the nineteenth century and even then there were debates about its effects until well into the twentieth century. Thus many of the symptoms of third stage syphilis such as tabes dorsalis, mental illness, heart damage as well as damage to other internal organs, wasting of tissues, bone lesions, et al., were not attributed to syphilis but to sexual activity per se. Adding to the concern of the medical community were other observations such as the lassitude following orgasm or the tendency to masturbate of those who were developmentally disabled and confined in the emerging institutions of the eighteenth century. Hermann

Boerhaave in his *Institutiones medicae* in 1728, for example, reported that the rash expenditure of semen brought on a lassitude, a feebleness, a weakening of motion, fits, wasting, dryness, fevers, aching of the cerebral membranes, obscuring of the senses and above all the eyes, a decay of the spinal cord, a fatuity, and other like evils.

The eighteenth century was the great age of medical theories. A major reason for this is that theories, in the absence of full understanding of the causes and nature of disease allowed the physician to treat the patient without knowing what had caused the illness. One of the more popular of such theorists was John Brown who developed a theory known as brunonianism: this had important implications for attitudes toward sex. In his *Elements of Medicine,* first published in 1780, Brown had held that all bodily states were explained either by excitability or lack of excitability (1803). Too little stimulation and too much stimulation were to be avoided. Both could be compared to the effect of air upon a fire. If there was not enough air (insufficient excitement), the fire would smoulder and go out, but if there was too strong a forced draft (too much excitement), the fire would burn excessively, become exhausted, and also go out. Sex had the potential of giving too much excitement. Mutual contact of the sexes as occurred in kissing or fondling gave an impetuosity to the nerves, but intercourse itself might bring temporary relief since it led to a lessening of excitement, providing it was not engaged in too frequently. Frequent intercourse released too much energy and excessive loss of semen was something to be avoided.

Brown did not distinguish between types of sexual activity. This was the contribution of S. A. D. Tissot (1766) whose monograph on onanism was translated into English as early as 1766. Tissot believed that physical bodies suffered a continual waste, and unless the losses suffered in such wastage were replaced, death would be the inevitable result. Normally much of the wastage was restored through nutrition, but even with an adequate diet, the body could still waste away through diarrhea, loss of blood, and most importantly for our purposes, through seminal emission. Some loss of male (and female) semen was necessary or otherwise the human race would die out, but the male had to husband his semen, making absolutely certain that any loss went toward the purpose of procreation. Similar assumptions were made about females. Onanism for Tissot was far more penicious than an excess in marital or premarital fornication, and if engaged in by young people would tend to destroy the mental faculties as well as lead to the various symptoms now associated with third stage syphilis.

The nineteenth century saw the expansion of the concept of what might be called masturbatory insanity, but as far as the clinician was concerned, the answer obviously was to not engage in sex, or to limit sex activities to procreation. One of the real dangers that the medical community saw in masturbation was that it would lead to homosexuality (Bullough, 1973). Though homosexuality was regarded with greater horror than other forms of sexuality, it seemed an inevitable consequence of excessive sexual activity, a sort of contagious disease that could only become worse. The medical answer obviously was to abstain from such activity. Homosexuals, however, did not particularly subscribe to the idea that their behavior was a perversion and they did not want to abstain. Many turned to alternative explanations for their behavior. Karl Heinrich Ulrichs (1975), for example, under his own name and the pen name of Numae Numantius poured out a series of polemical, analytical, and theoretical pamphlets defending homosexuality in the period between 1864 and 1879. Ulrichs argues that the "abnormal" instincts were inborn, and therefore no more dangerous to the individuals born with such instincts than procreative sex would be to married individuals. Homosexuality ("urning" was the term he used) did not derive from bad habits, but from a hereditary disease and the individuals who engaged in such activity were neither physically nor intellectually inferior to normally constituted individuals. Rather it was natural for some individuals to prefer their own sex rather than the opposite sex, and the dangers for these people in their sexual activities were no greater than between a man and wife, and no more unnatural.

Similar ideas were being expressed at about the same time by Karoly Maria Benkert who, under the name of Kertbenny, wrote a pamphlet defending homosexuality and in the process coined the term "homosexuality." Kertbenny wrote (1905):

> in addition to the normal sexual urge in man and woman, Nature in her sovereign mood, has endowed at birth certain male and female individuals with the homosexual urge, thus placing them in a sexual bondage which renders them physically and psychically incapable—even with the best intention—of normal erection. This urge creates in advance a direct horror of the opposite sex, and the return of this passion finds it impossible to suppress the feeling which individuals of his own sex exercise upon him. (pp. 36-37)

The writings of Ulrichs and Benkert and others had their effect upon those in the medical community concerned with sexuality, but a somewhat different effect than they intended. They added rather than detracted from the medicalization of sex, and homosexuality came to be regarded as pathological. Sex itself was dangerous but those born with "perverted" sex instincts were sick individuals. This concept appeared in the pioneering work of Carl Westphal (1869) who marked the real beginning of a therapeutic approach to homosexuality. Westphal coined the term "contrary sexual feeling" to describe a female homosexual transvestite who came to his attention, and held that such a phenomenon resulted from moral insanity due to "cogenital reversal of sexual feeling." Westphal described the patient's feeling of attraction for other females as a strong pleasure over which she had no control and against which she heroically struggled. He diagnosed the patient as having a form of moral insanity consisting of the morbid perversion of natural feelings, impulses, love, and moral tendencies. In effect the result was to include the new diagnosis of "contrary sexual feeling" as a form of neurosis, an obsessional state which persisted and occasionally disrupted but did not seriously undermine mental functioning.

The psychiatrist who became most associated with the concept of pathological homosexuality was Richard von Krafft-Ebing, the author of *Psychopathia Sexualis* (1894), originally published in 1886. He combined several prevailing nineteenth century theories to explain sexual pathology:

1. The idea that diseases were caused by the physical nervous system.
2. The idea that there were often hereditary defects in the system.
3. The concept of degeneracy.

Krafft-Ebing held that the sexual drive was one of the compelling forces in life but argued that individuals should not simply surrender to the gratification of the sexual impulse since to do so was to sink to the level of the beast. Human sexuality could lead to the most sublime virtue or the basest vice and life itself was a "never ceasing duel between the animal instinct and morality." It was the power of the will and the strength of character that rescued humans from the animal nature of their sexual drives. He also believed that true love could only exist between persons of opposite sex.

Sexual pathology originated either from environmental damage to the sexual organs or from degeneracy, an inherited, diseased condition of the nervous system. All anomalous sexual function were classified as "sexual neuroses," although some were more serious than others. Homosexuality, or a contrary sexual feeling, resulted from a diseased psychosexual center in the cerebral cortex, and clinically was a sign of degeneracy. Setting it off was masturbation in tainted individuals to the degree that the contrary sexual instinct corresponded to the degrees of hereditary predisposition.

> *In the milder cases there is a simple hermaphroditism; in more pronounced cases only homosexual feeling and instinct, but limited to the vita sexualis; in still more complete cases, the whole psychical personality and even the bodily sensations are transformed so as to correspond with the sexual inversion; and, in the complete cases, the physical form is correspondingly altered (1935, pp. 285–286).*

Thus one went from psychosexual hermaphroditism to homosexuality, to effeminization, to androgeny; in this last, men in the androgynous stage became totally feminine in thought, feeling, and physical appearance; women did the reverse. This description is close to what we now diagnose as transsexualism.

Treatment was difficult although in some cases, where environmental factors were at work, it was sufficient to prevent masturbation and relieve excitability. For hard core congenital cases the only possible way to combat homosexual impulses was through post-hypnotic suggestion designed to remove the impulse to masturbation and homosexual feeling and to encourage heterosexual emotions. Those forms of homosexuality that could be acquired were more a vice than a disease. Where Westphal had held that individuals suffering from contrary sexual feeling could struggle valiantly and successfully against their proclivity, Krafft-Ebing held such a struggle was impossible where homosexuality was a disease since such homosexuals enjoyed their aberration. He did hold that individuals with this biological proclivity should be objects of human pity and understanding rather than targets of moral or legal condemnation. This applied both to the public at large and to those who tried to treat them.

Not all fully accepted the biological determininism of Westphal and Krafft-Ebing. One who did was Havelock Ellis who in his *Studies in the Psychology of Sex* (1896-1938) argued that though homosexuality was probably inborn, there were aspects of homosexuality which were acquired and psychological. Some of these "exciting causes" could be eliminated, but even if they all were there would still be some homosexuals. He made a plea for tolerance and acceptance of variations from the norm which were harmless and perhaps even valuable. For Ellis, sexual inversion (his term) was incurable and the best a therapist could do was to help the individual accept himself or herself.

Others such as Benjamin Tarnowsky (1933), distinguished between congenital and acquired disorders. Writing in 1896, Tarnowsky felt nothing could be done for the congenital "pederast" but it was a different matter for those who acquired their pathology. The acquired homosexual or pederast was born healthy but had been corrupted by education or example, and this marked him for life.

More effectively challenging the degeneracy theory as an adequate explanation for the origin of sexual perversion were a number of individuals, most notably the French psychologist Alfred Binet (1887). Binet did not believe that heredity alone was a sufficient explanation but instead the shape of the "perversion" was in part acquired and fortuitous. Though this could only take place because the individual was potentially degenerate in the first place, he shifted the etiology of sexual perversion from somatic to psychological factors. Picking up on Binet's ideas was the psychiatrist Albert von Schrenck-Notzing (1892), a student of Krafft-Ebing. He held that the contrary sexual feeling could occur fortuitously during sexual development as a result of moral contagion or other cause. By making sexual perversion a contagious disease, as opposed to a solely congenital disorder, it became curable. This meant that psychiatry had a method for treating it: hypnosis. Since the basis of mental disease was environmental "contagion," it could be cured through a type of healthy counter contagion, i.e., the intervention of a therapist.

Others continued on this line including the American psychiatrist, Morton Prince (1898), who argued that the evidence for congenital theory rested entirely upon the self reports of homosexuals themselves. Instead most of the differences in characteristics and personalities between female and male, and among males and females, could be accounted for by socialization. Since a lack of volitional control lay at the root of homosexuality, Prince believed it could be cured by strengthening the will and character of the homosexual and by developing a sense of morality.

Albert Moll added to this by claiming that while homosexuality might be congenital, it was not necessarily a hereditary neuropathic condition. Prognosis for those that he classed as homosexual because of psychosocial factors was good. The effective therapist could direct the male psychosocial homosexual toward the heterosexual and transform the general psychic state to one of a more masculine behavior. Treatment included encouraging him to seek the company of women who could charm and captivate him by those qualities quite in accord with his nature. He should not, however, try intercourse until his recovery was far advanced because failure at it would weaken the hope for recovery.

In 1897 Moll published a treatise that ultimately led to the rejection of degeneracy theory in most of the twentieth century discussions of homosexuality. Moll defined the sexual instinct as:

> *an emotion which strives to express itself in external bodily movement of such a nature that the completion of the movement may bring about the enhancement of pleasure, already present, or the removal of the feelings of unpleasure. (1931, p. 20)*

He divided the drive into a (1) "detumescent drive" and (2) "contrectation drive." The detumescent drive was an organic impulse to evacuate a secretion just as a full bladder impelled one to empty the bladder. In the female this drive was tied to ovulation while in the male it was associated with ejaculation. The contrectation drive impelled the male to a physical and psychical approach of a female, and the female to the approach of the male. It was usually gratified by the touching, fondling, and kissing of sexual partners. Moll held that the two drives were or could be independent, with contrectation tied to the higher impulses in the form of love, one physical and one psychical. In any case, the psychical elaborations were limited by biological considerations which varied somewhat from individual to individual although Moll classified everyone as being in three different biological stages dependent upon evolutionary development. Each of the stages involved certain sexual stimuli and thus there were both psychical and biological factors involved.

Returning to heredity factors was the physician Magnus Hirschfeld. Hirschfeld agreed that there were both internal and external factors involved in homosexuality but the internal were most important since they were essentially physiological or biological while the external were environmental stimuli. The internal factors included what he called "inner secretins" i.e., hormones. Male homosexuals had a high amount of gynecin, the female fluid, while female homosexuals had a high amount of andrin. These "hormones" resulted in a neurochemical interaction center in the brain which affected both conduct and embryonic development (Hirschfeld, 1913).

As far as Hirschfeld was concerned therapy aimed at curing a homosexual would not be worthwhile since it was an innate drive occurring through no fault of the patient. Instead the purpose of the therapy was to help the individual accept himself and to help him be a useful citizen. In sum homosexuality was biologically determined and the homosexuality was not a disease nor was it a crime. It was a fact of life which the therapist should accept.

Probably the most influential theoretical school on therapy was Sigmund Freud. Though Freud agreed with Krafft-Ebing on the necessity of redirecting sexual energies, he also disagreed. Where Krafft-Ebing had held that variant sexual behavior came from sexual drives that had been misdirected in their aim or object, Freud held that the misdirection lay in the nervous system and the mind through which the instinctual drive operated. Though Freud paid comparatively little attention to most forms of variant sexual behavior, his followers seized upon his concepts to emphasize the environmental and accidental causes of variant impulses far more than he himself did. Though later behaviorists, stressing learning and conditioning of animals and man, carried this type of environmental and accidental determination to an extreme, the practical result of both Freudianism and learning psychologies was to suggest that everyone had the potential to channel his drives toward any form of gratification and use any object. Unavoidably, this undermined the assumption that certain forms of sex were against nature, for nature itself, the instinctual drive, was visualized as being able to express itself in many ways.

Freud regarded homoerotic behavior as a normal part of growing up. Most individuals moved beyond this stage into adult heterosexuality, and so, by implication, adult homosexuality was a distortion of natural development. His explanations for the failure of certain individuals to move beyond the homoerotic phase centered around the relationship of a child to its parents, most particularly the parent of the opposite sex. Homosexuality was conceived by Freud and his followers also as a flight from incest. In the absence of a father or in the presence of a weak one, a boy child who fell in love with his mother and sought to become her lover repressed his desire most effectively by suppressing sexual feeling towards all women. In other instances the child fell in love with the parent of the same sex and replaced or attempted to oust the parent of the other sex. The boy, suppressing his desires for his father, sought to be like the woman who accepted his father, but unable to reconcile the incestuous sin of a father love, sought the father in other males. Such a boy might become effeminate, play the female role in the sex act, and become attracted to other men (Freud, 1910, 1913, 1922, 1924-50, 1960).

Many of the psychoanalysts following the path blazed by Freud tended to emphasize that homosexuality was environmentally, rather than constitutionally caused, and by implication, curable. (Adler, 1917; Brill, 1913; Ferenczi, 1916; Stekel, 1922; Wittels, 1929; Money-Kryle, 1932; London, 1933, 1937; Bergler, 1956; Bieber, 1962) Many non-psychoanalytic psychiatrists seemed to agree (Allen, 1949; Hamilton, 1936; Henry, 1941; Caprio, 1952; Henry, 1955; West, 1955; see also Ellis, 1965).

Freud himself remained more biological and this was an important factor in his belief about the latent homosexual. Freud, however, contradicted himself somewhat and it is important to determine when he wrote to determine his attitudes. In his later life he became more and more biologically oriented, expressing doubts about the cure of homosexuality, as in his famous 1935 letter to a mother whose son was homosexual (Freud, 1955).

In retrospect it seems that though homosexuality came to be regarded as pathological in the nineteenth century, there was a widespread belief during most of the nineteenth century that the causes were biological, and therefore the therapist or clinician could do little more than make the patient more comfortable with his condition. By the turn of the century, however, while biological factors remained important, a number of individuals began to distinguish between physical and psychic aspects of sexuality, and to try to treat the psychic. Freud represents the kind of watershed in that he still subscribed to a strong biological base, but recognized the potential of treatment for some alleviation, at least early in his career. Following in the footsteps of Freud, however, were a number of investigators from a wide variety of approaches who emphasized the importance of therapy and who pushed the biological factor into the background although it never entirely disappeared. To a historian it seems that once environmental causes came to be recognized, therapists and clinicians took it as a challenge to argue that they had the answer to the problem of homosexuality and they alone or their like minded colleagues could cure it. The biological nature continued to be emphasized by a counter group but until the past few decades they have not been as influential.

Whether the "clinicians" and "therapists" either of the immediate past or of a century ago were helpful to understanding homosexuality is a question which this author does not care to try to answer. In retrospect, it often seems that we keep repeating the assumptions of the past with little new data or evidence.

REFERENCES

Adler, Alfred. The homosexual problem. *Alienist and Neurologist 38* (1917), 285.

Allen, C. *The sexual perversions and abnormalities.* London: Oxford University Press, 1949.

Bergler, Edmund. *Homosexuality.* New York: Hill and Wang, 1956.

Bieber, Irving et al. *Homosexuality.* New York: Basic Books, 1962.

Binet, Alfred. La fetichesme dans l'Amour. *Revue Philosophique 24* (1887), 143–167.

Boerhaave, Herman. *Institutiones medicae,* in *Opera medica universa.* Geneva: Fratres de Tournes, 1728.

Brill, A. A. Conception of homosexuality. *Journal of the American Medical Association, LX* (1913), 336.

Brown, John. *The elements of medicine.* Revised by T. Beddoes, (2 vols. in 1) Portsmouth, NH: William and Daniel Treadwell, 1803.

Bullough, Vern L., and Martha Voght. Homosexuality and its confusion with the 'secret sin' in pre-Freudian America. *Journal of the History of Medicine, 28* (1973), 143–156; reprinted in Vern L. Bullough, *Sex, society and history.* New York: Neale Watson, Science History Publications, 1976, 112–124.

Bullough, Vern L. *Sexual variance in society and history.* New York: Wiley, 1978; reprinted University of Chicago Press.

Caprio, F. S. *The sexually adequate male.* New York: Citadel Press, 1952.

Ellis, Albert. *Homosexuality: Its causes and cure.* New York: Lyle Stuart, 1965.

Ellis, Havelock. *Sexual inversion* in *psychology of sex.* Reprinted 2 vols., New York: Random House, 1936, vol. I, part IV.

Ferenczi, S. *Contributions to psychoanalysis: Sex in psychoanalysis.* Boston: Badger, 1916.

Freud, Sigmund. *Basic writings.* New York: Modern Library, 1938.

Freud, Sigmund. *Collected papers.* London: Imago Publishers, 1924–1950.

Freud, Sigmund. Die drei grundform der homosexualität. *Jahrbuch für sexuelle Zwischenstufen 13* (1913), parts 2, 3, 4.

Freud, Sigmund. Historical notes: A letter from Freud. *American Journal of Psychiatry, CVII* (April 1955), 786–787.

Freud, Sigmund. *Leonardo da Vinci,* translated A. A. Brill, London: Kegan Paul, Trench, Trubner and Co., 1922.

Freud, Sigmund. *Letters.* New York: Basic Books, 1960.

Freud, Sigmund. *Three contributions to sexual theory.* New York: Journal of Nervous and Mental Diseases Publishing Company, 1910.

Hamilton, G. V. Defensive homosexuality. In *Encyclopedia sexualis,* edited Victor Robinson. New York: Dingwall-Rock, 1936, 334–342.

Henry, W. S. *All the sexes.* New York: Holt, Rinehart and Winston, 1955.

Henry, G. W. *Sex variants.* New York: Hoeber, 1941.

Hirschfeld, Magnus. *Die homosexualität des mannes und das weibes.* Berlin: Louis Marcus, 1913.

Kertbenny. +143 des Preussichen Strafgetz buches vom 14, April 1851, und siene Aufrechter halting als + 152 im Entwurfe eines Strafgestzbuches für den Norddeutschen Bund. *Jahrbuch fur sexuelle Zwischenstufen, VII* (1905), 9–66.

Krafft-Ebing, R. von. *Psychopathia sexualis.* Translated from the 7th enlarged and revised German edition by G. Chaddock. Philadelphia: R. A. Davis, 1894. Also translated from the 12th edition by F. J. Rebman. Brooklyn: Physicians and Surgeons, 1935.

London, L. S. Analysis of a homosexual neurosis. *Urology and Cutaneous Review, XXXVI* (1933), 93.

London, L. S. *Mental therapy.* New York: Liveright, 1937.

Moll, Albert. *Die contrare sexualempfindung.* Berlin: Fischer's Medicinische Buchhandlung, 1891. Published as *Perversion of the sexual instinct,* translated by Maurice Popkin. Newark, NJ: Julian Press, 1931.

Moll, Albert. *Untersuchungen über die libido sexualis.* Berlin: Fischer's Medicinische Buchhandlung, 1897. English version was entitled *Libido sexualis: Studies in the psychosocial laws of love verified by clinical case histories,* translated by David Berger. New York: Ethnological Press, 1933.

Money-Kryle, R. E. *Development of the sexual impulses.* London: Kegan, Paul, Trench, Trubner, and Company, 1932.

Prince, Morton. Sexual perversions or vice? A pathological and therapeutic inquiry. *Journal of Nervous and Mental Disease 25* (1898), 237–256.

Schrenck-Notzing, Albert. *Die suggestions-Therapie bei Krankshaften Erschenungen des Geschlechtssinnes: mit besonderer Berucksichtlgung der contraren Sexualempfindung.* Stuttgaart: Ferdinand Enke, 1892.

Stekel, W. *Bisexual love.* Boston: Badger, 1922.

Tarnowski, B. *Anthropological, legal, and medical studies on pederasty in Europe,* translated by P. Gardner. New York: Falstaff Press, 1933.

Tissot, S. A. D. *Onanism: Or, a treatise upon the disorders of masturbation,* translated by A. Hume. London: J. Pridden, 1766.

Ulrichs, Karl Heinrich. *Forschungen über das Ratsel der Mannmannlichen Liebe* (1864–1879) translated as *Researches on the riddle of love between men,* in Jonathan Katz, Editor, *Homosexuality: Lesbian and gay men in society and literature.* New York: Arno Press, 1975.

West, D. J. *The other man.* New York: William Morrow, 1955.

THEORY AND RESEARCH

3

KINSEY AND OTHERS: EMPIRICAL INPUT

Marvin Siegelman

The major research areas concerning homosexuality included in this chapter are psychometric assessment, adjustment, and parental background. My intention is to present a *developmental* overview and analysis of empirical research appearing in print primarily between 1945 and 1984 related to these three topics. Empirical studies will refer to research efforts in which objective, quantitative data were obtained from groups of subjects using psychometrically sound or reasonably well established measuring devices. The sources referred to will be predominantly professional articles and some books written in English and I will follow the general literature search used by Weinberg and Bell (1972). The review of literature in this chapter, in contrast to most other compilations, will be mostly chronological, according to year of publication. The breakthrough Kinsey, Pomeroy and Martin survey in 1948 will be examined in relation to prior and subsequent work, and the papers *within* the measurement, adjustment, and parent background areas will typically (but not always) be enumerated in a chronological order. I believe some important insights can be gleaned from such a developmental presentation. The enormous nonempirical psychological literature on lesbianism and male homosexuality (Churchill, 1967; Karlan, 1971; Legman, 1941; Marmor, 1980; Parker, 1971; Weinberg & Bell, 1972; West, 1967) will not be covered, and while not exhaustive, the empirical research endeavors noted will be comprehensive. The present chapter will include a historical note describing some of the typical and atypical early thinking of clinicians between 1895 and 1947, an overview of research *findings* appearing between 1945 and 1984, a critique of research strategies and theory, and finally some thought about future research directions.

PRE-KINSEY: A HISTORICAL NOTE

Prior to the appearance of the Kinsey et al. report in 1948, most of the professional literature dealing with assessment, adjustment, and parental background of homosexuals consisted of subjective reports based primarily on case studies of patients in therapy, prisoners, or other clinical groups (Churchill, 1967; Parker, 1971; Weinberg & Bell, 1972). In 45 journal articles that I located written between 1895 and 1948 relating to measurement, adjustment, and parental background, 20 appeared in medical journals, 17 in psychoanalytic publications and the remaining 8 in psychological, sociological and legal journals. I estimate that at least 90% of the papers were written by psychiatrists and the findings were mostly based on case studies of patients in psychotherapy. In 61 additional papers not related to the topic of this chapter, 19 dealt with severe pathology, 15 with hormones, 8 with treatment, and again most appeared in medical journals. The only reports that could be considered empirical research as defined above, were nine assessment papers describing homosexual indicatores on the Goodenough Draw a Man Test (Dark & Geil, 1948; Geil, 1944), Rorschach (Bergman, 1945; Duo & Wright, 1945; Lindner, 1946), MMPI (Benton, 1945; Burton, 1947; Gough, 1946), and a MF vocabulary test (Slater & Slater, 1947). These nine assessment papers will be described later.

Historically, it is interesting to note the considerable diversity of opinion concerning the adjustment and parental background of homosexuals found in these early reports. Although most of the medical writers considered homosexuals to be maladjusted or neurotic (Adler, 1917; Bergler, 1947; Deutsch, 1933; Kraft-Ebing, 1886; Stekel, 1933), other psychiatrists stated that many homosexuals were deviant in their sex object but otherwise well adjusted or normal (Brill, 1913; Freud, 1949; Ellis, 1896; Hirschfield, 1944). The disagreement about the type and impact of parental background that homosexuals had was also clearly depicted in these early writings among the psychoanalysts (Adler, 1917; Brill, 1913; Deutsch, 1933; Freud, 1949), and among the psychiatrists (Bergler, 1947; Ellis, 1896; Kraft-Ebing, 1886; Hirschfield, 1944).

Of special historical significance was the work of one of the first, and I believe most brilliant, sexologists Havelock Ellis (1896, 1915). In several respects this sagacious British physician was the forerunner of Kinsey et al. (1948), Hooker (1958), Masters and Johnson (1966), and Money (1984). In 1895 Ellis wrote, "My cases were not gathered from my medical practice, nor by the aid of police officials. In this respect they differ from the groups of inverts presented by previous observers who have consequently been led to overestimate the morbid or vicious elements in such cases" (p. 225). He described 33 male subjects, including two physicians, and some 50 years later Kinsey, Pomeroy, and Martin (1948), and still later Masters and Johnson (1957), followed in his footsteps (Brecher, 1976). Ellis regarded sexual inversion as a product of both heredity and environment, a precursor of Money (1984), although he gave greater emphasis to "congenital" factors. The great complexity of etiology and behavioral expressions was recognized and he was "... prepared to admit that very divergent views of sexual inversion are largely justified" (p. 261). Concerning adjustment, Ellis believed that "... inversion may occur in apparently healthy and otherwise normal individuals" (p. 265), a belief later tested and supported by Hooker (1957). In conclusion Ellis wrote:

> *I do not now propose to consider what the attitude of society and the law should be towards the person I have here described. How far should we regard him as a deformed person to be medically treated? How far as an anti-social person to be punished or restrained? These are important questions, so important that many of us are inclined to rush to a conclusion concerning them without any clear idea as to what sexual inversion is. Before we decide what to do with the sexual invert we must know something about him and we must attain to some general agreement. (266-267)*

Diversity, controversy, and certainty characterized this early period of medical exploration. Many writers were convinced that they understood the nature of homosexuality, and few realized the severe limitations of basing their conclusions on small, biased, clinical case studies of patients that they had in therapy. Although the stage was *not* set, a new Zeitgeist, especially methodologically speaking, was to emerge or was initiated with the ground-breaking survey conducted by Kinsey et al. (1948), that challenged most of the existing writers in this field and contributed to enticing a larger number of diverse specialists to explore more carefully the enigmatic topic of homosexuality.

KINSEY

The sources, number of subjects, and methods of data collection on homosexuality were drastically modified and expanded by a scientist trained to precisely measure the characteristics of insects, who serendipitously turned his attention to the study of human sexual behavior, Alfred C. Kinsey. In 1948 Kinsey et al. conducted the first large scale study of carefully selected, non-clinical, representative samples of certain groups from wide geographic locations, employing precise, psychometrically sound measuring instruments. Kinsey et al. assessed homosexual behavior on a *continuum* of sexual activity and psychological reactions ranging from exclusively heterosexual (0) to exclusively homosexual (6) on a seven point scale. Previously investigators usually described sexual orientation as two dimensional, homosexual *or* heterosexual (Kinsey et al., 1948). No large scale study representative of a cross section of the total U.S. population had ever been conducted before, and the Kinsey staff were surprised to find a higher incidence of homosexual behavior in their sample that greatly exceeded the figure ranging from two to six percent noted by previous writers (Karlen, 1971). Kinsey carefully considered the *frequency* of sexual contacts which led to orgasm as well as a person's preferences and reactions in devising his seven point scale. Although the findings of Kinsey et al. (1948) have been criticized (Geddes, 1954), their data clearly indicate that the incidence of homosexual acts and reactions was rather widespread and much greater than most people had realized.

The social and scientific implications of the extent and diversity of homosexual acts (see pages 659-666 in Kinsey et al., 1948) seriously challenged the existing Zeitgeist and opened the door for qualitatively and quantitatively different types of research. If all homosexuals are not the same in their sexual experience and attitudes, and if a sizeable number of people have had homosexual experience, then a wide variety of people with different homosexual experience need to be studied; caution must be used in concluding that homosexual activity is necessarily pathological; the etiology may be quite complex (as complex as the cause of heterosexual orientation); simple biological, genetic, or parental background determinants could be untenable; and social/legal reactions should be made on the basis of a *given* individual who is unique. Simplistic notions about homosexuality based on unsupported subjective speculations were less acceptable without more convincing evidence. The surgency of clinical and subjective reports did not cease, of course, but a greater diversity of questions and outlooks began to emerge in different fields. Ford and Beach (1951), for example, reported that in 49 societies, out of 76 where information was available, "homosexual activities of one sort or another are considered normal and acceptable for certain members of the community" (p. 137).

POST-KINSEY

Empirical studies of measurement, adjustment, and parental background will now be presented chronologically. A critique of methodology and theory related to these studies will be given after the papers are reviewed in a separate section.

Psychometric Assessment

The primary focus of the papers reviewed in this section was to measure personality traits of homosexuals. Projective techniques and paper and pencil questionnaires were used to search for personality differences that differentiated between homosexuals and heterosexuals.

Figure Drawing Several authors (Barker, Mathis, & Powers, 1953; Dark & Geil, 1948; Geil, 1944; Grams, 1957; Machover, 1949; Pustel, 1971) examined the presence of feminine traits in the drawings of homosexual men. Using the Goodenough Draw a Man Test with male prisoners, Geil (1944) found that of 16 drawings judged to be most feminine, 13 were drawn by confirmed homosexuals, and of 16 drawings judged to be most masculine, 14 had case histories that provided no evidence of homosexuality. Geil noted that not all homosexuals projected feminine characteristics in their drawings, but when a man did draw feminine qualities it usually indicated strong feminine components in his personality. An innovative paper by Darke and Geil (1948) compared the Goodenough Draw-a-Man Test projections of masculinity-femininity in five groups of homosexuals (N = 100) ranging from those who engaged exclusively in homosexual activity to subjects whose experiences were predominantly heterosexual, and also to groups representing different homosexual roles, such as passive sodomists, active fellators, etc. The 100 male subjects were prisoners and significant differences were reported on drawing indicatores of femininity between some of the groups representing different degrees of homosexual activity and between different types of homosexual roles. Machover (1949) claimed that male homosexuals place special emphasis in their drawings of ears, hips and buttocks, that they draw large eyes and eyelashes, that they put heels on the shoes of male figures, confuse front and rear of drawings, reveal homosexual panic in their shading of legs or trousers. Data were collected on 50 male homosexual and 35 male heterosexual soldiers by Barker, Mathis, and Powers (1953) using the Machover Human Figure Drawing Test. They found that the homosexuals had a longer delay in identifying the self-same figure, they frequently distorted the female figure, but they did not give female characteristics to the male figure. Testing 15 of Machover's signs, Grams (1958) reported that three psychologists could not distinguish the degree of homosexual involvement of 50 male adolescent inmates of a state training school. Pustel (1971) found stronger feminine tendencies in the drawings of feminine (passive) mentally retarded homosexual males compared to masculine (active) mentally retarded homosexual males.

The importance of which sex is drawn by homosexuals in their first figure has been explored by several writers (Barker, Mathis, & Powers, 1953; Fraas, 1970; Hammer, 1954; Machover, 1949; Roback, 1974; Vilhotte, 1958; Whitaker, 1961). The underlying assumption is that there is a reversal in the sexual identification of male homosexuals who are feminine and female homosexuals who are masculine (Brown & Tolor, 1957). Machover (1949) noted that there is evidence of some degree of inversion in the records of all people who draw the opposite sex first in response to the standard instructions. Barker, Mathis and Powers (1953) found that 46 of their 50 homosexual soldiers drew the same sex figure first thus showing no propensity to draw the opposite sex figure first. Fifteen of 20 homosexual pedophiles drew their own sex first which was not significantly different from non-homosexual sex offenders reported by Hammer (1954). Drawing the female figure first was not diagnostic of homosexuality for 50 mentally defective homosexual males compared to 50 mentally defective heterosexual males (Vilhotte, 1958). Whitaker (1961) found that of 236 men referred through a court clinic, those rated as homosexual and/or effeminate produced significantly more female figures when asked to draw a person of whatever sex the subject wanted to draw. Two different group comparisons were made by Fraas (1970) of homosexual versus heterosexual patients in a hospital. The sex of the figure drawn first was significant for one group comparison but not significant for the second group comparison. No significant differences in sex of figure drawn first were found between male and female homosexuals versus male and female heterosexuals by Roback (1974).

In an excellent review and critique of work dealing with the sex of the first drawn figure, Brown and Tolor (1957) concluded that "The meager evidence that is available indicates that the great majority of male homosexuals do *not* draw a figure of the opposite sex first . . ." (p. 210). This 1957 analysis is still accurate and it is applicable to female homosexuals also. In a fine summary and evaluation of psychometric aspects of homosexuality, Grygier (1957) pointed out that there is no evidence to justify Machover's (1949) claims that homosexuality is indicated if the opposite sex is drawn first, and that various signs, mostly of an effeminate nature, are indicative of male homosexuality. It should be noted, in addition, that almost all of the studies reviewed above were done with male subjects only.

Rorschach Many of the papers that examined Rorschach content, supposedly indicative of homosexuality, used the 20 signs designed by Wheeler in 1949 (Aronson, 1952; Davids, Joelson, & McArthur, 1956; De Luca, 1966; Goldfried, 1966; Hendlin, 1976; Hooker, 1958; Meketon, Griffith, Taylor, & Wiedeman, 1962; Reitzell, 1949; Yamahito & Griffith, 1960). The remaining eight studies reviewed in this section (Anderson & Seitz, 1969; Bergman, 1945; Coats, 1962; Duo & Wright, 1945; Fein, 1950; Lindner, 1946; Nitsche & Robinson, 1956; Raychaudhuri & Murkerji, 1970; Sjostdt & Hurwitz, 1959) used content areas quite similar to those developed by Wheeler (1949).

Using 20 known male homosexuals at an Army Psychiatric Consultation Service, Bergman (1945) reported that for 15 men the characteristics of their Rorschach responses included a high percentage of sex organ responses associated with anxiety, homosexual arousing content, heterosexual revulsion, and a reluctance to distinguish positively between male and female figures. Duo and Wright (1945) found that the characteristic Rorschach responses in their single sample of 42 male homosexual psychiatric patients included dehumanization, confusion of sexual identification, feminine identification, castration and phallic symbolism, sexual and anatomical responses, and paranoid reactions. For both male and female homosexuals, Lindner (1946) published a list of six Rorschach response areas with typical content indicative of homosexuality. For example, on Card 1, the lower central D is seen by a feminine type male homosexual as "a muscular, mannish female." A useful critique of the Bergman (1945), Duo and Wright (1945), and Lindner (1946) papers was written by Wheeler (1949).

Using 100 male patients at a mental health clinic, Wheeler (1949) constructed and compared 20 signs on the Rorschach that he believed were indicative of homosexuality with therapists' judgement of homosexuality. He described the homosexual, in part, as having negative attitudes towards women, feminine identification, and as being paranoid. Reitzell (1949) found no statistically significant differences between 22 male homosexuals compared to alcoholics and hysterics, who had been referred as probation cases, on the 20 Wheeler signs. Some of the Rorschach response indicators of male homosexuality presented by Fein (1950), who tested 9 homosexuals, 10 neurotics and 24 normal college students, were feminine apparel and behavior, men with feminine attributes, men with sex connotation and aversion, and males and females seen in symmetrical blot areas. Aronson (1952) presented evidence to support the Freudian theory of paranoia where more Wheeler Rorschach signs of homosexuality were shown by paranoid males than by psychotic or normal men. Davids, Joelson and McArthur (1956) reported that four Wheeler signs, plus one new Rorschach sign, significantly differentiated between 20 overt homosexuals seeking therapy, 20 neurotics, and 20 normal college students. The 5 significant Wheeler signs were:

1. human or animal seen as contorted, monstrous or threatening on Card IV.
2. humanized animal on Card V.
3. human female with derogatory specification on Card VIII.
4. male or female genitalia on any card, and a new sign.
5. rear view response on any card.

The Rorschach protocols of 19 homosexual and 19 heterosexual convicted males referred to a mental health clinic were analyzed by Nitsche and Robinson (1956). Twelve content categories were evaluated, such as dehumanization, qualification toward the abnormal, projection of feminized behavior, sexual responses, and no significant differences were found. In 1958 Hooker evaluated the Rorschach responses of 30 matched pairs of well adjusted homosexual and heterosexual males. Although the homosexuals could be clearly differentiated on 2 out of 20 Schaefer themes, anal orientation and feminine emphasis, no significant differences, in addition, were found for M quality, human figure, and form level on the Rorschach. In comparing 74 male prisoners, 36 exhibitionists and 38 homosexuals, to 88 patients in a state hospital, Sjostedt and Hurwitz (1959) found the 74 deviants produced significantly more FC (form dominates over color-associated with relatively mature perceptual-cognitive functioning) responses. Yamahiero and Griffith (1960) reported data for 23 involuntary homosexual male patients which supports the percent of Wheeler signs present in homosexual protocols. The reduction in homosexual behavior in 45 males being treated at the Putman Clinic was significantly greater for those patients who had a castration anxiety response on Card II of the Rorschach (Coats, 1962). Little support was found by Meketon, Griffith, Taylor and Wiedeman (1962) for the Freudian assumption that latent homosexuality is asociated with paranoia when the Wheeler signs were used as the basis for judging such a relationship. Forty-two homosexual patients about to be discharged from the Army, compared to 25 soldiers with upper-respiratory infections, were found to not differ from each other on the 20 Wheeler signs by DeLuca (1966). The homosexuals did, however, respond with a higher number of Wheeler signs. The mean number of Schaefer signs was significantly different for homosexual (N = 15), heterosexual (N = 15), and sex-role disturbed (N = 15) psychiatric in-patients at the Denver V.A. Hospital (Anderson & Seitz, 1969). The use of Schaefer's signs was found to be more adequate than the Wheeler signs in distinguishing between 60 active homosexuals, passive homosexuals, sex-role disturbed, and heterosexual male prisoners in a Calcutta jail (Raychaudhuri & Mukerji, 1970). Hendlin (1976) compared 30 educated, adjusted male homosexuals to 30 educated, well adjusted heterosexuals and found no difference between these two groups when the traditional indices of homosexuality on the Rorschach were used.

A systematic evaluation of studies using the Wheeler signs to evaluate homosexuality as depicted in Rorschach protocols, including sampling and methodological problems, was made by Goldfried, Stricker, and Weiner (1971). They concluded that 6 of the 20 signs (7, 8, 10, 16, 17, 20) were unquestionably useful (Goldfried, 1966). The most sophisticated, and still up to date, critique of the literature related to the use of the Rorschach for assessing homosexuality was made by Hooker (1958). She concluded that using a list of Rorschach signs to differentiate between homosexuals and heterosexuals without other substantive evidence will usually fail, and even when successful does not reveal much about the totality of a homosexual's personality. In *all* of the above investigations, one should note, only male subjects were used and non clinical samples were reported on in only two papers (Hendlin, 1976; Hooker, 1958).

Minnesota Multiphasic Personality Inventory (MMPI) Twelve of the MMPI studies reported on below used nonclinical samples (Adelman, 1977; Boxley; 1973; Dean & Richardson, 1964, 1966; Horstman, 1975; Kripner, 1964; Loney, 1970; Manosevitz, 1970a, 1970b, 1971; Williams, 1981; Wilson, 1973). Patients or prisoners were evaluated in 15 MMPI investigations (Aaronson & Grumpelt, 1961; Benton, 1945; Botwinic & Machover, 1951; Burton, 1947; Fraas, 1970; Frieberg, 1967; Cubit & Gendreau, 1972; Gough, 1946; Hartman, 1967; Miller & Hannum, 1963; Pierce, 1972, 1973; Singer, 1970; Thomas, 1951; Yamahiro & Griffith, 1960). In 1945, Benton found that the responses of the Masculinity-femininity (Mf) Scale of the MMPI differentiated the "invert" from among other clinical groups, but Gough

(1946) reported negative results for psychotics. Burton (1947) compared 34 "inverts," 20 rapists, and 87 delinquents and found significant differences between the "inverts" and rapists (who were considered to represent an extreme form of masculinity) and between the "inverts" and the general group of delinquents on the Mf scale of the MMPI. The Mf scale of the MMPI was used by Botwinick and Machover (1951) to test for homosexuality in a group of 39 male alcoholics at Kings County Hospital compared to the normative population, and no significant differences were found. Higher Mf scores on the MMPI were found for 40 hospitalized homosexual male World War II veterans compared to 20 hospitalized heterosexual veterans by Thomas (1951). Yamahiro and Griffith (1960) reported that 23 involuntary homosexual male patients scored high on the Marsh-Hilliard-Liechti MMPI sexual deviation scale. A new MMPI scale independent of the Mf scale called the HSX scale devised by Panton (1960) to detect homosexuality in prison populations consisting of 22 items that differentiated between 58 homosexual and 174 heterosexual prison inmates. Aaronson and Grumpelt (1961) found that three masculinity-femininity subscales of the MMPI differentiated between 25 homosexuals and 25 heterosexual male patients, but some homosexuals had masculine orientations. Homosexual female prisoners could not be differentiated from heterosexual female prisoners on the MMPI (Miller & Hannum, 1963). Kripner (1964) found that scores on the Mf and Panton HSX scales of the MMPI successfully differentiated between male college students who discussed homosexual problems (N = 80) compared to male students who did not (N = 52) during a counseling interview. The scores on the MMPI Mf scale were found to be significantly higher for 40 highly educated, socially functioning male homosexuals compared to comparable heterosexuals (Dean & Richardson, 1964, 1966). No significant differences were reported by Hartman (1967) for 18 sociopaths compared to 18 sexual deviates in a state mental hospital on 11 MMPI scales. The use of the Mf scale of the MMPI by Panton for evaluating homosexuality was supported by Frieberg (1967), who compared hospitalized male schizophrenics (19 homosexuals, 16 heterosexual sex deviates, 67 general patients) and 50 normal subjects. The Mf MMPI scale did not differentiate between nine male homosexual patients compared to nine heterosexual patients in a state hospital (Fraas, 1970). Two separate analyses of male homosexuals (N = 49, N = 40) and heterosexuals (N = 49, N = 40) involving correlations between each of the 60 items comprising the MMPI Mf scale and sexual orientation yielded significant associations for 13 items (Manosevitz, 1970a). In a sample of 50 men, 28 homosexuals and 22 heterosexuals, Manosevitz (1970b) found that the homosexuals scored significantly higher on the D, Mf, Pt, and Sc MMPI scales. In a later study (Manosevitz, 1971) 49 homosexual males, in contrast to 64 heterosexual males, scored significantly higher on the Mf, F, K, D, Pd, Pa, Pt, Sc, and Si MMPI scales, and the Mf scale was not seriously contaminated by educational bias (r = .20). Singer (1970) reporting on 97 psychiatric male outpatients found that scores on the

MMPI Mf scale, but not on the Aaronson Masculinity-Femininity Index of the MMPI, nor on Panton's HSX MMPI Homosexuality scale, differentiated between overt homosexuals and heterosexuals. The mean MMPI F scale score was reported by Loney (1970) to be significantly higher for 29 self-labeled "normal" homosexuals compared to heterosexual males. Cubit and Gendreau (1972) noted that the MMPI Panton HSX scale did not differentiate between 21 homosexual and 72 heterosexual male prison inmates, but the Mf scale did. They also reported that age was significantly correlated with the HSX scale, but age and education were not correlated with the Mf scale. Pierce (1972) inferred that education and IQ were independent of HSX when he compared the HSX results of male college students and prisoners. Ten out of 12 long-term homosexual inmates were correctly identified by Pierce from HSX scale data as compared to 24 heterosexual inmates and a group of heterosexual college students. Panton's HSX scale responses were also found by Pierce (1973) to be effective in differentiating between 16 male prisoners who performed homosexual acts only after incarceration (situational). Wilson (1973) reported a new female homosexuality scale consisting of the Hs, Hy, and Pt MMPI scales which differentiated between 64 female members of a gay liberation group and 64 female heterosexuals. Black male homosexuals (N = 30), were compared to a matched group of black heterosexuals (N = 30) and were found by Boxley (1973) to score higher on the MMPI scales Hs, D, Hy, Mf, Pt, and Sc, but only the Mf scale was above T = 70. Horstman (1975) reported that for 50 homosexual and 50 heterosexual male undergraduates, there were no MMPI differences between the groups on the three validity scales, nine basic clinical scales, and two special scales (Es and At), that the Mf scale was significantly elevated for the homosexuals, and that there was a significant negative correlation between education level and Mf scores for the homosexuals. A comparison of professionally employed lesbians and heterosexual women on the MMPI indicated that the lesbians tended to see themselves as significantly more masculine than the heterosexual females (Adelman, 1977). Williams (1981) used two subscales derived from the MMPI Mf scale with items independent of traditional male-female stereotypes inherent in the full Mf scale which significantly differentiated between 10 homosexual and 10 heterosexual male restaurant workers.

Most studies support the finding that scores on the MMPI Mf scale effectively differentiate male homosexuals compared to male heterosexuals, but the findings for the Panton HSX scale, as well as the remaining MMPI scales, are inconsistent. Except for the Miller and Hannum (1963), Wilson (1973), and Adelman (1977) reports, all of the MMPI studies were based on male samples only. Another important consideration is that except for the Mf scale, most authors reported that mean MMPI scale scores were within the normal adjustment range, or T-scores were less than 70. For important critiques concerning the use of the MMPI in research on homosexuality see Gonsioreck (1977) and Suppe (1981).

Miscellaneous Davids, Joelson, and McArthur (1956) used 10 empirically derived Thematic Apperception Test (TAT) signs of male homosexuality (Tejessy, 1952; Lindzey, Tejessy, Davids, & Heinemann, 1953) in their study of 20 homosexuals, 20 neurotics, and 20 normal college students. The two signs that discriminated significantly between the homosexual and normal groups were sexual, genital references and a high degree of feminine identification. Lindzey, Tejessy, and Zamansky (1958) reported that 9 out of 20 TAT indices of homosexuality significantly differentiated between 20 Harvard undergraduate male homosexuals and 20 Harvard undergraduate male heterosexuals. A judge was able to sort the protocols into homosexual and heterosexual groups with 95 percent accuracy. In 1965 Lindzey found the 20 TAT signs also differentiated between 14 homosexual and 16 heterosexual male prisoners.

David and Rabinowitz (1952) compared two groups of male patients in state hospitals, 100 idiopathic epileptics and 100 overt homosexuals on the Szondi Test. Three signs of homosexuality out of nine were significant. The Szondi syndrome of homosexuality could not be entirely demonstrated in any of the 10 male homosexuals reported on by Bendel (1955).

Grygier (1958), using the Dynamic Personality Inventory (DAP) that he developed, described 20 male homosexual neurotics as showing a typically feminine pattern of behavior as compared to 22 male heterosexual neurotics. The DAP was used by Stringer and Grygier (1976) and was found to be effective in differentiating between male homosexual and heterosexual patients. The DAP emphasizes a multidimensional approach to masculinity and femininity. Cattell and Morony (1962) reported different Sixteen Personality Factor Questionnaire (16 PF) profiles for 100 male prisoners convicted of homosexual crimes, 67 non-homosexual male prisoners, and 100 heterosexuals not in prison. Twenty one homosexual male prisoners were compared to 72 heterosexual male prisoners on the Cattell 16 PF by Cubitt and Gendreau (1972) who found that the 16 PF I (tough vs. tender-minded) scale did not differentiate between the two groups but the 16 PF C (affected by feelings vs. emotionally stable) scale did.

Bernard and Epstein (1978), using the Bem Sex Role Inventory, reported 26 male homosexuals to be "androgynous," and 26 male heterosexuals to be highly "masculine sex typed." The Bem scale was also used by Nickeson (1980) who compared 30 gay male and lesbian teachers to 30 heterosexual male and female teachers. She found that the lesbians scored significantly higher on the masculine scale than did heterosexual women, with no differences on the feminine scale, and that gay men scored higher on the feminine scale than did heterosexual men, with no differences on the masculine scale. Shavelson, Biaggio, Cross, and Lehman (1980) found 26 lesbians, compared to 26 heterosexual women, to be more masculinely sex-role typed on the Bem questionnaire.

Slater and Slater (1947) devised a Mf test of 40 words known to men but relatively unfamiliar to women and 40 words known primarily to women. They found that this vocabulary Mf test significantly distinguished between the 50 heterosexual men versus the 37 homosexual men referred to a neurological hospital for treatment. Fraas (1970) indicated that the Gough Masculinity-Femininity Scale scores of the CPI were not significantly different for nine male homosexuals versus nine male heterosexual patients at a state hospital. Thompson, Schwartz, McCandless, and Edwards (1973) reported that 84 lesbians were more masculine than 94 heterosexual women, and 127 male homosexuals were less masculine than 123 male heterosexuals, on the Heilburn Adjective Check List. No significant differences on masculinity-femininity were found for the above four groups on the Franck Drawing Completion Test. Schatzberg, Westfall, Blumetti, and Berk (1975) developed an Effeminancy Rating Scale and reported significant differences on this scale for 16 homosexual versus 16 heterosexual males. Lester, David, McLaughlin, Cohen, and Dunn (1977) concluded that the handwriting of 17 homosexual and 17 heterosexual men was more masculine and the handwriting of 17 homosexual and 17 heterosexual women was more feminine. Cole (1983), using a developmental questionnaire, found that 129 male homosexuals, contrasted with 120 male heterosexuals, recall having perceived themselves as less masculine than their childhood peers.

Adjustment

Men Most of the empirical research conducted with non-clinical samples reported below found that male homosexuals were as well adjusted as male heterosexuals (Andress, Franzini, & Linton, 1974; Bell & Weinberg, 1978; Braatan & Darling, 1965; Chang & Block, 1960; Clark, 1975; Dean & Richardson, 1964; DeLuca, 1966; Evans, 1970, 1971; Haltiwanger, 1979; Hooker, 1957, 1959; Horstman, 1972; Kinsey et al., 1948; Liddicoat, 1961; McGovern, 1977; Nickeson, 1980; Oliver & Mosher, 1968; Richter, 1976; Saghir & Robins, 1970b, 1973; Skrapec & MacKenzie, 1981; Siegelman, 1972b, 1978; Thompson, McCandless, & Strickland, 1971; Weinberg & Williams, 1974; Weis, 1977; Weis & Dain, 1979; Willmott & Brierley, 1984). One study (Oliver & Mosher, 1968) using prisoners also found no differences in adjustment. In view of the data presented for 5300 males, Kinsey et al. (1948) concluded that

> ... *it is difficult to maintain the view that psychosexual reactions between individuals of the same sex are rare and therefore abnormal or unnatural, or that they constitute within themselves evidence of neuroses or even psychosis (p. 659)*

The first empirical study of non-clinical male homosexuals devoted specifically to the consideration of adjustment was conducted by Hooker (1957, 1959), and remains one of the best efforts to date, and which appears to have set the stage for many of the subsequent papers reviewed in this section. Hooker reported that for 30 matched pairs of homosexual and heterosexual males, three well known authorities found no differences on adjustment when they analyzed Rorschach, TAT, and MAPS protocols, and in fact agreed that two thirds of the homosexuals were average to superior in adjustment. Chang and Block (1960) reported that 20 homosexual males did not differ on self-acceptance (correspondence between ideal self and perceived self on an adjective check list) from 20 heterosexual males. No evidence of psychopathology was discovered by Liddicoat (1961) for 50 male homosexuals and 50 male heterosexuals in South Africa using biographical material. Using the MMPI with 40 matched highly educated, socially functioning male homosexual and heterosexual males, Dean and Richardson (1964) concluded that the homosexual subjects did not show indicators of neurosis, psychosis or other pathological personality deviations. Seventy six male homosexual and 50 male heterosexual college students were reported to show no group differences on the MMPI and the Mooney Problem Check List (Braaten & Darling 1965). De Luca (1966), using Rorschach protocols, found that male homosexuals being discharged from the Army because they were homosexuals and not for psychiatric reasons did not differ on psychopathology from 25 male heterosexual controls who were in hospital for upper respiratory infections. In 1967, De Luca reported similar non-significant differences between 20 male heterosexual and 40 male homosexual regular Army inductees on the Blacky Test. Oliver and Mosher (1968) found no differences on the MMPI and the Mosher Forced-Choice Guilt Inventory responses of 50 homosexual and 25 heterosexual male prisoners. On the basis of responses on the Cattell 16 PF of 44 homosexual men and 111 heterosexual men, Evans (1970) concluded that the results support the view that homosexual behavior is not necessarily an indication of psychological disturbance. The responses to an adjective check list administered by Evans (1971) to the same subjects in his 1970 paper indicated that the homosexual group had more problems in self-acceptance and in relating to others, but that only a small minority could be considered neurotic. Thompson, McCandless, and Strickland (1971) found that 127 homosexual males, compared to 123 heterosexual males, did not differ on defensiveness, personal adjustment, or self-confidence as measured by an adjective check list and a semantic differential.

In two studies (Siegelman, 1972b, 1978) I addressed three issues that had been given little attention in previous investigations. I used a multidimensional methodology in my attempt to cope with the enigmatic, and still unresolved, problem of what do we mean by "adjustment?" The tests devised for normal populations that I utilized were the Scheier and Cattell (1961) Neuroticism Scale Questionnaire, which has a Total score as well as subscale scores on Tender-Mindedness, Depression, Submissiveness, and Anxiety, and in addition, eight scales devised by four other psychometricians (Alienation, Trust, Goal-Directed, Self-Accepting, Sense of Self, Dependency, Nurturance, and Neurotic) primarily through factor-analytic methods (Siegelman, 1972b). I also demonstrated the critical importance of distinguishing between masculine and feminine homosexuals and heterosexuals when evaluating adjustment, by presenting highly divergent indications of adjustment for high versus low masculine and feminine subjects. And finally, I replicated my research using exactly the same measurements with a cross-national sample. For nonclinical samples in the U.S. and England I found few differences in adjustment between male homosexuals and male heterosexuals, especially those low on femininity.

There was no difference in quantity, type or degree of psychopathology, as measured by the MMPI according to Horstman (1972), who tested 50 heterosexual and 50 homosexual male undergraduates. Horstman (1975) also reported for the same two groups that there were no differences on the Taylor Manifest Anxiety scale or the Barron Ego-Strength scales. From data gathered using a structured interview, Saghir and Robins (1970, 1973b) could find no difference in psychopathology between 89 homosexual and 35 unmarried heterosexual men. A questionnaire was employed in a cross-cultural study of U.S. homosexual (N = 1117) and heterosexual subjects (N = 3101), Dutch homosexual (N = 303) and heterosexual subjects (N = 35) by Weinberg and Williams (1974). They found no signficant group differences on self-acceptance and psychosomatic symptoms between the homosexual and hetero-sexual males within each country, and comparisons on adjustment between the three homosexual groups in the three countries were also not significantly different. The responses of 82 male homosexuals and 100 male heterosexual college students on the Meninger Word Association Test, which includes several areas of emotional conflict, were not different from each other (Andress, Franzini, & Linton, 1974). The Tennessee Self-Concept Scale (TSCS) was used by Clark (1975) with 140 college educated males equally distributed in each of the seven Kinsey et al. (1948) heterosexual-homosexual behavior categories. He found no significant differences between the two groups, and between the homosexuals and the TSCS normative data, on self-criticism, defensiveness, self-concept, general emotional maladjustment, neurosis, psychosis, personality-character disorder, and overall personality integration. Richter (1976) reported no differences between 20 male hetero-sexuals and 40 "free ranging" homosexuals on the Mosher sex guilt measure on any of the MMPI scales as well as the Goldberg scale of general adjustment. A prison group of 20 homosexual males had abnormal MMPI profiles and they scored significantly higher on the Mosher sex guilt measure thus suggesting the danger of generalizing from prison samples to non-clinical samples. No differences were found between 50 homosexual and 50 hetero-sexual males on the Washington University Sentence Completion ego develop-ment scale (Weis, 1977; Weis & Dain, 1979). Homosexual males, McGovern (1977) reported, scored higher than heterosexual males on three measures of healthy interpersonal relationships. A 175 page interview schedule was used by

Bell and Weinberg (1978) with 689 homosexual males and 337 heterosexual males assigned to close-coupled, open-coupled, functional, dysfunctional, and asexual groups. Except for the asexual and dysfunctional groups, homosexuals were found to be similar to heterosexuals on psychosomatic symptoms, happiness, exuberance, self-acceptance, loneliness, worry, depression, tension, paranoia, and suicidal feelings and impulses. Haltiwanger (1979) administered the CPI to 86 gay men and 38 lesbians and reported that psychological adjustment as reflected in their CPI profiles did not differ from the CPI normative data. Fifteen male gay teachers of grades K-12 were matched with 15 heterosexual male teachers by Nickeson (1980) who found no differences on social/personal adjustment measured by The Teacher Characteristics Schedule. Skrapec and MacKenzie (1981) reported 24 homosexual males as having higher self-esteem than 24 heterosexual males. Willmott and Brierley (1984) reported no differences on the Eysenck Personality Inventory scales of Neuroticism and Extraversion between 20 homosexual males and 20 hetero-sexual males.

Several investigations have reported that homosexual males were more neurotic or maladjusted than heterosexual males (Bieber, Dain, Dince, Drellich, Grand, Gundlach, Kremer, Rifkin, Wilbur, & Bieber, 1962; Bruce, 1942; Cattell & Maroney, 1962; Doidge & Holtzman, 1960; Prytula, Wellford, & De Monbreun, 1979; Schiere & Cattell, 1961; Williams, 1981). Four of these reports (Bieber et al., 1962; Cattell & Maroney, 1962; Doidge & Holtzman, 1960; Schiere & Cattell, 1961) used clinical samples of patients in treatment or prisoners. Bruce (1942) reported that 53 male homosexuals, compared to the "general population" as indicated on the standardized test indicators, scored higher on neuroticism, introversion, and self consciousness, and lower on self-sufficiency, dominance, self-confidence, and sociability on the Bernreuter Personality Inventory. He also noted that the homosexuals scored higher on the Humm-Wadsworth Temperament Scale factors of hysteroid, manic, de-pressive, autism, and paranoid. Doidge and Holtzman (1960) found that 20 males in the psychiatric clinic at Lackland Air Force Base were more seriously disturbed than 20 male heterosexual patients. The responses of 133 male homosexual prisoners in Australia convicted of one or more homosexual offenses were found by Schier and Cattell (1961) to score higher on the Neuroticism Scale-Questionnaire than a group of "normal" heterosexuals. Cattell and Maroney (1962) administered the 16 PF to 100 Australian male prisoners and found that compared to a group of unskilled heterosexual males not in prison, that the homosexual prisoners were more neurotic, had a weak ego, and were characterized by low superego development. Bieber et al. (1962) reported that on a questionnaire completed by 77 psychoanalysts about their patients in therapy, 106 male homosexual patients were described as more seriously disturbed than their heterosexual patients. Using the responses on a self-report inventory of recalling adolescent experiences, Prytula, Wellford, and De Monbreun (1979) found that 28 homosexuals, versus 28 heterosexuals, scored lower on a body self-concept scale and on a general self-concept scale, but there were no significant differences on scales measuring body weight, sports activities, parental relationships, and interpersonal self-concept. In 1981 Williams wrote that 10 homosexual males compared to 10 heterosexual males, had significantly higher scores on the Pepper and Strong Mf-sub-1 and Mf-sub-2 scales of the MMPI which indicated a greater emotional vulnerability and reactivity to stressful social stimuli and more fears, aversions, and maladjustment in sexual and social relationships.

Some studies considered the degree to which adjustment varied *among* different homosexual groups (Chaffee, 1976; Dailey, 1979; Hammersmith & Weinberg, 1973; Hart, 1978; King, 1980; McGovern, 1977; Ross, 1978; Weiss, 1977) in contrast to the studies noted above that examined the adjustment of homosexuals compared to heterosexuals. Hammersmith and Weinberg (1973) found that for 2497 male homosexuals in the U.S., the Netherlands, and Denmark, commitment to a homosexual identity, and a report of significant others being supportive of that identity, was directly related to psychological adjustment. The Cattell 16 PF results indicated that, contrary to the expected outcome, 16 male homosexuals in stable homosexual relationships had slightly less positive 16 PF profiles than 15 never in a stable relationship (Chaffee, 1976). The stable relationship group, however, did score higher on self-reliance. McGovern (1977) found that for homosexual males, psychological androgyny was associated with lack of neuroticism, and with healthy interpersonal relationships, while for heterosexual males, androgyny was associated with self-actualization and was inversely related to one measure of marital adjustment. Weis (1977) found that for 100 homosexual males and females, and for 100 male and female heterosexuals, it appeared that persons at higher levels of ego development (conscientious, individualistic, autonomous, and integrated) tended to describe themselves in psychologically androgynous terms. He also noted that more positive attitudes toward homosexuality were related to higher levels of ego development for both heterosexual and homosexual individuals. Several questionnaires, including the Bem Sex Role Inventory and the Tennessee Self Concept Scale, were administered to 54 homosexual men by Hart (1978), who indicated that effeminacy, both positive and negative feminine-typed attributes, was associated with maladjustment. The findings of Ross (1978) showed that negative societal reaction to homosexuality was associated with psychological maladjustment in homosexual males. Dailey (1979) reported that little difference was detected between 14 heterosexual married couples, 12 heterosexual non-married couples, and 10 homosexual couples (5 male and 5 female) in terms of the success of the permanent pairing relationships studied. King (1980), using a subsample of the Bell and Weinberg (1980) Kinsey institute study, found that homosexual males who came to terms with their "deviant" sexuality functioned quite well as adults and reported less troubled early parent-child relationships. The above type studies reflect what Morin (1977) believes to be of greater interest to homosexuals themselves rather than to researchers who study homosexuals.

Women The majority of empirical studies of adjustment concurred that female homosexuals were not different than female heterosexuals (Armon, 1960; Bell & Weinberg, 1978; Ferguson & Finkler, 1978; Friedman, 1968; Hopkins, 1969; Kinsey et al., 1953; Liddicoat, 1961; Nickeson, 1980; Ohlson & Wilson, 1974; Saghir & Robins, 1973a; Shavelson, Biaggio, Cross, & Lehman, 1980; Siegelman, 1972a, 1979; Strassberg, Cunningham, & Larson, 1979; Thompson, McCandless, & Strickland, 1971; Weis, 1977; Wilson & Greene, 1971). All of these investigations used non-clinical subjects. Although Kinsey, Pomeroy, Martin, and Gebhard did not specifically refer to psychopathology in their 1953 survey of women, one can probably assume that their conclusion that male homosexuals were not more or less well adjusted than male heterosexuals would apply to their sample of 5940 women also. Armon (1960) analyzed the Rorschach and Figure Drawing responses of 60 homosexual and heterosexual women. She found no differences on dependency, hostility toward men, conflict about the female role, and personal-social adjustment. No evidence of psychopathology was discovered with a biographical questionnaire used by Liddicoat (1961) with 50 female homosexuals and 50 female heterosexuals in South Africa. Data from the Personal Orientation Inventory and the Eysenck Personality Inventory were used by Freedman (1968) who reported that 62 homosexual women, compared to 67 heterosexual women, were more independent and inner-directed, had greater acceptance of aggression, found more satisfaction in work, and were not different in self-acceptance. Results on the 16 PF reported by Hopkins (1969) for 24 lesbians and matched controls suggested that lesbians were more independent, resilient, reserved, dominant, bohemian, self-sufficient, and composed. Responses to the CPI, Eysenck Personality Inventory, and the Edwards Personal Preference Schedule were reported by Wilson and Green (1971) to reveal no pathological differences between 46 female homosexuals and 46 female heterosexuals. Thompson, McCandless, and Strickland (1971) reported that 84 well educated homosexual women, compared to 94 heterosexual women, did not differ in defensiveness, personal adjustment, or self-confidence on an Adjective Check List, nor in self-evaluations on a Semantic Differential. I conducted a U.S. study (Siegelman, 1972b) with 84 homosexual women and 133 heterosexual women, and a replication study in England (Siegelman, 1979) with 61 homosexual women and 49 heterosexual women, using the same adjustment questionnaire that I used for male subjects which I described above on page 45. The results for the two countries were strikingly similar. The homosexual women in the U.S. scored lower on Submissiveness and Total Neuroticism Score on the NSQ and higher on Goal-Direction, and Self-Acceptance, while the British homosexual women scored lower on Tender-Minded and higher on Goal-Directed and Self-Acceptance. In both countries the comparison groups were similar on the remaining nine scales. Statistically non-significant results were reported for 57 homosexual versus 44 heterosexual women on neurosis and personality disorders as measured by a structured interview (Saghir & Robins, 1973a). Sixty four lesbians, compared to 64 heterosexual women, were found by Ohlson and Wilson (1974) to be more alert, responsible, less anxious and more self-confident as depicted on MMPI responses. Weis (1977) reported no differences between 50 homosexual and 50 heterosexual women in ego development measured by the Washington University Sentence Completion test. Sixty-three lesbians described themselves as less anxious than a normative group of women in college on the Manifest Anxiety and Defensiveness Scale (Ferguson & Finkler, 1978). The 293 homosexual females reported on by Bell and Weinberg (1978) did not differ except for the dysfunctional group, from the 140 heterosexual females on any of the adjustment variables noted above on page 47 for their male subjects. These authors concluded

> ... that homosexual adults who have come to terms with their homosexuality, who do not regret their sexual orientation, and who can function effectively sexually and socially, are no more distressed psychologically than are heterosexual men and women (p. 216)

Strassberg, Cunningham and Larson (1979) administered the Tennessee Self-Concept Scale to 40 homosexual and 40 heterosexual women and found that the lesbians scored higher on Number of Deviant Signs but were not different on overall self-esteem, general maladjustment and perception of their body, physical appearance, state of health and sexuality. Social/personal adjustment, as measured by The Teacher Characteristic Schedule, was reported by Nickeson (1980) to be similar for 15 lesbian teachers compared to 15 heterosexual female teachers. Shavelson et al. (1980) indicated that 26 lesbians were more satisfied with their sex lives than 26 heterosexual women. Of 400 psychiatrists who answered a questionnaire concerning their attitudes toward female homosexuality (Gartrell, Kramer, & Brodie, 1974) 87 percent stated that their concept of mental health included the possibility of a well adjusted homosexual woman, and 66% challenged the traditional belief that lesbianism is equated with sickness or inadequacy.

Several studies indicated different types of psychopathology among lesbians (Eisenger, 1972; Hassell & Smith, 1975; Kenyon, 1968a; Kopp, 1960). All but one of these papers (Kopp, 1960) used non-clinical samples. Kopp (1960) evaluated 100 delinquent girls in a Minnesota institution with different degrees of homosexual experience with an Anomic Pressure Rating Schedule. The homosexual girls scored significantly higher on tenuous self-to-other and self-to-group relations, intense affectional deprivation and feelings of isolation. Kenyon (1968a) compared 123 lesbians with 123 heterosexual women in England on the Eysenck Personality Inventory and the Cornell Medical Index and found that the lesbians scored higher on neuroticism and were more severely disturbed in their moods and feelings. The Eysenck

Personality Inventory was also administered by Eisinger (1972) in England to 42 lesbians and 32 heterosexual women. The lesbians scored higher on Neuroticism and were more dysthimic, i.e., prone to anxiety and nervousness with obsessive tendencies. Both positive and negative elements of personality were reported for 24 lesbians compared to 24 matched female heterosexuals by Hassell and Smith (1975) based on responses to the Draw-A-Person Test and the Gough-Heilbrun Adjective Check List. The homosexuals showed no evidence of confusion in gender identity, scored high on Autonomy, and lower on Abasement, Defensiveness, Personal Adjustment and Self-Control.

See Riess, Safer, and Yotive (1974) and Hart, Roback, Tittler, Weitz, Walston, and McKee (1978) for critical reviews of literature on female homosexual adjustment. A psychoanalytic perspective on female homosexuality is presented by Socarides (1981) who takes issue with the conclusions of Riess et al. (1974) and Hart et al. (1978) that lesbians manifest no more psychopathology than heterosexual females.

Parent-Child Relationships

Men The most typical pattern reported for the parents of male homosexuals is an intensely affectionate, domineering, possessive, intimate mother and a distant, weak, inaffectual, rejecting father (Bene, 1965; Bieber et al., 1962; Braatan & Darling, 1965; Brown, 1963; Edwards, 1963; Evans, 1969; Freund & Pinkava, 1961; Henry, 1948, 1954; Jonas, 1944; King, 1980; Mathes, 1966; Nash & Hays, 1965; O'Connor, 1964; Snortum, Marshall, Gillespie, & McLaughlin, 1969; Terman & Miles, 1936; Thompson et al., 1973; Whitener & Nikelly, 1964; West, 1959; Whitam & Zent, 1984; Zuger, 1980). The above family structure was first depicted by Freud (1916) who described the mothers of male homosexuals as excessively loving and their fathers as retiring or absent, and by Stekel (1930) who noted strong dominant mothers and weak fathers. The studies that supported part or all of this family pattern, named by Bieber et al. (1962) as the "triangular system," included clinical and non-clinical samples. The non-clinical studies were conducted by Henry (1944), Bene (1965b), Mathes (1967), Evans (1969), Snortum, Marshall, Gillespie, and McLaughlin (1969), King (1980), and Whitam and Zent (1984). The clinical investigations (patients or prisoners) were done by Terman and Miles (1936), Jonas (1944), Henry (1954), West (1959), Freund and Pinkava (1961), Bieber et al. (1962), Edwards (1963), Nikelly (1964), O'Connor (1964), Nash and Hays (1965), Braaten and Darling (1965), and Zuger (1980).

Terman and Miles (1936), using a standardized personal interview, found the mothers of 18 incarcerated male homosexuals with preprison histories of homosexuality to be especially intimate, affectionate, and emotional or unstable, while the fathers were described as cold, stern or fear-inspiring, and none of the subjects preferred his father to his mother. Henry (1948) also described 40 male homosexual "volunteers" as having hostile, passive fathers and a dominant, protective mother who related to her son in a close, intimate, affectionate manner. Patients in an Army hospital including 60 homosexual and 60 heterosexual males were interviewed by Jonas (1944) who concluded that the homosexuals tended to prefer their mothers to their fathers, acted as "suitors to their mothers," and gave evidence of hating their fathers. An analysis of clinical histories and interviews of 46 hospitalized male mental patients by Henry (1954), grouped according to the "predominance of heterosexual or homosexual tendencies," indicated a nervous, sleepless, devoted mother whose homosexual son was devoted to her and a son who feared his father. The case histories of fifty male homosexual neurotic patients, compared to 50 male heterosexual neurotic patients, were analyzed by West (1959) who found unsatisfactory father-son relationships (i.e., absence from home, emotional aloofness, ineptitude, passivity) and overintense mother-son relationships among the homosexuals. Questionnaire responses reported by Freund and Pinkava (1961) for hospitalized neurotic male homosexuals (N = 154) and heterosexuals (N = 154), and for 128 homosexual men and 128 nonpsychiatric patients, indicated that the fathers of homosexuals were more often described as intolerant, unconcerned, or rude, and that they appreciated and preferred their mothers over their fathers. These authors concluded, however, that it was impossible to demonstrate any association between parental deprivation (i.e., absence of a parent, an unfavorable parent-child or interparental relationship, etcetera) and homosexuality.

Seventy seven psychoanalysts reported on a questionnaire that the homosexual males they had in therapy, compared to 100 heterosexual patients also in therapy, described their mothers as close-binding, especially demonstrative, dominant over the father, and their fathers as detached, unsympathetic, autocratic and frequently away from home (Bieber, et al., 1962).

Evans (1969) asked 43 homosexual men and 142 heterosexual men to answer 27 questions used on the Bieber et al. (1962) study and reported results striking similar to Bieber et al. Evans (1969) however, did not accept the conclusions that Bieber et al. came to based on these results, such as ". . . a constructive, supportive, warmly related father *precludes* the possibility of a homosexual son . . ." (p. 134). Some of the questions in the Bieber et al. (1962) investigation were converted by Snortum et al. (1969) and given to 46 male homosexuals being discharged from the Army because of their homosexual activities, to 21 enlisted men in training, and to 68 college students. The results indicated a close-binding, controlling mother and a rejecting, detached father for the homosexuals. Questions used in the Bieber et al. (1962) report were given to 127 well educated male homosexuals and 123 well educated male heterosexuals and the results supported the Bieber et al. (1962) finding that the homosexuals had more close-binding, intimate mothers and hostile, detached fathers (Thompson et al., 1973).

Using a Behavioral Incidence Technique, Edwards (1963) found that 20 male homosexual neuropsychiatric patients and prisoners described their fathers as low on nurturance, their mothers as excessively controlling and dominant in the parental interaction, and both parents as more depriving in comparison to 20 male heterosexual neuropsychiatric patients and prisoners. One sample of 30 homosexual male patients at a university health service was described by Whitener and Nikelly (1964) as being closer to their mothers (N = 17), not attached to either parent (N = 15), having passive (N = 11) rejecting (N = 12) fathers and indulgent (N = 10) mothers. The case histories of 50 homosexual and 50 heterosexual psychiatric patients in the Royal Air Force were analyzed by O'Connor (1964) who believed that the homosexuals had a poor relationship with their fathers and were very fond of their mothers. Bene (1965) administered the Bene-Anthony Family Relations test to 84 male homosexuals and 85 male heterosexuals and found that the homosexuals had poor relationships with their fathers, considered their fathers ineffectual, and took their fathers as models less often. The mothers of homosexuals, however, were not seen as more indulgent, intense, attached, protective or seen as models. "Passive" compared to "active" male homosexuals (N = 118), mostly convicted prisoners, were described by Nash and Hays (1965) as having a close relationship with their mothers and a worse relationship with their fathers. The clinical folders of male patients at a college mental health clinic (homosexual = 76; heterosexual = 42) were evaluated by Braaten and Darling (1965) using items from the Bieber et al. (1962) study. They rated the homosexuals as having more "close-binding intimate" mothers, being mother's favorite, and as having detached, indifferent, non-accepting/respecting fathers who spent little time with them and towards whom they expressed hatred. Using a questionnaire with samples of 100 male homosexuals and 100 heterosexuals, Mathes (1966) found that the homosexuals perceived the parental coalition as weaker, the mother-son coalition as stronger, and the father-son coalition as weaker. In addition to these reported coalitions, Mathes believes that identification with mother is enhanced and identification with father is impeded in male homosexuals by his finding that the homosexuals perceived their mothers' role as higher in instrumentality and expressiveness.

In a questionnaire study of 60 homosexual males, 11 fathers, 29 mothers, 22 brothers, and 41 sisters, King (1980) reported that one-half of the homosexuals mentioned that their fathers had contributed to their homosexuality by having been distant, absent or hostile-rejecting, and two-thirds mentioned that one or both parents had contributed to their homosexuality, but the members of their families generally did not replicate the causes which the homosexuals had cited for their homosexuality. In a developmental study of 50 homosexual male psychiatric patients, Zuger (1980) reported that the homosexuals were closer to their mothers than their fathers and had negative experiences with their fathers. All but seven patients were seen for "long periods of time," and Zuger explained the parental behavior as a *reaction* to the effeminate behavior of their sons. Whitam and Zent (1984) presented cross cultural Bieber et al. (1962) type questionnaire data, in agreement with

Zuger (1980), that strong mothers and distant, hostile fathers represented parental reactions to the early cross-gender behavior of their homosexual sons. The hostile father and strong mother pattern was found in a sample of 36 male homosexuals compared to 58 male heterosexuals from the U.S., described as the most hostile and repressive toward homosexuality, but was not found for Guatemalan (homosexual = 62; heterosexuals = 40) and Brazilian (homosexuals = 23; heterosexuals = 16) samples, where attitudes toward homosexuality were noted as being very permissive. Repressive U.S. attitudes, then, lead to fathers rejecting their sons' cross-gender effeminate behavior and to mothers being protective and close to their sons.

Papers will now be reviewed which relate to various aspects of parental behavior such as parental identification, parent harmony, parent personality, and studies that do not support, or give little support, to the "triangular system" hypothesis (Bieber et al., 1962). Normally functioning subjects were used by Liddicoat (1957, 1961), Chang and Block (1960), Krieger and Worchel (1960), Greenblatt (1966), Apperson and McAdoo (1968), Gigl (1970), Pritt (1971), Boxley (1973), Thompson et al. (1973), Stephens (1973), Pledger (1977), Hart (1978), Siegelman (1974b, 1981b), Bell, Weinberg and Hammersmith (1981), Van Wyk (1982), McCord (1982), Cole (1983), and Newcomb (1985). Clinical samples were evaluated by Paitich (1960), Edwards (1963), Greenstein (1966), and Robertson (1972).

Interview data from 50 male homosexuals and 50 male heterosexuals in South Africa indicated that the homosexuals more often came from disrupted or unhappy homes, "mother fixation" was not discernable in the majority of cases, and indifference to parents was more prevalent than cross-parent fixation (Liddicoat, 1957, 1961). Paitich (1960) described questionnaire data of male homosexual patients (N = 30) compared to "normal" heterosexual males (N = 115) as depicting mothers who were highly aggressive toward their fathers, and fathers perceived negatively with respect to competency and affection. The distance between mother and father was significantly greater for 20 male homosexuals than for 20 male heterosexuals, and the homosexuals identified more with their mothers on an ideal self, mother, father adjective check list (Chang & Block, 1960). Krieger and Worchel (1960) failed to support the Freudian hypothesis that homosexuals identify more with parents of the opposite sex for six male homosexuals, four heterosexuals who responded to a Q-sort of statements describing themselves, their ideal selves, their fathers, and their mothers. They report, in fact, that homosexual men identified more with their fathers than the heterosexual males. An examination by Edwards (1963) using institutional records and interviews, of 16 male homosexual patients in a state mental hospital, compared to 16 male heterosexual patients, revealed fathers to be less dominant than the mothers, mothers to be more nurturant, more controlling, less punishing and less affectionate, and both parents were found to be more emotionally depriving than the parents of heterosexuals. Greenblatt (1966) used a semantic differential technique with 30 male homosexuals and 30 male heterosexuals and found that the "triangular systems" hypothesis (Bieber et al., 1962) was not supported. Homosexuals, in addition, described their fathers as good, generous, pleasant, dominant, and underprotective, while mothers were good, generous, pleasant, neither dominant nor subordinate, neither overprotective nor underprotective. Greenstein (1966), reporting on 75 delinquent boys, indicated that the greater the degree of father closeness, measured by a psychiatric social worker rating scale, the greater the frequency of overt homosexual experiences, measured by a psychiatric interview conducted under sodium amytal medication. He also found no significant association between father-absent, father present, father dominance and the degree of overt or covert homosexuality. Twenty two homosexual, compared to 22 heterosexual males, who responded to a questionnaire were described by Apperson and McAdoo (1968) as having fathers who were more concerned about their son's feelings and mothers who were overpermissive. Male homosexuals (N = 887) completed a questionnaire describing their fathers in unfavorable, condemnatory terms and their mothers in highly favorable terms (Gigl, 1970). Pritt (1971) administered the Childrens Report of Parent Behavior Inventory to 42 male homosexuals and 42 male heterosexuals and found that the homosexuals perceived a strong sense of alienation and rejection from their fathers but they did not differ on their perceptions of their mothers. On the basis of evaluating case histories of outpatient homosexuals (N = 40), heterosexual deviates (N = 40), and neurotics (N = 40), Robertson (1972) concluded that the too powerful relationship between child and mother is not of primary importance in the development of the homosexual state. The responses of 30 black male homosexuals and 30 black male heterosexuals, on the Evans Parental Relationship questionnaire, which includes 27 items taken from the Bieber et al. (1962) study, indicated only 5 items that differentiated between groups (Boxley, 1973). The Perception of Parent Behavior Scale (90-item form) was also administered by Boxley and the results indicated only limited support for the close-binding restrictive, mother-son relationship for homosexuals, and no significant differences were found in the paternal-son relationship between groups. Thompson et al. (1973), using a semantic differential, reported that homosexual males were not more mother identified than heterosexual males, and they were more distant from both parents. Stephens (1973) found on responses to a semantic differential questionnaire that 88 male homosexuals, compared to 105 male heterosexuals, described their mothers as more dominant, less respectful, less affectionate, less encouraging of masculine behavior and their fathers as being absent more, more rigid, fearful, insecure, rejecting, less likable, less deserving of respect, and less encouraging of masculine behavior. The homosexual mothers were not pictured as being close-binding and intimate with their sons. The Siegelman and Roe Parent-Child Relationship Questionnaire II, the Profile Mood State (a measure of psychological adjustment) and the Personal Attributes Questionnaire (a measure of sex-typed role) were administered to 66 homosexual and 65 heterosexual men by Pledger (1977). He found that homosexuals described father as more rejecting, permissive, detached, less loving and strict, and mother as more overly close, restrictive, and intimate. When Pledger compared homosexuals and heterosexuals low on psychopathology and androgenous homosexuals and heterosexuals, there were *no* differences on any parental relationship variable. These findings are strikingly similar to my results (Siegelman, 1974b, 1981b). Hart (1978) reported that effeminate male homosexuals tended to come from disturbed families. Parent-Child Relationship Questionnaire and Biographical Data results for 307 male homosexuals and 138 male heterosexuals in the U.S. (Siegelman, 1974b) indicated that homosexuals described their fathers and mothers as more rejecting and less loving, and that they were less close to their fathers than heterosexuals. For subsamples of homosexuals and hetero-sexuals scoring low on neuroticism, however, I found *no* significant differences in family relations. In my U.S. study, in addition, homosexuals low on femininity reported negative behavior for fathers but not for mothers. In a replication study of 84 male homosexuals and 62 male heterosexuals residing in England (Siegelman, 1981b), I discovered similar results to my 1974 U.S. study, except that homosexuals differed from heterosexuals, for total samples, low neurotic samples, and low femininity samples, *only* on demanding mother (homosexuals higher) and closeness to father (homosexuals lower). Bell, Weinberg, and Hammersmith (1981) who interviewed 686 male homosexuals and 337 male heterosexuals with an extensive questionnaire reported that homosexual men tended to report greater closeness to mother, stronger mothers, no tendency to identify more with their mothers, and no "seductive" or negative mother-son relationships. The homosexuals did report a more negative relationship with their father, describing him more often as weak and cold, they identified less with him, and noted that their mothers dominate their fathers. In addition, fathers of homosexuals were not more detached or hostile, and the quality of parental relationships and the number coming from broken homes was not different for the two groups. The significant differences for fathers, finally, contributed little to the development of adult sexual preferences. Van Wyk (1982) found that for 7669 males and females, the more overt homosexual experience his male subjects had the more they reported having poor relationships with their fathers during their teenage years. In 1982 McCord reported that 17 pairs of homosexual sons and their fathers, compared to 17 pairs of heterosexual sons and their fathers, did not differ on father's nurturance, his acceptance of or positive involvement with his son. The responses on the Siegelman-Roe Parent-Child Relations Question-naire II and a developmental questionnaire of 129 homosexual males and 120 heterosexual males indicated that the homosexuals recalled their fathers, brothers and peers as more rejecting and they perceived themselves as less masculine than their childhood peers (Cole, 1983). The role of perceived relative parent personality (intellectuality, dependence, affiliation, endurance, aggressive-dominance), as depicted on the Parent Characteristics Questionnaire, was found to be similar for 106 heterosexual males compared to 34 homosexual males (Newcomb, 1985). The dissertation by Greenblatt (1966) includes an excellent evaluation of previous parental background investigations, especially the Bieber et al. (1962) study, as well as an important critique of research designs.

Female No typical pattern had been reported for the parent-child relationships of lesbians (Siegelman, 1974a). About one-half as many studies have been done on the parental background of lesbians as compared to the parental background of male homosexuals. Non-clinical samples were reported on by Liddicoat (1957, 1961), Bene (1965a), Kenyon (1968b), Loney (1973), Thompson et al. (1973), Siegelman (1974a, 1981a), Crouch (1977), Shavelson et al. (1980), Bell, Weinberg, and Hammersmith (1981), and Newcomb (1985). Clinical subjects were used by Howard (1962), Kaya et al. (1967), MacVicar (1967), Gundlach and Riess (1968), Kremer and Rifkin (1969), and Symonds (1969).

Liddicoat (1957, 1961), using biographical and interview material, found that indifference to parents rather than cross-parent fixation was more prevalent for 50 lesbians compared to 50 heterosexual women. Projective test data of 51 institutionalized lesbian delinquents were analyzed by Howard (1962) who reported that all of the girls were rejected by their mothers, with those assuming masculine roles feeling more strongly rejected than those assuming feminine roles, those assuming feminine roles as possessing a feminine identification and those assuming a masculine role as possessing a masculine identification. Those assuming the feminine role perceived their fathers as weak and inadequate and the fathers of those assuming masculine roles as aggressive and domineering. Bene (1965a) reported that 37 lesbians, compared to 80 married women, described themselves on the Bene-Anthony Family Relations Test as having fathers who were more rejecting, lower on dominance, and perceived by their daughters with greater hostility. The lesbians were also less likely to want to model themselves after either of their parents. Kaya et al. (1967), using questions and methods quite similar to Bieber et al. (1962), found that 25 homosexual, compared to 24 heterosexual women patients were described by their analysts as having fathers who were close-binding and intimate—the converse of the parent behavior noted for male homosexuals, but found that the mothers of the lesbians did not differ from the mothers of the non-lesbians. The mothers of 16 institutionalized delinquent girls were found by MacVicar (1967) to be less loving on the Parent-Child Relations Questionnaire than the mothers of heterosexual delinquent girls, but no differences were found for fathers. Patient and non-patient lesbians (N = 226) and heterosexual women (N = 234) were compared on a questionnaire by Gundlach and Riess (1968) which included many of the Bieber et al. (1962) questions and no group differences were found. The results of a questionnaire study by Kenyon (1968b) of 123 lesbians and a matched group of 123 heterosexual women revealed that the lesbians had a poor relationship with their mothers and fathers and there were no differences on parent dominance. In an open-ended interview investigation of 25 adolescent lesbian patients, Kremer and Rifkin (1969) found that the fathers of the homosexual women were hostile, exploitative, detached, and absent, but they were not close-binding, and the mothers were described as overburdened and inadequate in handling their responsibilities and not dominant. Symonds (1969) found that 14 homosexual daughters in therapy were disinclined to imitate their mothers. Using questions from the Bieber et al. (1962) study, Thompson et al. (1973) reported that 84 lesbians, compared to 94 heterosexual women, had more hostile and distant fathers, were alienated from both parents, but they did not identify with either parent. Loney (1973) used the Elias Family Adjustment Test with 11 lesbian and 12 heterosexual women and reported that the lesbians described their fathers as neglecting, moody, disappointing, unloving, mean, selfish, and untrustworthy, and the mothers as preoccupied with their marital worries and fears to the point of reduced involvement with their daughters. The Elias Family Adjustment Test was also used by Crouch (1977), with 67 lesbians and 55 heterosexuals, who found only one significant difference, that the lesbians felt more rejected by either or both parents during childhood. Shavelson et al. (1980) indicated no differences in family background between 26 lesbians and 26 heterosexual women in their responses to the Schaefer Child Report of Parental Behavior Inventory and to an interview concerning family background variables. On the basis of intensive interviews with 293 lesbians and 140 heterosexuals, Bell, Weinberg and Hammersmith (1981) found that

> *The homosexual women tended to report relatively negative relationships with their mothers, to describe their mothers more unfavorably, and have identified with them less than did the heterosexual women. In the path analysis, however, none of these variables appear to have had much effect on the daughters emerging sexual preference (pp. 124-125).*

These authors also found that the lesbians described their fathers as more likely to be detached, hostile, rejecting, as having been colder and weaker and as less likely to have identified with their fathers. Only the higher incidence of detached, hostile, and rejecting fathers finding, however, was somewhat related to the development of adult homosexuality. Finally, Bell, Weinberg, and Hammersmith (1981) noted that lesbians reported more negative relationships between their parents and mothers who dominated their fathers, but they concluded that these parental interactions were of litle use in predicting adult female homosexuality.

For a U.S. sample of 63 homosexual women and 68 heterosexual women who responded to The Parent-Child Relations Questionnaire (PCR) and a Biographical Questionnaire (Siegelman, 1974a), I found that the lesbians reported their mothers and fathers to be less loving and more rejecting, they were more distant from both parents, and they indicated less family security. When lesbians and heterosexuals low on neuroticism were compared, however, all PCR differences were not significant, but the lesbian group again noted more distance from both parents and less family security. In a replication study (Siegelman, 1981a) with British subjects (61 lesbian and 49 heterosexual women) I found very few differences between the total group comparisons and the low neurotic group comparisons. For the total sample, the lesbians reported less loving and protecting fathers, more rejecting mothers, felt more distant from their fathers and that there was less family security. For the low neuroticism groups, the lesbians depicted their fathers as less loving and more rejecting and their mothers as more rejecting and more distant from their fathers, and that there was less family security. The consistency of findings between the U.S. and British studies was primarily on the Biographical Questionnaire variables of closeness to parents and family security. Newcomb (1985) found that the responses of 63 lesbians, contrasted to 122 heterosexual women, on the Parent Characteristics Questionnaire, indicated that their mothers were perceived as more independent, more aggressive-dominant, and less affiliative relative to their fathers.

RESEARCH STRATEGIES AND THEORETICAL CONSIDERATIONS

Measurement

An underlying assumption of most measurement studies was that homosexual males were effeminate and so the goal of measurement was to test for femininity. Relatively few measurement studies have been conducted with lesbians and the significance of masculine homosexual females has not been emphasized. Femininity in men *and* women has often been associated with less adequate adjustment and competency and so has probably drawn more attention from researchers than masculinity in women (Siegelman, 1972b). The meanings of "femininity" and "masculinity" are as diverse as there are different tests and different conceptions of what the test results mean (Constantinople, 1973; Kelly & Worell, 1977; Worell, 1978). Except for the MMPI Mf scale used with males, all other testing attempts to link Mf and homosexuality have been inconsistent, contradictory, or too few in number to be impressive (Storm, 1980), and Suppe (1981) casts considerable doubt on the validity of the Mf scale. No causal relationship, in addition, between adult femininity and male homosexuality has ever been demonstrated (Storm, 1980).

The search to differentiate homosexuality and heterosexuality on a concept of femininity has been usually based on the postulate of identification, i.e., that homosexual individuals identified with and copied their opposite sexed parent and rejected their own gender role (Freud, 1922, 1959). The further assumption appears to be that when a male acts, thinks, and feels like a woman (originally his mother) then he desires what a woman (mother) desires, is attracted to a man (father). A woman acting like a man (identifying with her father) wants what a man wants, a woman. If you are a woman acting like a man, you will be physically attracted and excited by women the way men are and desire to be physical and sexual with women. Being sexual like the opposite sex also involves a rather in depth insight and capacity to take over cross-gender roles through observation. The above assumptions appear to me to be torturous, unreasonable, and totally unsupported by any evidence. I believe that the homosexual is not simply a man acting like a woman or a woman acting like a man (Grygier, 1957; Storm, 1980; Terman & Miles, 1936). I propose that homosexuals do not act like the opposite sex, they act and feel like their own sex, and for whatever the reason (speculated on below), they are sexually and emotionally attracted to members of their own sex (Hoffman, 1968; Kinsey et al., 1948, 1953; Storm, 1980; Tripp, 1975). I believe men and women are *fundamentally* different in some important aspects of sexual behavior, not only in anatomy and physiology, but in emotions, needs, goals, etc., along with being similar, of course, in many other psychological ways. If we assume that most men are fundamentally male and most women are fundamentally female, then tests and hypotheses would be consistent with this assumption and many previous predications would be rejected or modified. I suggest that we separate sex object choice from masculine-feminine role behavior. Both homosexual and heterosexual individuals manifest different degrees of masculinity-femininity which is independent of their sexual preferences (Hooker, 1965). This model is consistent with the idea presented by Storm (1980) that sexual orientation is related to erotic orientation and not to sex role orientation.

Adjustment

There is overwhelming evidence from all empirical studies that at least *some* homosexual individuals are well adjusted, and most studies have demonstrated that male and female homosexuals are as well adjusted as male and female heterosexuals. *No* study has ever shown that all homosexuals evaluated were neurotic on all measures or questions employed.* Although our ability to define and measure "adjustment" is highly questionable, inconsistent, and in great need of validity support, (Siegelman, 1972b) the testing that has been done so far seriously questions the opinion that all

---

*In evaluating research studies, especially comparative investigations, it is important to recognize ways in which the two groups were *alike* when the authors point out only hypothesized differences. Even in papers with significant mean differences, the amount of overlap between groups is usually considerable indicating how *alike* the groups are or the many exceptions to the mean differences.

homosexuals are neurotic or that being homosexual *per se* means being maladjusted (Gonsioreck, 1977; Green, 1972; Riess, 1980).

There is some evidence that feminine male homosexuals tend to be, on the average, more maladjusted than masculine male homosexuals (Hart, 1977; Hooberman, 1979; McGovern, 1977; Siegelman, 1972b). In these studies, however, at least some of the feminine homosexual subjects were well adjusted. The relationship between adjustment and sex role behavior for heterosexuals is inconsistent, but there are some studies that found androgynous men and women to be better adjusted than either strongly masculine or feminine men and women (Worell, 1978). It is my opinion that adjustment is independent of sexual preference. More feminine male homosexuals than masculine male homosexuals probably experienced more societal disapproval or conflict and sex role confusion and so, on the average, described themselves as more maladjusted than masculine homosexuals. In my own data (unpublished) I found that feminine heterosexual males were more maladjusted than masculine heterosexual males. For women there does not appear to be a relationship between masculine versus feminine lesbians and adjustment, as most of the non-clinical studies indicated that lesbians were as well adjusted as heterosexual women. Thus there are well adjusted and poorly adjusted homosexuals and heterosexuals.

Parent-Child Relations

There is considerable evidence that *more* male homosexuals than male heterosexuals described their parents in a manner consistent with the "Triangular System Hypothesis." In all studies, however, some male heterosexuals also presented this pattern and some male homosexuals did not show the pattern. For some male homosexuals, then, close-binding mothers and hostile-distant fathers may be prominent or characteristic of their backgrounds more so than other homosexuals and heterosexuals. I found that this pattern was not typical for well-adjusted homosexuals (Siegelman, 1974b, 1981b). Inferring any cause and effect relationship at this time is unwarranted and the evidence presented by Bell, Weinberg, and Hammersmith (1981) contradicts such a causative interaction. The interesting possibility that the reason that fathers are hostile and mothers are close and protective is that they may be reacting to the cross-gender behavior of their sons (Greenblatt, 1966; Whitener & Zent, 1984; Zuger, 1980). In my studies of lesbians (Siegelman, 1974a; 1981a) I found that they felt more distant from, insecure with, misunderstood by, and unhappy with their parents compared to heterosexual women. I speculated that the lesbians rejected their parents because of their parents' heterosexual role orientations.

The research on parental background of homosexuals highlights, I believe, the error of searching for simple uniform dynamics to explain extremely complex behavior. It seems that since so little of the variation in degree of homosexual to heterosexual behavior has been accounted for by parental behavior, we need to look for additional factors to explain sexual object choice. I also think that the causes of homosexuality will include the same parameters as the causes of heterosexuality. If we search for the etiology of *sexual preference* we will be less inclined to oversimplify the dynamics and we might ask different questions. If you speculated that a homosexual male identified with his mother who is close and dominant because his father is distant and rejecting then heterosexuals would be expected to identify with a close-intimate father because their mothers were distant and rejecting. Another assumption I would make is that homosexuality, like heterosexuality, is not necessarily pathological and so I would not be hypothesizing pathological parental background as a cause of sexual orientation. Sexual preference appears to me to be independent of the parental background factors that we have studied thus far. Homosexual and heterosexual development occurs in people of all levels of adjustment and in people with good and bad parent-child interactions.

Interesting iatrogenic effects have been suggested by Bell, Weinberg, and Hammersmith (1981), Gonsiorek (1977), and Hoffman (1969). Homosexual men who had therapy, according to Bell, Weinberg, and Hammersmith (1981), had paternal histories that were consistent with the triangular system, compared to homosexual men never in therapy. These authors speculated that therapists may teach their homosexual clients to see or interpret their family backgrounds in ways that are consistent with the therapists' particular theoretical perspective. Gonsiorek (1977) pointed out that many homosexuals accepted the pejorative homosexual literature that they read, and that therapists who want to "cure" a homosexual argue that in order to "cure" a homosexual he or she must be convinced that their behavior is sick. Hoffman (1969) believes that "A well known fact in the study of oppressed minorities is that they, tragically, adopt toward themselves the degrading view that the larger society has of them. The homosexual accepts this stigma. He views himself as queer, bad, dirty, something a little less than human. And he views his partner in the same way" (p. 70).

General Methodological Considerations

Excellent reviews of research design considerations can be found in papers by Greenblatt (1966), Hooker (1968), Bell (1976), Gonsiorek (1977), Morin (1977), Bentler and Abramson (1980), and Suppe (1981). Some of the major research issues are definitions and typologies, sampling, measuring instruments, type of study (i.e., comparative, longitudinal, cross-cultural, case study, sociological, etc.), and theoretical conceptualizations. In almost all methodological aspects, I believe, we need to explore the dynamics of sexual orientation in the same manner for homosexuals and heterosexuals (Hooker, 1980). Sex research goals and problems in general (Bentler & Abramson, 1980) are equally applicable to homosexuals and heterosexuals.

Kinsey et al. (1948) greatly advanced the precision of defining sexual orientation with their 7 point continuous scale. They demonstrated the prevalency and diversity of homosexual and heterosexual behavior using this continuous scale. The need to more precisely define the Kinsey scale has been emphasized by Bell (1976), especially the examination of *why* a person rates himself from 0-6 on the Kinsey scale. Closely related to defining sexual preference is typologies or subgroups within homosexuals and within hetero-sexuals. I pointed out that a group of feminine homosexual males were more maladjusted than masculine homosexuals (Siegelman, 1972b), and this dif-ference has been found for feminine and masculine heterosexual males (Heilbrun, 1969; Lynn, 1969; Vroegh, 1968). Feminine male homosexuals also tend to report more disturbed parental backgrounds than masculine male homosexuals (Siegelman, 1974b, 1981b). Poorly adjusted male homosexuals reported more negative parental behavior than better adjusted homosexuals (Siegelman, 1974b, 1981b). Male homosexuals who were coupled were better adjusted than single homosexuals (Bell & Weinberg, 1978). It is rather surprising that so little attention has been given to socioeconomic factors and age differences, considering the emphasis and importance of these variables in heterosexual research, both sexual and non-sexual. What differences in adjustment and parent-child interactions exist for homosexuals of different ages and different socioeconomic backgrounds? Lumping all homosexuals together is as unreasonable as lumping all heterosexuals together. It seems quite clear that the homosexual experience is as varied and complex as the heterosexual experience and a consideration of multifactorial aspects is called for rather than reductionistic simplification.

The desirability of deriving large, representative samples randomly from diverse populations is clearly indicated, which is of course true for most psychological research. Generalizing to all homosexuals and heterosexuals from patient and prison populations is blatantly untenable. We would certainly never evaluate heterosexual patients or prisoners on psychological variables and then generalize these findings to all heterosexuals (Clark & Epstein, 1969). Large, random, representative samples are non-existent today, but the Kinsey et al. (1948, 1953) and Bell, Weinberg, and Hammersmith (1981) efforts are laudatory and should be refined, replicated and expanded.

The critical question of measurement remains a major stumbling block. What is the "normal" well adjusted person like? Can the retrospective recollections of an adult accurately reflect what his parents were like when he was growing up and how he reacted to them and they to him? What does masculinity-femininity mean? I believe the validity of all existing measures of sex role behavior, adjustment and parent-child relationships is questionable and backed by insufficient evidence (Bentler & Abramson, 1980; Constanti-nople, 1973; Siegelman, 1972b, 1974b; Worell, 1978). We should utilize the best existing techniques and work toward constructing more sophisticated and meaningful measuring devices.

The great majority of empirical papers on measurement, adjustment, and parental background have been comparative, homosexuals versus heterosexuals. The assumptions by many investigators that homosexuals were more feminine if male and more masculine if female, less well adjusted, and had more disturbed parental backgrounds than heterosexuals may have prompted these researchers to do their comparative studies. If these assumptions are not made, or if they are seen as less important, then other types of questions and designs might be considered. *Intragroup* differences might be given greater consideration. The life style studies recommended by Morin (1977), such as the dynamics of gay relationships, the development of positive gay identity, etc. would fall into this category. Longitudinal, developmental, cross-cultural, sociological, case study and biological researach would all be appropriate with both intragroup *and* intergroup designs. Intergroup studies are valuable and will continue to be so, but we need to supplement them with intragroup approaches.

Perhaps the most pressing need that we have is for imaginative theoretical constructs that can generate testable hypotheses. I believe sexual development and expression are enormously complex, extremely variable, deeply ingrained and thus require a multifactorial and interdisciplinary theory. I will briefly sketch some of the diverse components that I believe need to be considered in the construction of such a theory. The magnitude of such a theoretical orientation goes beyond the scope of this chapter, and even of this book, but I want to indicate what appears to me to be some provocative and potentially meaningful and important leads that we now have, and to illustrate the multidimensional input that will probably be necessary to begin to unravel the current mysteries of the sexual experience.

Men and women are born with different characteristic sexual tendencies due to an evolutionary process according to Symons (1979). He believes, for example, that men are more inclined to be promiscuous and women are predisposed to be more monogamous; men are more aroused than women by visual stimuli; women can tolerate sexual abstinence better than men can. Money (1970) reported similar conclusions concerning promiscuity and visual arousal. With this evolutionary background, a social-learning theory (Bandura, 1977), that recognizes the importance of biological predispositions, might be fruitfully employed to explore sexual orientation and expression through an integration of factors such as the following.

1. Genetic, fetal, birth, hormonal and central nervous system contributions (Diamond, 1977; Money, 1970, 1984).
2. Parent-child interactions starting immediately after birth (Green, 1975; Money & Ehrhardt, 1972).
3. Cross-gender behavior in childhood (Bell, Weinberg, & Hammersmith, 1981; Green, 1975; Grellert, Newcomb, & Bentler, 1982; Saghir & Robins, 1973; Stephens, 1973; Thompson et al., 1973; Zuger, 1966).

4. Orgasmic reinforcement of fantasies during masturbation (McGuire et al., 1965).
5. Romantic fantasies and cognitional rehearsals during childhood and early adolescence (Money & Tucker, 1975; Saghir & Robins, 1973).
6. Sex of playmates during adolescence (Werner, 1979).
7. Compensation for deficient masculine behavior in adolescents and rejection by valued males (Cole, 1983; Tripp, 1975).
8. Sociological and cultural contributions (Carrier, 1980; Hooker, 1967; Levine, 1980; Weinberg & Williams, 1974).

From a model building perspective, I believe that the areas and examples noted in numbers 1-8 above could be schematized as ranging from bipolar to orthogonal. Figure 1 depicts this model. Orthogonality, as used here, implies that for a given behavior such as sexual preference, and for a given characteristic in relation to another dimension such as sex role, each dimension operates independently. A person can be both homosexual and heterosexual, and if homosexual and/or heterosexual, can be both masculine and feminine or androgynous (Storm, 1980).

The manifold components of sexual preference and expression are further complicated, I believe, because a *unique configuration* of contributing factors may exist for any given individual. Some of the variables enumerated above in 1-8 may be operative in one person and not in another, and a given factor might contribute in different degrees in different people and at different times. Experience that may have *critical periods* for development (Money, 1970) may vary in type and degree from person to person, the experience, the critical period and the developing trait. This probable labarinth leads me to conclude that intensive developmental case studies of single individuals are necessary *in addition* to our typical nomothetic approach. An especially promising formulation of this methodology is presented by Lamiell (1981), labelled idothetic, which stresses and examines the unique, idiographic personality of a given individual in contrast to the traditional nomothetic assessment of differences between individuals. The roots of idiographic methodology go back to the personology of Murray (1938), Allport (1962) and others (Epstein, 1978; Hall & Lindzey, 1979). Fowler and Epting (1976) presented an in-depth case study of an homosexual male as an alternative to what they believe is the extraordinary narrow and impoverished scope of current personality research. Personology includes intensive case studies but also uses insights from nomothetic procedures such as objective tests, developmental approach, non-clinical subjects, etc. Related to the idiographic approach is the emphasis given by Bell (1978), Hooker (1957, 1961), and Suppe (1981) to the importance of researchers immersing themselves in the lives of subjects they are studying. The humanistic psychology of Rogers (1985) is also germane to the idiographic procedure, where Rogers emphasizes an experiental knowledge, an "in-dwelling" in the perceptions, attitudes, experiences of the

Structure and behavior	More Bipolar				More Orthogonal
	Chromosome structure (XX, XY)	Gender (genitals, brain, hormones)	Gender role (boy-girl, man-woman)	Sex role (masculine, feminine)	Sex preference (homosexual, heterosexual, bi-sexual)
Developmental sequence	Conception	Prenatal	Birth Neonatal	Childhood	Adolescence Adulthood

Figure 1 A bipolar-orthogonal model of sexual behavior.

participant, where there are no longer "subjects" of research but "co-researchers," or "research partners."

From the above theoretical assumptions the focus of research would *not be* on measuring the extent to which gay men act like women or lesbians act like men, nor on the need to be more like the opposite sexed parent, nor on the question of the adjustment of homosexuals compared to heterosexuals. Examples of topics to be explored or emphasized are those noted above in numbers 1–8. Sexual development and expression would be studied for homosexual and heterosexual males and females. Orthogonality would be assumed for most psychological variables, and social-learning theory would be most appropriate for these psychological qualities. Precise traditional experimental approaches would be desirable for the more bipolar dimensions and developmental-naturalistic, including idiographic, methods would be relevant for the more orthogonal variables.

Almost all of the empirical research reviewed in this chapter could be considered atheoretical or inductive. Based on this review of the literature, I outlined some theoretical constructs that appeared to be consistent with the reported findings. Are we now ready for more deductive approaches, using more explicit theoretical formulations, to derive testable hypotheses that can be evaluated with both idiographic and nomothetic research methods?

REFERENCES

Aaronson, B. S., & Grumpelt, H. R. Homosexuality and some MMPI measures of masculinity-femininity. *Journal of Clinical Psychology,* 1961, *17,* 245–247.

Adelman, A. M. R. A comparison of professionally employed lesbians and heterosexual women on the MMPI. *Archives of Sexual Behavior,* 1977, *6,* 193–201.

Adler, A. The homosexual problem. *Alienist and Neurologist,* 1917, *38,* 268–287.

Allport, G. W. The general and the unique in psychological science. *Journal of Personality,* 1962, *30,* 405–422.

Anderson, D. O., & Seitz, F. C. Rorschach diagnosis of homosexuality: Schafer's content analysis. *Journal of Projective Techniques and Personality Assessment,* 1969, *33,* 406–408.

Andress, V. R., Franzini, L. R., & Linton, M. A comparison of homosexual and heterosexual responses to the Menninger Word Association Test. *Journal of Clinical Psychology,* 1974, *30,* 205–207.

Apperson, L. B., & McAdoo, W. G., Jr. Parental factors in the childhood of homosexuals. *Journal of Abnormal Psychology,* 1968, *73,* 201–206.

Armon, V. Some personality variables in overt female homosexuality. *Journal of Projective Techniques,* 1960, *24,* 292–309.

Aronson, M. L. A study of the Freudian theory of paranoia by means of the Rorschach test. *Journal of Projective Techniques,* 1952, *16,* 397–411.

Bandura, A. L. *Social learning theory.* Englewood Cliffs: Prentice Hall, 1977.

Barker, A. J., Mathis, J. K., & Powers, C. A. Drawing characters of male homosexuals. *Journal of Clinical Psychology*, 1953, *9*, 185–188.

Bell, A. P. Research in homosexuality: Back to the drawing board. In Rubinstein, E. A., Green, R., & Brecher, E. (Eds.) *New directions in sex research.* New York: Plenum Press, 1976, pp. 99–109.

Bell, A. P., & Weinberg, M. S. *Homosexualities: A study of diversity among men and women.* New York: Simon and Schuster, 1978.

Bell, A. P., Weinberg, M. S., & Hammersmith, S. R. *Sexual preference: It's development in men and women.* Bloomington, Ind.: Indiana University Press, 1981.

Bendel, R. The modified Szondi Test in male homosexuality. I. *International Journal of Sexiology*, 1955, *8*, 226–227.

Bene, E. On the genesis of female homosexuality. *British Journal of Psychiatry*, 1965, *111*, 815–821.

Bene, E. On the genesis of male homosexuality: An attempt at clarifying the role of the parents. *British Journal of Psychiatry*, 1965, *111*, 803–813.

Bentler, P. M., & Abramson, P. R. Methodological issues in sex research: An overview. In Green, R., & Wiener, J. (Eds.) *Methodology in sex research.* Rockville, Md.: National Institute of Mental Health, 1980, pp. 308–332.

Benton, A. L. The MMPI in clinical practice. *Journal of Nervous and Mental Diseases*, 1945, *102*, 416–420.

Bergler, E. *Neurotic counterfeit sex.* New York: Grune and Stratton, 1951.

Bergman, M. S. Homosexuality on the Rorschach Test. *Bulletin of the Menninger Clinic*, 1945, *9*, 78–83.

Bernard, L. C., & Epstein, D. J. Androgyny scores of matched homosexual and heterosexual males. *Journal of Homosexuality*, 1978, *4*, 169–178.

Bieber, I., Dain, H. J., Dince, P. R., Drelich, M. G., Grand, H. G., Gundlach, R. H., Kremer, M. W., Rifkin, A. H., Wilbur, C. B., & Bieber, T. B. *Homosexuality: A psychoanalytic study.* New York: Basic Books, 1962.

Botwinick, J., & Machover, S. A psychometric examination of latent homosexuality in alcoholism. *Quarterly Journal of Studies in Alcohol*, 1951, *12*, 268–272.

Boxley, R. L. *Sex-object choice in adult black males: Perception of parental relationships and early sexual behavior.* (Doctoral dissertation, University of Washington) Ann Arbor, Michigan: University Microfilms, 1973, No. 74-15-, 534.

Braaten, L. J., & Darling, C. D. Overt and covert homosexual problems among male college students. *Genetic Psychology Monographs*, 1965, *71*, 269–310.

Brecher, E. M. *The sex researchers.* Boston: Little, Brown, 1969.

Brill, A. A. Conception of homosexuality. *Journal of the American Medical Association*, 1913, *61*, 335–338.

Brown, D. G. Homosexuality and family dynamics. *Bulletin of the Menninger Clinic*, 1963, *27*, 227–232.

Brown, D. G., & Tolor, A. Human figure drawings as indicators of sexual identification and inversion. *Perceptual and Motor Skills*, 1957, *7*, 199–211.

Bruce, E. W. *Comparison of traits of the homosexual from tests and from life history materials.* Master's thesis, University of Chicago, 1942.

Burton, A. The use of the masculinity-femininity scale of the MMPI as an aid in the diagnosis of sexual inversion. *The Journal of Psychology,* 1947, *24,* 161-164.

Carrier, J. M. Homosexual behavior in cross-cultural perspective. In Marmour, J. (Ed.) *Homosexual behavior.* New York: Basic Books, 1980, pp. 100-122.

Cattell, R. B., & Marony, J. H. The use of the 16 PF in distinguishing homosexuals, normals, and general criminals. *Journal of Consulting Psychology,* 1962, *26,* 531-540.

Chaffee, P. N. *Personality factors relating to stability in male homosexual relationships.* (Doctoral dissertation, Boston University) Ann Arbor, Michigan. University Microfilms, 1976, No. 76-21, 325.

Chang, J., & Block, J. A study of identification in male homosexuals. *Journal of Consulting Psychology,* 1960, *24,* 307-310.

Churchill, W. *Homosexual behavior among males: A cross-species investigation.* New York: Hawthorn Books, 1967.

Clark, T. R. Homosexuality and psychopathology in nonpatient males. *American Journal of Psychoanalysis,* 1975, *35,* 163-168.

Clark, T., & Epstein, R. Self-concept and expectancy for social reinforcement in noninstitutionalized male homosexuals. *Proceedings 77th Annual Convention American Psycholanalytic Association,* 1969, *4,* 575.

Coates, S. Homosexuality and the Rorschach test. *British Journal of Medical Psychology,* 1962, *35,* 177-190.

Cole, M. M. *The developmental antecedents of sexual preference among males.* (Doctoral dissertation, North Carolina State University) Ann Arbor, Michigan: University Microfilms, 1083, No. DA8402091.

Constantinople, A. Masculinity-femininity: An exception to a famous dictum? *Psychological Bulletin,* 1973, *80,* 389-407.

Crouch, A. M. *A comparison of parental home and family relationships and family constellations of adult female homosexuals and adult female heterosexuals.* (Doctoral dissertation, The University of New Mexico) Ann Arbor, Michigan: University Microfilms, 1977, No. 7727167.

Cubitt, G. H., & Gendreau, P. Assessing the diagnostic utility of MMPI and 16 PF indexes of homosexuality in a prison sample. *Journal of Consulting and Clinical Psychology,* 1972, *39,* 342.

Dailey, D. M. Adjustment of heterosexual and homosexual couples in pairing relationships: An exploratory study. *Journal of Sex Research,* 1979, *15,* 143-157.

Darke, R. A., & Geil, G. A. Homosexual activity: Relation of degree and role to the Goodenough test and to the Cornell selectee index. *Journal of Nervous and Mental Diseases,* 1948, *108,* 217-240.

Davids, A., Joelson, M., & McArthur, C. Rorschach and TAT indices of homosexuality in overt homo's, neurotics, and normal males. *Journal of Abnormal and Social Psychology,* 1956, *53,* 161-172.

David, H. P., & Rabinowitz, W. Szondi patterns in epileptic and homosexual males. *Journal of Consulting Psychology*, 1952, *16*, 247–250.

Dean, R. B., & Richardson, H. Analysis of MMPI profiles of forty college-educated overt male homosexuals. *Journal of Consulting Psychology*, 1964, *28*, 483–486.

DeLuca, J. N. The structure of homosexuality. *Journal of Projective Techniques & Personality Assessment*, 1966, *30*, 187–191.

Deutsch, H. Homosexuality in women. *International Journal of Psychoanalysis*, 1933, *14*, 34–56.

Doidge, W. T., & Holtzman, W. H. Implications of homosexuality among Air Force trainees. *Journal of Consulting Psychology*, 1960, *24*, 9–13.

Due, F. O., & Wright, M. E. The use of content analysis in Rorschach interpretation: I. Differential characteristics of male homosexuals. *Rorschach Research Exchange*, 1945, *9*, 169–177.

Edwards, H. E. *The relationship between reported early life experiences with parents and adult male homosexuality.* (Doctoral dissertation, The University of Tennessee) Ann Arbor, Michigan: University Microfilms, 1963, No. 64-4874.

Eisinger, A. J., et al. Female homosexuality. *Nature*, 1972, *238*, 106.

Ellis, H. *Studies in the psychology of sex.* (3rd ed.) Vol. II, *Sexual inversion.* Philadelphia: F. A. Davis, 1915.

Ellis, H. Sexual inversion in men. *Alienist and Neurologist*, 1896, *17*, 115–150.

Epstein, S. Explorations in personality today and tomorrow. *American Psychologist*, 1979, *34*, 649–653.

Evans, R. B. Childhood parental relationships of homosexual men. *Journal of Consulting & Clinical Psychology*, 1969, *33*, 129–135.

Evans, R. B. Sixteen personality factor questionnaire scores of homosexual men. *Journal of Consulting Psychology*, 1970, *34*, 212–215.

Fein, L. G. Rorschach signs of homosexuality in male college students. *Journal of Clinical Psychology*, 1950, *3*, 248–253.

Ferguson, K. D., & Finkler, D. C. An involvement and overtness measure for lesbians: Its development and relation to anxiety and social zeitgeist. *Archives of Sexual Behavior*, 1978, *7*, 211–227.

Ford, C. S., & Beach, F. A. *Patterns of sexual behavior.* New York: Harper & Row, 1951.

Fowler, M. G., & Epting, F. R. The person in personality research: An alternate lifestyle case study. *Journal of Clinical Psychology*, 1976, *32*, 159–167.

Fraas, L. A. Sex of figure drawing in identifying practicing male homosexuals. *Psychological Reports*, 1970, *27*, 172–174.

Freedman, M. J. *Homosexuality among women and psychological adjustment.* (Doctoral dissertation, Case Western Reserve University) Ann Arbor, Michigan: University Microfilms, 1968, No. 63-3308.

Freud, S. *Group psychology and the analysis of the ego.* (J. Strachey, Ed. and trans.) London: Hogarth Press, 1959. (Originally published, 1922.)

Freud, S. *Leonardo Da Vinci.* New York: Knopf, 1916.

Freud, S. *Three essays on the theory of sexuality.* London: Imago Publishing Co., 1949.

Freund, K., & Pinkave, V. Homosexuality in man and its association with parental relationships. *Review Czechoslovakian Medicine,* 1961, 7, 32–40.

Friberg, R. R. Measures of homosexuality: Cross-validation of the two MMPI scales and implications for usage. *Journal of Consulting Psychology,* 1967, *31,* 88–91.

Gartrell, N., Kraemer, H., & Brodie, H. K. Psychiatrists' attitudes toward female homosexuality. *Journal of Nervous and Mental Diseases,* 1974, 159, 141–144.

Geddes, D. P. (Ed.) *An analysis of the Kinsey reports on sexual behavior in the human male and female.* New York: Dutton, 1954.

Geil, G. A. The use of the Goodenough test for revealing male homosexuality. *Journal of Clinical Psychopathology and Psychotherapy,* 1944, 6, 307–321.

Gigel, J. L. *The overt male homosexual: A primary description of a self-affected population.* (Doctoral dissertation, University of Oregon) Ann Arbor, Michigan: University Microfilms, 1970, no. 71-16, 811.

Goldfried, M. R. On the diagnosis of homosexuality from the Rorschach. *Journal of Consulting Psychology,* 1966, *30,* 338–349.

Goldfried, M. R., Stricker, G., & Weiner, I. *Rorschach handbook of clinical and research applications.* New Jersey: Prentice-Hall, 1971.

Gonsiorek, J. G. Psychological adjustment and homosexuality. JSAS *Catalog of Selected Documents in Psychology,* 1977, 7, 45. (Ms, No. 1478)

Gough, H. G. Diagnostic patterns on the Minnesota Multiphasic Personality Inventory. *Journal of Clinical Psychology,* 1946, 2, 23–37.

Grams, A., & Rinder, L. Signs of homosexuality in human-figure drawings. *Journal of Consulting Psychology,* 1958, *22,* 394.

Green, R. Homosexuality as a mental illness. *International Journal of Psychiatry,* 1972, *10,* 77–98.

Green, R. *Sexual identity conflict in children and adults.* New York: Basic Books, 1975.

Greenblatt, D. R. *Semantic differential analysis of the "triangular system" hypothesis in "adjusted" overt male homosexuals.* (Doctoral dissertation, University of California) Ann Arbor, Michigan: University Microfilms, 1966, No. 67-6178.

Greenstein, J. M. Father characteristics and sex-typing. *Journal of Personality and Social Psychology,* 1966, *3,* 271–277.

Grellert, E. A., Newcomb, M. S., & Bentler, P. M. Childhood play activities of male and female homosexuals and heterosexuals. *Archives of Sexual Behavior,* 1982, *11,* 451–478.

Grygier, T. G. Psychometric aspects of homosexuality. *Journal of Mental Science,* 1957, *103,* 514–526.

Grygier, T. Homo, neurosis and "normality": A pilot study in psychological measurement. *British Journal of Delinquency,* 1958, *9,* 59–61.

Grundlach, R. H., & Riess, B. F. Self and sexual identity in men and women in relationship to homosexuality. In B. F. Riess (Ed.), *New directions in mental health.* New York: Grune & Stratton, 1968, pp. 205–231.

Hall, C. S., & Lindsey, G. *Theories of personality.* New York: Wiley, 1978.

Haltiwanger, C. D. *Discriminants of psychological adjustment within a homosexual population.* (Doctoral dissertation, North Carolina at Chapel Hill) Ann Arbor, Michigan: University Microfilms, 1979, No. 7925927.

Hammer, E. F. Relationship between diagnosis of psychosexual pathology and the sex of the first drawn person. *Journal of Clinical Psychology,* 1854, *10,* 168–170.

Hammersmith, S. K., & Weinberg, M. S. Homosexual identity: Commitment, adjustment, and significant others. *Sociometry,* 1973, *36,* 56–79.

Hart, M., Roback, H., Tittler, B., Weitz, L., Walston, B., McKee, E. Psychological adjustment of nonpatient homosexuals: Critical review of the research literature. *Journal of Clinical Psychiatry,* 1978, *39,* 604–608.

Hart, M. T. *Gender attributes and adjustment in homosexual men.* (Doctoral dissertation, George Peabody College for Teachers) Ann Arbor, Michigan: University Microfilms, 1978, No. 7902500.

Hartman, B. J. Comparison of selected experimental MMPI profiles of sexual deviates and sociopaths without sexual deviation. *Psychological Reports,* 1967, *20,* 234.

Hassell, J., & Smith, E. W. Female homosexuals' concepts of self, men, and women. *Journal of Personality Assessment,* 1975, *39,* 154–159.

Heilbruron, A. B., Jr. Sex role, instrumental-expressive behavior, and psychopathology in females. *Journal of Abnormal Psychology,* 1968, *73,* 131–136.

Hendlin, J. C. Homosexuality in the Rorschach: A new look at the old signs. *Journal of Homosexuality,* 1976, *1,* 303–312.

Henry, G. W. *Sex variants: A study of homosexual patterns.* New York: Paul B. Hoeber, 1948.

Hirschfeld, M. *Sexual anomalies and perversions.* London: Francis Aldor, 1944.

Hoffman, M. Homosexual. *Psychology Today,* 1969, *3,* 43–45.

Hoffman, M. *The gay world.* New York: Basic Books, 1968.

Hooberman, R. E. Psychological androgyny, feminine gender identity and self-esteem in homosexual and heterosexual males. *The Journal of Sex Research,* 1979, *15,* 306–315.

Hooker, E. The adjustment of the male overt homosexual. *Journal of Projective Techniques,* 1957, *21,* 1–31.

Hooker, E. Male homosexuality in the Rorschach. *Journal of Projective Techniques,* 1958, *22,* 33–54.

Hooker, E. Symposium on current aspects of the problems of validity: What is a criterion? *Journal of Projective Techniques,* 1959, *23,* 278–286.

Hooker, E. The case of El: A biography. *Journal of Projective Techniques,* 1961, *25,* 252–267.

Hooker, E. An empirical study of some relations between sexual patterns and gender identity in male homosexuals. In Money, J. (Ed.) *Sex research: New developments.* New York: Holt, 1965, pp. 24–52.

Hooker, E. The homosexual community. In Gagnon, J. H., & Simon, W. (Eds.) *Sexual deviance.* New York: Harper & Row, 1967, pp. 167–184.

Hooker, E. Parental relations and male homosexuality in patient and nonpatient samples. *Journal of Consulting Psychology*, 1969, *33*, 140–142.

Hooker, E. Discussion of Saghir paper. In Green, R. (Ed.) *Methodology in sex research.* Rockville, Maryland: National Institute of Mental Health, 1980, pp. 292–301.

Hopkins, J. H. The lesbian personality. *British Journal of Psychiatry*, 1969, *115*, 1433–1436.

Horstman, W. R. MMPI responses of homosexual and heterosexual male college students. *Homosexual Counseling Journal*, 1975, *2*, 68–76.

Horstman, W. R. *Homosexuality and psychopathology: A study of the MMPI responses of homosexual and heterosexual male college students.* (Doctoral dissertation, University of Oregon) Ann Arbor, Michigan: University Microfilms, 1972, No. 72-28, 153.

Howard, S. Determinants of sex-role identification of homosexual female delinquents. *Dissertation Abstracts*, 1962, *23*, 2588–2589.

Jonas, K. H. An objective approach to the personality and environment in homosexuality. *Psychiatric Quarterly*, 1944, *18*, 626–641.

Karlen, A. *Sexuality and homosexuality: A new view.* New York: W. W. Norton and Co., 1971.

Kaye, H. E., et al. Homosexuality in women. *Archives of General Psychiatry*, 1967, *17*, 626–634.

Kelly, J. A., & Worell, J. New formulations of sex roles and androgyny: A critical review. *Journal of Consulting and Clinical Psychology*, 1977, *45*, 1101–1115.

Kenyon, F. E. Studies in female homosexuality: IV. Social and psychiatric aspects. V. Sexual development, attitudes and experience. *British Journal of Psychiatry*, 1968, *114*, 1337–1350.

Kenyon, F. E. Studies in female homosexuality: Psychological test results. *Journal of Consulting & Clinical Psychology*, 1968, *32*, 510–513.

King, W. M. *The etiology of homosexuality as related to childhood experiences and adult adjustment: A study of the perceptions of homosexual males, their parents and siblings.* (Doctoral dissertation, Indiana University) Ann Arbor, Michigan: University Microfilms, 1980, No. 8016685.

Kinsey, A., Pomeroy, W., Martin, C., & Gebhard, P. *Sexual behavior in the human female.* Philadelphia: Saunders, 1953.

Kinsey, A. C., Pomeroy, W. W., & Martin, C. E. *Sexual behavior in the human male.* Philadelphia: W. B. Saunders, 1948.

Kopp, M. A. A study of anomie and homosexuality in delinquent girls. Unpublished doctoral dissertation. University of St. Louis, 1960.

Krafft-Ebing, R. *Psychopathia sexualis.* Translated by Harry E. Wedeck. New York: G. P. Putnam's Sons, 1965.

Kremer, M. W., & Rifkin, A. H. The early development of homosexuality: A study of adolescent lesbians. *American Journal of Psychiatry*, 1969, *126*, 91–96.

Kreiger, M. H., & Worchel, P. A test of the psychoanalytic theory of identification. *Journal of Individual Psychology*, 1960, *16*, 56–63.

Krippner, S. J. The identification of male homosexuality with the MMPI. *Journal of Clinical Psychology*, 1964, *20*, 159–161.

Lamiell, J. Toward an idiothetic psychology of personality. *American Psychologist*, 1981, *36*, 276–289.

Legman, G. *Toward a bibliography of homosexuality (1500–1941)*. New York: Breaking Point, 1941.

Lester, D., McLaughlin, S., Cohen, R., & Dunn, L. Sex deviant handwriting, femininity and homosexuality. *Perceptual and Motor Skills*, 1977, *45*, 1156.

Levine, M. P. The sociology of male homosexuality and lesbianism: An introductory bibliography. *Journal of Homosexuality*, 1980, 249–275.

Liddicoat, R. Homosexuality: Results of a survey as related to various theories. *British Medical Journal*, 1957, *5053*, 1110–1111.

Liddicoat, R. Homosexuality: A study of non-institutionalized homosexuals. *Journal of the National Institute of Personnel Research*, 1961, *8*, 217–249.

Lindner, R. M. Content analysis in Rorschach work. *Rorschach Research Exchange*, 1946, *10*, 121–129.

Lindzey, G., Tejessy, C., & Zamansky, H. S. Thematic Apperception Test: An empirical examination of some indices of homosexuality. *Journal of Abnormal and Social Psychology*, 1958, *57*, 67–75.

Lindzey, G., Tejessy, C., Davids, A., & Heinemann, S. H. *Thematic Apperception Test: A summary of empirical generalizations*. Unpublished manuscript, Harvard University, 1953.

Lindzey, C. Seer versus sign. *Journal of Experimental Research in Personality*, 1965, *1*, 17–26.

Loney, J. An MMPI measure of maladjustment in a sample of "normal" homosexual men. *Journal of Clinical Psychology*, 1971, *27*, 486–488.

Loney, J. Family dynamics of homosexual women. *Archives of Sexual Behavior*, 1973, *2*, 343–350.

Lynn, D. B. *Parental and sex-role identification: A theoretical formulation*. Berkeley: McHutchen Publishing Corp., 1969.

Machover, K. *Personality projections in the drawings of the human figure*. Springfield, Ill.: Charles C. Thomas, 1949.

MacVicor, J. *Homosexual delinquent girls: Identification with mother and perception of parents*. (Doctoral dissertation, Boston University) Ann Arbor, Michigan: University Microfilms, 1967, No. 67-13, 291.

Manosevitz, M. Early sexual behavior in adult homosexual and heterosexual males. *Journal of Abnormal Psychology*, 1970, *3*, 396–402.

Manosevitz, M. Item analysis of the MMPI Mf scale using homosexual and heterosexual males. *Journal of Consulting & Clinical Psychology*, 1970, *35*, 395–399.

Marmor, J. (Ed.) *Homosexual behavior: A modern reappraisal*. New York: Basic Books, 1980.

Masters, W. H., & Johnson, V. E. *Human sexual response*. Boston: Little, Brown and Co., 1966.

Mathes, I. D. B. *Adult male homosexuality and perception of instrumentality, expressiveness, and coalition in parental role structure*. (Doctoral dissertation, University of Missouri) Ann Arbor, Michigan: University Microfilms, 1966, 67-2897.

McCord, T. H. *Fathers, sons, and sexual object choice: A multivariate study.* (Doctoral dissertation, California School of Profesisonal Psychology) Ann Arbor, Michigan: University Microfilms, 1982, No. DA8305254.

McGovern, R. H. *Psychological androgyny and its relation to psychological adjustment in the homosexual male.* (Doctoral dissertation, Case Western Reserve University) Ann Arbor, Michigan: University Microfilms, 1977, No. 77-18, 835.

McGuire, R. J., Carlisle, J. M., & Young, B. G. Sexual deviations as conditioned behavior: A hypothesis. *Behavior Research Therapy,* 1965, *2,* 185–190.

Meketon, B. W., Griffith, R. M., Taylor, V. H., & Wiederman, J. S. Rorschach homosexual signs in paranoid schizophrenics. *Journal of Abnormal & Social Psychology,* 1962, *65,* 280–284.

Miller, W. G., & Hannum, T. E. Characteristics of homosexually involved incarcerated females. *Journal of Consulting Psychology,* 1963, *27,* 227.

Money, J. Sexual dimorphism and homosexual gender identity. *Psychological Bulletin,* 1970, *74,* 425–440.

Money, J. Gender-transposition theory and homosexual genesis. *Journal of Sex and Marital Therapy,* 1984, *10,* 75–82.

Money, J., & Ehrardt, A. A. *Man and woman: Boy and girl.* Baltimore: The Johns Hopkins University Press, 1972.

Money, J., & Tucker, P. *Sexual signatures.* Boston: Little, Brown, 1975.

Morin, S. F. Heterosexual bias in psychological research on lesbianism and male homosexuality. *American Psychologist,* 1977, *32,* 629–637.

Murray, H. A. *Explorations in personality.* New York: Oxford University Press, 1938.

Nash, J., & Hays, F. The parental relationships of male homosexuals: Some theoretical issues and a pilot study. *Australian Journal of Psychology,* 1965, *17,* 35–43.

Newcomb, M. D. The role of perceived parent personality in the development of heterosexuals, homosexuals, and transvestites. *Archives of Sexual Behavior,* 1985, *14,* 147–164.

Nickeson, S. S. *A comparison of gay and heterosexual teachers on professional and personal dimensions.* (Doctoral dissertation, The University of Florida) Ann Arbor, Michigan: University Microfilms, 1980, No. 8105601.

Nitsche, C. J., Robinson, J. F., & Parsons, E. T. Homosexuality and the Rorschach. *Journal of Consulting Psychology,* 1956, *20,* 196.

O'Conner, P. J. Aetiological factors in homosexuality as seen in Royal Air Force psychiatric practice. *British Journal of Psychiatry,* 1964, *110,* 381–391.

Ohlson, E. E., & Wilson, M. Differentiating female homosexuals from female heterosexuals using the MMPI. *The Journal of Sex Research,* 1974, *10,* 308–315.

Oliver, W. A., & Mosher, D. L. Psychopathology and guilt in heterosexual and subgroups of homosexual reformatory inmates. *Journal of Abnormal Psychology,* 1968, *73,* 323–329.

Paitich, D. Parent-child relations and sexual deviation. Forensic Clinic Seminar, no. 47. Toronto: Toronto Psychiatric Hospital, 1960, Mimeographed, 27 pp.

Panton, J. H. New MMPI scale for the identification of homosexuality. *Journal of Clinical Psychology*, 1960, *16*, 17–21.

Parker, W. *Homosexuality: A selective bibliography of over 3,000 items.* Metuchen, N.Y.: The Scarecrow Press, 1971.

Pierce, D. M. MMPI HSX scale differences between active and situational homosexuality. *Journal of Forensic Psychology*, 1972, *4*, 31–38.

Pierce, D. M. Test and nontest correlates of active and situational homosexuality. *Psychology*, 1973, *10*, 23–26.

Pledger, R. H., Jr. *Early parent-child relationships of male homosexuals and heterosexuals.* (Doctoral dissertation, The University of Texas) Ann Arbor, Michigan: University Microfilms, 1977, No. 7807365.

Pritt, T. E. *A comparative study between male homosexuals' and heterosexuals' perceived parental acceptance-rejection, self-concepts, and self-evaluation tendencies.* (Doctoral dissertation, University of Utah) Ann Arbor, Michigan: University Microfilms, 1971, No. 72-531.

Prytula, R. E., Wellford, C. D., & DeMonbreun, B. G. Body self-image and homosexuality. *Journal of Clinical Psychology*, 1979, *35*, 567–572.

Pustel, G., Sternlicht, M., & Deutsch, M. Feminine tendencies in figure drawings by male homosexual retarded dyads. *Journal of Clinical Psychology*, 1971, *27*, 260–261.

Raychaudhuri, M., & Mukerji, K. Rorschach differentials of homosexuality in male convicts: An examination of Wheeler and Schaefer signs. *Journal of Personality Assessment*, 1970, *35*, 22–26.

Reitzell, J. M. A comparative study of hysterics, homosexuals and alcoholics using content analysis of Rorschach responses. *Rorschach Research Exchange*, 1949, *13*, 127–141.

Richter, R. W. *Measures of maladjustment and guilt and their relationship to homosexual behavior in two homosexual groups.* (Doctoral dissertation, Southern Illinois University) Ann Arbor, Michigan: University Microfilms, 1976, No. 77-6253.

Reiss, B. F. Psychological tests in homosexuality. In Marmor, J. (Ed.) *Homosexual behavior.* New York: Basic Books, 1980, pp. 296–311.

Reiss, B. F., Safer, J., & Yotive, W. Psychological test data on female homosexuality: A review of the literature. *Journal of Homosexuality*, 1974, *1*, 71–85.

Roback, H. B., Lengevin, R., & Zajac, Y. Sex of free choice figure drawings by homosexual and heterosexual subjects. *Journal of Personality Assessment*, 1974, *38*, 154–155.

Robertson, G. Parent-child relationships and homosexuality. *British Journal of Psychiatry*, 1972, *121*, 525–528.

Rogers, C. R. *Toward a more human science of the person.* La Jolla, Cal.: Center for Studies of the Person, 1985. Unpublished manuscript.

Ross, M. W. The relationship of perceived societal hostility, conformity, and psychological adjustment in homosexual males. *Journal of Homosexuality*, 1978, *4*, 157–168.

Saghir, M. T., Robins, E., Walbran, B., & Gentry, K. A. Homosexuality: IV.

Psychiatric disorders and disability in the female homosexual. *American Journal of Psychiatry*, 1970a, *127*, 147–154. (a)

Saghir, M. T., Robins, E., Walbran, B., & Gentry, K. A. Homosexuality: III. Psychiatric disorders and disability in the male homosexual. *American Journal of Psychiatry*, 1970b, *126*, 1079–1086. (b)

Saghir, M. T., & Robins, E. *Male and female homosexuality: A comprehensive investigation*. Baltimore: Williams and Wilkins, 1973.

Schatzberg, A. F., Westfall, M. P., Blumetti, A. B., & Birk, C. L. Effeminancy. I. A quantitative rating scale. *Archives of Sexual Behavior*, 1975, *4*, 31–41.

Schier, I. H., & Cattell, R. B. *The neuroticism scale questionnaire*. Champaign, Ill.: Institute for Personality and Ability Testing, 1961.

Shavelson, E., Biaggio, M. K., Cross, H. H., & Lehman, R. E. Lesbian women's perceptions of their parent-child relationships. *Journal of Homosexuality*, 1980, *5*, 205–215.

Siegelman, M. Adjustment of homosexual and heterosexual women. *British Journal of Psychiatry*, 1972, *120*, 477–481. (a)

Siegelman, M. Adjustment of male homosexuals and heterosexuals. *Archives of Sexual Behavior*, 1972, *2*, 9–25. (b)

Siegelman, M. Parental background of homosexual and heterosexual women. *British Journal of Psychiatry*, 1974, *124*, 14–21. (a)

Siegelman, M. Parental background of male homosexuals and heterosexuals. *Archives of Sexual Behavior*, 1974, *3*, 3–18. (b)

Siegelman, M. Psychological adjustment of homosexual and heterosexual men: A cross-national replication. *Archives of Sexual Behavior*, 1978, *7*, 1–11.

Siegelman, M. Adjustment of homosexual and heterosexual women: A cross-national replication. *Archives of Sexual Behavior*, 1979, *8*, 121–125.

Siegelman, M. Parental background of homosexual and heterosexual women: A cross-national replication. *Archives of Sexual Behavior*, 1981, *10*, 369–375. (a)

Siegelman, M. Parental backgrounds of homosexual and heterosexual men: A cross-national replication. *Archives of Sexual Behavior*, 1981, *10*, 505–513. (b)

Singer, M. I. Comparison of indicators of homosexuality on the MMPI. *Journal of Consulting and Clinical Psychology*, 1970, *34*, 15–18.

Sjostedt, E. M., & Hurwitz, I. A developmental study of sexual functioning by means of a cognitive analysis. *Journal of Projective Techniques*, 1959, *23*, 237–246.

Skrapec, C., & Mackenzie, K. R. Psychological self-perception in male transsexuals, homosexuals, and heterosexuals. *Archives of Sexual Behavior*, 1981, *10*, 357–370.

Slater, E., & Slater, P. A study in the assessment of homosexual traits. *British Journal of Medical Psychology*, 1947, *21*, 61–74.

Snortum, J. R., Gillespie, J. F., Marshall, J. E., & McLaughlin, J. P. Family dynamics and homosexuality. *Psychological Reports*, 1969, *24*, 763–770.

Socarides, C. W. Psychoanalytic perspectives on female homosexuality: A discussion of "The lesbians as a 'single' woman." *American Journal of Psychotherapy*, 1981, *35*, 510–515.

Stekel, W. *The homosexual neurosis.* Revised Edition. Brooklyn, NY: Physicians and Surgeons Books Co., 1933.

Stekel, W. Is homosexuality curable? *Psychoanalytic Review,* 1930, *17,* 443–451.

Stephan, W. G. Parental relationships and early social experiences of activist male homosexuals and male heterosexuals. *Journal of Abnormal Psychology,* 1973, *82,* 506–513.

Storm, M. D. Theories of sexual orientation. *Journal of Personality and Social Psychology,* 1980, *38,* 783–792.

Strassberg, D. S., Roback, H., Cunningham, J., McKee, E., & Larson, P. Psychopathology in self-identified female-to-male transsexuals, homosexuals, and heterosexuals. *Archives of Sexual Behavior,* 1979, *8,* 491–496.

Stringer, P., & Grygier, T. Male homosexuality, psychiatric status, and psychological masculinity and femininity. *Archives of Sexual Behavior,* 1976, *5,* 15–27.

Suppe, F. The Bell and Weinberg study: Future priorities for research on homosexuality. *Journal of Homosexuality,* 1981, *6,* 69–97.

Symonds, M. Homosexuality in adolescence. Pennsylvania Psychiatric Quarterly, 1969, *9,* 15–24.

Symons, D. *The evolution of human sexuality.* New York: Oxford University Press, 1979.

Tejessy, C. *The Thematic Apperception Test: A summary and preliminary investigation of empirical generalizations.* Unpublished honor's thesis, Harvard University, 1952.

Terman, L. M., & Miles, C. C. *Sex and personality: Studies in masculinity and femininity.* New York: McGraw-Hill, 1936.

Thomas, R. W. *An investigation of the psychoanalytic theory of homosexuality.* (Doctoral dissertation, University of Kentucky) Ann Arbor, Michigan: University Microfilms, 1951, No. 60-712.

Thompson, N. L., McCandless, B. R., & Strickland, B. R. Personal adjustment of male and female homosexuals and heterosexuals. *Journal of Abnormal Psychology,* 1971, *78,* 237–240.

Thompson, N. L., Schwartz, D. M., & McCandless, B. R. Parent-child relationships and sexual identity in male and female homosexuals and heterosexuals. *Journal of Consulting and Clinical Psychology,* 1973, *41,* 120–127.

Tripp, C. A. *The homosexual matrix.* New York: McGraw-Hill, 1975.

Van Wyk, P. H. *Developmental factors associated with heterosexual, bisexual, and homosexual outcomes.* (Doctoral dissertation, Illinois Institute of Technology) Ann Arbor, Michigan: University Microfilms, 1982, No. DA8220268.

Vilhotti, A. J. An investigation of the use of the D.A.F. in the diagnosis of homosexuality in mentally deficient males. *American Journal of Mental Deficiency,* 1958, *62,* 708–711.

Vroegh, K. Masculinity and femininity in the preschool years. *Child Development,* 1968, *39,* 1253–1257.

Weinberg, M. S., & Bell, A. P. *Homosexuality: An annotated bibliography.* New York: Harper & Row, 1972.

Weinberg, M. S., & Williams, C. J. *Male homosexuals: Their problems and adaptations.* New York: Oxford University Press, 1974.

Weis, C. B., & Dain, R. N. Ego development and sex attitudes in heterosexual and homosexual men and women. *Archives of Sexual Behavior,* 1979, *8,* 341–356.

Weis, C. B., Jr. *A comparative study of level of ego development and sex-role attributes in heterosexual and homosexual men and women.* (Doctoral dissertation, The University of Texas Health Science Center) Ann Arbor, Michigan: University Microfilms, 1977, No. 77-25, 886.

Werner, D. A cross-cultural perspective on theory and research on male homosexuality. *Journal of Homosexuality,* 1979, *4,* 345–362.

West, D. J. *Homosexuality.* Chicago: Aldine, 1967.

West, D. J. Parental figures in the genesis of male homosexuality. *International Journal of Social Psychiatry,* 1959, *5,* 85–97.

Wheeler, W. M. An analysis of Rorschach indices of male homosexuality. *Rorschach Research Exchange,* 1949, *13,* 97–126.

Whitaker, L., Jr. The use of an extended draw-a-person test to identify homosexual and effeminate men. *Journal of Consulting Psychology,* 1961, *25,* 482–485.

Whitam, F. L., & Zent, M. A cross-cultural assessment of early cross-gender behavior and familial factors in male homosexuality. *Archives of Sexual Behavior,* 1984, *13,* 427–439.

Whitener, R. W., & Nikelly, A. G. Sexual deviation in college students. *American Journal of Orthopsychiatry,* 1964, *34,* 486–492.

Williams, S. G. Male homosexual responses to MMPI combined subscales Mf-sub-1 and Mf-sub-2. *Psychological Reprints,* 1981, *49,* 606.

Willmott, M., & Brierley, H. Cognitive characteristics and homosexuality. *Archives of Sexual Behavior,* 1984, *13,* 311–319.

Wilson, M. L. *A new female homosexuality scale.* (Doctoral dissertation, University of Northern Colorado) Ann Arbor, Michigan: University Microfilms, 1973, No. 74-1657.

Wilson, M. L., & Greene, R. L. Personality characteristics of female homosexuals. *Psychological Reports,* 1971, *28,* 407–412.

Worell, J. Sex roles and psychological well-being: Perspectives on methodology. *Journal of Consulting and Clinical Psychology,* 1978, *46,* 777–791.

Yamahiro, R. S., & Griffith, R. M. Validity of two indices of sexual deviancy. *Journal of Clinical Psychology,* 1960, *16,* 21–24.

Zuger, B. Homosexuality and parental guilt. *British Journal of Psychiatry,* 1980, *137,* 55–57.

4

PSYCHOANALYTIC THEORY

Reuben Fine

INTRODUCTION

Homosexuality has been in the forefront of psychiatric and psychoanalytic discussion for almost 100 years. The theory is basically very simple. But it is obscured by the forces of obscurantism and hostility which are so prevalent in the hate culture, such as ours (Fine, 1985).

In 1898 Morton Prince read a paper on homosexuality to the Medico-Psychological Society (Prince, 1975) that expressed the prevailing pre-psychoanalytic position. Prince's theory was that sexual perversion has its basis in a diseased nervous system which, in most cases, is the result of inheritance. At the same time he found that the treatment of sexual paraesthesia, as he called it, in contradiction to the genetic (hereditary theory) is attended in a large proportion of cases with encouraging results. According to his figures (his as well as those of von Schrenck-Notzing), about 70% were essentially improved or cured. Treatment at that time consisted of little more than educational instruction (the same kind of "treatment" that Masters and Johnson used almost a century later).

Into this dark forest Freud cast the first beam of light that made sense of the "perversions." In the Three Essays (1905), the first essay deals with homosexuality. There he divided the sexual act into aim and object. Homosexuality is a deviation in respect to the object.

Several other pertinent observations were made by the early analysts. The normal individual is bisexual, in that he/she has both heterosexual and homosexual desires. In the normal course of development, the heterosexual desires come to take precedence, but homosexual desires never disappear entirely. Our society, as Ferenczi pointed out, has made it difficult or impossible for men (and women as well) to allow the enthusiastic and devoted friendship between men that was so common in antiquity. (Ferenczi, 1914). "It is in fact astounding to what extent present-day men have lost the capacity for mutual affection and amiability. Instead there prevails among men decided asperity, resistance and love of disputation" (p. 315). This close relationship between homosexuality and hostility has since been a cornerstone of all psychoanalytic observations on the subject.

A further and extremely important consequence of analytic investigation was that homosexual desire, both conscious and unconscious, has to be differentiated from exclusive compulsive homosexuality, which is what is ordinarily referred to as homosexuality. In the rest of this paper I shall speak of homosexuality in this sense—the exclusive compulsive attachment to a person of the same sex, with the exclusion of close and sexual relationships with the opposite sex, in fact, usually with the total denial of any interest in the opposite sex. It is about this kind of homosexuality that all the arguments center.

Now, as Sandler (1983) has recently pointed out, psychoanalysis is an ongoing continuous growing body of theory. What Freud and Ferenczi saw as symptoms, was soon transformed into the notion of character structure. A symptom cannot be understood in its own right; it can only be understood in the light of the total character structure in which it is embedded. Hence homosexuality, like any other piece of behavior, can only be understood when the total person is understood.

A paradoxical way of putting this proposition, one which I have often used therapeutically with patients is this: there is no such thing as homosexuality. There is only homosexual behavior, in its various forms and manifestations. It is this homosexual behavior which has to be dissected and grasped.

Still another way of approaching the question is this. A professor of mine, Morris Raphael Cohen, who was very famous in his day as one of the leading American philosophers, was once asked: Can a man urinate during sexual intercourse? Cohen was not a medical man, but he replied in a common sense way: Who would want to? We can thus ask about the homosexual: why does he (she) want to?

The expansion of psychoanalytic theory cannot be described here in full detail (cf. Fine, 1979). But since the question of neurosis has been brought up repeatedly in connection with homosexuality, it is worth quoting what Laplanche and Pontalis have to say about the subject (1973):

The task of trying to define neurosis, as revealed by clinical experience, in terms of the comprehension of the concept *of neurosis, tends to become indistinguishable from the psychoanalytic theory itself.*

Since today we deal with the ego, id, superego, affects, self-image, identity, defensive and autonomous ego structures and much more, the question of homosexuality, and whether it is a "neurosis" or not is by no means a simple one to answer. Again it can be answered only in terms of a full description of the personality.

From the beginning, it was observed that no person resorts to homo-sexuality without some frustration of heterosexuality. This has been borne out in all clinical experience, as well as in anthropological research and animal psychology. Where heterosexuality is freely permitted, exclusive homosexuality is virtually unknown; there are only rare exceptions. And when homosexuality is there, its dynamics can readily be explained.

The contemporary American custom of setting up homosexual couples as though they were man and wife (Blumstein and Schwartz, 1983) is unknown in any other society. Not that this makes it bad or "perverse" per se; merely a fact to be noted. Many cultures have homosexual contacts, but they all require some clarification. For example, the Greek version of homosexuality was limited to that of an older man with a younger pubescent boy (Dover, 1978). It can best be explained as the wish of the older man to regain the vigor and enthusiasm of his lost youth (Fine, 1985). In the climate of complete heterosexual freedom, where wives, mistresses, slaves and prosti-tutes were all freely available, the older man's wish for the young boy related more to his aggression than to his sexuality; the Greeks, as Sagan has put it (1979) had a lust to annihilate. In spite of their momentous cultural achievements, it was essentially a hate culture, in which love played little or no real role.

Psychoanalysis is both a system of psychology and a philosophy of living. As a philosophy, its major value is love (Fine, 1985). I have tried to formulate this philosophy in terms of the *analytic ideal:* human beings attain the greatest degree of happiness when they 1) can love; 2) enjoy sexuality; 3) have pleasure; 4) have feeling, yet 5)are guided by reason; 6) have a role in a family; 7) have a role in a social structure; 8) have a good self-image; 9) can work; 10) can communicate with their fellow human beings; 11) have a creative outlet and 12) are free from psychiatric symptomatology. It is only in the light of this analytic ideal (or some comparable approach in terms of ego functions, such as Bellak, 1984, or Anna Freud, 1965) that human beings can be properly understood and treated. "Neurosis," if we wish to use the term (and I do not wish to but am forced to do so to achieve some consensual validation) can best be defined as the distance from the analytic ideal.

To what degree are human beings in our culture neurotic? To a large degree. The initial investigation by Rennie et al. in 1962 estimated some 80% of the population; it is certainly at least that.

In the light of these findings, it is best to speak of maladjustment neuroses (the traditional psychiatric categories) and adjustment neuroses (which have been uncovered by psychoanalytic research). The average person in our culture suffers at least from an adjustment neurosis. To call him or her "normal" because they get along in society serves only to obfuscate the truth.

Veroff Douvan and Kulka (1981) in their survey of representative Americans, stress the degree to which psychoanalytic concepts have come to dominate thinking on this subject. They write (p. 7):

> In these characteristics—isolation, detachment, intellectual/verbal analy-sis—psychoanalysis represents quintessential science. Its popularity marks the movement of the scientific revolution of the last frontier—the sphere of human behavior and the thickets of the human soul—and represents, above all, a remarkable faith in and optimism about the power of science. Its emergence as the model of human counsel marks modern sensibility and displaces a religious/moral model.

With these preliminaries we can now consider the main questions that have concerned the literature:

1. Is homosexuality treatable?
2. Is homosexuality per se a "neurosis?"
3. What are the psychodynamics of homosexuality?

TREATABILITY

I have recently had occasion to review the results of psychotherapy with homosexuals, and been surprised by the findings. It is paradoxical that even though the politically active homosexual group denies the possibility of change, all studies from Schrenck-Notzing on have found positive effects, virtually regardless of the kind of treatment used (Wiedemann, 1962, 1974).

The most intensive study of treatment was published by Irving Bieber and his colleagues at the Flower-Fifth Ave. Psychoanalytic Center (1962). They collected data on treatment of 106 cases with a variety of analysts, 70% of whom classified themselves as Freudian, while 30% saw themselves as cultural. Regardless of theoretical orientation, 27% (29) of the group became exclusively heterosexual. Of the 72 patients who had been exclusively homo-sexual, 19% became heterosexual and of the 30 patients who began treatment as bisexuals, 50% became heterosexual. They also found a correlation between the length of treatment and favorable results in terms of change from homosexuality to heterosexuality.

They regarded the following factors as favorable prognostic indicators: 1) bisexual at the beginning of analysis; 2) patient begins analysis before age 35; 3) patient continues in analysis for at least 150 hours, preferably 350 hours or more; 4) patient has a non-detached or at least an ambivalent father; 6) patient's father respects and/or admires the patient, is affectionate, more intimate with patient than with other male siblings and likes women; 7) patient "idolizes" women; 8) patient has tried heterosexual genital contact at some time and 9) patient had erotic heterosexual activity in the manifest content of his dreams.

Hatterer (1971) reports on the treatment of 200 homosexuals over the course of 17 years. The author also examined and evaluated 710 men who were "troubled and untroubled by a vast spectrum of homosexual fantasy, impulse, act and milieu." In his treatment he used a great many modalities, such as supportive, directive and interpretive activities. The treatment duration varied from one month to 15 years, with a minimum of three to a maximum of 375 sessions. The age range varied from 15 to 65 years. Some patients were followed up for a period of two to 15 years. Of 143 patients in the pilot study between 1959 and 1969, 49 recovered, 19 recovered partially and 76 remained homosexual.

In more recent years behavior therapists have also tried their hand at homosexuality. Stevenson and Wolpe (1960) encouraged and established assertive behavior in three homosexual patients through an active therapeutic approach. They did not deal at all with homosexuality, yet this treatment led to the abandonment of homosexual and the establishment of heterosexual behavior. Feldman and MacCullough (Wiedemann, p. 689) used anticipatory avoidance therapy with 43 homosexuals, 41 men and 2 women, of whom 36 completed the full course. On the average, the patients received 18 to 20 sessions each, lasting 20 to 25 minutes. Twenty-five patients improved; 11 patients were unimproved. After a follow-up of one year, 58% of the patients were considered improved.

Masters and Johnson (1979) reported their results with the treatment of "male homosexual dissatisfaction" over a period of ten years. By this they mean male homosexuals who wish to become heterosexual. They divided the group into those who wished to "convert" (i.e., had never been heterosexual) and those who wished to "revert," that is, get back to heterosexuality which they had once experienced and given up in favor of homosexuality. Of the 54 men, 9 were conversion clients, and 45 reversion. Their statistics are presented somewhat unusually, but put most simply of the 9 conversion cases, 6 became heterosexual, with three cases lost to a 5-year follow-up. Four were converted to heterosexuality, while 2 of the remaining had unknown outcome (lost to a 5-year follow-up). Of the 45 reversion clients, 19 became heterosexual, while of the remainder 14 were lost in the 5-year follow-up. It is well known that Masters and Johnson possess little or no psychological sophistication, and content themselves with imparting anatomical information and educational procedures (as Prince did 100 years ago).

Thus, whether with hypnosis (Schrenck-Notzing), psychoanalysis of any variety, educative psychotherapy, behavior therapy, and/or simple educational procedures, a considerable percentage of overt homosexuals became heterosexual. Of course, only the psychoanalytic cases are really understood, since the others present no dynamic picture. But it is striking that if the patients are motivated, whatever procedure is adopted a large percentage will give up their homosexuality.

In this connection public information is of the greatest importance. The misinformation spread by certain circles that "homosexuality is untreatable by psychotherapy" does incalculable harm to thousands of men and women.

IS HOMOSEXUALITY PER SE A "NEUROSIS"?

To answer this question it is first necessary to clarify what is meant by a neurosis today. Above, I have offered a definition of neurosis as the distance from the analytic ideal. This definition is in conformity with the mainstream psychoanalytic tradition. In a society such as ours, in so many respects a hate culture (Fine, 1985), the percentage of persons who are distant from the analytic ideal is high indeed. Figures tend to be misleading; the fact is that virtually everybody above a minimal eduational and social level can benefit from psychotherapy, and should be offered a chance to do so. If this is not done, it is one more mark against the society in which we live. As of now, it is estimated that about one of every three Americans consults a mental health expert in the course of his/her life (Veroff, Douvan & Kulka, 1981). As the number of therapists increases, the number of persons who seek counseling or psychotherapy can only grow.

The commonly heard argument that the therapist sees only "sick" homosexuals, and has no contact with "healthy" homosexuals is too absurd to be taken seriously, yet it is taken seriously by some. In point of fact, every homosexual patient in analysis (or even superficial therapy) provides information on perhaps a thousand or more other homosexuals whom he/she talks about. Further, the therapist, as a member of our society, can see homosexual individuals in action, and form his own judgment.

A comment is in order about the political homosexual community, which has in the past ten years or so resorted to political action rather than scientific debate. Their action has all too often been destructive and violent. At a meeting arranged by our group some years ago on the dynamics of homosexuality, we were advised by the police at the last minute that the meeting would have to be called off because of the threat of violence. This is no longer sober scientific discussion; it is a form of totalitarian behavior which is dangerous in the extreme. It also bears out the analytic observation that hostility is the other side of the coin of homosexuality. The ordinary person who is heterosexual represses his/her homosexuality; the homosexual represses both the heterosexuality and the violence.

The argument has centered on a variety of material, anthropological, biological, sociological, clinical and so on. There can be no doubt that exclusive compulsive homosexuality (which is what we are talking about) is reached by men and women only after a long and terrible ordeal. Equally there is no doubt that if caught early enough, and that if properly motivated to change, most of them can do so.

It is important to note the other side of the analytic position, which has been largely ignored, i.e., that homosexual wishes are an essential part of the human make-up. Kinsey (1948, 1953) found that a substantial percentage of men and women engaged in homosexual activity in their younger years, then gave it up and went on to heterosexuality. Statistics are notoriously inaccurate in this area, but according to Sorenson (1973) about 2% of adolescents remain homosexual. Thus by far the largest majority of individuals give up their homosexuality of their own accord, simply because it represents to them an undesirable way of living.

The argument that homosexuality is merely a "normal" variation (Gonsiorek et al., 1982), which has also been called the "vegetarian" theory (some people prefer meat, some beets) has no real scientific foundation. Indeed, it makes no real sense, since the advocates of such a position have no way of explaining how, if it is a normal variation, the man becomes homosexual when the vast majority of the remainder of the population remains heterosexual. Perhaps Samuel Johnson's aphorism is most apt here: marriage has many pains, but celibacy has no pleasures.

The biological-evolutionary argument that Darwinian fitness resides in the capacity to reproduce the species, which in turn makes heterosexuality an overpowering drive, cannot be refuted. Indeed, as time goes on it makes more and more sense. Further, our clinical experience is unanimous: homosexuality is a curable deviation from the analytic ideal.

If homosexuals do not wish to be cured, that is about par for the course, since most people resist psychotherapy with all the forces at their command (Strean, 1985). Indeed, the discovery that resistance is inherent in psychotherapy is one of Freud's most momentous contributions (Fine, 1973).

The reclassification of homosexuality by the American Psychiatric Association need not be taken seriously. Socarides (1974) has shown in detail how this conclusion was reached on the basis of political rather than scientific considerations. Furthermore, the "change" has even been misstated, since the older DSM II did not list homosexuality as a "neurosis" but as a "sexual deviation" without further explanation. There could hardly be any argument with that, since it is merely a descriptive term.

The balloting of the psychiatric community by the directors of the American Psychiatric Association was likewise carried on in a scandalously dishonest manner. The Board urged the members not to overrule it because the Board had never previously been overruled! In addition, they did not mention that subsequent to the initial ballot, another survey was done of psychiatric opinion, for whatever that is worth, which disagreed strongly with the position of the American Psychiatric Association (Robitscher, 1980).

The present classification of "egodystonic" homosexuality is a category reserved for those homosexuals for whom changing sexual orientation is a "persistent concern." This bizarre reversal of accepted clinical wisdom can only be understood as part of a political maneuver on the part of the task force that composed the DSM III (Socarides, 1974). Those best known and most knowledgeable about homosexuality were excluded from the deliberations that preceded the establishment of the diagnostic category.

Almost all persons in our society feel great concern about whether they are "really homosexuals," as Ferenczi had pointed out 70 years ago, and as analytic experience confirms over and over again. Those who do not feel the concern engage in the defensive mechanism of denial, one of the most pathological defense mechanisms of all. The DSM III is thus glorifying pathology, not rendering any sensible scientific opinion. It is not surprising to hear that DSM IV is already in the process of preparation.

Much evidence has been presented purporting to show that in both interview material and on standard psychological tests no difference is found between homosexuals and heterosexuals. This contention is faulty on two grounds.

First of all, if pencil-and-paper tests (so-called "objective" tests of personality) do not discriminate between heterosexuals and homosexuals, even though they are structured to do so (as in the Minnesota Multiphasic) that indicates that there is something wrong with the tests. In general, analytic psychologists have little faith in pencil-and-paper tests of personality, feeling that they are falsified too easily, are too close to the surface, and do not touch the deeper dynamic strivings of the personality.

Second, as far as the Rorschach and other projective tests are concerned, the evidence at hand is that they do discriminate homosexuals from heterosexuals (Goldfried et al., 1971).

In this connection mention must be made of the shoddy and questionable research which has so often been quoted to "prove" that homosexuality is simply a "normal" variation. Perhaps the best known of these studies is the one by Evelyn Hooker (1958). A number of years ago I was asked to examine her papers critically, which I did; my study was published in 1973. I found that her study was seriously flawed. She asked three judges to differentiate, on the basis of a blind analysis, homosexual from heterosexual projectives (Rorschach and TAT). The judges stated in advance that they did not think they could do so. And in fact they could not.

Her choice of subjects was peculiar. The homosexuals were taken from the Mattachine society, on the basis of the fact that they had never been in therapy. This only shows that they used the defense of denial very strongly, not that they were "well adjusted" (whatever that might mean). As far as the heterosexual controls are concerned she says that because they were obtained from community organizations she could not "describe further the way in which they were obtained." What earthly reason could ordinary heterosexual men have for remaining so doggedly anonymous in a study of this kind? They were interviewed, and given a battery of psychological tests—conventional psychological research that goes on all the time. Hooker's refusal to give more information about the controls casts serious doubt on her work, if it does not entirely invalidate it.

Then we discover on more careful examination that in spite of everything the tests did discriminate. When the Wheeler signs were used for matched pairs in a definite direction, they did differentiate at a statistically significant level. This was discarded because the individual signs did not stand up to a more careful study.

Further she states that certain records, about one-third of the total, revealed a pronounced emphasis on femininity and/or anality, and these records were definitely and clearly homosexual. She says: "Some kinds of homosexual records can be distinguished with certainty."

In the TAT-MAPS there was a clear differentiation with almost 100% certainty. (Incidentally, this does not agree with my own experience; it is more complex than she alleges.) But this finding was discarded because it was on the surface. So what? It is still a finding.

Her main conclusion was: "Some homosexuals may be very ordinary individuals, indistinguishable, except in sexual pattern, from ordinary individuals who are heterosexual." This is an obvious truism which requires no arcane psychological testing. But her major thesis that there is no evidence to show that homosexuals are maladjusted does not emerge from this study; she had no clear way to measure maladjustment.

Scientifically her study is worthless, yet it is quoted again and again. It should also be noted that she had been appointed chair of a task force on homosexuality by the NIMH in 1969, in spite of her obvious and clearly stated biases (Fine, 1973).

In this connection the value of psychoanalysis as a *research tool* must be stressed, especially with a topic as heavily emotion-laden as homosexuality. There is no way of knowing the inner dynamics of the homosexual's life without careful and detailed clinical examination, preferably psychoanalytic. In a society in which most everybody has neurotic conflicts of one kind or another, the distinction between those which characterize the homosexual and those which characterize the heterosexual requires detailed examination of the entire life situation, both inner and outer. Just as Hooker's study is biased and worthless, almost all studies in this area, which do not rely on detailed clinical material, are equally biased and worthless. Examination of the book by Paul, Weinrich, Gonsiorek, and Hotvedt (1982) which was prepared for the Society for the Psychological Study of Social Issues, shows that the book is essentially a plea to recognize the "normality" of homosexuality, and not an attempt to find any real evidence.

The book by Bell and Weinberg (1978) prepared for the Kinsey Institute, is equally flawed, methodically outrageously wrong, and equally highly biased. For instance, on p. 116 they state:

*The heterosexual majority has so generally regarded homosexuality per
se as a sexual problem that almost no consideration has been given to
whether homosexuals may differ in how many problems they have in
their sexual functioning.*

This statement shows such an appalling ignorance of the body of
psychoanalytic literature that it would be laughable if it were not so tragic.
From the very beginning psychoanalysis always emphasized that all homosexuals, as well as all heterosexuals, are different.

Thus the question of whether homosexuality (now speaking again of
exclusive compulsive homosexuality) is "neurotic" has not even been addressed
by these questionnaire and interview studies. It has been addressed by
psychoanalytic research. The answer is that homosexuals have numerous
problems, and that no one reaches the final stage of exclusive homosexuality
without serious inner conflicts, which remain, even if they are denied. As far
as why homosexual couples live together, which is the main element under
investigation, any serious examination would have to begin with the question
posed above: Who would want to?

THE PSYCHODYNAMICS OF HOMOSEXUALITY

Psychoanalysis has been examining the psychodynamics of homosexuality
from the very beginning (it will be recalled that the first section of the Three
Essays is devoted to homosexuality). Much relevant material has been
uncovered, almost entirely ignored by the apologists for homosexuality. For
the rest of this section we shall again be speaking of exclusive compulsive
homosexuality, in which the opposite sex is completely excluded.

There are at least three dynamic questions that require an answer:

1. Why does the homosexual shift his object to the same sex?
2. What is the meaning of his or her actual sexual practices?
3. How does the homosexuality interrelate with the other aspects of the
   personality?

The Shift of Object

In the normal developmental process, the child moves toward the parent
of the opposite sex (boy to mother, girl to father). In every case ever
investigated, this move takes place.

Then what happens is that the sexual wishes are frustrated, and the
child turns away to the same sex. This turning away occurs only after a long
and painful series of conflicts. It happens generally because of the rejection by
the parents. In this connection the significance of the father has been

especially stressed. A boy or girl who has a good warm relationship with a heterosexual father does not become an overt homosexual.

The feelings among homosexual couples are ones of intense jealousy, rivalry and hostility. Just as love may cover up hatred in the heterosexual couple, it usually does so in the homosexual couple as well.

Further, we find that unconsciously the homosexual takes pleasure in depriving the partner of a normal sex life; in fact, this pleasure is one of the greatest rewards in homosexuality. "If I can't have it, you can't either" is what the person is saying. The love between homosexuals is a pseudo-love, more often than not simply a reaction formation against hatred. The abundant case material in the literature demonstrates this point over and over again.

The attitude toward the opposite sex is one of extreme hostility. Homosexual men, frustrated in their sex lives early in life, turn against women with a vengeance. Their imitation of women is usually an identification with the aggressor (Anna Freud, 1936).

Similarly, lesbian women express an intense hatred of men; this is so much on the surface that it requires little proof. In 40 years of analytic practice I have never been consulted by a homosexual woman for her problems, although some female patients have developed homosexual conflicts in the course of their analyses. Socarides, who probably has more experience than anyone else with homosexuals, likewise mentions only a few women in his study (Socarides, 1978). The reason is not far to seek: men are so hateful to them that the woman will not even go near them.

The shift in object in homosexuality is thus based on denial, identification with the aggressor and extreme hatred of the opposite sex. That all of this can be covered up by "gay" activities or laughter need cause no surprise to the analyst; Melanie Klein called it the "manic defense."

It is necessary to mention here that severe pathology of all kinds can coexist with social adjustment. Just to take one example from the past: in the Civil War, Lincoln was a serious depressive who took to his bed for months at one time, while his wife was obviously a psychotic; Sherman was psychotic at one time; Grant was a severe alcoholic all his life. In spite of these emotional handicaps, or perhaps because of them, they fought a great war and won. ·

Examples could be multiplied endlessly. By now it should be clear that the ability to get along in society is not per se any indication of mental health. It does not even bar great achievements. Isaac Newton was undoubtedly a completely paranoid man, if not a paranoid schizophrenic, yet he changed the course of scientific history. Eileen Simpson, ex-wife of the poet John Berryman (1982) describes the severe pathology of her ex-husband (who later committed suicide) and of many of his peers, all of whom were famous names in modern American poetry.

The correlation between mental health in the analytic sense and the capacity to function socially is always a difficult one to ascertain. Many analysts have made the point that certain types of pathology get along better in our society than ideally healthy individuals (Hartmann, 1939), as well as that every culture has its own distinctive neurosis (Roheim, 1932).

The Sexual Patterns

The detailed examination of the sexual practices of homosexuals (as well as of heterosexuals) reveals all kinds of dynamic configurations. The man who offers his anus to another man in lieu of a woman's vagina (the "fuckee" as contrasted with the "fucker") is clearly acting out the wish to be a woman, a wish which all men have but refrain from, or carry out in other ways (e.g., the "effeminate" man). Likewise the lesbian woman who acquires a dildo or other artificial penis for herself is expressing the frustration that she is not a man.

Inherently the genitals offer all kinds of pleasurable sensations. Whether the penis is masturbated, or sucked, or in intercourse, the ejaculation provides the same pleasure. The choice of modality is unconsciously determined.

I have often asked homosexual men who enjoyed fellatio: If you were being sucked by a woman, could you tell the difference? Invariably the answer has been: no woman would do such a thing. Obviously we are dealing here with a delusional kind of thinking.

The detailed examination of the sexual practices of homosexuals is usually quite revealing. Oral, anal, phallic, exhibitionistic and other infantile elements will usually play a role. In one case one man put a ball of twine in his anus when he had sex, and as the sex act proceeded, he unravelled the ball. Another would ejaculate on the stomach of his partner, then lick the semen. One woman would suck off a man, then drop the semen into the mouth of another woman. And so on. The early analytic literature (before 1914) contains a detailed categorization of all of these strange practices which had never been known to exist before.

Nor can the notion that other cultures engage in similar practices and that they are "normal" carry any real weight. Recently the glorification of semen by some of the tribes of New Guinea has come to light (Herdt, 1984). Men will suck the penises of older men, with the conviction that the semen that they thus acquire has virtually magical properties. This is a culture in which for some unknown reason semen has been endowed with magical qualities, and the people act accordingly. It is the adjustment neurosis of their culture. On the contrary, in our culture semen has generally been considered "dirty," "defiling," "impure," like "urine" and so on. It is only within recent years that people have been able, because of analytic education, to regard semen as a normal bodily product, and enjoy it accordingly.

Homosexuality and the Personality Structure

Various generalizations have been made by psychoanalysts about the kinds of persons who become homosexual; before WWI they were all considered obsessional neurotics; today they would probably be considered narcissistic or borderline. These designations have no real meaning.

The relationship between the homosexuality and the personality structure is extensive and complicated, like personality in general. Perhaps the only generalization that is valid today is that the homosexual is a person who has not grown up. Boys play with boys when they are children, girls with girls. The homosexual continues this exclusive preoccupation with his/her own sex, because of all the heartaches and disappointments experienced earlier in life.

People who are not grown up in one area abound in our society, as well as in all others. Psychoanalysis has set up the criterion of genital maturity as a major aspect of maturity, and in spite of the various attacks on this concept, the criterion, in my opinion, still holds.

But immaturity does not imply that the person has to be hospitalized, or stigmatized. It is a problem which has to be confronted, preferably by psychotherapy. But as we know the resistance to psychotherapy remains strong (Strean, 1985).

Our educational efforts should be devoted to elucidating the total range of human conflicts, of which homosexuality is only one.

Mention must be made of the efforts of some mental health organizations to insist that homosexuality is "normal." In a disordered society, some mental health professionals are also disordered. The anti-Freudian crusade is strong (Fine, 1985). Yet we can only hope, with Freud, that while the voice of reason is weak, it persists until it gets a hearing.

REFERENCES

Bell, A. P. and Weinberg, M. S. 1978. *Homosexualities.* New York: Simon and Schuster.

Bellak, L. and Goldsmith, L. eds. 1984. *The broad scope of ego function assessment.* New York: Wiley.

Bieber, I. et al. 1962. *Homosexuality.* New York: Basic Books.

Blumstein, P. and Schwartz, P. 1983. *American couples.* New York: Morrow.

Dover, K. J. 1978. *Greek homosexuality.* New York: Vintage.

Ferenczi, S. 1914. The nosology of male homosexuality. In S. Ferenczi: *First contributions to psychoanalysis,* Ch. XII, 296–318. New York: Brunner/Mazel, 1980.

Fine, R. 1973a. Review of Hooker's paper on homosexuality. *Int. J. Psychiatry, 11,*(4), 471–475.

Fine, R. 1973b. *The development of Freud's thought.* New York: Jason Aronson.

Fine, R. 1979. *A history of psychoanalysis.* New York: Columbia University Press.

Fine, R. 1985a. *The meaning of love in human experience.* New York: Wiley.

Fine, R. 1985b. The academy of love. *Current Issues in Psychoanalytic Practice, 2,* 25–40.

Fine, R. 1985c. The anti-Freudian crusade continues. *Journal of Psychohistory,* *12,* 395–410.

Freud, A. 1936. *The ego and the mechanisms of defense.* New York: International Universities Press.

Freud, A. 1965. *Normality and pathology in childhood.* New York: International Universities Press.

Freud, S. 1905. *Three essays on sexuality.* SE, VII.

Goldfried, M. et al. 1971. *Rorschach handbook of clinical and research applications.* Englewood Cliffs, NJ: Prentice-Hall.

Gonsiorek, J. C., Paul, W., Weinrich, J. D. and Hotvedt, M. E. 1982. *Homosexuality.* Beverly Hills, Cal.: Sage.

Hartman, H. 1939. Psychoanalysis and the concept of health. *Int. J. Psychoanalysis, 20,* 308–321.

Hatterer, L. J. 1976. *Changing homosexuality in the male.* New York: Dell.

Herdt, G. H. ed. 1984. *Ritualized homosexuality in Melanesia.* Berkeley: University of California Press.

Hooker, E. 1958. Male homosexuality in the Rorschach. *J. of Projective Techniques, 22,* 33–54.

Kinsey, A. C. et al. 1948. *Sexual behavior in the human male.* Philadelphia: Saunders.

Kinsey, A. C. et al. 1953. *Sexual behavior in the human female.* Philadelphia: Saunders.

Laplanche, J. and Pontalis, J.-B. 1973. *The language of psychoanalysis.* New York: Norton.

Masters, W. H. and Johnson, V. E. 1966. *Human sexual response.* Boston: Little, Brown.

Prince, M. 1975. *Psychotherapy and multiple personality: Selected essays.* Cambridge, MA: Harvard University Press.

Rennie, T. C. et al. 1962. *Mental health in the metropolis.* New York: McGraw-Hill.

Robitscher, J. 1980. *The powers of psychiatry.* Boston: Houghton Mifflin.

Roheim, G. 1932. Psychoanalysis of primitive cultural types. *Int. J. Psychoanalysis, 13,* 1–224.

Sagan, E. 1979. *The lust to annihilate.* New York: Psychohistory Press.

Sandler, J. 1983. Reflections on some relations betwen psychoanalytic concepts and psychoanalytic practice. *Int. J. Psychoanalysis, 64,* 35–45.

Simpson, E. 1982. *Poets in their youth.* New York: Random House.

Socarides, C. 1974. The sexual unreason. *Book Forum, 1,* 172–185.

Socarides, C. 1978. *The overt homosexual.* New York: Jason Aronson.

Sorenson, R. C. 1973. *Adolescent sexuality in contemporary America.* New York: World Publishing.

Stevenson, I., and Wolpe, J. 1960. Recovery from sexual deviations through overcoming nonsexual neurotic responses. *Amer. J. Psychiatry, 116,* 737–742.

Strean, H. 1935. *Resolving resistances in psychotherapy.* New York: Wiley.

Veroff, J., Douvan, E. and Kulka, R. A. 1981. *Mental health in America.* New York: Basic Books.

Wiedemann, G. H. 1962. Survey of psychoanalytic literature on overt male homosexuality. *Journal of American Psychoanalytic Association, 10,* 386–409.

Wiedemann, G. H. 1974. Homosexuality: A survey. *Journal of American Psychoanalytic Association, 22,* 651–696.

5

THE NEO-FREUDIANS

Manny Sternlicht

The sexual revolution has produced so many changes in our value systems, attitudes, and prejudices that the true nature of homosexuality has in many ways been obscured. As a consequence of major changes in our concepts of human rights, minority rights, women's rights, and political rights, discrimination against homosexuals has in some ways become intensified while simultaneously in some ways it has become diminished.

Our focus here is upon the various psychological overviews of neo-Freudian considerations of homosexuality. The psychoanalytic study of homosexuality started with Freud's 1905 paper entitled "Three Essays on the Theory of Sexuality." In this paper, Freud illustrated two conceptions which had surrounded homosexuality for centuries—namely that it was innate and that it was a form of degeneracy. He distinguished between the sexual instinct and the sexual object. Freud viewed sexual instinct as an endowed characteristic of all human beings and he viewed the sexual object as an acquired characteristic of the sexual instinct. He also hypothesized that some experiences in childhood had a determining effect upon the direction taken by the homosexual's libido.

In a 1915 note to the "Three Essays" work, Freud noted that psychoanalytic research decidedly opposed any attempt at segregating homosexuals from the rest of mankind, as a group of special characters. He also

Thanks are due to Hv Pomerance for his assistance.

noted that all human beings are capable of making a homosexual object choice.

It is quite clear that the overriding theories of homosexuality during the late 19th and the early 20th century were those of Sigmund Freud. Since the Freudian era, however, the social scientific theories of homosexuality were challenged by what is called today the neo-Freudian theory of sexuality. Over the past 30 years or so there have been numerous chemical, genetic, and somatic studies attempting to establish that homosexuality has an organic or non-psychogenic origin. All have failed in this attempt (so far, at least). Rado wrote that the human male and female do not inherit any organized neurohormonal machinery of courtship or mating. Nor do they inherit any organized component mechanism that would or could direct them to such goals as mating or a choice of mate. In the light of this evidence, the psychoanalytic theory of sexual instincts has outlived its usefulness.

> *Each of the sexes has an innate capacity for learning, and is equipped with a specific power plan and tools. But in sharp contrast to the lower vertebrates and as a consequence of the encephalization of certain functions first organized at lower evolutionary levels of the central nervous system, they inherit no organized information* (Rado, 1956)

Rado believed that homosexuality represented a desire for surplus variation, a consequence of the fact that the sexual drive in human beings is not exclusively in the service of procreation, but more for pleasurable strivings. Notwithstanding, he also maintained that homosexuality represents the outcome of tremendous fears of the opposite sex, a finding with which Bieber (1962) is in agreement.

The focus of neo-Freudian homosexuality is on gender identity.

> *The male-female identity is the most deeply ingrained or imprinted image of the various components that constitute one's global identity. It is closely related to body image. Uncertainty about one's gender identity frequently generates great anxiety and often leads to panic; therefore, defenses against such states are sharply preserved* (Gershman, 1981–82).

These discoveries of behavior geneticists, learning theorists, and ethologists may be the reason for some change in our current approach to homosexuality. The neo-Freudian theorists on homosexuality suggest that areas of learning are permanently imprinted during the early formation of the psyche. Thus, disturbances in the body image and subjective feelings leave an imprint and affect the earliest basic gender identification (Gershman, 1981–82). It is important to keep in mind that notions of homosexuality being an innate phenomenon still exist in this neo-Freudian era. Other theorists do not regard these concepts as very valid. Alfred Adler explains that there are two major viewpoints regarding the issue of inheritance (although he pokes fun of the concept in general, with its implication that individuals come into the world homosexual). One group assumes that the germinal complex—in the case of a masculine homosexual—is decreased in favor of a complex of a somewhat feminine type, while the other group believes in certain inherited components which have been specifically strengthened (Adler, 1946). Adler goes on to conceptualize two substantial statements of evidence regarding the rejection of the hypothesis of inherited homosexuality. Firstly,

> No one has ever claimed that the inherited feminine factors, the female-appearing aspect, is any more prominent among masculine homosexuals than are female traits in a woman, and yet in examining homosexuals we almost exclusively find individuals either with female tendencies or such as are directed into female channels, whereas the masculine tendencies appear to be absent. On the other hand, (normal) women frequently exhibit masculine tendencies. For the demonstration of these being inherited and not acquired traits the above facts are quite unfavorable for we may justifiably ask where are the masculine impulses? (Adler, 1946)

Another objection which must be faced is the enormously frequent occurrence of facultative sexuality. The Adlerian theory of homosexuality addresses itself to the question of why homosexuals fixate upon certain experiences, experiences that normal people also share. He feels that if one were to watch children, adolescents, and grown-up adults, all of whom share similar marked tendencies toward imitation, one would discover that no one ever imitates anything that doesn't in one way or another fit into his purpose. The basic question for Adler is why does an homosexual find that the fixation on an homosexual experience fit into his nature as well? (Adler, 1946). Adlerian theory, however, clearly rejects Freud's conceptions of a hereditary instinctual homosexual notion. According to Ansbacher and Ansbacher (1956), the belief in the compelling causes of homosexuality, in its innate characteristics, in its unalterability may be easily unmasked as a scientific superstition of one sort or another. According to Adler, the homosexual personality is the result of a social developmental process which begins during childhood. In describing an overview of his conceptualizations, Adler noted that homosexuality has a number of difficult aspects. In some fashion or other, and to varying degrees, a homosexual will often be found to be antagonistic to social life, to have changed his occupation, and to have begun later and finished earlier. Oftentimes his entire life flows along as though regulated by some type of brake mechanism. The power required for operating this brake, however, he must (by himself) continually produce again and again. During childhood, Adler emphasizes, most homosexuals are already mistakenly embarked along the path of a female's psychological development when, to their amazement, they are made aware of the fact that they really belong to the opposite sex (Adler, 1946). In essence, Adler basically points out feelings of inferiority and compensatory strivings for power as the central focus of his theory. Thus, homosexuality represents the aborted attempt at compensation of people with a distinct inferiority feeling, and corresponds in its disturbed social acivity to the individual's attitude toward the problems of society. In conjunction with these inferiority notions and with an overevaluation of women, Adler describes the "masculine protest" with regard to male homosexuality, in terms of the masculine protest making use of the feminine role in order to attain its purpose. The concept of the masculine protest also plays a role in the development of homosexuality in females, it representing a reaction by women as a consequence of their being given an inferior status in society. According to Adler, the homosexual aims at a fictitious feeling of superiority through the use of a trick, a modus operandi, or a gesture of revolt. Adler explains that:

> . . . homosexuality . . . is the result of the fear of the opposite sex . . . even when carried into practice (homosexuality) is always found to be a symbol by means of which it is sought to place the individual's own superiority beyond question. This mechanism is similar to that of a religious psychosis in which the nearness of God has the significance of an elevation (Adler, 1916).

There have been many arguments in the recent neo-Freudian era as to what kind of person the homosexual individual really is. For example, Myerson and Neustadt (1942) described the homosexual as a psychopathic personality who may be either neurotic or psychotic. The constitutional nature of homosexuality, rather than homosexuality on the basis of learned, acquired behavior, has been argued by many investigators. Perhaps one of the most strongly emphasized positions is that of Greenspan and Campbell (1944), who declared that the homosexual is an individual who is endowed with sexual desires that are directed wholly or in part toward members of the same sex. The manifestations of homosexuality may occur early, through arrested psychosexual development, or late, through regression, and its origin is always constitutional or biological and never environmental, or acquired. According to these authors, homosexuality represents a congenital anomaly rather than being a disease entity.

In general, Greenspan and Campbell (1944), and others such as Henry and Galbraith (1934) and Henderson and Gillespie (1940) have argued this biological position, including the view of unique psychological characteristics of homosexuals. The genetic aspects were emphasized by Kallman (1953). As a result of Kallman's studies with monozygetic twins, he claimed that the results throw considerable doubt on the validity of purely psychodynamic theories of certain types of homosexual behavior patterns in adulthood,

... while strengthening the hypothesis of a gene controlled disarrangement in the balance between male and female maturation (hormonal) tendencies. In line with this theory, overt homosexual behavior in the adult male may be viewed as an alternative minus variant in the integrative process of psychosexual maturation, comparable in the sexually reproductive human species to the developmental aspects of left-handedness in a predominantly right-handed human world (Kallman, 1953)

Another school of thought emphasizes the psychological, personal, and social-cultural variables which may differentiate the homosexual from the heterosexual. Such arguments have been advanced by Allen (1962), Hooker (1958), Kinsey (1941), Westwood (1960), and others who found no systematic data or significant physical or endocrinological differences between homosexuals and heterosexuals. The further illustration of the neo-Freudian diversity in homosexual history is reflected in the 1955 memorandum of the British Medical Association (which in part dealt with homosexuality). This document included observations that moral values and even religious conversions had been recommended by physicians as possible cures for homosexuality (Westwood, 1960). At one time it was generally considered to be a totally irreversible condition, for which no cure was possible.

Psychological theories have ranged from essentially orthodox psychoanalytical interpretations to those of social learning. The diversity of these theories is patently evident. Neo-Freudian references have been made to unconscious identifications with the parents, to fixations, to the equation of the breast with the penis or the buttocks or both, to an extreme degree of narcissism, and so on. Ernest Jones (1912) focused upon strong oral eroticism and intense sadism, while Melanie Klein (1952) highlighted the oral frustrations of the infant as causative factors in the development of homosexuality. Other suggestions have to do with classifications of homosexuality, an exercise which often arouses great discussion about bisexuality. Kinsey, for instance, in 1941 developed a six-point rating scale to describe stages of homosexuality. The range of sexual behavior went from exclusively homosexual to exclusively heterosexual.

Most studies today, however, do leave the question open. The basic direction of approach can be reached as most studies do not prove one concept or another, but, on the contrary, tend to increase the confusion. The majority of studies, however, do push for the direction of homosexuality as a developmental or acquired sexual status. Desmond Curran and Denis Parr (1957)—one a British psychologist, the other a research fellow—made a careful study of one hundred variously referred cases that had been seen in psychiatric practice. They concluded that the homosexuals that they studied were on the whole successful and valuable members of society, quite unlike the popular conception of such persons as vicious criminals or effete or depraved. What this study suggested was a strong continuity between a person's childhood and adolesecent sexual feelings and behaviors and his/her adult sexual preference. Their findings could be understood in at least two different ways. The very strong continuity between pre-adult homosexual patterns and an adult homosexual preference can be interpreted as reflecting an extraordinarily strong conditioning effect of some sort that "tracks" people into homosexuality. Or, the findings could be interpreted as simply reflecting the emergence of a deep-seated propensity toward either homosexuality or heterosexuality, which begins to emerge while a person is growing up and then continues into adulthood. That is to say, a boy or a girl is predisposed to be a homosexual or heterosexual, and during childhood and adolescence this basic sexual orientation begins to become evident. This illustration of the undecided status of certain studies is not uncommon.

Another common aspect to this study was the etiological emphasis on preadolescent experiences. Many theorists find important experiences during the preadolescent years in regard to homosexual tendencies, with homosexual preadult feelings playing a more cogent role than behaviors. For example, Harry Stack Sullivan (1953) regarded homosexuality as resulting from experiences earlier in life which have constructed a barrier (either relative or absolute) to integration with persons of the opposite sex. Sullivan visualized the preadolescent experience as an extremely important force based on the concept of "chumming." During the preadolescent period the child develops an intimate relationship with a "chum." Sullivan viewed this chum relationship as "prognostically favorable" in its adjustment implications, and he believed it to be an important counterinfluence against the development of a long-lasting homosexual adaptation, particularly since the chum relationship tends to become a fixated one. Homosexuality, according to Sullivan, may also result if the preadolescent is driven to form a relationship with an older adolescent or adult. Furthermore, Sullivan saw yet another possible source for homosexuality in "maturational retardation." This concept separates the boy from his chronological peers. When this occurs, the immature individual may become fixated at the preadolescent level. The failure to fulfill the need for a "chum" in preadolescence while the lust dynamism undergoes biological maturation may, in some cases, result in a homosexual orientation (Sullivan, 1953). Sullivan concludes that during the preadolescent period, homosexuality may result from "collisions of lust, security, and the intimacy need." Sullivan notes that collisions of lust and security usually occur when the adolescent is burdened with culturally prohibited and parentally proscribed attitudes against heterosexuality. In this case a primary genital phobia may develop and homosexuality may be the outcome. Sullivan, agreeing with Freud, recognized that the fear of female genitals may exist in men when they regard women as pleasurable sexual objects. This fear may result in feelings which are literally uncanny, which are quite paralyzing, and which are able to force the male to escape from these uncanny feelings into homosexuality.

Another theorist who found an extensive etiological source for homosexuality in the preadolescent period was Clara Thompson. In general, Thompson (1950) concurred with Freud's view that everybody is biologically polysexual and bisexual. Moreover, she contended that the uncritical enjoyment of body stimulation is a fact in childhood. As a consequence, she asserted that sexual pleasures in childhood may be derived from either sex. In a permissive culture this basic biological tendency would probably result in some recourse to homosexuality whenever the possibility of heterosexual relations was not available, thus agreeing with Sullivan in the positive adjustment value of homosexuality. Thompson viewed sexuality on a biological level, with human beings resorting at any given time to the best type of interpersonal relationship that is available to them. She did not regard these biological polysexual and polymorphous tendencies as having any undue influence upon personality development. She concluded that homosexuality is a consequence of dependency, hostility, attitudes toward the family or other figures, security questions, and other factors. Thompson found that homosexuality disappeared whenever general character problems became solved.

In summary, Sullivan emphasized the importance of peer group relationships during adolescence and preadolescence, while Thompson noted that heterosexuality is "biologically more congenial." Both, however, highlight interpersonal components, and both regard homosexuality as an attempt at integrating one's sexual needs at any given point in time.

Since Freud, however, theorists have conceptualized homosexuality as a neurosis as well as a sexual status. Ovesey (1954), for instance, classified homosexuality as a neurotic state divisible into true (actual) and pseudohomosexual types. He attributed the former type to early and excessive sexual discipline. According to Ovesey, homosexuality is resorted to with the object of orgasmic attainment. The pseudohomosexual type is equated with latent, unconscious homosexuality which he regards as motivationally determined by the desire for dependency, or as the end product of inhibited assertiveness which the person unconsciously equates with castration, with femininity and homosexuality. Bieber (1962), on the other hand, concluded that dependency and inhibited assertiveness are the "consequences" rather than the causes of psychological injury. According to Ovesey (1955), homosexuals resorted to deviant sex practices less from erotic need than from fear of self-assertion and from a compulsion to seek out situations of dependency.

As we can see, elements of Freudian psychosexual theory permeated into the semi-revolutionary era of sexual theory. Otto Fenichel (1945) incorporated the Freudian Oedipal Complex into his theory on homosexuality. According to Fenichel, one of the common manifestations of Oedipal fears in adult males is the inability to perform adequately sexually (except with prostitutes). Nice women are too much like mothers, too saintly, and hence forbidden fruit, pure and chaste. Homosexual males go one stage further and usually become cold towards all women, because any kind of heterosexual feelings arouses their incest guilt. (These heterosexual feelings then tend to become repressed and displaced onto other men.) For them, the female form inspires terror instead of pleasure. The absence of male sexual organs suggest castration. Women's genitals are frequently perceived of as castrating tools which are capable of biting and tearing off the penis. Melaine Klein (1952) has also equated the vagina with the concept of a devouring mouth. Since identification plays more of a role with homosexuals, the intensity of their mother fixation is especially pronounced. Thus, according to Klein, the primary oral and anal anxieties are the chief factors in the homosexual fixation.

Although, during the post-Freudian period, theories of homosexuality vary to great extremes, many theorists particpated in what is currently called "schools of homosexual theory." Clara Thompson (1950) thought that many cases of male homosexuality were the result of abnormal dependency needs. Karen Horney (1945) came to similar conclusions when she suggested that the struggle for ascendency in sexual relations between men provided a means of acting out abnormal urges to subdue and to conquer others, or alternatively to submit to and placate others. Karen Horney generally focused attention upon the importance of non-sexual needs in sexual activity. Her remarks on homosexuality were based on observations of bisexuals in whom she discovered needs to conquer and subdue, or needs to please, of such magnitude that the sex of the partner became a matter of indifference, no longer having any importance in and of itself. These elements, then, became part of a homosexual personality. In addition, she thought, the homosexual has such a fear of injury to his neurotic pride, a fear of not being glamorously successful with the opposite sex, that he usually withdraws from competition with his equals, thereby inhibiting heterosexual attraction. He unconsciously believes that his pride will be injured whenever he even approaches a woman. This fear, then, this potential threat to his pride, becomes one of the chief contributing factors in the origins of his homosexual orientation.

Perspectives on homosexuality continue to be presented as many and broad. The classical psychodynamic view of homosexuality centers on the problem of unresolved Oedipal conflicts. According to this theory, the homosexual is unable to overcome his attachment to his mother, to identify with his father, and thus to proceed to the mature stage of genital sexuality. (There is an element of identification with the object in all homosexual love.) Hence he combines to suffer from acute castration anxiety, and consequently he strenuously avoids contact with female genitals for fear of injury or loss of his penis, thereby representing the homosexual defense against heterosexuality. This theory, expanded by Bieber (1962), contends that homosexuality develops as a substitute for the heterosexual adaptation that the individual's fears prevent him from achieving. Today this perspective also is referred to as the family-centered perspective.

Another school of thought on the causes of homosexuality is labeled "hormone theory." This theory, and others similar to it, usually regard homosexuality as being "a part of man's natural biological inheritance" (West, 1955). One theory, for example, discusses the effect of homoerotic propensities on biological aspects of homosexuality. According to West, it is really remarkable that so many people succeed in developing exclusively heterosexual inclinations and in losing all recollections of ever having had contrary feelings. The capacity for homosexual responsiveness is not, however, completely eradicated; rather, it remains dormant and can become aroused under unusual circumstances, such as being incarcerated for a fairly long period of time, in spite of all of the individual's efforts to control against its expressive appearance. Such theories have not gained particular credence, and have been referred to as circular theories, in that they are molded around reality and do not permit reality to mold itself around the theory.

Another such type theory, which developed during the 1950s, was slightly more detailed and pointed to the sex glands as having strong etiological functions. In his article entitled "Homosexuality as an endocrinological, psychological, and genetic problem," Bauer (1940) stated that

> *It is a popular belief that the development of exclusive homosexuality, especially if it occurs in the man of effeminate physique or temperament, is the result of an inborn constitutional anomaly, probably connected with some male function of the sex glands, and possible heredity.*

This theory of inborn homosexuality, often referred to as "true inversion," is thought to be analogous to the masculine behavior that can be artificially induced in some female animals by injecting some sex hormone, and thereby possibly modifying chromosomal aberrations. On the other hand, the theory of "true inversion" finds favor with some homosexuals because it releases them from any and all sense of responsibility.

The present status of these theories is quite negative. Insofar as present knowledge goes, it would certainly be fair to state that no convincing relationship between hormone estimations and homosexuality has been demonstrated. This is not really surprising (and certainly would not be to an Adlerian), for ". . . endocrine abnormalities are relatively rare and are usually accompanied by physical signs, whereas homosexuality is an exceedingly common condition that presents no recognizable physical stigmata" (West, 1955).

The question of genetic homosexuality, however, is not a completely outmoded question. Although professional opinion is sharply divided regarding this issue, the majority of those working in this area are agreed that homosexuality does not depend upon an organic compound in the individual. Glands or glandular products cannot totally direct the choice of male over female sex objects in the male, or the reverse in women. Most workers agree that glandular secretions can determine the degree or amount of sexual impulse, that female hormones occur among males, as indicated by androgen-estrogen urine levels, and that male hormones occur regularly among females. In any case, however, the direction of the sexual drive is not determined by hormones. There can be no doubt, then, that homosexuality must be considered as a purely and uniquely psychological condition.

The psychoanalytical approach declares that sexual interests begin early in life, and that the emotions experienced during the developmental period greatly influence attitudes possessed later in life. Although they disagree on matters of detail, psychologists as a group tend to support the analytical view that the origins of nearly all cases of sexual deviance can be traced back to childhood, especially early childhood. In general, the psychoanalytical approach finds significant importance in the manner in which the child senses his parents' unspoken feelings and the way in which the child responds virtually intuitively. Conceptualizations such as "incestuous guilt feelings" and "castration complex" are the analysts' intellectual conceptions of the general tenor of their patients' unconscious fears and fantasies. In the analytical psychosexual schemata, the Oedipal situation is normally resolved by the time the child starts attending a formal educational experience. This is where the commencement of homosexuality may come about. According to the psychoanalytical approach, people who have experienced an especially intense parental attachment that is accompanied by severe guilt feelings may continue to attempt to fight against all sexual responsivity for the remainder of their lives. As adults, such individuals are unable to enjoy any sexual relations fully because, unconsciously to be sure, they continue to associate all of their sexual feelings with the same incestuous feelings that they had to guard against when they were children. Since the Oedipal complex remains unresolved and active, the behavioral outcomes of this situation account for many of the manifestations that are to be encountered in homosexuality.

The status of homosexual theory available contemporarily can be viewed as the crystallization of segments from several different schools of thought, representing diverse outlooks. What is important, however, is to pinpoint the beginnings of a revolutionary era. Interest in the causes and treatment of homosexuality grew as Freud introduced his psychoanalytical views. The neo-Freudian era then evolvd as later theorists pecked away at different aspects of Freud's initial theoretical works. The end result is almost as controversial and varied as was the pre-Freudian era!

REFERENCES

Adler, A. (1916). *The neurotic condition.* New York: Moffat Yard.
Adler, A. (1946). *The practice and theory of individual psychology.* London: Routledge & Kegan Paul.
Allen, C. (1962). *A textbook of psychosexual disorders.* London: Oxford University.

Ansbacher, H. L., & Ansbacher, R. R. (1956). *The individual psychology of Alfred Adler.* New York: Basic Books.

Bauer, J. (1940). Homosexuality as an endocrinal, psychological, and genetic problem. *Journal of Criminal Pathology, 2,* 188–197.

Bieber, I., et al. (1962). *Homosexuality—A psychoanalytic study.* New York: Basic Books.

Curran, D., & Parr, D. (1957). Homosexuality: An analysis of 100 male cases seen in private practice. *British Medical Journal,* 797–801.

Fenichel, O. (1945). *The psychoanalytic theory of neurosis.* New York: W. W. Norton.

Freud, S. (1953). Three essays on the theory of sexuality (1905). In J. Strachey (Ed.), *The standard edition of the complete psychological works of Sigmund Freud, vol. 3.* London: Hogarth.

Gershman, H. (1981–82). Homosexual marriages. *American Journal of Psychoanalysis, 41,* 149.

Greenspan, H., & Campbell, J. D. (1944). The homosexual as a personality type. *American Journal of Psychiatry, 101,* 682–689.

Henderson, D. K., & Gillespie, R. D. (1940). *A textbook of psychiatry for students and practitioners.* London: Oxford University.

Henry, G. W., & Galbraith, H. M. (1934). Constitutional factors in homosexuality. *American Journal of Psychiatry, 13,* 1249–1270.

Hooker, E. (1958). Male homosexuality in the Rorschach. *Journal of Projective Techniques, 25,* 33–54.

Horney, K. (1945). *Our inner conflicts.* New York: W. W. Norton.

Jones, E. (1912). *Papers on psycho-analysis.* London: Bailliere, Tindall & Cox.

Kallman, F. J. (1953). *Heredity in health and mental disorder.* New York: W. W. Norton.

Kinsey, A. C. (1941). Homosexuality: Criteria for a hormonal explanation of the homosexual. *Journal of Clinical Endocrinology, 1,* 424–428.

Klein, M., Heimann, P., Isaacs, S., & Riviere, J. (1952). *Developments in psycho-analysis.* London: Hogarth.

Myerson, A., & Neustadt, R. (1942). Bisexuality and male homosexuality. *Clinics, 1,* 932–957.

Ovesey, L. (1954). The homosexual conflict. *Psychiatry, 17,* 243–250.

Ovesey, L. (1955). The pseudohomosexual anxiety. *Psychiatry, 18,* 17–25.

Rado, S. (1956). An adaptational view of sexual behavior. In G. E. Daniels (Ed.), *Psychoanalysis of behavior.* New York: Grune & Stratton.

Sullivan, H. S. (1953). *Conceptions of modern psychiatry.* New York: W. W. Norton.

Sullivan, H. S. (1953). *The interpersonal theory of psychiatry.* New York: W. W. Norton.

Thompson, C. (1950). *Psychoanalysis: Its evolution and development.* New York: Hermitage House.

West, D. J. (1955). *The other man.* New York: Whiteside.

Westwood, G. (1960). *A minority: A report on the life of the male homosexual in Great Britain.* London: Longmans.

6

A BEHAVIORISTIC APPROACH

Joel Greenspoon
P. A. Lamal

The issue of homosexuality has changed dramatically in the United States during the past 25 years. For many years homosexuality and lesbianism were criminal offenses in most states of the United States. In today's jargon, homosexuality and lesbianism have been decriminalized in most states. Many homosexuals and lesbians who practiced their sexual preference in privacy have "come out of the closet." Homosexuals exercise considerable political power in San Francisco. Despite these developments, including the declassification of homosexuality as a behavior disorder by decree of the American Psychiatric Association, the homosexual or lesbian does not have the full protection of the law that is accorded others. The homosexual or lesbian still finds that acknowledging his or her sexual preference can result in a variety of discriminatory reactions. As a consequence, the homosexual may find himself/herself developing a number of behavior problems that revolve around the sexual preference.

THE ETHICAL ISSUE

In dealing with homosexuals the clinician may be presented with some serious ethical considerations, especially personal ethical considerations. One of the authors had a homosexual client who stated clearly that he preferred being a homosexual but desired help in his being able to live more comfortably with his sexual preference. He did not ask to have his sexual preference modified. At that time and in that state homosexuality was a criminal act. Should the client have been accepted into therapy under these conditions, especially into a state supported mental health clinic? Some clinicians would have found it difficult to have accepted the client since homosexuality was illegal. Others might have found it difficult to accept the homosexual client because they considered homosexuality to be immoral. Today, in most states the legal issue has been resolved. The moral issue has not. Our position is that the clinician who cannot function effectively with the client, who cannot develop a program that will meet the objectives of the client, should not work with the client. On the other hand, a clinician who utilizes behavioral techniques and principles should not build his/her own objectives into the program.

One important way in which the radical behaviorist viewpoint differs from other positions is that it eschews the assumption that behavior has qualitative characteristics (Greenspoon, 1976). Consequently, the radical behaviorist does not describe behaviors as "good" or "bad," "right" or "wrong," "healthy or unhealthy," or as having any inherent qualitative characteristics. It makes no more sense to talk about good or bad behaviors than to talk about good or bad atoms. It is only when other factors or conditions are considered that a behavior is considered to have qualitative characteristics. When we do include the other factors and conditions and then attribute the qualitative characteristics to the behavior, we may be creating many more problems than we are solving. After all, it may be just as appropriate to contend that the environment is bad, but the behavior is good. From a behavioristic standpoint neither the environment nor the behavior has any qualitative characteristics. However, it is the attribution of qualitative characteristics to behavior qua behavior that is fundamental to many different psychodynamic and cognitive approaches. It becomes necessary in these approaches to change the dynamics or cognitions of the client to effect any change in the behavior. Moreover, it is from these qualitative characteristics attributed to behavior that the psychodynamics or cognitions are inferred. Since a radical behavioristic position does not deal with qualitative characteristics, it tends to emphasize a completely different set of pertinent variables and, consequently, a diferent approach to the treatment of homosexuality. What is of interest to the radical behaviorist are such features of any behavior as the frequency of its occurrence, its duration, the setting in which the behavior occurs, antecedents of the behavior, and the consequences of the behavior. These features, which will be discussed below, are critical concerns in the measurement and treatment of any behavior. They are also critical determinants of individuals' decisions to seek treatment, either to change the sexual preference or to improve the functioning of the homosexual.

The question has been raised as to whether therapists should attempt to change the sexual orientation of homosexuals. Davison (1976) has argued that programs whose purpose is to change the sexual orientation of homosexuals should be terminated. According to Davison (1978), therapists "have no abstract responsibility to accede to requests from clients for certain types of treatment,," (p. 170) including requests for change of sexual orientation. Davison (1978) maintains that "great numbers of people are being hurt by the availability of change-of-orientation programs." (p. 172) Rather than attempting to change homosexuals into heterosexuals, Davison urges therapists to attend to the social and political factors in homosexuals' lives, particularly the prejudice confronting them and its effects on their lives. Homosexuals should be treated, according to this view, but treated only with the goal of helping them to overcome problems while still maintaining their homosexuality. Others (e.g., Sturgis & Adams, 1978) have argued that the decision concerning the modification of sexual orientation is the client's to make, in light of his or her particular circumstances and values.

Much has been written about ethics and behavior change (e.g., Bergin, 1980; 'Ethical Issues," 1977; Krapfl & Vargas, 1977; Kitchener, 1980; Ward, 1980; Wood, 1979; Woolfolk & Richardson, 1984) and about the ethics of therapy with homosexuals (e.g., Davison, 1976, 1977, 1978, 1982; Coleman, 1982; Sturgis & Adams, 1978). The approach of radical behaviorists to these questions is probably unique. For one thing, as mentioned earlier, for radical behaviorists behaviors per se do not have qualitative characteristics. Thus, homosexual behavior per se is not judged by the radical behaviorist to be "good," "bad," "healthy," "unhealthy," or anything else. An important premise held by radical behaviorists that is relevant here is that ethical issues are matters of behavior and antecedent conditions and consequences of behavior. In contrast, the traditional view is that ethical issues, questions about "ought," are of a domain that is completely different from questions of fact, questions about "what is." According to the traditional view, knowing "what is" has no bearing on what "ought to be." Radical behaviorists do not subscribe to such a dichotomy. Rather, for radical behaviorists, matters of ethics and values are matters of behavior that are encompassed in the science of behavior. Our radical behavioral ethics differ from the normative ethics of many in the homosexuality debate. Normative ethics are concerned with the rational (in the sense of giving reasons for) justification of moral values (Day, 1977), whereas radical behavioral ethics are concerned with the analysis of individuals' controlling contingencies.

Our view is that the purpose of treatment is to attempt to help the client achieve his or her goals, consistent with the legal rights of others. Thus, if a client requests to change from a homosexual to a heterosexual orientation, s/he should be helped to do so. Homosexual clients who seek help aimed at enhancing their homosexual behavior should be helped to achieve more rewarding homosexual relationships (cf. Masters & Johnson, 1979). There is nothing inherently wrong in helping homosexuals to change to a heterosexual orientation or, alternatively to become better "adjusted" in their homosexuality. What is to be attempted depends, rather, upon the particular circumstances of the particular case. Radical behaviorism has always emphasized the importance of understanding the individual case (Kazdin, 1982); this continues to be true when attempting to help homosexuals.

In our view the primary responsibility of the clinician is to honor the client's requests. The authors disagree with those (e.g., Davison, 1982) who advocate a complete cessation of efforts to change individuals' sexual orientation. That is not something for clinicians to decide. Radical behaviorists do not, however, advocate a completely uncritical approach to the issue. Obviously different clinicians have different views about homosexuality, ranging from abhorrence through neutrality to advocacy. It is incumbent upon the clinician to make clear to the client what his or her reactions are to homosexuality. The view that no clinician can have "neutral" views about homosexuality is unacceptable, as witness the views and practices of Masters and Johnson (1979).

Some may raise the question of whether the homosexual *really wants* a change in sexual orientation, even contending that if the client does not really want to change, then change cannot occur. There is no hard evidence bearing on this question of the significance of *want* as a critical factor in the effectiveness of any treatment program. Since *want* is not a meaningful construct in radical behaviorism, it is simply treated as another bit of verbal behavior whose significance must be determined by its relationship to other behaviors. If the client's emitting of "wanting to change" sexual orientation or anything else for that matter serves as a source of control over other behaviors pertinent to the treatment program, then it has some significance to the radical behaviorist clinician.

In discussing the goal of sexual preference reorientation for homosexuals, Coleman (1982) says:

> *Clients must explore their reasons for wanting such goals. They must understand the meaning and significance of their decision to act in a way that is incongruent with their sexual orientation. They must understand the external forces that affect their decision to do so* (p. 404).

The authors concur that the client perhaps should look at the factors that may be involved in his/her requesting a change in sexual orientation or any other behavior change. But when Coleman descibes clients as acting "in a way that is incongruent with their sexual orientation," he implies that one's sexual orientation is a more or less immutable trait that one has, and that any attempt to change one's sexual orientation is, for some unknown reason, inherently wrong and pernicious. Such an absolutist position is totally unacceptable.

Radical behaviorists generally agree with Coleman that clients should "understand the external forces that affect decisions" on their part to seek sexual preference reorientation. In all cases it is desirable that clients have examined these external factors, to the extent that such external factors can be identified. It is important that the therapist has knowledge of the variables affecting the client's decision. This is so for two reasons. One is that if it is clear that the client is being coerced into seeking such sexual preference reorientation, the therapist should decline to aid and abet the coercion. The second reason is that, in the absence of coercion, success in reorientation will depend to a great extent upon the therapist's knowledge of the variables affecting the client's decision to seek change.

Such information is also valuable in the therapist's appraisal of the likelihood of success. In our view the therapist should discuss with the client the likelihood of success in light of the variables responsible for the client's decision to seek change, as well as in the light of such variables as the length of time the client has engaged in homosexual acts, the frequency of such acts, the client's history of heterosexual relationships, level of social skills, the consequences for the homosexual activities, etc.

After a consideration of all of the above the homosexual client may decide not to attempt sexual preference reorientation. The focus of therapy may then shift to helping the client function better in an often hostile society. In either case the rule is that the client sets the general goal.

ORIGINS OF HOMOSEXUALITY

One of the dominant themes of radical behavioristic psychology is the analysis of the environment as a source of variables in the development and maintenance of any behavior. Sexual behavior is analyzed from the same perspective. Our first objective in the determination of the variables involved in the development of homosexuality is to analyze the environment. The environment includes not only the physical characteristics, but the behavioral reactions of other people and animals.

Critical to a behavioral analysis of homosexuality is the measurement of the environmental variables that are to be analyzed. Being able to provide quantitative measurements is essential to effective behavioral analysis. A rigorous behavioral analysis excludes the many methods of qualitative measurements that are prevalent in other approaches to homosexuality and other forms of behavior. Since qualitative characteristics of behavior have already been rejected, we obviously cannot use qualitative measurements to measure nonqualitative behaviors. Thus, the numerous scales that have been developed to measure a vast array of qualitative characteristics of behavior are excluded.

An examination of quantitative measurement reveals one very clear feature. Quantitative measurement involves counting and the ratios of counts. Counting the number of times an event occurs provides a quantitative measurement. In measuring the length of a room the number of times that a specific standard unit is used to cover the distance from one wall to another is counted.

There are more difficulties in measuring behavior, any behavior, than in measuring the length of a room. The primary basis of these difficulties is the establishment of the standard unit of the behavior. If a unit of behavior can be established, then the basis for counting how often that unit of behavior occurs has been created.

This issue of measurement and establishment of the unit of behavior is especially pertinent in the realm of homosexual behavior. Just what is the unit of homosexual behavior? Before answering this question, however, there is a need to address the question of what are the distinguishing characteristics of homosexual behavior? That is, what behaviors differentiate homosexual from heterosexual behavior? It is frequently accepted that homosexual behavior is sexual behavior with a member of the same sex. If this "definition" of homosexual behavior is our starting point, the issue becomes "what is sexual behavior?" "What specific behaviors comprise sexual behavior?" "Is holding hands sexual behavior?" "Is kissing sexual behavior?" "Is embracing sexual behavior?" The list of specific questions about specific behaviors can become rather lengthy.

Despite the fact that the list of specific behaviors may become rather lengthy, from a behavioristic point of point, it is necessary to enumerate them. The reason that the behaviorist requires such specificity of behavior is because it is this specification that leads to the establishment of the unit or units of behavior that will provide the basis for measurement. The list of specific behaviors that may be called sexual behaviors is arbitrary. The behavioristic position, being a positivistic position, accepts the arbitrariness of definition. The limiting condition on the arbitrariness of a definition is the utility of the definition. Does the arbitrary definition result in the creation of functional relationships that may lead to a broadening of our knowledge of a particular phenomenon? If our definition can generate significant functional relationships, then our arbitrary definition has utility.

Let us assume that we have created this list of specific behaviors that comprise sexual behavior. The next issue involves whether engaging in these behaviors with a member of the same sex is to be specified as homosexual behavior. If two men hold hands, are they engaging in homosexual behavior? The question seems rather straightforward and easily answered with a yes or no. If our answer is yes, then when two men hold hands in a football huddle, they are engaged in a homosexual act. If holding hands is defined as a sexual act and if a sexual behavior between two persons of the same sex is a homosexual behavior, then the conclusion is that the men in a football huddle are engaged in homosexual behavior. Most football fans would probably strongly object to their heroes engaging in homosexual behavior. Consequently, it turns out that a seemingly simple question becomes a more complex one. The behaviorist must not only consider the behavior and the sex of the partners who are involved in the behavior, but the environment in which the sexual behavior occurs.

Taking these three factors into consideration the behaviorist can arrive at a definition of homosexuality that may open the way to the kinds of research that will enable us to develop a better grasp of what is involved in the development and maintenance of homosexuality. If the variables involved in the development and maintenance of homosexuality can be determined, it will be possible to prevent or modify homosexuality, if that is considered important or necessary by the particular individual. The measurement of the specific behaviors involved in homosexuality allows us to investigate various and sundry variables that may be involved. For example, the radical behaviorist may be able to identify behaviors and environmental events that affect the selection of the sex partner. At the present time there is a vast array of positions that purportedly account for the development of homosexuality. There are some, for example Bieber (1976), who contend that a domineering mother may be the major factor in the development of homosexuality. On the other hand, difficulties with the same-sexed parent in early childhood have been described as a causal factor in homosexuality (Saghir & Robins, 1973). And there are many other causal factors that are purportedly responsible for homosexuality, including hormonal factors (See chap. 7, this vol.)

At the present time it can be safely said that the pertinent variables involved in the development and maintenance of homosexuality have not been identified. However, it is possible to develop a rationale from radical behavioristic principles that may be relevant to an understanding of the development and maintenance of homosexuality. Though the supporting evidence for this rationale may be lacking, the position to be presented in this chapter is capable of being supported or refuted by empirical evidence.

As mentioned previously, radical behavioristic psychology places the major emphasis on environment factors as determiners of behavior, any behavior, including sexual behavior. One very important environmental factor is the reactions of other people to a particular behavior. Another factor is the various stimuli provided by the environment, including people's reactions, that may control the emission of certain behaviors.

At this point we are forced to make some conjectures concerning sexual behaviors and how these behaviors may be developed, perhaps even in childhood.

There are many reactions of parents during infancy and childhood that may control the emission of behaviors that may be precursors to sexual behavior. The parent in the course of bathing the child or cleaning the child following urination or defecation may stimulate the genitalia of the child. The application of soothing oils or creams to the genital area may also serve as a source of stimulation. Putting powder around the genital area may provide a measure of escape or avoidance of irritation of the genital area. If the same-sex parent is providing the stimulation or the avoidance of an aversive consequence, the child may associate this outcome with the parent. However, the association may be dependent on how it is done. Moreover, the reaction of the parent to the stimulation may be a significant factor. There are reports of male children having erections. Parental response to these erections may have a profound effect on the kind of association that develops between these reactions and the sex of the parent. For example, if a male parent reacts to the erection by hitting the child or screaming at the child, it may affect the way in which the child reacts to males. On the other hand, if the male parent essentially ignores the erection, then the association that may develop between the parent and child will be markedly different. It has been stated previously that the consequences of an act are an important variable in the subsequent occurrence of the act. The provider of punishment frequently acquires aversive characteristics that may generalize to others who have comparable characteristics, e.g., maleness. There is a marked tendency to avoid aversive consequences. On the other hand, there is a marked tendency to remain in the presence of individuals who provide positive reinforcement.

As the child grows older, there may be other events that profoundly affect the determination of the ultimate sex partner. One of the authors had a client who was homosexual and who had a position from which he would have been discharged if his superiors learned about his sexual preference. He was a pastoral counselor in a fundamentalist church working with teenagers and young adults. He described how at the age of 9 or 10 he was "playing doctor" with a neighbor girl. He had reached the point in his "examination" where the girl had removed all of her clothes. His parents walked in and found them in this condition. His parents were furious and he was soundly beaten. Moreover, the girl told her parents about the event and they forbade her from ever associating with him. Furthermore, her parents told the parents of other girls in the neighborhood and they proceeded to forbid their daughters from having anything to do with him. The beating and rejection by girls forced him into the company of boys only. "I simply felt more comfortable around boys," he said. Would he have become homosexual if this sequence of consequences had not occurred? There is no way to answer this question. Did this sequence of consequences contribute to his becoming homosexual? Again we have no way of answering this question.

The first heterosexual interaction may be critical in the development of homosexuality. If the interaction is positively reinforcing, then the likelihood that the ultimate sexual partner is a member of the opposite sex is greatly increased. A 19-year-old woman came to the Center for Behavioral Analysis at the University of Texas of the Permian Basin. She stated that she believed she was homosexual, although she had never had what she called a homosexual interaction. She was planning to get married and was concerned about her ability to perform the sexual act. She had not had sexual intercourse with her fiance despite his numerous efforts to have intercourse with her. She said that she was in a conflict situation because she would like to have sexual intercourse with him, but that "the thought of sexual intercourse just turned me off." Further discussion of the situation revealed that she had had her first and only sexual interaction at the age of 15. Her parents were described as "straight laced" and both had told her on numerous occasions that sex with a boy was dirty, and if she did it before she was married, she would go to hell. Her mother especially emphasized that anyone who engaged in premarital sexual relations was a very bad and evil person. Her boyfriend at that time, age 15, told her that sexual intercourse was a great experience. Some of her girlfriends had also encouraged her to have intercourse with her boyfriend, telling her that it was really a great experience. Moreover, they told her that if she did not have intercourse with him, she would probably lose him. She stated that her boyfriend "really aroused her" and she would have liked to have sexual intercourse with him. At the same time she expressed great concern over the reactions of her parents if she were to engage in sexual intercourse. After months of intense pressure from her boyfriend she finally succumbed in the back seat of a car at a drive-in theatre. She stated that she was really excited and was anticipating one of the most wonderful experiences in her life. However, she reported that it was one of the most disappointing experiences in her life. She found that the entire act was over in a very short period of time and the experience, as far as she was concerned, was a complete failure. "It was the biggest let-down in my life. After the build-up I had received and the level of excitement that preceded it, I guess I expected too much. It wasn't worth the effort." Following that episode, she found that boys never excited her very much. She enjoyed the casual interactions that she had with boys, but never "felt the excitement that I had that night in the back seat of the car." She enjoyed being with her fiance, but she never felt terribly aroused in his presence. She indicated that she wanted to have intercourse with him because he wanted it so badly. Since she was going to marry him, she thought she should comply, but she could never bring herself to the point where they actually had intercourse. She reported that she frequently faked being excited because she did not want to disappoint him. Moreover, she was afraid that if she did not show some responsivity, he would break off with her. During the engagement she had used every excuse she could to avoid having intercourse, including lying to her fiance about never having had sexual intercourse. However, once they were married, she would have no more excuses and she was very concerned about what she was going to do. The situation was further compounded by the fact that she said that she was more comfortable in the presence of women. There were actually a couple of women who tended to excite her sexually. However, neither woman friend made any effort to have a sexual relationship with her.

The above example illustrates the tremendous impact that the consequences of a behavior may have on that behavior. Essentially the young lady did not find heterosexual behavior to be very reinforcing. From her account it would appear that heterosexual behavior had no reinforcing value. There was no indication how she found herself more interested sexually in women than men. Perhaps the demands made upon her in the presence of women did not produce any tension. After all, to maximize the reinforcing value of sexual interactions the individual should be relaxed. Apparently she found women to be less aversive than men and this situation may have affected her sexual interest in women. Although her account does not permit the development of a rationale to account for her seeming sexual interest in women, it certainly suggests the possible basis for her rejection of heterosexual behavior.

Many teenage males and females may have been provided little or no attention by members of the opposite sex. They are rejected. If this condition is accompanied by attention from members of the same sex, the individual may be very vulnerable to the development of homosexual behaviors. Attention is a very powerful reinforcer. If attention is provided to a young woman by other women but not by young men, then the controller of such reinforcement is in an excellent position to manipulate and control the behavior, any behavior, of the other. Though the individual may have reservations about engaging in a homosexual act, the possibility of losing the attention provided by the other person may be powerful enough to overcome the reservations. If the homosexual act is reinforcing, then the individual may develop a stronger and stronger homosexual relationship.

Another commonly occurring situation conducive to the development of homosexuality is the availability of a sex partner of the opposite sex at the time the individual is sexually aroused. There are many reports of the development of homosexuality in prison where an opposite sexed partner is not available. However, the same situation can arise outside the prison environment. One of the authors had a client who was bisexual. Though he was married and had heterosexual relations with his wife, he also maintained an active homosexual life. He was in a position where his homosexuality, if it became known would probably destroy his career. His wife was aware of his homosexual interest but was not aware that he actually engaged in homosexual acts. He lived in a relatively small community, but reported that he had little difficulty finding homosexual partners.

He stated that his first sexual experience was a homosexual one. When he was 16 years old he camped out on the beach with a male friend. They decided that they would scour the nearby community to find a couple of young ladies who might enjoy spending the night on the beach. Their efforts to find such young ladies were not rewarded. They returned to their tent on the beach, sexually aroused but without opposite sexed partners. They proceeded to have a homosexual interaction which he reported that he enjoyed. However, he said that he began to "experience a lot of guilt and shame."

His last statement raises a very important point that is not only pertinent to the question of ultimately selected sex partner but to other behavior problems as well. It involves the issue of immediacy of reinforcement. There is an abundance of research that attests to the effectiveness of immediate reinforcement on the development and maintenance of a behavior.

Delaying reinforcement reduces the effectiveness of reinforcement. Delay of punishment also reduces whatever effectiveness that punishment may have. If the reinforcement for a homosexual act is immediate, any punishment that is subsequently provided to that act will be less effective than the immediate reinforcement. Similarly, if the punishment is immediate or the reinforcement is delayed or not provided at all, then any subsequent reinforcement may be considerably less effective. Recall the young lady whose initial heterosexual experience was non-reinforced, perhaps even punished if "feeling very disappointed" is punishment. These conditions may make it difficult for the individual to get into a situation where heterosexual relations may occur.

Immediate punishment of a particular behavior may lead to the development of an avoidance behavior. Immediate punishment of heterosexual or sexual behaviors that may precede heterosexual interactions, as characterized by the small boy who was playing "doctor," may lead to an avoidance reaction. The individual who has been punished for heterosexual behaviors may avoid interactions with members of the opposite sex. By avoiding interactions with members of the opposite sex, the individual reduces the probability of having interactions that may lead to heterosexual acts. The result is that the individual is never put into a position where he/she may be positively reinforced for heterosexual acts. The lack of opportunity for positive reinforcement for heterosexual acts will probably prevent their development.

The lack of positive reinforcement for heterosexual intercouse is frequently observed in couples, resulting in a reduced interest in having sexual intercourse with their partners. Some of these men and women turn to homosexual acts since homosexual acts may generate more immediate positive reinforcement.

Another important issue that confronts the radical behaviorist is how a member of the same sex comes to acquire control over the sexual arousal response. How can a member of the same sex produce sexual arousal? The radical behaviorist position on this issue is rather straightforward. It has been alluded to in the previous discussion of several other issues. Generally speaking, the behaviorist's position is that any environmental event in the presence of which a response is reinforced will acquire control over that response. If, in the presence of a member of the same sex an individual is sexually aroused and that sexual arousal is immediately reinforced, then the same sex member will acquire control over sexual arousal. Sexual arousal is being reinforced by the homosexual act and the same person may ultimately control sexual arousal. It does not take too many occurrences of this sequence of events before members of the same sex can acquire control over the chain of sexual arousal and homosexual act.

If this chain of events occurs as described, does it mean that the individual will be sexually aroused every time the individual is in the presence of a same sexed person? The answer is no. It means that the homosexual act has an increased probability of occurring in the presence of same sexed persons. We do not sit down every time we are in the presence of a chair, despite the fact that a chair may have developed as *a* source of control over sitting. In the radical behavioristic vernacular, the same sexed member has developed into a discriminative stimulus (S^D) for a homosexual act, just as the chair has developed into an S^D for sitting. The discriminative stimulus is usually defined as a stimulus in the presence of which there is an increased probability that a specific and specifiable behavior will occur. There are other environmental sources of control, although they are frequently not specified. There is no more basis for assuming that a homosexual is sexually aroused every time he/she is in the presence of a same sexed member than for assuming a heterosexual is always sexually aroused in the presence of an opposite sexed individual. If other factors that have developed as S^Ds for the homosexual act could be specified for the individual, then it would be possible to devise a more effective program to modify the sexual experience. The S^Ds must be identified for the particular individual, because since the S^D property is an acquired property, it will differ from individual to individual.

THERAPY

Having explored some of the variables that may contribute to the development of homosexuality, we now turn our attention to the ways of modifying sexual preference. It is at this point that ethical issues come to the fore, and while we discussed this topic earlier in the chapter, we feel its importance warrants further attention. Who determines if a homosexual should have his/her sexual preference altered? What should be done with the homosexual whose sexual preference may create other problems of coping with the environment? Even with the so-called sexual revolution the latter situation still arises. What should be done about the homosexual who says that he/she "really enjoys the homosexual act but feels guilty after engaging in it?" These kinds of questions arise and confront the clinician. Does the clinician have the right to tell a homosexual cllient that the client's sexual preference must be altered? From a radical behavioristic standpoint the answers to these questions are pretty clear cut. It is the client, not the clinician, who determines the behaviors to be emitted by the client. The basis for this determination is that it is the client, not the clinician, who must live with the consequences of the client's behaviors. To assume that the clinician has the right to tell someone else what to do when it is the other person who must live with consequences of that behavior is an usurption of another's rights. The clinician who cannot live with this restriction may find it advantageous to function under a different theoretical structure, especially one that assumes that behavior qua behavior has qualitative characteristics.

Suppose a homosexual client states that he/she wishes a change in sexual preference. Since the client has made this request, the present sexual preference will be, for simplicity's sake, called the problem. How does the radical behavioristic clinician proceed with this problem? One of the first factors that the clinician considers is the frequency of occurrence of the homosexual act. It is apparent that it is very important that there is a clear specification of what constitutes a homosexual act. If that is not done, then it is very difficult to determine how often the homosexual act occurs. The determination of the frequency of occurrence of the homosexual act is called the baseline. The baseline is very important since it provides some very pertinent and important information. The frequency of occurrence of the homosexual act tells the clinician something about the severity of the problem, since the more frequently a response occurs, the greater the likelihood that it has been reinforced more often. The more a response is reinforced, the more difficult it usually is to modify. If the frequency of occurence of a behavior is several times a day and is reinforced, it will be more difficult to modify that behavior than one that occurs once a month and is reinforced. The frequency of occurrence may provide us with information concerning the S^Ds that are controlling the act. An act that has a high frequency of occurrence probably has more S^Ds controlling it than one that occurs less frequently. The more S^Ds that control a behavior, the more difficult it will be to modify it.

In addition to providing information about the difficulty of modifying the behavior, the baseline may provide information that could lead to the ready identification of the S^Ds. Since a low frequency of occurrence of a behavior probably has fewer S^Ds controlling it, it may be possible to pinpoint some, perhaps all, of the S^Ds very quickly. The sooner that the S^Ds are identified, the more quickly the clinician can create a program to effect behavior change.

The baseline may play a part in the clinician's decision to accept the client. If the frequency of occurrence is very high, the clinician may conclude that it is not possible to create an effective behavior change program for a client who is being seen on an outpatient basis.

The usual second step in a behavioral approach to behavior change is to identify the reinforcers for the target behavior. Since the reinforcers are considered to be a critical factor in the maintenance of a behavior, it is necessary to identify them and try to eliminate them. It is practically axiomatic in behavioristic psychology that if you cannot eliminate the reinforcers that are maintaining a behavior, you will have a difficult time effecting a behavioral change.

In the case of designing a program to change homosexual sexual preference, the clinician is in a difficult position with respect to eliminating the reinforcers for the homosexual act. The controller(s) of the reinforcer is or may be unknown to the clinician. Moreover, the controller(s) of the reinforcement may also be deriving a considerable amount of reinforcement from the homosexual relationship. Control of the reinforcer by the clinician is very important in the radical behavioristic approach. If the clinician cannot control the reinforcer, then it is critical that the controller(s) of reinforcement cooperate in any behavior change program if the program is to have a reasonable chance of success. This condition may not prevail in the case of change in sexual preference.

If the positive reinforcement for the homosexual act can be removed, then the control exercised by the same sexed individual(s) will extinguish. As mentioned earlier, this control is acquired through the reinforcement that is provided in the presence of the same sexed individual. The only conceivable way to eliminate this reinforcement, but which is very unlikely, is to enlist the assistance of a homosexual who does not reinforce the client for sexual arousal in the presence of the homosexual. Even if such assistance could be obtained, there is a high probability that the client would find alternatives, e.g., other homosexuals who would be more cooperative with the client.

An alternative would be to punish the client for sexual arousal in the presence of the same sexed individual. Again it would require the cooperation of another homosexual person and that may be difficult to achieve. Moreover, the effects of punishment are difficult to predict. It is conceivable that the punishment may create more serious problems without effecting the requested behavioral change. Consequently, we strongly advise against the use of punishment to effect a change of sexual preference, or any other behavioral change.

A third alternative may be to develop a sexual response in the presence of an opposite sexed individual that may be stronger than the sexual response in the presence of the same sexed individual. This approach also necessitates an accomplice. Moreover, it could be very time consuming. It would be necessary at the outset to extinguish all avoidance responses that the client may have acquired to opposite sexed individuals. The extinction of an avoidance response is very difficult. Some variation of an in vivo Wolpian approach may be utilized here. Though the client may accept the introduction of the opposite sexed individual, the client's avoidance responses may appear once the introduction is completed. The clinician must proceed very slowly. As soon as the avoidance response occurs, the opposed sexed individual is removed from the environment. It will probably be necessary to repeat each step a number of times before the avoidance responses are extinguished. Any response that is incompatible with the avoidance response is reinforced. It is not adequate to extinguish the avoidance response; it is equally important to reinforce any behaviors that involve movement toward the opposite sexed individual. The initial movement may be very small, probably will be, but once movement begins and is reinforced, it usually accelerates.

The steps involved in the beginning are very small. As the program progresses, the size of the steps, which are behaviors on the part of the client, may be increased. The number of reinforcements for each step may be reduced so that the process speeds up. The expectation of these procedures is to get the client to the point where the accomplice can provide some stimulation that may be sexually arousing. When that point is reached, if it is, then it is necessary to be very careful. Any miscalculation may set back the program and, perhaps, make it virtually impossible to achieve the goal of heterosexual intercourse.

In this approach it is very important that the accomplice is well trained to carry out the program, or the accomplice may become impatient and attempt to move too rapidly through the program. The speed of movement through the program is determined by the behavior of the client, not the accomplice.

It is also important to determine a number of effective reinforcers for the client. Since heterosexual interactions may never have been reinforced and homosexual interactions strongly reinforced, it will be necessary to utilize the most powerful available reinforcers. Skinner, in a course in the Control of Sexual Behavior, once commented that no one had found a reinforcer more powerful than the orgasm. If the client has achieved orgasm in the homosexual interactions, the task of finding effective reinforcers may be very difficult.

An alternative using aversive consequences, a procedure not recommended, may be effective for some individuals. Aversive consequences have been used in the treatment of fetishes, pediphilia, and other sexually related behaviors. This method is usually carried out in the office. Rather than using in vivo attempts to generate sexual arousal, pictures, presumably erotic, are used. Several different measures of sexual arousal have been used. The most frequently used measure of sexual arousal in the female has been vaginal temparture. Vaginal temperature is related to blood flow and blood flow has been related to sexual arousal in the female. For the male a penile plethysmograph or string gauge has been used. Both provide a measure of penile circumference. As penile circumference increases, sexual arousal is considered to increase. The most commonly used punisher is electric shock. Electric shock has the advantage of being provided immediately in measured quantities. The electric shock is usually provided to an arm or leg through a cuff that has been affixed to the limb.

Erotic pictures of males and females are used. Here again the individual client must be considered since not all clients consider the same material to be erotic or erotic to the same degree. In the process of obtaining the baseline for the client, the clinician may use those measurements described above to establish the hierarchy of sexual arousal for the various pictures. Though it is expected that pictures of nudes and homo- and heterosexual intercourse would have maximum sexual arousal, this result may not occur. One of the authors had a pediphiliac client for whom little boys in tank tops and tight fitting jeans were more sexually arousing than pictures of nude boys.

Once the hierarchy is established through the baseline measurements, the pictures that control the smallest magnitude of sexual arousal are presented. Those pictures that are classified as arousing homosexual reactions in the client are presented first. The least sexually arousing picture is actually presented first. If there is any sexual arousal in the client, the client is shocked. It is generally accepted that it is advisable to provide the maximum amount of shock at the very outset. After the shock, the client is provided time for the sexual arousal level to subside and return to a baseline established for non-erotic pictures. After the client returns to baseline, the same sexually arousing picture is presented. The same procedure is followed until the client shows no sexual arousal to the picture. When the picture controls no sexual arousal, the client is reinforced, both positively and negatively. The negative reinforcement consists of the absence of shock. The positive reinforcement consists of whatever has been established as a reinforcer for the client. The next picture in the "homosexual arousal hierarchy" is presented. The same procedures are followed. If there is any sexual arousal as evidenced by an increase over baseline, the client is shocked. If there is no sexual arousal to the picture, the client is positively reinforced. These procedures are followed through the entire list of homosexual arousing pictures. An occasional heterosexual arousal picture may be introduced to determine if there is a sexual arousal response. If there is an arousal response to the heterosexual picture, then the client is positively reinforced. If there is no arousal response to the heterosexual picture, the client may be shocked. However, it is not recommended to provide shock for the absence of sexual arousal response to the heterosexual picture. There is always the danger that shock in the presence of the heterosexual picture may prevent the development of an arousal response to heterosexual stimulation.

The initial arousal response to heterosexual stimuli may be very small. Despite the small magnitude of the arousal response, the client is reinforced. It is unreasonable to expect a sudden and dramatic shift to arousal responses in the presence of heterosexual stimuli. The shocking of the arousal response to the heterosexual stimulation is designed to suppress the homosexual response. If the homosexual response is suppressed, it may allow for the shaping of a larger and larger magnitude of arousal response to the heterosexual stimulation.

If an arousal response to heterosexual stimulation can be attained, there is still the problem of the generalization of the arousal response to the outside environment. It is desirable in this situation to utilize a trained accomplice since the untrained sex partner may proceed in a manner that would destroy all of the prior training. As mentioned earlier in describing the activities of the accomplice, he/she must move very slowly, making sure that there is an arousal response before moving on to the next step along the way to heterosexual intercourse.

A technique used by Barlow and Agras (1973) with male homosexuals had modest success. Their technique was based on the method called errorless discrimination and utilizes a fading procedure. The errorless discrimination training procedure was developed by Hebert Terrace (1963). The major premise of this technique is a fundamental premise of the radical behavioral approach to behavior change. This premise is that the organism is always right. That is, there is nothing "wrong" with the behavior. It is simply controlled by inappropriate environmental events. Thus, the behaviors involved in the homosexual act are not "wrong." They are controlled by environmental events that some consider to be inappropriate.

Barlow and Agras (1973) had three male homosexual clients who asked that their sexual preference be changed. They used a string gauge that was attached to the penis. The string gauge provided a measure of penile circumference. Sexual arousal was measured in terms of the penile circumference. As the penile circumference increased, the magnitude of sexual arousal increased.

Each client was presented pictures of nude males since nude males controlled the sexual arousal response. Very gradually and slowly the picture of a nude female was superimposed over the male figure, which was gradually faded out. The picture of the nude female was graduallly faded in over the picture of the nude male that was gradually being faded out. The ultimate objective was to have the client maintain maximum penile circumference in the presence of the picture of the nude female.

The investigators reported modest success in terms of the overall effectiveness of the procedures. Success was measured in terms of maintenance of heterosexual interactions. No mention was made of any procedures that were used to increase the likelihood of generalization of the sexual arousal response in the real life situation. And generalization is an integral factor in the ultimate success of any behavior change program. Too often we just hope that generalization will occur. Steps need to be taken that will increase the likelihood that generalization will occur. Some psychoanalysts (e.g., Alexander and French, 1946), acknowledge that the most difficult part of an effective modification program is to have the developments in the program generalize to the outside environment.

It must be conceded that there is a dearth of knowledge about the factors that affect generalization. However, there are steps that Barlow and Agras (1973) could have taken that may have increased the success of their procedures. Those suggestions are embodied in the discussion of the procedures used in the combined aversive-positive consequences method. The use of a skilled accomplice in the Barlow and Agras (1973) procedures may have increased the likelihood of maintenance of the heterosexual arousal response. To turn the client loose to fend for himself in a new and different sexual orientation results in a great dependency on the client's finding a very cooperative and understanding sex partner. A sex partner for someone undergoing a change of sexual preference must proceed carefully and not be very demanding. The client needs a sex partner who is patient and knows the importance of maintaining penile erection throughout the entire prelude to sexual intercourse. The client must be maintained in a relaxed state if there is to be a successful outcome. If the sex partner is not aware of the client's situation, she could create a condition that could lead to a failure of the client to function effectively. All prior gains from the modification program could be destroyed quickly. Future efforts to alter the sexual preference would be very difficult.

In addition to providing information about the severity of the behavior problem, the baseline can also serve another extremely important purpose. During and after the course of a modification program, the client's problematic behavior can be compared with the baseline of the behavior. This often involves a comparison of the frequency of occurrence of the behavior before or at the start of the modification program, with its occurrence during the course of the program and, when possible, after the program has ended, during follow-up. Such comparisons provide the clinician and client with a basis for deciding if the program has been effective. It is also valuable during the course of the program in alerting the clinician when the program, for whatever reason, is not succeeding. This emphasis on the ongoing monitoring of the effects of a program is one of the defining characteristics of a radical behavioral approach to change.

A problem frequently encountered with outpatient clients is the necessity of relying on the client's self-report data, which may or may not be accurate in varying degrees. Depending upon the particular individual such self-report data may be augmented by information from others, e.g., by a spouse or by direct measures of sexual arousal obtained in the clinic. Nevertheless, the extensive reliance on clients' self-reports should be accompanied by the clinician's awareness that the accuracy of such information may vary across clients and over time for any given client.

It should also be noted that for homosexual reorientation to be successful, decreasing arousal to homosexual stimuli and increasing heterosexual arousal, while necesary, are often insufficient. Many homosexuals have not developed the social skills that are prerequisite in our culture for the intimacy that can result in heterosexual intercourse. For such clients, rather extensive social skills training is necessary. Such training typically involves modeling of social behaviors appropriate to heterosexual situations, role-playing of such behaviors, with the provision of feedback to the client, and "homework assignments" for the client.

The behavior problems that may arise with a homosexual who has no interest in changing sexual preference have not been discussed. To discuss these problems would carry us far afield from the primary objective of this chapter.

A radical behavioristic approach to the modification of homosexual behavior has been described. There are many nuances and subtleties in a behavior modification program that have not been described or discussed. There are many who contend that radical behavioristic approaches are very simple and superficial. The way in which these programs are frequently

described can lead to this conclusion. However, our clinical experience suggests that an effective program of behavioral change, any behavioral change, is very complex.

REFERENCES

Alexander, F., & French, T. M. (1946). *Psychoanalytic therapy: Principles and applications.* New York: Ronald Press.

Barlow, D. H., & Agras, W. S. (1973). Fading to increase heterosexual responsiveness in homosexuals. *Journal of Applied Behavior Analysis, 6,* 355–366.

Bergin, A. E. (1980). Behavior therapy and ethical relativism: Time for clarity. *Journal of Consulting and Clinical Psychology, 48,* 11–13.

Bieber, I. (1976). A discussion on "Homosexuality: The ethical challenge." *Journal of Consulting and Clinical Psychology, 44,* 163–166.

Coleman, E. (1982). Changing approaches to the treatment of homosexuality. *American Behavioral Scientist, 25,* 397–406.

Davison, G. C. (1976). Homosexuality: The ethical challenge. *Journal of Consulting and Clinical Psychology, 44,* 157–162.

Davison, G. C. (1977). Homosexuality and the ethics of behavioral intervention. *Journal of Homosexuality, 2,* 195–204.

Davison, G. C. (1978). Not can but ought: The treatment of homosexuality. *Journal of Consulting and Clinical Psychology, 46,* 170–172.

Davison, G. C. (1982). Politics, ethics, and therapy for homosexuality. *American Behavioral Scientist, 25,* 423–434.

Day, W. (1977). Ethical philosophy and the thought of B. F. Skinner. In J. Krapfl & E. A. Vargas (Eds.). *Behaviorism and ethics.* Kalamazoo, MI: Behaviordelia.

Ethical isues for human services. (1977). *Behavior Therapy, 8,* 763–764.

Greenspoon, J. (1976). *The sources of behavior: Abnormal and normal.* Monterey, CA: Brooks/Cole.

Krapfl, J., & Vargas, E. (Eds.). (1977). *Behaviorism and ethics.* Kalamazoo, MI: Behaviordelia.

Kazdin, A. E. (1982). *Single-case research designs: Methods for clinical and applied settings.* New York: Oxford University Press.

Kitchener, R. F. (1980). Ethical relativism and behavior therapy. *Journal of Consulting and Clinical Psychology, 48,* 1–7.

Masters, W. H., & Johnson, V. E. (1979). *Homosexuality in perspective.* Boston: Little, Brown.

Saghir, M. T., & Robins, E. (1973). *Male and female homosexuality.* Baltimore: Williams and Wilkins.

Sturgis, E. T., & Adams, H. E. (1978). The right to treatment: Issues in the treatment of homosexuality. *Journal of Consulting and Clinical Psychology, 46,* 165–169.

Terrace, H. S. (1963). Discrimination learning with and without errors. *Journal of the Experimental Analysis Behavior, 6,* 1–27.

Ward, L. C. (1980). Behavior therapy and ethics: Response to Kitchener. *Journal of Consulting and Clinical Psychology, 48,* 646–648.

Wood, W. S. (1979). Ethics for behavior analysts. *The Behavior Analyst, 2,* 9–15.

Woolfolk, A. L., & Richardson, F. C. (1984). Behavior therapy and the ideology of modernity. *American Psychologist, 39,* 777–786.

7

PSYCHOBIOLOGICAL CONTRIBUTIONS

Brian A. Gladue

Human sexuality is a highly diverse enterprise. Sexual activity, fantasies and preferences come in seemingly as wide a variety as there are people. Probably the most obvious and salient feature of human sexual diversity is gender of sexual partner (sexual orientation). People come in many sexual orientations; heterosexual, homosexual and the varying intermediate forms of bisexuality. Yet in efforts to categorize or label someone as heterosexual or homosexual we run into confusion. Consider the following descriptions of a few people:

A thirty year old bachelor decides, after years of numerous dates and tentative "involvements" with men, to move in with his lover of the past six months. Both men contemplate a long and healthy relationship and enjoy a vigorous and romantic sharing of sex and emotions.

A twenty-eight year old husband and father of two children, after years of inner turmoil and dissatisfaction with a heterosexual lifestyle, leaves his wife and children. He arranges for their financial well-being (as much as he is able), and tries to assure them that his decision does not reflect on them, but rather his desire to be true to his needs and self.

A young male lingers in the lounge area of a gay night club hoping for one more sexual encounter before going home for the night. Although he has had intercourse with a few women in his teen years, he prefers the company of men and has felt this way since he was a boy.

Arthur has never had sex with a man, although he has had many daydreams and masturbatory fantasies in which men were his sex partners. He has had these images and dreams since puberty. Arthur is forty years old, never married, reports having had sex with several lady companions, but confesses waning interests in them, and an increasing desire to "do it with a guy."

By most definitions and standard assessment techniques, all of the above descriptions seem to indicate some degree of male homosexuality. But are these people all alike? Is there a simple definition of "homosexual?" And do such monolithic concepts really teach us anything about human sexual diversity, or do we merely engage in a simplistic exercise in convenience labelling? The casual observer would agree that each of these men has a different way of being sexual, and most assuredly a different past and history, yet each is still erotically oriented toward persons of the *same* gender. The same could be said for heterosexual men: each has a different past, each with different tastes and lifestyles regarding interactions with an *opposite* gender partner.

But how do people come to be homosexual (or heterosexual, for that matter)? What events influence someone to be exclusively homosexual or bisexual since puberty? What factors contribute to the development of one's psychosexuality? This is, of course, a continuing question of human sexuality. It is a question that asks about the fundamental nature of human development: how we become who we are. Efforts to understand human sexual orientation have involved numerous disciplines from anthropology to zoology. And nowhere can any one discipline claim convincing evidence for a complete explanation of the development of sexual orientation, be it homosexuality or heterosexuality. The prevailing view among many psychologists, for example, is that psychosexual development is multifactorial: the diversity among sexual orientations is likely to be understood from a combination of sociological, cultural, and biological factors.

This chapter will review a piece of that larger pool of data and theory regarding psychosexual development, and address what we know and also what we do not know about the biology and psychobiology of sexual orientation.

BIOLOGICAL APPROACHES TOWARD UNDERSTANDING SEXUAL ORIENTATION

Is there a biological basis for a predisposition for a given sexual orientation, whether it be heterosexuality, homosexuality, or varying degrees of bisexuality? And, in particular, are there hormonal or genetic factors which contribute to the development of homosexuality? Certainly these are forefront often posed questions, more so lately as our society becomes more aware of increasing knowledge in biology and medicine and thus, more likely to embrace biological explanations for human behavior. Several biological approaches contributing toward an understanding of sexual orientation include the effects of hormones upon behavior, and how the brain and nervous system interact with hormones.

Hormonal Studies of Homosexuality

Numerous animal studies strongly support the thesis that gonadal hormones influence the development and expression of sexual behavior. Males of many species, for example, show diminished male-typical sexual behavior after hormone removal by castration (Clemens and Gladue, 1978), behavior which can be restored by hormone replacement. Furthermore, the degree of behavioral response to hormone in adulthood depends a great deal upon hormonal interactions that occurred prenatally during sexual and neural differentiation. This view of the dependency of dimorphic sexual behavior upon pre- and post-natal hormone functioning in nonhuman mammals has revived interest in the possibility of a hormonal component to human sexuality. While the evidence for hormonal involvement in human sexual behavior is not as convincing as it is for animal species, similar endocrine-behavior correlates probably exist (see Beach, 1979 for review of comparative research in sex behavior).

Given that there is increasing interest in hormone influences upon human behavior, we need to look (briefly) at how hormones work. First, hormones such as gonadal steroids like testosterone or estrogen are chemical messengers that instruct cells and tissues of the body to undergo chemical and biophysical changes. Often such changes are readily discerned, such as puberty, hair growth or menstruation. Other actions of hormones are less obvious, such as the metabolism of fats and proteins, or manufacture of sperm in men or maturation of egg cells in women. Other hormones, such as the protein gonadotropins, secreted by the pituitary gland are important for maturation and operation of the reproductive system of men and women. Together, hormones and the tissues they interact with are called the endocrine system. Their influences upon behavior have become increasingly important to understand because hormones are highly potent and have long-lasting influences upon the body.

But how do hormones affect human sexual morphology (such as the genitals) and behavior (such as arousal or possibly erotic partner preferences)? Two main ingredients for any hormone action are: a critical level or amount of hormone needs to be present, and more important, the hormone has to effectively interact with a particular target tissue. As an example, consider a group of men some of whom have heavy (and regular) beard growth, others are clean-shaven, still others with little or no facial hair growth. All men may have similar levels of androgenic hormones that can stimulate beard growth. But not all men have skin/hair cells that respond to the hormone in the same way. Thus, while they have similar levels of the hormone, the hormone's effects in these men differ due to their different sensitivities to androgen. This sensitivity is now thought to be primarily a function of how the cell (be it skin, liver, bone or brain) operates, in essence a consequence of that cell's genetic instructions. The genetic diversity among individuals and biochemistry of cell operation can explain why the same hormone has different effects on different tissues in the same body (which is why, for example, in the same body, estrogen stimulates growth and maintenance of bone in some cells and regulates production of gonadotropin in brain cells). And since not all humans have the same genetic constitution, hormone action on the same types of cells and tissue differs to some degree across different people (as in the beard example above). At its core, hormone actions require not only the presence of a given hormone, but the interaction of that hormone with the cell's genetic codes and biochemical machinery. All of which helps to explain the difficulty and complexity in understanding human psychoendocrinology (which is also why one should be cautious in overinterpreting hormone "explanations" for behavior or preferences, a point to which we shall return). How human sexual behavior is biologically influenced or determined by hormones is not clear although recent research is beginning to yield evidence and promising avenues toward understanding human behavioral biology (Ehrhardt and Meyer-Bahlburg, 1979; Meyer-Bahlburg, 1979; Baker, 1980; Hines, 1982).

With regard to sexual orientation behavioral variations, one view has held that homosexual men and women have some atypicality in hormone function. In this view, for example, homosexual men would show some deficiency of the "male" hormone testosterone or other androgens, and/or an excess of the "female" hormone estrogen, whereas female homosexuals would show the reverse. Since 1971, many studies have examined the relationship of hormone levels to sexual orientation in both men and women.

Male Homosexuals A few early studies reported homosexual men to have lower circulating testosterone levels than heterosexuals (Kolodny et al., 1971; Pillard et al., 1974; Starka et al., 1975). However, two of these studies lacked appropriate control groups and the third study (Kolodny et al., 1971) appears confounded by drug use in the homosexual group. Since Kolodny et al., (1979) reported that many psychotropic drugs can depress testosterone levels, that earlier study is suspect.

In contrast, numerous studies (over twenty at this time) reported *no* diferences between homosexual and heterosexual men (reviewed in Meyer-Bahlburg, 1977; 1984), a finding confirmed in the most recent endocrine report on male sexual orientation (Gladue et al., 1984). Indeed, two early studies showed homosexual men with *elevated* testosterone levels compared to the comparison group of heterosexual men (Tourney and Hatfield, 1973;

Brodie et al., 1974). Hormone studies examining other androgens, notably androstenedione, a weak androgenic hormone primarily from the adrenal gland, found the production rate of androstenedione not different according to sexual orientation (Tourney and Hatfield, 1973; Newmark et al., 1979; Meyer et al., 1981; Aiman and Boyar, 1982; Sanders et al., 1984). Only one study found androstenedione elevated in a group of twenty homosexual men (Friedman et al., 1977). Interestingly, in this study they also reported higher levels of cortisol, also a hormone of adrenal origin, among the homosexual men. Those authors argued that both androstenedione and cortisol may have been elevated due to the unusual emotional stress in the homosexual group, presumably a consequence of living as a minority in a homophobic culture, which affected their adrenal gland function.

What can we make of these endocrine studies? First, the available data on male homosexuals compared to male heterosexuals make it seem *highly unlikely* that variations in testosterone or estrogen level *cause* variations in sexual orientation. The vast majority of male homosexuals have testosterone levels similar to that seen in male heterosexuals. Relating differences in testosterone levels to differences in sexual orientation in such a simplistic manner is a dubious undertaking for several reasons. When correlating hormone levels with sexual orientation one needs to consider the wide range of normal hormone levels among men along with multiple factors that influence such levels (diet, drug intake, time of day or month in which samples were drawn are but a few). In fact, there are no convincing data that, in men, sexuality is directly related to the amount of hormone present. We should not expect sexual partner gender preference to yield any substantially different results. But hormones are not totally irrelevant to human sexuality and partner preference. While hormone levels *per se* may not be critical, how hormones operate to effect behavior may be more influential. We will return to this point shortly.

Female Homosexuals There are few studies which relate testosterone levels to sexual orientation in lesbian women (in fact, most studies have investigated hormone levels in female-to-male transsexuals—most of those women reported significant same sex partner fantasies and activity). Of these ten studies, four reported no difference in testosterone levels (Downey et al., 1982; Seyler et al., 1978; Meyer et al., 1981; Gooren et al., 1984). The two studies which measured androstenedione found no differences related to sexual orientation (Meyer et al., 1981; Downey et al., 1982). However, six studies reported elevated testosterone in women with atypical gender orientation. In these studies, not all lesbian or female transsexual subjects showed elevated testosterone. In fact, only about one third of the subjects in these studies had elevated testosterone when compared to heterosexual women (Loraine et al., 1971; Griffiths et al., 1974; Gartrell et al., 1977; Fulmer, 1973; Jones and Samimy, 1973; Sipova and Starka, 1977).

Estradiol (for women, the predominant gonadal estrogenic hormone) levels did not differ between lesbian or transsexual subjects and heterosexual women in the four studies which measured this hormone (Griffiths et al., 1974; Seyler et al., 1978; Meyer et al., 1981; Gooren et al., 1984). One study on urinary estrone, another potent estrogen, showed decreased excretion of this hormone in female homosexuals (Loraine et al., 1971).

From these studies, we can conclude that the majority of adult female homosexuals appear to have testosterone and estrogen levels well within the normal female range. Yet, there may be a subgroup of female homosexuals who have slightly elevated testosterone levels, although these levels are far below that seen in men. Whether these elevated testosterone levels have any causal relationship regarding lesbianism is not known. Because of so few studies, and because in women, testosterone is typically secreted in such small amounts as to introduce sampling and technique errors, these findings bear replication. Furthermore, we cannot be sure that these data represent artifacts of experimental design which may differentially exclude women with endocrine pathologies from the heterosexual but not homosexual groups. It is possible that hormone deviations among women may represent an adrenal gland response to the stressful psychosocial situation of lesbians in a predominantly unsympathetic society. Finally, there are intriguing (but unconfirmed) data that women in certain occupations have elevated testosterone levels (Purifoy and Koopmans, 1980). Perhaps career women who tend to be overrepresented in homosexual sample groups may be accounting for elevated testosterone levels reported for lesbians in those studies.

HORMONE–BRAIN INTERACTIONS: THE PRENATAL HORMONE THEORY

As stated earlier, there are many ways in which hormones and biology can influence sexuality and sexual behavior. While it is unlikely that adult levels of a given hormone may have any direct bearing on sexual orientation, many researchers are beginning to suspect the influence of hormones *before birth* upon the developing nervous system and body, and overall developmental influences upon adult sexuality. In this prenatal hormone theory, an interaction exists between hormones, the body's responsiveness to a given hormone (i.e., molecular genetics and endocrinology) and ultimate neural and behavioral development.

This theory is based upon the large amount of animal research showing influences of hormones on the differentiation of the brain and subsequent behavior, particularly sexual behavior (Baum, 1979). In short, the exposure of a mammalian fetal brain to hormone during a "critical period" has far-ranging and lasting consequences for its adult behavioral repertoire, perhaps, to some degree, an influence upon that animal's sexual interactions. Certainly, extending research findings from animals to humans is risky business, particularly given the marked cultural and social influences upon developing infants, children and adults. However, there appears to be some conservative basic mammalian pattern of brain development and maturation, a pattern that is reflected, at least in part, in humans.

There is good reason to suspect, that even if only as a matter of degree, human brain and behavioral development may be influenced by prenatal hormones. In addition to some psychobiologists, the prenatal hormone theory enjoys some acceptance among behavioral scientists (Bell et al., 1981; MacCulloch and Waddington, 1981), who are not satisfied with psychosocial explanations of diversity in sexual orientation.

In the past decade, investigations on hormone influences upon human sexuality have focused on neuroendocrine (brain-hormone) function and the inter-relationships of hormones and behavior (psychoendocrinology). Current thinking in behavioral endocrinology requires that we consider *interactions* of hormones with brain and other body tissues, as well as hormone interactions with other hormone systems. While *levels* of hormone may be similar from one person to the next and across groups of people with diverse sexual orientations, it does not readily follow that persons varying in sexual orientation have a similar *response* to a given hormone. Individuals may differ in hormone effects upon central nervous system (CNS) structures that mediate behavioral and physiological responses. Functional, rather than static, assessments of hormone-behavior interactions became the next logical stage of inquiry.

Consider two manners in which gonadal hormones might affect behavior. In adulthood, hormones provide for the activation, maintenance, and operation of reproductive anatomical, physiological, and behavioral systems (such as puberty, menstruation, pregnancy, and sexual arousal). Earlier, during differentiation of the fetus, hormones also influence and permanently modify genital and neural system development. Research with non-human species has established that the presence of androgen during specific critical periods of development masculinizes and defeminizes the CNS. The absence of such androgenic hormone results in a "feminized" CNS (Feder, 1981; McEwen, 1983). For humans, the evidence for behavioral sex differentiation is less clear, owing in large measure to the obvious difficulties in collecting reliable experimental data, and to a reliance on studies involving certain "naturally-occurring" endocrine disorders of fetuses and adults (reviewed in Hines, 1980). Yet, recent studies of persons affected by prenatal hormone abnormalities (so-called "experiments of nature") implicate prenatal hormones as contributing factors in the development of sexuality, including sexual orientation (Schwartz and Money, 1983; Money and Lewis, 1983; Money et al., 1984; Ehrhardt et al., 1985). Though a developmental relation between neuroendocrine response and sexual orientation is not certain, it is an appropriate avenue of inquiry, and these studies report findings consistent with such an interpretation.

There are three lines of human sex research which address biological factors that might influence psychosexual development and sexual orientation in particular. They are: neuroendocrine studies in adults which correlate with sexual orientation, prenatal endocrine disorders, and, finally, studies involving offspring of hormone-treated pregnancies. We will briefly consider each in turn.

Neuroendocrine Studies

In considering prenatal hormone theory for human sexual orientation, one needs a functional measure in adults for some consequence of prenatal hormone influences. One example of such a developmental consequence is the pattern of adult luteinizing hormone (LH) secretion.* This LH secretion pattern depends upon the presence of androgen during a critical period of sexual differentiation, a period also associated with behavioral sex differentiation in animal models (Harris, 1970; Gorski, 1971; Karsch, 1973). Males typically exposed to androgen during a critical period of fetal life show regular acyclic LH secretion patterns as adults. Females, not ordinarily exposed to androgen during fetal development, secrete LH in a cyclic pattern, related to the ovulatory cycle. Hence, the LH secretion pattern is a rough indicator of the degree of prenatal hormone differentiation of this neuroendocrine function, and presumably, behaviorally relevant regions and functions of the brain.

LH secretion patterns also depend, in part, upon adult neural responsiveness to estrogen. During part of the female menstrual cycle, rising estrogen levels (of an endogenous or exogenous source), cause a rapid decline in LH levels (the "negative feedback effect") which is followed by a sharp increase in LH (Loriaux et al., 1977; Knobil, 1980; Krey, 1984). This pattern appears to be dependent upon hypothalamic estrogen sensitivity (Keye and Jaffe, 1975). The ability of rising levels of circulating estrogen to ultimately enhance the release of LH, termed the "positive feedback estrogen phenomenon" is thought to have been determined by the afore-mentioned developmental hormone-mediated sexual differentiation process (Gorski, 1971; Feder, 1981). This response, typically seen in females, reflects the "feminized" brain. The typical absence of this response in males presumably reflects their relatively "defeminized" brains. This positive feedback estrogen phenomenon has been shown in rhesus monkeys (Yamada et al., 1971; Karsch et al., 1973) and

---

*A commonly misunderstood feature about LH studies and psychobiology is how levels of this hormone relate to sexuality. LH levels in the adult do *not* contribute to one's sexual orientation, nor are they linked to sexual arousal per se. Rather, LH is a protein pituitary homone (gonadotropin) found in both sexes, important for maintenance and operation of reproductive systems. Generally, patterns of LH production differ by gender: men have relatively stable LH production across a time span of, say, a month. In women, LH levels are highly variable and related to monthly changes in their menstrual cycle. Changing one's LH levels would have no effect on sexual orientation; the gender "type" of LH production is presumably fixed at birth and modifiable by levels of testosterone and estrogen in the bloodstream, and is essentially an indicator of neuroendocrine responsiveness than an influence on one's current sexuality.

humans (Monroe et al., 1972). Human males do not ordinarly show distinct high amplitude positive feedback response patterns (Kulin and Reiter, 1976), although considerable variation has been reported for men (Barbarino and De Marinis, 1980).

This apparently sex-dimorphic neuroendocrine response pattern has been used to explore the psychobiology of human sexuality. In the mid 1970s Doerner and colleagues (Doerner et al., 1975a, 1975b, 1976) reported that a single intravenous injection of an estrogen compound raised the circulating level of LH above initial values in homosexual but not in heterosexual men. They concluded that the positive feedback response to estrogen seen in homosexual males reflects a predominantly "female-differentiated" brain resulting from critical prenatal events, and that this "female-differentiated" brain would mediate sexual arousal to males (which they considered to be a typically female response). These authors further speculated that this LH difference in homosexual males results from insufficient CNS stimulation by androgen during prenatal differentiation, leading to an incompletely masculinized, partially "feminine" brain.

Doerner's findings (for review, see Doerner, 1980; also, see Meyer-Bahlburg, 1982, 1984) prompted other workers to re-examine neuroendocrinology related to sexual orientation. Our laboratory began a controlled and carefully considered investigation into the relationship between sexual orientation and LH response to estrogen. Initial findings confirm the presence of neuroendocrine differences related to sexual orientation. Evaluations of LH response patterns in men showed the presence of a physiological distinction between *lifelong* (since puberty) heterosexual and *lifelong* homosexual men in response to an experimental adult administration of estrogen (Gladue et al., 1984). Most, but not all, homosexual men show an LH response pattern intermediate to that of most heterosexual men and women. As such, men with a distinct homosexual orientation showed a response pattern intermediate to that of the heterosexual men and women, whereas none of the heterosexual men showed such a response pattern. Furthermore, testosterone secretion following this estrogen injection differed in men according to sexual orientation: Testosterone levels in homosexual men were significantly depressed for longer periods of time compared to testosterone levels in heterosexual men (Gladue et al., 1984). None of the men, by the way, showed a typically "female" response pattern. Responses in the women were earlier and of greater magnitude than those in the men. However, a differential response pattern was found among the homosexual men that suggests a neuroendocrine responsiveness intermediate between that of the heterosexual men and that of the women. This invites the idea that there may be physiological developmental components in the sexual orientation of some homosexual men.

Another interpretation for these neuroendocrine differences related to sexual orientation involves not the brain-pituitary directly, but indirectly, through an influence on testicular function. Recent research on some primate species suggest that differences in estrogen-induced LH responsiveness can be attributed to some hormonal factor from the testis (Steiner et al., 1978; Westfahl et al., 1984). This testicular factor (not the typical androgens testosterone or dihydrotestosterone, but possibly an unidentified protein hormone) might be responsible for such pituitary hormone response differences between heterosexual and homosexual men. As such, the difference as measured in the laboratory, might be located at the gonadal level. Unknown, of course, is how such a gonadal factor difference between homosexual and heterosexual men might originate. The possibilities for a better understanding of the relationships between brain, gonad, hormones and behavior are intriguing and likely to be an area of intense activity in the near future.

There are, of course, some *caveats* regarding psychoendocrine studies related to sexual orientation. First, and foremost, is the uncertainty, at least in humans, that LH secretion patterns are functionally correlated with the development of psychosexuality. That is, differences in LH patterns between groups of heterosexual and homosexual men may reflect hormone responsiveness causally independent of sexual differentiation. As such a causal relation between hormone responsiveness and ultimate sexual orientation should not be inferred. Unknown physiological factors in the adult may account for the differential responses of LH. Second, differences in brain response to hormone may reflect lifestyle variables (stress, drug/substance use, sexual activity levels) and not necessarily indicate any consequence of prenatal hormone involvement upon psychosexual development.

Finally, being able to demonstrate differences in neuroendocrine response related to differences in sexual orientation tells us little about the origins of sexual preferences. Nor do we have convincing data regarding the sensitivity of brain tissue to hormones related to human sexual behavior. Studies of endocrine functioning and neuroendocrine response studies of homosexual men (Doerner et al., 1976; Halbreich et al., 1978; Boyar and Aiman, 1982; Gladue et al., 1984) and in transsexuals (Goh et al., 1980; Seyler et al., 1978; Gooren et al., 1984) indicate one common feature: individuals have highly variable levels of hormone and response to a given hormone. While some argue that enhanced variability in LH and steroid levels among homosexual men may be related to abnormal prenatal hormone conditions (Halbreich et al., 1978; Boyar and Aiman, 1982), others point out that atypical (so-called "female") neuroendocrine response patterns in LH can be elicited in intact and castrated men if their blood levels of estrogen are made to mimic that of women around mid-menstrual cycle (Barbarino et al., 1982, 1983). Thus, the issue of neuroendocrine response pattern differences related to sexual orientation may be a matter of differences in hormone sensitivity. Homosexual men may differ from heterosexual men, not so much in their neuroendocrine responsiveness but in their general sensitivity to hormone. And this sensitivity difference may (or may not) be related, in part, to prenatal developmental events, and in part, to that person's genetic constitution.

The key point here is caution. We really do not know with certainty the degree or kind of hormone involvement and influence upon the development of heterosexuality or homosexuality or all of the intermediate stages of bisexuality. We, as psychobiologists, *suspect* that sexual orientation, like other elements of human behavior, has some endocrine input. But the exact timing and degree of that involvement currently eludes us. If we are to know what "being human" is all about, then we need to look further into how our biology affects ourselves, both in the adult, and in the developing fetus/infant/prepubertal child.

Prenatal Endocrine Disorders

Another line of inquiry regarding influences of biology upon psychosexual development has revolved around spontaneously occurring prenatal hormone abnormalities (intersexes or so-called "experiments of nature") in which genetic males and females have atypical endocrine exposure during prenatal development. As such, these disorders offer opportunities to consider what influences hormones may have upon sexual orientation development.

In genetic males, the number of detailed and well-controlled studies is too few to allow a full exploration of the effects of prenatal endocrine anomalies upon sexual orientation. In two studies of androgen insensitivity (wherein androgen, though present, has limited androgenic effects upon body tissues due to cellular insensitivity to the steroid), these genetic males are usually found to be heterosexual relative to their sex of rearing and resulting gender identity (Masica et al., 1971; Money and Ogunro, 1974; reviewed by Meyer-Bahlburg, 1977, 1979). Thus, if the boys were raised as boys, they saw themselves as men and had sexual interest in women; if raised as girls, and had a female gender identity, they preferred opposite sex (male) partners. The general opinion from these studies is that social learning appears powerful enough to override whatever influences occur from deficiencies in androgen prenatally. However, Diamond (1979, 1982) discussed follow-up studies of genetic males reared as girls who later develop gender identity conflict. He argues that there are natural limits to sexual identity. Within these limits social forces interact with biological influences to effect an individual's gender identity and sexual orientation.

Regarding genetic females, the most common and relevant endocrine pathology is congenital adrenal hyperplasia (CAH; formerly called adreno-genital syndrome). This condition results from an enzyme defect which shifts steroid production in the adrenal gland from cortisol to androgens and other steroids. Thus, prenatally, genetic females are exposed to considerable (and atypical) amounts of androgens. There is some controversy regarding CAH as a factor which might influence the development of sexual orientation. Early studies reported that the majority of CAH patients, given corrective endocrine treatment in infancy or early childhood, were found to be heterosexual, again pointing to a strong influence of social rearing and learning on gender identity (and sexual orientation) formation (Ehrhardt et al., 1968; Money and Ehrhardt, 1972; Money and Dalery, 1976; Money and Schwartz, 1977).

Recently, controlled follow-up studies of early-treated CAH women report increased bisexuality in experience and/or erotic imagery in subjects, although again, the majority of these CAH women were heterosexual (Money and Lewis, 1983; Schwartz and Money, 1983; Money et al., 1984). Thus, while social learning interpretations still seem most explanatory for many CAH women, one can also argue that some evidence exists in some women to support a prenatal endocrine hypothesis, particularly if one considers that the *degree* of behavioral differentiation due to androgenic exposure may be additionally influenced not just by congenital androgen levels, but by genetic differences (i.e., target cell sensitivity differences) among fetuses. The variability among the women suggests a multi-factorial approach toward understanding prenatal endocrine disorder influences upon psychosexual development.

Lastly, another syndrome, the 5-alpha-reductase deficiency, has become a point of discussion in psychosexual development. Genetic males with this syndrome have an enzyme defect and do not readily convert testosterone to the genitally masculinizing hormone dihydrotestosterone (DHT). These males are born with apparently female-like genitalia, yet begin virilizing at puberty (develop a penis and scrotal tissue) when increasing levels of testosterone override the earlier morphological consequences of the enzyme defect. It was reported that, in childhood these genetic males are reared as females and develop female gender identities, yet during puberty and adolescence establish a sexual orientation toward other females and ultimately change their gender identity to male (Imperato-McGinley et al., 1979; reviewed with a critique by Meyer-Bahlburg, 1982). Presumably these males' brains were "masculinized" *in utero* by testosterone, but not having masculinized genitalia (due to the inability to convert testosterone to the virilizing hormone DHT) concordant with brain development, they were readily reared as girls and saw themselves as such. We know few details of the cultural and social rearing inputs for these children, and even less of how researchers assessed their sexual orientation and gender identity. In addition, other methodological issues have been raised which prevent researchers from holding these reports as strong evidence for either the social-learning model, or the prenatal hormone theory of sexual orientation development. We will simply have to wait for further studies in this area.

Studies Involving Offspring of Hormone-Treated Pregnancies

During the two decades following World War II, many problem pregnancies were treated with a variety of progestins and estrogens. Since it is known from research on animals that hormone exposure during pregnancy can alter the behavioral development of the fetus, it was suspected that similar behavioral consequences might be found in children exposed *in utero* to hormone-treatments designed to assist in their gestation and delivery. Because progestins often act as anti-androgens (thus interfering with the action of androgen hormones) the hypothesis was posed that males, exposed to progestins before birth, would be *de*masculinized by this hormone treatment, and that similarly exposed female offspring would be masculinized (Meyer-Bahlburg and Ehrhardt, 1980). Several retrospective studies were conducted to explore what effects such prenatal hormone treatments may have had on gender identity development in men and women.

In a thorough study by Kester et al. (1980), prenatal exposure to progesterone compounds had no effect on sexual orientation of males when compared to control subjects. Yalom et al. (1973) and later Beral and Colwell (1981) studying males prenatally exposed to progesterone *and* the synthetic estrogen diethylstilbestrol (DES) reported no differences in sexual orientation between those males and unexposed controls. Research by Kester et al. (1980) verified these reports: prenatal exposure to either progesterone alone or in combination with DES had no significant effect on the development of sexual orientation in males.

In genetic females, prenatal *progesterone* exposure has been reported to shift behavioral development toward more typically masculine traits, such as aggressiveness (Reinisch, 1981; Reinisch and Sanders, 1984) and less feminine gender identity characteristics (Ehrhardt and Meyer-Bahlburg, 1981). Yet, thus far, no compelling evidence exists that sexual partner preference is directly influenced by prenatal progestin exposure (reviewed by Meyer-Bahlburg, 1982).

With regard to prenatal *estrogen* exposure in genetic females, some recent and curious findings have emerged. First, however, one requires a short course in developmental psychoendocrinology. One of the main findings of behavioral endocrinology in the past decade has been that there are two pathways of biochemical action upon brain organization: one an androgenic pathway, chiefly DHT, the other an estrogenic pathway which depends on circulating levels of the androgen testosterone (T) to be converted to estradiol (E) in the brain. Ordinarily estradiol is removed from the circulation by placental metabolism to the relatively ineffective steroid estrone (Slikker et al., 1982). Thus fetuses, which are ordinarily exposed to maternal estrogens during pregnancy, are not developmentally affected by typical levels of the "natural" estrogen. Testosterone exerts much of *its* effects on the brain by first being converted, in brain cells, to estradiol, an estrogen. It seems slightly paradoxical: In order for androgens to masculinize the nervous system, they must actually interact with brain cells as the hormone estrogen. And since circulating estradiol is routinely not available to the fetal brain, male and female fetuses are not ordinarily exposed to any masculinizing estrogen. Only male fetuses, manufacturing testosterone, are normally masculinized, since the testosterone produced by fetal testes gets into the brain and there is converted to estradiol. Female fetuses make no masculinizing quantities of testosterone (ordinarily; see CAH section above for exceptions) and thus develop un-masculinized.*

What has all this to do with prenatal DES exposure in genetic females? The non-steroidal synthetic estrogen DES avoids metabolic conversion and is readily taken into brain cells where it is extremely biologically potent. Animal studies found that exceedingly small quantities of DES could masculinize and defeminize the sexual behavior of females, and alter functioning of sex-dimorphic areas of primate brains (Fuller et al., 1981). The effects of DES on human sexuality are only recently being considered in experimental detail. While Hines (1981, 1982) reported no differences in marital status of DES women when compared to untreated sisters, another more detailed study found marital status differences along with other more remarkable distinctions. Ehrhardt et al. (1985) found that women prenatally exposed to DES were more likely to report more lifelong lesbian and/or bisexual erotic responsiveness than non-exposed sibling controls. These authors, in a methodologically sound study, report a high consistency of this finding across a range of different rating categories for sexual orientation, and suggest that perhaps DES exposure may have contributed somewhat to the development of sexual orientation. But, these authors also caution against an overextension of these findings, since their study is based on carefully chosen (to meet clinical criteria) pairs of subjects and untreated sisters, and is not a survey of all DES offspring. Obviously, a replication of these findings is in order.

Summary of Prenatal Hormone Theory Findings

From the evidence described above, one could probably conclude that hormonal factors *might* be implicated in the development of sexual orientation. Such hesitation is appropriate because only now psychobiologists are beginning to employ techniques and perspectives toward understanding biological influences upon psychosexuality. Recall that considerable endocrine variation occurs not only across the several studies described, but often within a given study. For example, as Gladue et al. (1984) found, not all homosexual men exhibit the same LH response pattern when their neuroendocrine system is experimentally challenged with the same quantity of estrogen. And the many studies by Ehrhardt and colleagues over the past decade show that not all CAH females exhibit tomboyish behavior as children or lesbian imagery or

*The curious notion of hormones having gender such as testosterone being a "male" steroid (androgen) and estradiol a "female" hormone (estrogen), persists, largely due to historical factors [The hormones were initially derived from extracts of testis (testosterone) or ovaries during estrus (estrogen)]. That estrogens can affect "androgenic" functions such as masculinization of brain tissue, and that androgens are responsible for development of such female structures as the clitoris causes no shortage of confusion, even among some biologists. In fact, both genders make both hormones, in differing quantities, to be sure, and with different hormonal consequences. Hopefully, with time, such generic terms as estrogen and androgen will be redefined in terms of function instead of origin, and will lose their "masculine" and "feminine" associations.

activity as adults. Not all women who were prenatally exposed to DES develop homosexual interests in adulthood. Humans are extraordinarily variable. And while psychobiologists attempt to understand the nature of such variance, one cannot expect an easy explanation. At this stage, it can be stated that, while it is unlikely that hormones *cause* or directly *determine* sexual orientation, they are probably a contributing factor.

OTHER PSYCHOBIOLOGICAL FACTORS RELATED TO SEXUAL ORIENTATION

In addition to hormone studies of sexual orientation, other avenues of inquiry have been explored in an effort to evaluate physiological reasons why some people are homosexual and others not. Chief among these non-hormonal approaches have been studies on heredity (genetics) and early onset of puberty.

Genetic Studies

Many researchers have explored the notion that homosexuality is hereditary. In 1952 Kallman reported 100% concordance for homosexuality in 37 adult, presumably monozygotic (identical) twins (Kallman, 1952): where one member of the twin pair was homosexual, so was the other. Yet these twins were not representative of the general population. They were recruited from psychiatric referrals and penal systems, presenting possible confounding influences of social factors. Other studies since then have been less conclusive. A number of case studies report monozygotic male twins to be discordant for homosexuality (one twin is gay, the other is not) (Friedman et al., 1976; Zuger, 1976; McConaghy and Blaszaznski, 1980; McCulloch, 1980). Still, there are reports of sexual orientation concordance among monozygotic male twins (Heston and Shields, 1968; Perkins, 1973). In a more recent study of the siblings of 50 homosexual men and 50 heterosexual men, significantly more (25%) of the brothers of homosexual men were also homosexual (Pillard et al., 1982). Because of these disparate findings, it would seem safe to conclude that sexual orientation is the product of multiple influences, of which heredity and genetics may be a part.

Early Onset of Puberty

Another theory of sexual orientation development combines social factors with biological. As exposed by Storms (1981) this theory of erotic development suggests that the timing of sexual maturation is critical to the development of sexual orientation. His theory takes into account sexual maturation at both social and biological levels (puberty). With the onset of puberty, sexual fantasies, imagery and activity (mostly masturbation) increase in frequency and intensity. Vague at first, most people's fantasies begin to take specific shapes as they mature. Storms argues that the development of sexual identity is shaped by erotic fantasies. Those children reaching biological puberty early (before the age of 12, for example) but still in same-gender social groups would tend to have erotic fantasies involving the same gender. The onset of heightened sexual feelings and fantasies at around 13 years or later occurs in a social scheme involving *both genders*. Sexual maturation at this age would more likely lead to heterosexuality (and presumably, bisexuality). The later one develops, the more likely one is socialized with opposite sex groupings, and the more likely one is to incorporate these persons into sexual fantasies and erotic desires.

Support for Storms' theory comes from studies in which homosexual men and women report onsets of sexual feelings before age 13, unlike heterosexual comparison groups (Goode and Huber, 1977; Saghir and Robins, 1973). Storms and Wasserman (1982) studied 97 men, and found that the time of sexual maturation was predictive of their erotic orientation. Not in support of this theory are the findings from both prospective and retrospective studies that many homosexual men report erotic orientation and so-called "femininity" at early ages, often as early as age 4 (Green, 1979, 1985; Hellman et al., 1981; Zuger, 1984), certainly well before biological puberty begins. To argue that these males were in extraordinarily early stages of puberty is to redefine the concept of puberty and push it back into fetal or early postnatal life.

What *is* appealing about Storms' theory is that it can satisfy both camps: interpretations can be made for both biological and social factors related to psychosexual development of sexual orientation. And, of course, there is the distinct possibility that sexual orientation across the entire spectrum from exclusive heterosexuality to exclusive homosexuality, is shaped and influenced in differing degrees through a variety of means.

SUMMARY: IS SEXUAL ORIENTATION BIOLOGICALLY DETERMINED

In their historic and monumental *Sexual Behavior in the Human Male*, Kinsey and colleagues considered factors which might account for homosexual activity and suggested guidelines for such explanations. Since sexual orientation differences exist across a continuum (and not merely an "all-or-none" situation), biological explanations must consider this variance.

> *Attempts to identify the biologic bases of homosexual activity, must take into account the large number of males who have demonstrated their capacity to respond to stimuli provided by other persons of the same sex. It must also be taken into account that many males combine in their single histories, and very often in exactly the same period of time, or even simultaneously in the same moment, reactions to both heterosexual and homosexual stimuli. . . . It must be shown that fluctua-*

tions in preferences for female or male partners are related to fluctuations in the hormones, the genes, or other biologic factors which are assumed to be operating. It must be shown that there is a definite correlation between the degree in which the biological factor operates, and the degree of the heterosexual-homosexual balance in the history of each individual. (Kinsey et al., 1948, pp. 660-661).

Kinsey couldn't know, of course, that twenty years hence, neural and other biological distinctions would be found to correlate to sexual behavior and partner preferences. Since Kinsey's time, advances in the field of psychobiology have brought forth knowledge about hormonal and genetic influences on the development of the nervous system and behavior. While no definitive set of studies have met Kinsey's strict criteria for identifying biological bases of homosexuality or heterosexuality, an emerging body of evidence suggests that the development of sexual orientation is not without some biological inputs. We cannot know now what might be revealed in the next two decades of sexuality research, any more than Kinsey and colleagues could have anticipated the dramatic surge of research activity in the realm of psychoendocrinology. Yet, the several lines of evidence mentioned earlier indicate that the diversity of human sexuality is not solely a product of cultural socialization or child-rearing practices. Few scientists hold to the simplistic notion that hormone levels *per se* are causal factors for homosexuality. Rather, a new cluster of research findings suggests that the workings of biology upon behavior are more subtle, interactive and not necessarily so singly determining.

As described above, the dynamic interactions of brain tissue, gonads and hormones appear to offer better opportunities to understand the relationships of biology and psychosexual development. Theories of prenatal hormone influences warrant additional consideration since studies on daughters of women treated with DES during gestation indicate that these daughters are more likely to exhibit lesbian imagery and interests as adults (Ehrhardt et al., 1985). Possible genetic factors cannot be ignored given findings of a familial relationship to sexual orientation (Pillard et al., 1982; personal communication). And, as Storms suggests, sexual orientation development may be related to atypical pubertal development, another area where biological factors are involved.

It should be noted that there may be limitations to biological explanations of psychosexual development. Men and women may arrive at an adult sexual orientation through different routes. Indeed, the hormonal response variance among homosexual men in all studies to date indicates that there is no obvious, simple, and perfect biological correlate for sexual orientation. Homosexuality, like heterosexuality may not be readily understood or explained through theories of singular mechanisms or origins. For some men, the path to a particular sexual identity and orientation may involve biological factors. Efforts to explain sexual orientation based upon social-learning theories (Bell et al., 1981) are no more convincing than are simplistic genetic or hormonal theories. Like much of human behavior, a combination of biological and psychosocial factors are most likely involved in the development of sexuality.

Whatever factors (biological, sociological, or psychological) are considered as influential in the development of sexual orientation, note that the basic phenomenon to be explained is an individual's desire and preference for a partner of one's sex, or for a partner of the opposite sex, or a partner of either sex. In this context, preference is not a changeable whim based on passing interests, but a deep yearning for sexual satisfaction with a particular gender partner. Kinsey argued that this is part of the problem of choices in general: "A choice of a partner in a sexual relation becomes more significant only because society demands that there be a particular choice in this matter, and does not so often dictate one's choice of food or of clothing" (Kinsey et al., 1948, p. 661). The factors involved in the development of object choice and satisfaction are yet to be determined. However, considerable evidence regarding behavioral development invites participation of at least some biological factors and perspectives.

Finally, it was the contention of Kinsey et al. that "homosexuality has been a significant part of human sexual activity ever since the dawn of history, primarily because it is an expression of capacities that are basic in the human animal" (p. 666). From the vantage point of current psychobiological research on human sexuality and sexual orientation development, there is reason to agree with that statement.

REFERENCES

Aiman, J. and Boyar, R. (1982). Testicular function in transsexual men. *Arch. Sex. Behav.*, 11:171–179.

Baker, S. W. (1980). Psychosexual differentiation in the human. *Biol. Reprod.* 22:61–72.

Barbarino, A. and De Marinis, L. (1980). Estrogen induction of luteinizing hormone release in castrated adult males. *J. Clin. Endo. Metab.* 51:280–286.

Barbarino, A., De Marinis, L., Mancini, A., Giustacchini, M. and Alcini, A. E. (1982). Biphasic effect of estradiol on luteinizing hormone response to gonadotropin-releasing hormone in castrated men. *Metabolism*, 31:755–758.

Barbarino, A., De Marinis, L. and Mancini, A. (1983). Estradiol modulation of basal and gonadotropin-releasing hormone-induced gonadotropin release in intact and castrated men. *Neuroendocrinology*, 36:105–111.

Baum, M. J. (1979). Differentiation of coital behavior in mammals: A comparative analysis. *Neurosci. Biobehav. Rev.* 3:265–284.

Beach, F. A. (1979). Animal models for human sexuality. In *Sex, hormones and behaviour,* Ciba Foundation Symposium (Vol. 62), Excerpta Medica, NY, 113–143.

Bell, A. P. (1975). The homosexual as patient. In *Human sexuality: A health practitioner's text* (Ed. R. Green). Baltimore: Williams and Wilkins. pp. 55–74.

Bell, A. P. and Weinberg, M. S. (1978). *Homosexualities: A study of diversity among men and women.* New York: Simon and Schuster.

Bell, A. P., Weinberg, M. S. and Hammersmith, S. K. (1981). *Sexual preference: Its development in men and women.* Bloomington, IN: Indiana University Press.

Beral, V. and Colwell L. (1981). Randomised trial of high doses of stilboestrol and ethinesterone therapy in pregnancy: Long-term follow up of the children. *J. Epidemiol. Community Health,* 35:155–160.

Brodie, H. K. H., Gartrell, N., Doering, C. H., and Rhue, T. (1974). Plasma testosterone levels in heterosexual and homosexual men. *Am. J. Psychiatry,* 131:82–83.

Clemens, L. G. and Gladue, B. A. (1978). Neuroendocrine control of adult sexual behavior. In: *Review of neuroscience,* 4 (Ed. D. M. Schneider). New York: Raven Press. pp. 73–104.

Diamond, M. (1979). Sexual identity and sex roles. In: *The frontiers of sex research* (Ed. V. Bullough). Buffalo, NY: Prometheus. pp. 33–56.

Diamond, M. (1982). Sexual identity, monozygotic twins reared in discordant roles and a BBC follow-up. *Arch. Sex. Behav.,* 11:181–186.

Doerner, G. (1976). *Hormones and brain differentiation.* Amsterdam: Elsevier.

Doerner, G. (1983). Hormone-dependent brain development. *Psychoneuroendocrinol.* 8:205–212.

Doerner, G., Rohde, W., Stahl, F., Krell, L., and Masius, W. G. (1975). A neuroendocrine predisposition for homosexuality in men. *Arch. Sex Behav.* 4:1–8.

Doerner, G., Rohde, W., and Schnorr, D. (1975). Evocability of a slight positive oestrogen feedback action on LH secretion in castrated and oestrogen-primed men. *Endokrinologie,* 66:373–376.

Doerner, G., Rohde, W., Siedel, K., Haas, W., and Schott, G. (1976). On the evocability of a positive estrogen feedback action on LH secretion in transsexual men and women. *Endokrinologie,* 67:20–25.

Doerner, G., Schenk, B., Schmiedel, B. and Ahrens, L. (1983). Stressful events in prenatal life of bi- and homosexual men. *Exp. Clin. Endocrinol.,* 81:83–87.

Downey, J., Becker, J. V., Ehrhardt, A. A., Schiffman, M., Abel, G. G. and Dyenfurth, I. (1982). Behavioral, psychophysiological, and hormonal correlates in lesbian and heterosexual women. In: *Abstracts, International Academy of Sex Research,* Copenhagen, Denmark.

Ehrhardt, A. A., Evers, K. and Money J. (1968). Influence of androgen and some aspects of sexually dimorphic behavior in women with the late-treated andrenogenital syndrome. *Johns Hopkins Med. J.,* 123:115–122.

Ehrhardt, A. A., Grisanti, G. C. and Meyer-Bahlburg, H. F. L. (1977). Prenatal exposure to medroxyprogesterone acetate (MPA) in girls. *Psychoneuroendocrinol.*, 2:391–398.

Ehrhardt, A. A. and Meyer-Bahlburg, H. F. L. (1979). Prenatal sex hormones and the developing brain: Effects on psychosexual differentiation and cognitive function. *Ann. Rev. Med.* 30:417–430.

Ehrhardt, A. A. and Meyer-Bahlburg, H. F. L. (1981). Effects of prenatal sex hormones on gender-related behavior. *Science*, 211:1312–1318.

Ehrhardt, A. A., Meyer-Bahlburg, H. F. L., Feldman, J. F. and Ince, S. E. (1984). Sex-dimorphic behavior subsequent to prenatal exposure to exogenous progestogens and estrogens. *Archives Sexual Behav.*, 13:457–477.

Ehrhardt, A. A., Meyer-Bahlburg, H. F. L., Rosen, L. R., Feldman, J. F., Veridiano, N. P., Zimmerman, I. and McEwen, B. S. (1985). Sexual orientation after prenatal exposure to exogenous estrogen. *Arch. Sex. Behav.* 14:57–78.

Feder, H. H. (1982). Perinatal hormones and their role in the development of sexually dimorphic behaviors. In: *Neuroendocrinology of Reproduction* (Ed. N. T. Adler). New York: Plenum Press, pp. 127–158.

Friedman, R. C., Wollensen, F., and Tendler, R. (1976). Psychological development and blood levels of sex steroids in male identical twins of divergent sexual orientation. *J. Nervous and Mental Disease*, 163:282–288.

Friedman, R. C., Dyrenfurth, I., Linkie, D., Tendler, R., and Fleiss, J. L. (1977). Hormones and sexual orientation in men. *Am. J. Psychiatry*, 134:571–572.

Fuller, G. B., Yates, D. E., Helton, E. D., and Hobson, W. C. (1981). Diethylstilbestrol reversal of gonadotropin patterns in infant rhesus monkeys. *J. Steroid Biochem.*, 15:497–500.

Fulmer, G. P. (1973). Testosterone levels and female-to-male transsexualism. *Arch. Sex. Behav.*, 2:399–400.

Gartrell, N. K., Loriaux, D. L. and Chase, T. N. (1977). Plasma testosterone in homosexual and heterosexual women. *Am. J. Psychiatry*, 134:1117–1119.

Gladue, B. A., Green, R. and Hellman, R. E. (1984). Neuroendocrine response to estrogen and sexual orientation. *Science*, 225:1496–1499.

Goh, H. H., Chew, P. C. T., Karim, S. M. M. and Ratnam, M. (1980). Control of gonadotropin secretion by steroid hormones in castrated male transsexuals. I. Effects of oestradiol infusion on plasma levels of follicle-stimulating hormone and luteinizing hormone. *Clin. Endo.*, 12:165–175.

Goode, E. and Huber, L. (1977). Sexual correlates of homosexual experience: An exploratory study of college women. *J. Sex Research*, 13:12–21.

Gooren, L. J. G., Rao, B. R., van Kessel, H. and Harmsen-Louman, W. (1984). Estrogen positive feedback on LH secretion in transsexuality. *Psychoneuroendocrinol.*, 9:249–259.

Gorski, R. A. (1971). Gonadal hormones and the perinatal development of neuroendocrine function. In: *Frontiers in neuroendocrinology*, (Eds. L.

Martini and W. F. Ganong). New York: Oxford Univ. Press. pp. 237–290.

Gorski, R. A. (1984). Critical role for the medial preoptic area in the sexual differentiation of the brain. In: *Progress in brain research,* Vol. 61. New York: Elsevier Press.

Green, R. (1975). *Sexual identity conflict in children and adults.* New York: Basic Books, Baltimore: Penguin.

Green, R. (1979). Childhood cross-gender behavior and subsequent sexual preference. *Amer. J. Psychiatry,* 136:106–108.

Green, R. (1980). Taking a sexual history. In: *Human sexuality: A health practitioner's text,* 2nd Ed. Baltimore: Williams and Wilkins.

Green, R. (1985). Gender identity in childhood and later sexual orientation: Follow-up of 78 males. *Amer. J. Psychiatry* 142:339–342.

Griffiths, P. D., Merry, J., Browning, M. C. K., Eisinger, A. J., Huntsman, R. G., Lord, E. J. A., Polani, P. E., Tanner, J. M. and Whitehouse, R. H. (1974). Homosexual women: An endocrine and physiological study. *J. Endocrinol.,* 63:549–556.

Halbreich, U., Segal, S. and Chowers, I. (1978). Day-to-day variations in serum levels of follicle-stimulating hormone and luteinizing hormone in homosexual males. *Biol. Psychiatry,* 13:541–549.

Harris, G. W. (1970). Hormonal differentiation of the developing nervous system with respect to patterns of endocrine function. *Philos. Trans. Roy. Soc. London. (Biol. Sci.),* 259:165.

Hellman, R. E., Green, R., Gray, J. L. and Williams, K. (1981). Childhood sexual identity, childhood religiosity and "homophobia" as influences on the development of transsexualism, homosexuality, and heterosexuality. *Arch. Gen. Psychiatry,* 38:910–915.

Heston, L. L. and Shields, J. (1968). Homosexuality in twins. *Archives General Psychiatry,* 18:108–113.

Hines, M. (1981). *Prenatal diethylstilbestrol (DES) exposure, human sexually dimorphic behavior and cerebral lateralization,* Ph.D. dissertation, University of California, Los Angeles. Dissertation Abstracts International, 42: 423B (University Microfilms 81-13858).

Hines, M. (1982). Prenatal gonadal hormones and sex differences in human behavior. *Psychol. Bull.,* 92:56–80.

Imperato-McGinley, J., Peterson, R. E., Gautier, T. and Sturla, E. (1979). Androgens and the evolution of male gender identity among male pseudohermaphroditism with 5-alpha-reductase deficiency. *New Engl. J. Med.* 300:1233–1237.

Jones, J. R. and Saminy, J. (1973). Plasma testosterone levels and female transsexualism. *Arch. Sex. Behav.,* 2:251–256.

Kallman, F. J. (1952). A comparative twin study on the genetic aspects of male homosexuality. *J. Nerv. Ment. Dis.,* 115:283–298.

Karsch, F. J., Dierschke, D. J. and Knobil, E. (1973). Sexual differentiation of pituitary function: Apparent difference between primates and rodents. *Science,* 179:484–486.

Kester, P., Green, R., Finch, S. J. and Williams, K. (1980). Prenatal 'female hormone' administration and psychosexual development in human males. *Psychoneuroendocrinol.*, 5:269–285.

Kinsey, A. C., Pomeroy, W. B. and Martin, C. E. (1948). *Sexual behavior in the human male.* Philadelphia: W. B. Saunders, pp. 606–651.

Kinsey, A. C., Pomeroy, W. B., Martin, C. E. and Gebhard, P. H. (1953). *Sexual behavior in the human female.* Philadelphia: W. B. Saunders, pp. 446–501.

Knobil, E. (1980). The neuroendocrine control of the menstrual cycle. *Rec. Prog. Horm. Res.* 36:53–88.

Kolodny, R. C., Masters, W. H., Hendryx, J. and Toro, G. (1971). Plasma testosterone and semen analysis in male homosexuals. *New Engl. J. Med.* 285:1170–1174.

Kolodny, R. C., Masters, W. H. and Johnson, V. E. (1979). *Textbook of sexual medicine.* Boston: Little, Brown.

Krey, L. C. (1984). Neuronal and endocrine mechanisms involved in the control of gonadotropin secretion. In: *Neuroendocrinology and psychiatric disorder.* (Ed. G. M. Brown, S. H. Koslow, and S. Reichlin). New York: Raven Press. pp. 325–338.

Kulin, H. E. and Reiter, E. O. (1976). Gonadotropin and testosterone measurements after estrogen administration to adult men, prepubertal and pubertal boys and men with hypogonadotropism: Evidence for maturation of positive feedback in the male. *Pediatric Res.* 10:46–51.

Livingstone, I. R., Sagel, J., Distiller, L. A., Morley, J. and Katz, M. (1978). The effect of luteinizing hormone releasing hormone (LRH) on pituitary gonadotropins in male homosexuals. *Horm. Metab. Res.,* 10:248–249.

Loraine, J. A., Adamopoulos, D. A., Kirkham, K. E., Ismail, A. A. A. and Dove, G. A. (1971). Patterns of hormone excretion in male and female homosexuals. *Nature,* 234:552–555.

Loriaux, D. L. L., Vigersky, R. A., Marynick, S. P., Janick, J. J. and Sherons, R. (1977). Androgen and estrogen effects in the regulation of LH in man. In: *The testis in normal and infertile men,* (Eds. P. Troen and H. R. Nankin). New York: Raven Press. pp. 213–225.

MacCulloch, M. J. and Waddington, J. L. (1981). Neuroendocrine mechanisms and the etiology of male and female homosexuality. *Brit. J. Psychiatry,* 139:341–345.

Manosevitz, M. (1972). The development of male homosexuality. *J. Sex Research,* 8:31–40.

Masica, D. N., Money, J. and Ehrhardt, A. A. (1971). Fetal feminization and female gender identity in the testicular feminizing syndrome of androgen insensitivity. *Arch. Sex. Behav.,* 1:131–142.

Matsumoto, A. M. and Bremner, W. J. (1984). Modulation of pulsatile gonadotropin secretion by testosterone in man. *J. Clin. Endo. Metab.* 58:609–614.

McConaghy, N. and Armstrong, M. S. (1983). Sexual orientation and consistency of sexual identity. *Archives Sexual Behavior,* 12:317–328.

McConaghy, N. and Blaszczinski, A. (1980). A pair of monozygotic twins discordant for homosexuality: Sex-dimorphic behavior and penile volume responses. *Archives Sexual Behavior*, 9:123–133.

McCulloch, M. (1980). Biological aspects of homosexuality. *J. Medical Ethics*, 6:133–138.

McEwen, B. S. (1983). Gonadal steroid influences on brain development and sexual differentiation. In: *Reproductive Physiology IV* (International Review of Physiology), Vol. 27 (Ed. R. O. Greep). Baltimore: University Park Press.

Meyer, W. J. III, Finkelstein, J. W., Stewart, C. A., Webb, A., Smith, E. R., Payer, A. F. and Walker, P. A. (1981). Physical and hormonal evaluation of transsexual patients during hormonal therapy. *Arch. Sex. Behavior*, 10: 347–356.

Meyer-Bahlburg, H. F. L. (1977). Sex hormones and male homosexuality in comparative perspective. *Arch. Sex. Behavior*, 6:293–325.

Meyer-Bahlburg, H. F. L. (1979). Sex hormones and female homosexuality: A critical examination. *Arch. Sex. Behavior*, 8:101–119.

Meyer-Bahlburg, H. F. L. (1982). Hormones and psychosexual differentiation: Implications for the management of intersexuality, homosexuality and transsexuality. *Clin. Endo. Metab.*, 11:681–701.

Meyer-Bahlburg, H. F. L. (1984). Psychoendocrine research on sexual orientation. Current status and future options. In: *Progress in Brain Research, Sex Differences in the Brain*, Vol. 61. New York: Elsevier Press. pp. 375–398.

Money, J. and Dalery, J. (1976). Iatrogenic homosexuality: Gender identity in seven 46, XX chromosomal females with hyperadrenocortical hermaphroditism born with a penis, three reared as boys, four reared as girls. *J. Homosexuality*, 1:357–371.

Money, J. and Lewis, V. (1982). Homosexual/heterosexual status in boys at puberty: Idiopathic adolescent gynecomastia and congenital virilizing adrenocorticism compared. *Psychoneuroendocrinol.*, 7:339–346.

Money, J. and Ogunro, C. (1974). Behavioral sexology: Ten cases of genetic male intersexuality with impaired prenatal pubertal androgenization. *Arch. Sex. Behav.*, 3:181–205.

Money, J., Schwartz, M. and Lewis, V. G. (1984). Adult erotosexual status and fetal hormonal masculinization and demasculinization: 46, XX congenital virilizing adrenal hyperplasia (CVAH) and 46, XY androgen insensitivity syndrome (AIS) compared. *Psychoneuroendocrinology*, 9:405–414.

Monroe, S. E., Jaffe, R. B., and Midgley, A. R. Jr. (1972). Regulation of human gonadotropins. XII. Increase in serum gonadotropins in response to estradiol. *J. Clin. Endocrinol.*, 34:342.

Newmark, S. R., Rose, L. I., Todd, R., Birk, L. and Naftolin, F. (1979). Gonadotropin, estradiol, testosterone profiles in homosexual men. *Amer. J. Psychiatry*, 136:767–771.

Perkins, M. W. (1973). Homosexuality in female monozygotic twins. *Behavior Genetics*, 3:387–388.

Pillard, R. C., Rose, R. M. and Sherwood, M. (1974). Plasma testosterone levels in homosexual men. *Arch. Sex. Behav.*, 3:453–458.

Pillard, R. C. Poumadere, J. and Caretta, R. A. (1982). A family study of sexual orientation. *Archives Sexual Behav.*, 11:511–520.

Purifoy, F. E. and Koopmans, L. H. (1980). Androstenedione, testosterone, and free testosterone concentrations in women of various occupations. *Social Biology*, 26:179–188.

Reinisch, J. M. (1983). Influence of early exposure to steroid hormones on behavioral development. In: *Development in adolescence: Psychological, social and biological aspects* (Eds. Everaed, W., Hindley, C. B., Bot, A., and van der Werff ten Bosch, J. J.). Boston: Martinus Nijhoff.

Reinisch, J. M. and Sanders, S. A. (1984). Prenatal gonadal steroidal influences on gender-related behavior. In: *Progress in brain research*, Vol. 61. New York: Elsevier Press. pp. 407–416.

Saghir, M. T. and Robins, E. (1973). *Male and female homosexuality*. Baltimore: Williams and Wilkins.

Sanders, R. M., Bain, J. and Langevin, R. (1984). Peripheral sex hormones, homosexuality, and gender identity. In: *Erotic preference, gender identity, and aggression in men* (Ed. R. Langevin). Hillsdale, NJ: Erlbaum. pp. 227–247.

Schwartz, M. F. and Money, J. (1983). Dating, romance and sexuality in young adult adrenogenital females. *Neuroendo. Lett.*, 5:132.

Seyler, L. E., Canalis, E., Spare, S. and Reichlin, S. (1978). Abnormal gonadotropin secretory responses to LRH in transsexual women after diethylstilbestrol priming. *J. Clin. Endo. Metab.*, 47:176–183.

Sipova, I. and Starka, L. (1977). Plasma testosterone values in transsexual women. *Arch. Sex. Behav.*, 6:477–481.

Slikker, W., Jr., Hill, D. E. and Young, J. F. (1982). Comparison of the transplacental pharmacokinetics of 17-Beta-estradiol and diethylstilbestrol in the subhuman primate. *J. Pharmacol. Exp. Ther.*, 221:173–182.

Starka, L., Sipova, I. and Hynic, J. (1975). Plasma testosterone in male transsexuals and homosexuals. *J. Sex. Research*, 11:134–138.

Storms, M. D. (1981). A theory of erotic orientation development. *Psychol. Rev.*, 88:340–353.

Storms, M. D. and Wasserman, E. (1982). *Toward better theories of sexual orientation*. Paper presented at the annual meeting of American Psychological Association, Washington, D.C.

Tourney, G. and Hatfield, L. M. (1973). Androgen metabolism in schizophrenics, homosexuals, and normal controls. *Biol. Psychiatry*, 6:23–26.

Van Look, P. F. A., Hunter, W. M., Corker, C. S. and Baird, D. T. (1977). Failure of positive feedback in normal men and subjects with testicular feminization. *Clin. Endo.*, 7:353–366.

Yalom, I. D., Green, R., and Fisk, N. (1973). Prenatal exposure to female hormones. *Arch. Gen. Psychiatry*, 28:554–561.

Yamada, T., Dierschke, D. J., Hotchkiss, J., Bhattacharya, A. N., Surve, A. H. and Knobil, E. (1971). Estrogen induction of LH release in the rhesus monkey. *Endocrinology*, 89: 1034.

Young, J. R. and Jaffe, R. B. (1976). Strength-duration characteristics of estrogen effects on gonadotropin response to gonadotropin-releasing hormone in women. II. Effects of varying concentrations of estradiol. *J. Clin. Endo. Metab.*, 42:432–442.

Zuger, B. (1976). Monozygotic twins discordant for homosexuality. *Compr. Psychiatry* 17:661–679.

Zuger, B. (1984). Early effeminate behavior in boys: Outcome and significance for homosexuality. *J. Nerv. Ment. Dis.*, 172:90–97.

NOTES ADDED IN PROOF

Additional evidence suggesting biological influences in the development of sexual orientation has appeared while this manuscript was in process. Pillard and Weinrich ("Evidence of familial nature of male homosexuality," *Archives of General Psychiatry* 43:808–812, 1986) report a significant familial component to male but not female homosexuality and that this component no doubt represents a combination of environmental and genetic factors. Continuing evidence for neuroendocrine factors associated with sexual differentiation comes from two reports by Kula and colleagues ("Changes in gonadotropin regulation in both behavioral and phenotypic disturbances of sexual differentiation in men," *Psychoneuroendocrinology* 11:61–67 (1986), and "A nonspecific disturbance of the gonadostat in women with transsexualism and isolated hypergonadotropism in the male-to-female disturbance of gender identity," *Experimental and Clinical Endocrinology* 87:8–14 (1986). However, the lack of an exact and explanatory relationship between neuroendocrine response, gonadal function, and sexual orientation has been noted by Gooren ("The neuroendocrine response of luteinizing hormone to estrogen administration in heterosexual, homosexual, and transsexual subjects," *J. Clin. Endo. Metab.* 63:583–588). Clearly, the field of biological factors associated with psychosexual development continues to be an exciting and controversial one. Given the interest and activity of researchers in this area, we shall know more soon.

8

GENDER ROLE

Ihsan Al-Issa

Gender role refers to social expectations about how males and females should behave. It has served as a model for mental health in general and for homosexuality in particular in terms of its stereotyped psychological correlates which prescribe personality characteristics and normative patterns of interactions between males and females. Such personality characteristics and modes of interaction have been labeled either masculine or feminine (Maffeo, 1982). For example, while males are expected to be aggressive, independent, dominant and active, women are believed to show the opposite characteristics. Deviation from gender role expectations is traditionally considered abnormal (Al-Issa, 1980; Chesler, 1972).

In a discussion of gender role and its relationship to homosexuality or other sexual variations, it is important to distinguish between the concepts of gender role and gender identity. Whereas gender role is related to personality *characteristics* and *behavior,* gender identity reflects a *conviction* about, and acceptance of, being biologically a male or a female. Homosexual behavior is related to deviation from gender role or social expectations about normal sexual orientation and behavior; that is, having sexual relationships with members of the opposite sex. However, there is no gender identity disorder involved in homosexuality; the identity of homosexuals is compatible with their anatomy. Cross-dressing in transvestism also involves deviation from gender roles, but, again, the gender identity of the transvestite usually remains intact.

There has been much research dealing with prenatal and postnatal hormonal abnormalities and sexually dimorphic behavior including sexual orientation. Most of the evidence in support of the influence of prenatal hormones is derived from animal experiments. However, studies of the relationship between circulating levels of hormones in adulthood and sexually dimorphic behavior is inconsistent. The biological perspective has been reviewed by Al-Issa (1982). This chapter deals with the social and cultural aspects of gender roles and homosexuality. A major theoretical and research issue in this area is the tendency to associate homosexuality with gender role reversal which implies adopting the role of members of the opposite sex. First we discuss this general hypothesis of gender role reversal. Second, we deal with gender role reversal in homosexual relationship. Third, we cover the relationship between gender role reversal and attitudes toward homosexuality. Fourth, we deal with research relating gender role reversal to child-parent relationship. Finally, we explain the association between gender role reversal and psychopathology.

THE GENDER ROLE REVERSAL HYPOTHESIS IN HOMOSEXUALITY

One popular belief about the homosexual woman is that she is aggressive, competitive and masculine in physical appearance and dress. She is a woman who wants to be a man, smoke a cigar and play football. The stereotype of the homosexual male is the "limp-wristed faggot" who may work as an interior decorator, a hairdresser, or a ballet dancer. It is therefore not surprising that the homosexual woman has been described as a seductive and aggressive female who combines active homosexuality and transvestism (cross-dressing).

Many researchers have attempted to relate male homosexuality to femininity and female homosexuality to masculinity in both childhood and adulthood. Saghir and Robins (1971) carried out interviews with 89 male and 57 female homosexuals. In contrast to heterosexuals, homosexual male subjects avoided rough games, preferred girl mates and feminine interests. The girls had mainly boy playmates and were interested in sports rather than in dolls and domestic work. Evans (1969) found that male homosexuals were frail, clumsy, avoided athletics and fights and preferred to play with girls. Early feminine tendencies in male homosexuals are also found by Stephan (1973). In another study, Saghir and Robins (1973) found that about two-thirds of adult homosexuals reported being teased for effeminate appearance and behavior during adolescence.

Heilbrun and Thompson (1977), using the masculinity-femininity scale items of the Adjective Check List (Gough & Heilbrun, 1965) reported that homosexual females were significantly more masculine than heterosexual females. Whitam (1977) administered questionnaires to 206 male homosexuals and 78 male heterosexuals. The study revealed the following "childhood indicators" of later adult homosexuality: interest in dolls; cross-dressing; being regarded by other boys as a sissy and sexual interest in other boys rather than girls in childhood sex play. These studies are retrospective and homosexual persons may be more willing to admit such childhood behavior. However, a follow-up study by Zuger (1984) seems to support the gender role reversal hypothesis. In a follow-up of 55 boys with early effeminate behavior it was found that 63.6 percent of the group showed homosexuality as compared with 5.5 who manifested heterosexuality (the outcome of the remaining subject was uncertain) (Zuger, 1984).

Oldham et al. (1982) used the Bem Sex Role Inventory (BSRI) to compare a homosexual female sample with a group of college women. The BSRI was developed to assess psychological androgyny through the measurement of masculinity and femininity which are conceived as independent constructs rather than as opposite poles of a single dimension of personality (Bem, 1974). It was found that homosexual women scored higher on the Bem masculinity scale than did a heterosexual control group, a result consistent with previous research. However, there was no difference between the two groups on the femininity scale. It appears that homosexual women may adopt desirable masculine characteristics and preference for sexual relationship with other females, but, at the same time, maintain feminine characteristics.

Stoller (1978) pointed out that since adult homosexuality in males is associated with femininity, the earlier and greater the femininity, the more likely it will be resistant to "treatment." He suggested that "treatment" should begin as early as possible and should include both parents. Stoller observed that while the mother should encourage the boy to separate from her, the father should present an adequate model for the child. Liljestrand et al. (1978) used data from interviews with 24 clients and 16 therapists on how issues of gender-role stereotyping and sexual orientation arose and were dealt with in therapy. She found that there is a trend toward more positive outcomes when client and therapist were of the same sex. Similarly, the sexual orientation of client and therapist is related to positive psychotherapeutic outcomes.

Hooker (1976) pointed out that the masculinity of the lesbian and the femininity of the homosexual male are by no means universal. Whereas some male homosexuals are effeminate in appearance and behavior, gestures and posture, others seem to be masculine. Physical appearance does not seem to bear relationship to sexual preference. The masculine and feminine appearance of the homosexual is not related to the preferred homosexual behavior (Hooker, 1976).

GENDER ROLE REVERSAL
AND HOMOSEXUAL RELATIONSHIP

One stereotype of homosexual couples is that they adopt the same husband-wife (butch-femme) relationship as heterosexual married couples. For example, a lesbian relationship described by Rubenstein (1964) in the case of N is quite typical. N was a young girl of average feminine appearance, but from the age of 10 onward, she had shown a strong desire to behave in a masculine manner, cutting her hair short and wearing masculine clothing. This tendency was encouraged by an older girlfriend of a domineering personality to whom she was very attached and was ready to submit. She also showed preference for boys' games throughout her childhood. From puberty on she had had love affairs with girls about her own age with whom she insisted on taking the active role. She liked her partners to be feminine and she enjoyed stimulating them by manual masturbation. She always developed very tender feelings for her friends and felt depressed when they eventually left her for boyfriends.

The presumed roles played by homosexuals may be seen in the psychiatric classification of homosexuals into the passive and active types. The passive homosexual takes the female role in sexual contact, while the active homosexual takes the masculine role. Although homosexuality used to be considered an abnormal behavior by psychiatrists, the passive homosexual male and active homosexual female were considered more abnormal than the active homosexual male and the passive homosexual female. The homosexual was considered more abnormal when she or he showed gender role reversal by taking the role of the opposite sex in the sexual relationship (Buss, 1966). Recent research has shown that there is no clear-cut classification of active and passive homosexuals. Homosexual couples alternate between these two roles (Saghir & Robins, 1969; Saghir et al., 1969).

Abse (1974) noted that the role played by the homosexual female couple may take various forms. It may sometimes reflect the mother-daughter relationship and sexual intercourse itself may emphasize all those facets of lovemaking concerned with tenderness, including gentle caresses and endearments. At other times there is a greater emphasis on playing a male role by the dominant partner (the butch), while the more passive partner (the femme or fem) responds as "his" wife. Also, tribadism (opposition and friction of the female genitals) occurs as one woman lies on top of the other in order to simulate coitus. Some lesbians may freely exchange roles as the "male" player may be left unsatisfied unless there is role reversal. The butch may maintain the illusion of masculinity by the manner of dress, short haircut, absence of makeup or the assumption of the male's economic role. The butch may also initiate heterosexual intercourse by wearing a dildo (artificial penis) sometimes with a vibrating, electically powered rubber tip. Except for the butch, lesbians are undistinguishable from other females in physique, dress or mannerisms.

More recent studies on lesbians and gay men report patterns of behavior in their relationships that resemble conventional gender roles, even though they hardly resemble the stereotype of exaggerated role-playing of the butch-femme relationships attributed to homosexual couples. Indeed, a study by Cardell, Finn and Marecek (1981) suggests that traditional gender roles may be less common in lesbian and gay male couples than in heterosexual couples. However, the evidence that gender roles can occur even in relationships in which both partners belong to the same sex needs some explanation (Marecek, Finn & Cardell, 1983). One possible factor to explain gender role playing in couples is that individuals internalize heterosexual models of role playing in intimate relationship and this cultural learning may be brought to homosexual relationship. Such cultural models are represented in literature, mass media, myth, and even in the Bible. Observation of parent relationships in childhood provides an excellent model for identification and initiation (Marecek et al., 1982).

Also specific factors may play a part in the allocation of roles in the relationship between lesbian and gay male couples. One factor in role allocation involves pragmatic conditions (income disparity, skill differences, work schedules) which facilitate the use of internalized gender role norms. First, pragmatic conditions may lead one partner to assume certain tasks and responsibilities in a relationship. Additional behavior which is part of gender role is then assumed by the same partner. For example, work schedule may lead one partner to prepare dinner, which is part of the feminine role. Although this initial assignment of cooking may not have been the result of gender role division, assuming other feminine tasks by the same partner (housework, decorating, and purchasing house supplies) may be defined as the female role in a homosexual relationship. Finally, since the masculine role is more valued than the feminine role, it is possible that the more powerful (more dominant) member of a couple would assume such a role. Assuming the masculine role may be facilitated by differences in gender identity among couples. If one of the couple, for example, feels more masculine than the other, he or she may tend to adopt a masculine role in the homosexual relationship (Marecek et al., 1982).

Martin and Lyon (1972) presented similar arguments to explain the relationship among homosexual couples. They noted that the butch-femme idea came about because it is an advantage to be a man. Some lesbians who are convinced that they are more masculine than feminine tend to equate masculinity with aggression, power and superiority and femininity with passivity, inferiority and softness. They are following social stereotypes of equating femininity with inferiority. Other lesbians may learn early that if one is sexually attracted to a woman, one should play the masculine role; that is, getting yourself "a wife." They find that "heterosexual marriage is the only available and accepted model for women setting up housekeeping." Another reason for going through the "butch" stage is for identification. "If you look like any other woman on the street, how in the world are you going to find other lesbians, or, how are they going to find you? Thus stereotyping oneself may serve a function." Martin and Lyon (1972) describe situations in which the femmes insist that their butches wear only male clothing and that they appear and act as nearly like the stereotyped male as possible. However, most of these femmes have been divorced more than once; they have been so badly treated by men that they cannot bear the idea of remarrying.

Finally, sociocultural expectations may play some part in homosexual relationship. A study by Carrier (1976) of male homosexuals in Mexico revealed that sharp dichotomization of male and female gender role is associated with the belief that effeminate males generally prefer to play the female role than the male role. Effeminacy and homosexuality are linked by the belief that as a result of this role preference, effeminate males are sexually interested only in masculine males with whom they play the passive sex role. Males involved in homosexual behavior in Mexico seem to operate in a sociocultural environment which gives rise to expectations that they should play either the insertee or inserter sex role, but not both.

GENDER ROLE REVERSAL AND ATTITUDES TOWARD HOMOSEXUALITY

Since masculinity has been more highly valued than femininity across time and culture (Goldberg, 1973), such attitudes have been transferred to the gender roles adopted in homosexual relationships. Among ancient Egyptians adult homosexual intercourse is negatively viewed for the passive partner because it implied submissive behavior; anal intercourse was an outrage reserved for the conquered (Bullough, 1973). Soranus, a Greek physician who lived in the first half of the second century A.D., described negative attitudes toward effeminate behavior in homosexuals:

> *People find it hard to believe that effeminate men or pathics [Greek* malthacoe] *really exist. The fact is that, though the practices of such persons are unnatural to human beings, lust overcomes modesty and puts to shameful use parts intended for other functions. They even adopt the dress, walk, and other characteristics of women. Now this condition is different from a bodily disease; it is rather an affliction of a diseased mind.* (Bullough, 1976, p. 143)

The Greeks have shown negative attitudes toward the effeminate partner because such homosexual activity used to demonstrate the power of one male over another. In a case in which power was an important factor, the passive partner would adopt a "female" role, involving a bent or lowered position, would permit either anal or oral penetration, and would accept money for services rendered. Although a citizen could acceptably assume either the older or the younger role, taking the passive position was considered humiliating and unworthy. (This type of homosexual activity should be distinguished from another acceptable type of homosexuality involving the sexual attraction of an older mentor to a younger male.) (Meikle, 1982). A recent cross-cultural study by Carrier (1977), involving samples of Mexican, Brazilian, Turkish, Greek, lower-class American, and Chicano cultures, who equate inserter with dominant masculine roles, and of insertee with passive feminine roles, suggests that homosexual activity may be utilized to demonstrate the power of one individual over the other (feminine male).

The association between active homosexuality on the one hand, and the aggression and the superiority of the male on the other, is also found in many non-Western cultures (Ford & Beach, 1952). Ford and Beach reported that cultures in which violence and mastery are regarded as attributes of the male also consider active homosexuality as an expression of virility. The Iatmul of New Guinea is such an example: they have at least eleven words for sodomy and these are frequent terms of abuse. In this society, passive homosexuality is regarded as the fate of captives in war. In describing homosexuality in an Iraqi village, Al-Issa and Al-Issa (1970) pointed out that at a certain age, young boys must leave the world of home (that is, female and young members of the family) and must join the exclusive society of men. Their strong need to belong to the male world is exploited by older adult males to induce them to homosexual practices. As the culture looks down on this passive sexual role (that is, the feminine role), those young boys soon assert their virility and, in their turn, they start playing the role of the active homosexuals.

However, negative attitudes toward femininity are not universal. Ford and Beach (1952) describe a form of institutionalized male homosexuality where taking the female passive role is not degrading, but brings considerable prestige and power in the community. The *berdache* is a male who dresses like a woman, performs women's tasks, and adopts some aspects of the feminine role in sexual behavior with male partners. Less frequently, a woman dresses like a man and seeks to adopt the male sex role. In some societies the man who assumes the feminine role is regarded by other members of the community as a powerful shaman. Among the Siberian Chukchee such an individual puts on women's clothing, assumes feminine mannerisms and may become the "wife" of another man. The pair copulate per anum, the Shaman always playing the feminine role. In addition to the Shaman "wife," the husband usually has another wife with whom he indulges in heterosexual coitus. The Shaman may, in turn, support a feminine mistress.

Social reaction to male and female homosexuality may reflect different attitudes of these societies toward these activities. Female homosexuality has attracted less attention and has aroused less legal and ethical concern in most societies. In a cross-cultural study, Brown (1952) found that in 68 percent of societies studied, males were punished for homosexuality. In contrast, only 33 percent of societies punished female homosexuality. In the past, psychologists and psychiatrists have mainly investigated male homosexuality; while male homosexuality used to be considered a crime, female homosexuality was not considered an offense in almost all European countries and North America.

Differences in attitudes toward male and female homosexuality are interpreted as reflection male-female social status (Martin & Lyon, 1972). In societies which tend to be in many respects androcentric, female homosexual practices do not imply any lowering of the female personal or sexual status, and can therefore be ignored. Initiating a girl into lesbianism is thought trivial compared with the "corruption" of a youth by making a woman of him, or inciting him to inflict such degradation upon another man. Martin and Lyon (1972), in an analysis of homosexuality in literature, found that the lesbian has not been acknowledged or taken seriously. Lesbian episodes depicted in the literature take the form of the initiation of an innocent girl by an older woman more experienced in giving sexual pleasure to men, a diversion of the prostitute, an experiment by upper class ladies with their maids to alleviate boredom, or the desperate activity of nuns or prison inmates who have been isolated from men. The accounts are devoid of personal devotion in any such relations.*

GENDER ROLE REVERSAL
AND PARENT-CHILD RELATIONSHIP

Research on the origin of gender role reversal in homosexuality has been stimulated by psychoanalytical theory. It is postulated by psychoanalysts that when the same-sex parent is either frightening or weak and ineffectual, the child may identify with the parent of the opposite sex, and choose as a love object a person of the same sex. A boy may not be able to identify with his father and may develop instead a feminine identification by default. A girl, on the other hand, may not be able to choose such a man as her love object. She may not only identify with her strong dominant mother, but may also take over her mother's attitudes of masculine dominance (Bacon, 1956; Johnson, 1955).

Studies of parent-child relationship of homosexuals generally indicate that homosexual individuals tend to have disturbed emotional relationship with same-sexed parent (Evans, 1969; Saghir & Robins, 1973). Male homosexuals are less likely to report nurturant relationship with their fathers (Bieber, 1976; Bieber et al., 1962; Evans, 1969; Townes, Ferguson & Gillam, 1976).

Bieber et al. (1962) gave a large number of psychoanalysts a questionnaire

*There are other explanations of the neglect of female homosexuality which are not based on gender role theory. Chesser (1971) suggested that, historically, lesbianism did not excite the same horror as male homosexuality because of the prevalent ignorance of the nature of the sexual acts. It was believed that semen contributed the whole of the embryo. The womb was merely a receptacle in which the embryo was nourished. Since male homosexuality, like masturbation, resulted in loss of semen, it seemed more horible than female homosexuality. Different attitudes toward male and female homosexuality may also reflect the nature of participation by the sexes in the sexual act and concern of society with the procreational function of sex. That is, while homosexual women may reproduce, exclusive homosexual (and impotent) men may not.

about homosexual patients they had recently treated. They found one-half of male homosexual subjects with dominant mothers who are disparaging of their husbands and who have close relationship with their sons. This study popularized the view of the seductive and protective mother, and detached and hostile father of homosexual males. In a study of female homosexuals using reports from the same psychoanalysts who provided Bieber et al. with 106 male cases, Kaye et al. (1967) obtained data for only 24 female cases. The female data are somehow opposite those for males; the fathers had intimate relations with the daughters, whereas the mothers were hostile to them.

Stephan (1973) reported more father absences because of both death and divorce among male homosexuals than their heterosexual counterparts. Fathers were more distant, hostile and less encouraging of masculine behavior in their sons. On the other hand, mothers were dominant and encouraged feminine attitudes and behavior. Parents of both males and females had rigid attitudes toward sex and regarded it as shameful.

A study by Siegelman (1972) revealed that the parental background of lesbians is more disturbed than that of heterosexuals. However, when the family background of a group of homosexuals scoring low on neuroticism was compared with a sample of heterosexuals scoring low on neuroticism (emotional instability), there was no significant difference between the groups. Indeed, it appears that the degree of emotional stability rather than sexual orientation is the deciding factor in daughter-parent relationship. In a more recent work, Siegelman (1974) found that the tendency of homosexuals to report more rejecting, less loving, or more demanding parents tended to be related to the level of emotional stability rather than to homosexuality. However, regardless of the degree of emotional stability, homosexuals reported less closeness to their parents and less family security. These women felt more distant, insecure, misunderstood and unhappy with their parents than heterosexual women. Similarly, using the Repertory Grid, Mallen (1983) found that homosexual men perceived themselves as psychologically more distant from their fathers than did their heterosexual counterparts. In an earlier study, Thompson et al. (1973) found that heterosexual persons see themselves more similar to their same-sexed parent than to their opposite sex parent, whereas the perception of homosexuals of one parent is not significantly different from that of another parent.

One important factor that might affect the relationship between a lesbian and her parents found by Siegelman in the studies referred to earlier is the negative attitude of these parents toward homosexuality. Ruth Simpson (1976) reported that when a number of heterosexual women were asked how they would feel, and what they would do, should they learn that their daughters were lesbians, their responses were negative: "I would take her to a psychiatrist immediately and have her cured"; "I would rather she would get pregnant—at least that would be normal"; "I would see to it that she was married as soon as possible"; "If her father ever found out he'd kill me." Simpson (1976) emphasized alienation as a dominant factor in parental relationship of homosexuals. "The family closet, the only temporarily safe place for the young homosexual, cannot help alienating the child from the parent. As the young lesbian reaches her teens, she sometimes feels obliged to have sexual relations with a boy. Often, in such cases, she is motivated partly by the hope that her parents won't suspect her true sexuality. This adds further to the sense of alienation and resentment that inevitably builds up between child and parent."

One criticism of studies of patterns of family interaction is that they are not found in all cases of homosexuals. Some homosexuals come from homes with idealized fathers, while others report an intensely ambivalent relationship with an older sibling or an absent mother (Marmor, 1971). Also patterns of family interaction of homosexuals are found in the families of controls or in families of mental patients. Disturbance in parents may affect the psychological adjustment of children, but this does not necessarily result in homosexuality (Hooker, 1969). In the study of parents of homosexuals the direction of causality is not clearcut; it is uncertain whether parent-child relationship is a cause of homosexuality or it is simply the effects of it.

GENDER ROLE REVERSAL, PSYCHOPATHOLOGY, AND OTHER BEHAVIOR

The view that deviation from gender role expectations is related to psychopathology is not supported by research on mental illness in homosexual individuals. A classic study by Hooker (1958) has challenged the disease approach to homosexuality. Hooker studied ten male homosexuals who are not under treatment and matched with 30 male heterosexuals. She gave them a battery of tests and obtained detailed information on their life history. When the data were analyzed by clinical psychologists, it was concluded that there were no differences in the psychological adjustment and mental symptoms of the two groups. Thompson, McCandless and Strickland (1971), using self-report rating scales with 127 male and 84 female homosexuals, confirmed the Hooker conclusion about the mental health of homosexuals. These two homosexual groups did not differ from matched controls in defensiveness, self-confidence and psychological adjustment. Indeed, male homosexuals revealed less defensiveness and female homosexuals were relatively more self-confident than controls.

The finding that gender differences in psychopathology among homosexuals are similar to those of heterosexuals may provide an evidence against the gender role reversal hypothesis. For example, gender differences in anxiety and phobic disorders among homosexual and heterosexual groups tend to show similar trends. Both homosexual and heterosexual males have significantly lower rates of these disorders than their female counterparts. The same trend is found in depression among males and females in the homosexual and the heterosexual groups. Attempted suicide is also higher in females regardless of sexual orientation (Saghir & Robins, 1973). It is only in the rate of drinking where female homosexuals are equal to males; but this could be due to the use of alcohol by the female to reduce her tension rather than being a symptom of gender role reversal.

Finally, many gender differences among married heterosexual couples are found in homosexual relationships. Males seem to be more promiscuous in both homosexual and heterosexual relationship. Females tend to form more stable relationship than males regardless of sexual orientation (Eysenck & Wilson, 1979). Similarly, the male interest in the physical rather than the emotional aspects of sexual relationship is also found among heterosexual and homosexual males (Bell, 1975). It appears that except for their sexual orientation, homosexual and heterosexual individuals are not significantly different in psychological adjustment and behavior.

SUMMARY

An attempt is made to discuss the relationship between homosexuality and gender role reversal. Research reveals that homosexual males tend to be feminine and female homosexuals tend to be masculine in both childhood and adulthood. More recent research indicates that homosexual individuals tend to be androgynous rather than either masculine or feminine. Gender role reversal noted in some homosexuals is by no means universal. However, homosexual couples tend to adopt the same husband-wife relationship as heterosexual couples. Many factors may lead to such conventional paterns of homosexual relationship.

The idea that homosexuals may play either the masculine or the feminine role may have influenced attitudes towards homosexuality—the passive role is considered more negatively than the active role. Similarly, the greater concern or attention given to male rather than female homosexuality may be explained in terms of social evaluation of masculinity and femininity.

The view that homosexuality is a manifestation of gender role reversal stimulated research related to the influence of parent-child relationship on the development of homosexuality. The finding that the fathers of some homosexual males are ineffectual while their mothers are dominant is not specific to homosexuality but is found in normals and mental patients. The hypothesis that gender role reversal in homosexuality would result in reversal in gender differences in psychopathology has received no support; gender differences in psychopathology among homosexuals and heterosexuals are quite similar.

REFERENCES

Al-Issa, I. *The psychopathology of women.* New Jersey: Englewood Cliffs, 1980.

Al-Issa, I. Gender, hormones and psychopathology. In I. Al-Issa (Ed.), *Gender and psychopathology.* New York: Academic Press, 1982.

Al-Issa, I., & Al-Issa, B. Psychiatric problems in a developing country: Iraq. *International Journal of Social Psychiatry,* 1970, *16,* 15–22.

Bacon, C. A developmental theory of female homosexuality. In S. Lorand and M. Balint (Eds.), *Perversions: Psychodynamic and therapy.* New York: Random House, 1956.

Bell, A. P. The homosexual patient. In R. Green (Ed.), *Human sexuality.* Baltimore: Williams and Wilkins, 1975.

Bem, S. L. The measurement of psychological androgyny. *Journal of Consulting and Clinical Psychology,* 1974, *42,* 155–162.

Bieber, I. A discussion of homosexuality: The ethical challenge. *Journal of Consulting and Clinical Psychology,* 1976, *44,* 163–166.

Bieber, I., Dain, H. J., Dince, P. R., Drellich, M. G., Grand, H. G., Gundlach, R. G., Kremer, M. W., Riffein, A. H., Wilbur, C. B., & Bieher, T. B. *Homosexuality: A psychoanalytical study of male homosexuals.* New York: Basic Books, 1962.

Brown, J. S. A comparative study of deviations from sexual mores. *American Sociological Review,* 1952, *17,* 138.

Bullough, V. L. Homosexuality as submissive behavior: Example from mythology. *The Journal of Sex Research,* 1973, *9,* 283–288.

Bullough, V. L. *Sexual variance in society and history.* Chicago: The University of Chicago Press, 1976.

Cardell, M., Finn, S. E., & Marecek, J. Sex role identity, sex role behavior, and satisfaction in heterosexual, lesbian and gay male couples. *Psychology of Women Quarterly,* 1981, *5,* 488–494.

Carrier, J. M. Cultural factors affecting urban Mexican male homosexual behavior. *Archives of Sexual Behavior,* 1976, *5,* 103–124.

Carrier, J. M. "Sex role preference" as an explanatory variable in homosexual behavior. *Archives of Sexual Behavior,* 1977, *61,* 53–65.

Chesler, P. *Women and madness.* New York: Doubleday, 1972.

Chesser, E. *The human aspects of sexual deviation.* New York: Random House, 1971.

Evans, R. B. Childhood parental relationships of homosexual men. *Journal of Consulting and Clinical Psychology,* 1969, *33,* 129–135.

Eysenck, H. J., & Wilson, G. *The psychology of sex.* Toronto, Canada: Dent, 1979.

Ford, C.S., & Beach, F. A. *Patterns of sexual behavior.* New York: Ace Books, 1952.

Goldberg, S. *The inevitability of patriarchy.* New York: William Morrow, 1973.

Gough, H. G., & Heilbrun, A. B. *Joint manual for the adjective checklist and the need scales for the ACL.* Palo Alto, CA: Consulting Psychologists Press, 1965.

Heilbrun, A. R., & Thompson, N. L. Sex role identity and male and female homosexuality. *Sex Roles*, 1977, *3*, 65–79.

Hooker, E. Male homosexuality in the Rorschach. *Journal of Projective Techniques*, 1958, *22*, 33–54.

Hooker, E. Parental relationships and male homosexuality. *Journal of Consulting and Clinical Psychology*, 1969, *33*, 140–142.

Hooker, E. Homosexuality. In M. Livingood (Ed.), *Homosexuality*. Rockville, MD: U.S. Department of Health, Education, and Welfare, 1976.

Johnson, A. M. Etiology and therapy of overt homosexuality. *Psychoanalytical Quarterly*, 1955, *24*, 506–515.

Kaye, H. E., Berl, S., Clare, J., Eleston, M., Gerschwin, P., Kagan, L., Torda, C., & Wilber, C. Homosexuality in women. *Archives of General Psychiatry*, 1967, *17*, 626–634.

Libjestrand, P., Gerling, E., & Saliba, P. A. The effect of social sex role stereotypes and sexual orientation on psychotherapeutic outcomes. *Journal of Homosexuality*, 1978, *3*, 361–372.

Maffeo, P. Gender as a model for mental health. In I. Al-Issa (Ed.), *Gender and psychopathology*. New York: Academic Press, 1982.

Mallen, C. A. Sex role stereotypes, gender identity and parental relationships in male homosexuals and heterosexuals. *Journal of Homosexuality*, 1983, *9*, 55–74.

Mareck, J. Finn, S. E., & Cardell, M. Gender roles in the relationships of lesbians and gay men. *Journal of Homosexuality*, 1982, *8*, 45–49.

Marmor, J. Homosexuality in males. *Psychiatric Annals*, 1971, *4*, 45–59.

Martin, D., & Lyon, P. *Lesbian/woman*. San Francisco: Glide Publications, 1972.

Meikle, S. Culture and sexual deviation. In I. Al-Issa (Ed.), *Culture and psychopathology*. Baltimore: University Park Press, 1982.

Oldham, S., Farnill, D., & Ball, I. Sex role identity of female homosexuals. *Journal of Homosexuality*, 1982, *8*, 41–46.

Rubenstein, L. M. The role of identifications in homosexuality and transvestism in men and women. In I. Rosen (Ed.), *The pathology and treatment of sexual deviation: A methodological approach*. London: Oxford University Press, 1964.

Saghir, M. I., & Robins, E. Homosexuality I. Sexual behavior of the female homosexual. *Archives of General Psychiatry*, 1969, *20*, 192–201.

Saghir, M. I., Robins, E., & Walbran, B. Homosexuality: II. Sexual behavior of the male homosexual. *Archives of General Psychiatry*, 1969, *21*, 219–229.

Saghir, M. T., & Robins, E. Male and female homosexuality: Natural history. *Comprehensive Psychiatry*, 1971, *12*, 503–510.

Siegelman, M. Adjustment of homosexual and heterosexual women. *British Journal of Psychiatry*, 1972, *120*, 477–481.

Siegelman, M. Parental background of homosexual and heterosexual women. *British Journal of Psychiatry*, 1974, *124*, 14–21.

Simpson, R. *From the closet to the courts: The lesbian transition*. New York: Viking Press, 1976.

Stephan, W. Parental relationships and early social experiences of activist male homosexuals and male heterosexuals. *Journal of Abnormal Psychology,* 1973, *82,* 506–513.

Stoller, R. J. Boyhood gender aberrations: Treatment issues. *Journal of the American Psychoanalytical Association,* 1978, *26,* 541–558.

Thompson, N., Schwartz, D., McCandless, B., & Edwards, D. Parent-child relationships and sexual identity in male and female homosexuals and heterosexuals. *Journal of Consulting and Clinical Psychology,* 1973, *41,* 120–127.

Thompson, N. L., McCandless, B. R., & Strickland, R. R. Personal adjustment of male and female homosexuals and heterosexuals. *Journal of Abnormal Psychology,* 1971, *78,* 237–240.

Townes, B. D., Ferguson, W. D., & Gillam, S. Differences in psychological sex adjustment, and familial influences among homosexual and nonhomosexual populations. *Journal of Homosexuality,* 1976, *1,* 261–272.

Whitam, F. L. Childhood indicators of male homosexuality. *Archives of Sexual Behavior,* 1977, *2,* 89–96.

Zuger, B. Early effeminate behavior in boys. *Journal of Nervous and Mental Disease,* 1984, *172,* 90–97.

CLINICAL CONCERNS

9

THE RELATIONSHIP OF HOMOSEXUALITY TO MENTAL DISORDERS

Louis Diamant
Ronald B. Simono

INTRODUCTION

As noted previously, there is considerable discussion about the theories of the dynamics of homosexuality with most perspectives on its development focusing on hereditary tendencies, environmental influences, or sex hormonal imbalances or a combination of these three influences. An even more concentrated debate has centered around whether or not homosexuality should be included as a distinct and separate entity when classes of mental and emotional disorders are discussed. In addition, there can be considerable difference of opinion as to the correct definition of homosexuality. Many practitioners appear to adhere to Kinsey's (1948, 1953) useful concept of degrees of sexuality which consisted of a seven-point scale to categorize the heterosexual-homosexual balance ranging from one end of the scale of exclusive heterosexuality to the other end of exclusive homosexuality. Few practitioners would deal with homosexuality as an either/or proposition.

As Gonsiorek (1982a) points out, there are many methodological problems involved in identifying a representative sample of homosexual males and females, and many studies reflect samples drawn from those involved in the legal system, psychotherapy, politically active homosexual organizations, and social settings such as gay or lesbian bars, even though these might be seen as less than representative samples (Gonsiorek, 1982a, 1982b). There, nevertheless, appears to be a paucity of data to support the contention that homosexuals have more emotional difficulties and experience greater psychological instability than do heterosexuals. Extensive studies using both paper and pencil personality inventories as well as projective techniques have led to the conclusion that:

> *Testing results overwhelmingly suggest that if there are consistent, measurable differences between heterosexual and homosexual populations, they are not in the range of scores indicative of greater disturbance in the homosexual groups* (Gonsiorek, 1982b).

This contention that the gay and lesbian population shows no more representation in categories of maladaptive behaviors than heterosexuals has been supported by other writers. Clark (1975) for instance, studied 140 college graduates who were assessed as being representative of a broad range of professions and who were functioning well, socially as well as occupationally. Through interviews, it was determined what the ratio of heterosexual-to-homosexual behavior was for each person in the study. When the association between this sexual preference continuum and a personality measure was analyzed, the conclusion was reached that the level of homosexuality was not a predictor of psychotherapy.*

HOMOSEXUALITY AND DIAGNOSTIC CLASSIFICATIONS

Current psychiatric diagnosis and classification has no place for homosexuality as a symptom or a disorder except in one context: 302.00 Ego-dystonic Homosexuality (American Psychiatric Association, 1980). This mental disorder is listed in the category of psychosexual disorders whereas in an earlier edition of the Diagnostic and Statistical Manual of mental disorders (American Psychiatric Association, 1968), it was a personality disorder. Thus, when it was included in the mental disorders, homosexuality was thrown into a mixed bag of sexual concerns such as zoophilia, sexual sadism, and inhibited female orgasm. Homosexuality, officially anyway, in and of itself is not a disorder; homosexuality is only considered a disorder when it has complications—that is when it is unwanted or ego-dystonic. The conceptual structure of Diagnostic and Statistical Manual III cannot determine whether ego-dystonic homosexuality is the symptom of a neurotic conflict or if the conflict is a symptomatic reaction to a human sexual behavior which the American Psychiatric Association must have considered normal (otherwise it would surely be listed independently in the psychosexual disorders without an ego-dystonic qualifier). After all, there is no classification for ego-dystonic

---

*M. Siegelman has written a comprehensive review of the research elsewhere in this volume.

zoophilia although there certainly are those who despise themselves for such behavior and wish they were not so, as well, perhaps, as those who find they have no anxiety and aversion for which they would seek help. DSM-III notes that symptoms are symptoms because they are ego-dystonic (American Psychiatric Association, 1980, p. 9).

The ambiguous and anomalous characteristic of pathological homosexuality is not discussed here just to rake through DSM-III in a caviling fashion but rather to point to the historical difficulties in reviewing homosexuality as a clinical concern. Schacht (1985) has previously written a scholarly review of this problem. It is only to be expected that there will be difficulties and readjustments for diagnostic committees since scientific procedures are by their nature heuristic, and revisions are always in order. At this time, the structural problems of classifying homosexual behavior are reviewed in order to validate a freedom to discuss some persistent psychiatric and clinical postulates that put homosexuality in relationships not mentioned at all in DSM-III, and yet they are important in the overall study of psychopathology and homosexuality.

It seems, then, that a small amount of semantic and conceptual manipulation and adjustment will allow us to see a flexibility (or looseness) in DSM-III that permits both advocacy and challenge regarding homosexuality and psychopathology with no need to rekindle an old "abnormality" argument. In order to validate the exploration of some enduring postulates of relationships between homosexuality and other mental disorders, the concept of a pathological homosexuality has to be considered along with the concept of nonpathological homosexuality. DSM-III, perhaps without intention, permits us to elaborate on other integral and normal behaviors that can develop symptoms or are symptoms or are in some way involved in the symptom formation of other classified mental disorders. Even such an essential human behavior as "the desire for affection and acceptance" can be part of the psychopathological process (American Psychiatric Association, p. 324). Heterosexuality itself can be ego-dystonic and accompanied by ego-dystonic symptoms or used pathologically as in so-called Don Juanism (American Psychiatric Association, 1980, p. 283). Abraham (1922) has said of this pursuing heterosexual type, "He avenges himself on all women for the disappointment which he once received from the first woman that entered his life" (p. 361). If there are eating behaviors, sleeping behaviors, and even heterosexuality that under some conditions can be viewed as ego-dystonic or symptomatic, then it stands to reason that homosexuality can be reviewed in that light without a need to consider it essentially psychopathological. This chapter examines theoretical constructs and research related to some specific DSM-III mental disorders and homosexuality. The concentration will be on homosexuality as a correlate or as part of the structural formation of some mental disorders that have been identified by clinicians as associated with homosexuality.

ALCOHOL ABUSE AND HOMOSEXUALITY

Although the most recent literature suggests that the homosexual population shows no more psychological disturbance than the general population, there is some strong suggestion that homosexuals might be over-represented in populations which are demonstrating alcohol-related problems. Although the argument continues as to whether or not homosexuality is a mental disorder, there is agreement that alcoholism is a disorder/disease although there may be some argument as to definition. The following definition was drawn up by the National Council on Alcoholism/American Medical Society on Alcoholism Committee on Definitions (*Annals of Internal Medicine*, 1976):

Alcoholism is a chronic, progressive and potentially fatal disease. It is characterized by: tolerance, physical dependency and/or pathological organ changes all of which are the direct or indirect consequence of the alcohol ingested.

1. *By chronic and progressive it is meant that there are both physical and emotional/social changes which are cumulative and progressive with the continuation of drinking.*
2. *By tolerance is meant brain adaptation to the presence of high concentrations of alcohol.*
3. *By physical dependency is meant that there are withdrawal symptoms upon decreasing or ceasing consumption of alcohol.*
4. *In addition, the individual with alcoholism cannot consistently predict on any drinking occasion the duration of the episode or the quantity which is consumed.*
5. *Pathological organ changes can be found in almost any organ, but most often involve the liver, brain, peripheral nervous system and the gastrointestinal tract.*
6. *The drinking pattern generally continues but may be intermittent with periods of abstinence between drinking episodes.*
7. *The social, emotional and behavioral symptoms and consequences result from the effect of alcohol on the function of the brain.*

The degree to which these symptoms and signs are considered deviant will depend upon the cultural norms of the society or group in which the individual operates.

The DSM-III approach to alcohol use is more complex. No definition of alcoholism per se is provided. The pathological use of alcohol is discussed under two major disorder categories: substance use disorders and organic mental disorders. The organic mental disorders atributed to alcoholism are: Alcohol Intoxication, Alcohol Idiosyncratic Intoxication, Alcohol Withdrawal Delirium, Alcohol Hallucinosis, Alcohol Amnestic Disorder, and Dementia Associated with Alcoholism (p. 129). Categorized under substance use disorders are Alcohol Abuse and Alcohol Dependence (p. 169). Although many psychological and physiological disturbances are attributed to alcoholism, no mention of sexual behavioral excesses or deviances are noted related to the disorder; and any relationship of alcohol to homosexuality must be convoluted by the interpreter via Freud's comments on homosexuality, jealousy, alcohol, and paranoia. In this respect, DSM-III rejects the ICD-9-M category of "alcoholic jealousy" by rerouting the diagnostician.

The concept of "alcoholic jealousy," can be expressed in DSM-III terms by a diagnosis of Alcohol Dependence and an additional diagnosis of a Paranoid Disorder (p. 129).

Myers (1980), in looking at the kind of psychological problems that a sample of homosexual men and women brought out during contact with family physicians, concluded that homosexual men and women showed no higher frequency in psychological problems than did men and women seen in the general medical practice. However, there were indications in this study that alcoholism was slightly more prevalent in the homosexual population; and it was suggested that the abuse of alcohol might be in response to other difficulties the homosexual may have to deal with from time to time such as loneliness, anxiety, depression, and guilt which are all often associated with the responses the homosexual might obtain from those in his or her immediate environment.

Very useful and comprehensive work has been done by Israelstam and Lambert (1983) and Nardi (1982). Israelstam and Lambert (1983) traced historical connections between alcoholism and latent or overt homosexuality to an early psychoanalytic view which was strongly held in the medical/ psychiatric community as well as in psychology until the notions emanating from humanistic psychology and existential psychology began to be heard. These writers outline that although current conceptual frameworks for understanding homosexuality have steered away from the more classic psycho-analytic and medical models, psychoanalytic literature still attempts to emphasize personality factors in alcoholism which are "explained or interpreted in psychoanalytic terms using psychoanalytic language" (Israelstam & Lambert, 1983, p. 1094). The Israelstam and Lambert paper is well researched and has many references on alcoholism and homosexuality. It is made clear that those who study the association between homosexuality and alcoholism are often divided between the psychoanalytic followers on the one hand and those who go in a different direction on the other. However, their review does seem to indicate that homosexuals have a higher rate of alcoholism and that the primary argument might be about why this might be a valid observation.

Nardi (1982) wrote an interesting paper focused on reviewing the literature primarily from the *Journal of Studies on Alcohol* from the period 1951 through 1980. Apparently there were only 42 references under the heading of homosexuality during this thirty year time span and Nardi (1982) considered most of the literature anecdotal and generally unreliable. This article looked at four frameworks for interpreting alcoholism among homosexuals. These included the biological-genetic, the psychoanalytic, learning theory, and sociocultural view. The biological-genetic perspective suggested, as many experts have on alcoholism, that there might be a genetic predisposition to alcohol addiction. Interestingly, in a short note in the *American Journal of Psychiatry* (Turner, 1981), a suggestion was made that there might be some genetic interdependence between alcoholism, homosexuality, and bipolar affective disorder.

Nardi (1982) did not seem to accept the suggested causal relationship between latent homosexuality and alcoholism which is emphasized in psychoanalytic thinking. The reference to learning theory suggested that alcohol might become an important part of a homosexual's life style if one were to look closely at tension-reduction and pleasure seeking. On the other hand, the learning theory perspective might lead us to suspect that there is a relationship between heavy drinking and acknowledged homosexuality as an acquired habit which is an attempt to be socially bonded to other homosexuals. The sociocultural approach presented a more integrative look at this issue and took into account societal norms, values and attitudes. Nardi's focus is particularly stimulating since it raised some useful questions about many of the myths and assumptions surounding homosexuality and alcohol abuse. Comparisons are drawn between how society has negatively responded to both alcoholics and homosexuals and, therefore, have contributed to the tendency for these populations to use denial and concealment as a way to fit into society. Both alcoholics and homosexuals have been historically judged poorly by those in society charged with defining what is legally and morally acceptable.

Lewis, Saghir, and Robbins (1982) analyzed data collected by Saghir and Robins (1973) for a study in the late 1960s. During this more recent look at the data, interest was in comparing lifetime drinking histories of homosexual and heterosexual women. The earlier study (Saghir & Robins) had been found wanting (Nardi, 1982) because of problems with sample size, questions about how representative the gay subjects were, and the very small number of questions concerning drinking behavior. This second look at the data (Lewis, et al., 1982) suggested that the lesbian sample had significantly higher lifetime prevalence of problem drinking. Genetic factors for both groups looked similar. These authors did have one interesting speculation that *female homosexuals may have an earlier age of onset of alcoholism, which would falsely elevate prevalence rates for this group in comparison with heterosexual women of similar age* (p. 279).

This might suggest why many studies show homosexuals as having more alcohol related problems. This was certainly the case in two studies reviewed (Lohrenz et al., 1978; Small & Leach, 1977).

Small and Leach (1977) proposed that one-third of the men who sought help from them for alcoholism were also concerned about homosexuality and associated issues. These authors did case histories of ten male homosexual alcoholics and found that one-half of them had family related alcohol problems with either one or both parents alcoholic. Seven of the ten had started showing signs of alcohol-related problems as early as adolescence. These authors/therapists did not see patterns of these ten men as similar to other alcoholics they had treated.

A related study (Lohrens et al., 1978) reported that about one-third of homosexual men surveyed in four urban areas in the Midwest were alcoholics. These authors suggested that the prevalence of alcohol related problems in the homosexual population was "considerably higher" than the prevalence of such problems in the population at large. They cited other studies that showed three out of ten homosexuals had or will have serious alcohol related problems and hypothesized that this probably was true because homosexuals socialized in bars and other settings where drinking was the focus of activity and that this was done in order to bond up with other homosexuals. There also was some suggestion made that the family and social support system problems made the homosexuals more vulnerable to alcohol abuse. Finally issues of social and psychological pressures emanating from the environment were discussed.

With the tendency for those homosexuals who abuse alcohol to start serious drinking as adolescents, this period should be looked at in terms of the social and psychological pressures which relate both to homosexuality as well as the potential for alcohol abuse. When the adolescent moves into the area of his or her sexual development, there are many adaptations that have to be made. Whether male or female, each adolescent must adjust to a certain amount of confusion and lack of stability associated with a powerful and strange new set of emotions often associated with sexuality. These changes often come suddenly without adequate preparation, and the adolescent finds that society demands both control and direction of this new drive in line with social expectations. In addition, each adolescent has to deal with the environmental pressures to assume an appropriate biological role. Finally, there is a general and necessary trend for the style of sexual gratification to become more and more specific and clearly differentiated as individuals move through adolescence. Many homosexuals recall this time as their initial experiences with homosexual expression. The early alcohol use reported by homosexuals might be seen as a way to ease inhibitions but it is more likely that the tendency to find alcohol abuse among homosexuals is more analogous to the phenomenon we sometimes associate with those individuals experiencing anxiety disorders. That is, as mentioned earlier, alcohol abluse can sometimes be a "complication" of homosexuality as a tension reducer and a response to distress imposed by environmental factors.

HOMOSEXUALITY AND PARANOIA

The notion, or if you will, the psychodynamic postulate that paranoia is a defense against unwanted, unwitting, or unwilling homosexual arousal goes back to Freud's interpretation and analysis of the Schreber case (Freud, 1911). Probably because of Freud's analysis and conceptualization of a relationship between that major disorder and homosexuality, Schreber became a household word in psychoanalytic institutions. In other places, it might bear some introduction.

D. P. Schreber was a German jurist of apparent brilliance. While institutionalized and still undergoing delusional and hallucinatory experiences, he wrote a book describing them. It was this book, *Memories of My Nervous Illness,* published in 1903 which attracted Freud's attention. Dr. Schreber initially became psychotic in 1884 and seemed to recover completely the following year. A second severe paranoid condition occurred again in 1893 from which there was also somewhat of a recovery. In 1907 there was a final paranoid phase following the death of his mother and the illness of his wife. The last psychotic episode lasted until his death in 1911. During the psychotic episode his delusional experiences were concerned with his being changed from a man to a woman and of his being used sexually. Freud, in his interpretation, stated that the sexual etiology in paranoia was not as obvious in males as the seemingly more prominent social slights and injuries; however, he stated that behind these hurts were the homosexual dynamics and at the core of the conflict in male paranoia was the homosexual wish of loving a man.

Schreber's linking of his erotic lapses with his nervous disorder gave Freud a confirmation of his own belief in the sexual etiology of the mental disorder. In the latter stages of his delusional thinking, Schreber thought of himself in a voluptuous relationship with God. Freud saw that as a transference of sexual feelings from an older brother to father and finally at the time of his full blown paranoia, to God, at which state homosexual libidinal impulses and the megalomania could be expressed. Since the paranoia developed after his briefer and, according to Freud, nonpsychotic first illness and his dependent relationship with his doctor, Freud noted that the patient was in fear of sexual abuse at the hands of his doctor. The exacerbating cause of his illness was an outburst of homosexual libido, the object of which was probably from the very first his physician, and the struggle against the libidinal impulse produced a conflict which gave rise to the symptoms (Freud, 1911, p. 43). The doctor, whom he had loved, turned into his persecutor whom he said had tried to commit "soul murder" on him (p. 44).

"What lies at the core of the conflict in cases of paranoia among males is a homosexual wishful fantasy of loving a man" (p. 62). Freud stated that the confirmation of that hypothesis would require the investigation of a large number of instances of every variety of paranoia disorder. He added that one must be prepared to limit the assertion then, to a single type of paranoia. Nevertheless, he noted that the principal forms of paranoia were all represented as a contradiction of the single proposition: "I (a man) love him (a man)." This through further contradiction evolves as: "I do not love him, I hate him because he persecutes me." The hatred or the persecution is explained by the mechanism of projection (p. 63).

One of the topics discussed in this chapter is alcoholism and homosexuality, and Freud commented on an unrecognized homosexual fixation in alcoholic delusions and jealousy. He said that it was not infrequently disappointment over a woman that drove a man to drink, but as a rule, he resorts to a bar to the company of men who offer him an emotional satisfaction which he has failed to get from his wife at home. If now these men become the objects of strong libidinous affections, in his unconscious, he will ward it off with a type of contradiction. "It is not I who love the man—it is she who loves him," and after that he will suspect the woman in relation to all the men who he the drinker might be tempted to love (p. 64).

While Freud had made his observations on both men and women, he did not present a major paper dealing with paranoia and homosexuality in women until some years after he interpreted the Schreber memoirs. In "A Case of Paranoia Running Counter to the Psychoanalytic Theory," Freud (1920) reiterated his theoretical proposition that the unresolved and unconscious conflict concerning homosexuality lay behind every paranoid disorder. The subject of his investigation, a thirty year old woman, attractive and competent, had developed a paranoiac relationship with a man following their brief encounter as lovers. In this case study, Freud once again used some of the postulates made in the Schreber case to illustrate the relationship between paranoia and the unconscious homosexual conflict. The encapsulation of the homosexual anxiety in the persecution is demonstrated through an analysis of the sexual content of the patient's delusions. The need for the persecuted person to be the same sex is shown by Freud to be essential. In this case, the male lover whom the patient saw as the persecuting person, is viewed as merely the transference from an older female attachment and thus probably a screen figure for a mother. Freud used this case study again to stress what he considered were the necessary ingredients for the clinical syndrome of paranoia:

denial, homosexuality, and projection. Freud is consistent in these two major papers in his view that the person who is hated when the disorder is in progress was once loved and honored or at least symbolizes one once so regarded.

In his paper on jealousy, paranoia, and homosexuality, Freud (1922) again drew a relationshiip between homosexuality and paranoia in an examination of jealousy. He elaborated on three forms of jealousy: (1) competitive, or normal (though not completely rational), which is the jealousy one feels about losing a partner to a rival, (2) projected—the unfaithfulness that is attributed to a mate when one himself is unfaithful or has such an impulse, and (3) delusional jealousy. While Freud claimed that all jealousies were derivatives of early unconscious Oedipal fantasies, he said that the delusional type is also repressed unfaithfulness; and it is directed toward a person of the same sex as the subject.

> *Delusional jealousy is left of homosexuality that has run its course and it rightly takes its position among the classical forms of paranoia. As an attempt against an unduly strong homosexual impulse, it may be in a man described in the formula: "I do not love him, she loves him."* (p. 225).

Analyst Paula Heimann (1957, p. 257) has said of Freud's analysis of the Schreber memoirs: "It has led to an almost monopolistic position of homosexuality in the pathogenesis of paranoia ..." (p. 257). Whether rejected, accepted, or amended, there seems little doubt that Freud's contributions on paranoia and homosexuality are deeply imbedded in the matrix of information used in clinical processes.

Frosch (1981) in a comprehensive review of Freud's psychoanalytic postulate emphasized the importance of distinguishing unconscious homosexuality from latent and overt homosexuality. After an in-depth examination of the psychoanalytical literature, and a presentation of case illustrations, he concluded that the role of repressed and unconscious homosexuality is primary in the etiology of the paranoid constellation. He stated that unconscious homosexuality is denied, rejected, and projected onto the replica of a significant childhood object who became the persecuted, passive participant. The nature of the persecution is an anal sadomasochistic attachment which the subject experiences as degrading and humiliating. According to Frosch, this humiliation has as its basis the humiliating experiences during the crucial developmental stages (before the establishment of a sexual identification) and the objects are usually the same sex as the subject. The latter postulate tends to fit Freud's (1911) comment that paranoia in males appears at first to be more related to humiliation and slights than to sexual matters.

Some empirical investigations have been done with a variety of paranoid disorders and paranoid schizophrenia to test the validity of Freud's postulate concerning homosexuality and paranoia. One of the difficulties encountered might be an inexactness of classification and diagnosis. DSM-III specifically separates the two disorders (schizophrenia and paranoia) and states that certain schizophrenic symptoms counter-indicate paranoia (American Psychiatirc Association, 1980, p. 196). Freud had distinguished paranoia from schizophrenia although allowing that the two could occur together. He wrote that the schizophrenic libido is at an earlier developmental period and shorter developmental level than repressed homosexuality. Because of the depth of regression in schizophrenia and the earlier nature of the fixation, he found the prognosis for recovery more favorable in paranoia.

> *The dispositional fixations must therefore be situated further back than in paranoia and must be somewhere in the beginning of the cause of development from autoeroticism to object love. Moreover, it is not at all likely that homosexual compulsions which are so frequently—perhaps invariably—to be found in paranoia play an equally important part in the etiology of that far more comprehensive disorder dementia praecox (schizophrenia)* (Freud, 1911, p. 77).

Freud emphasized crucial differences in the disorders, i.e., wishful fantasy, hallucination in schizophrenia and projection in paranoia.

Klein and Horowitz (1948) are among those few who attempted empirical assessment to examine "the increasingly expressed concept that the homosexual conflict serves as a nuclear problem in the paranoid syndrome (p. 697)." They examined the records of 40 male and 40 female patients at a psychiatric in-patient institution. These patients were randomly selected from a larger group all previously diagnosed as paranoid state, or schizophrenia, paranoid type. Among other data, they scrutinized the behavior, productions and feelings of the patients in terms of homosexual feelings, conflicts, and fears. In studying all such references in the content during illness, they reported that most of the patients showed no behavior of a homosexual nature nor expressed in interviews such erotic wishes. Their conclusion was that the paranoid mechanism could not solely be explained by a homosexual concept.

Klaf (1961) and Klaf and Davis (1960) used the examination of patients' records to test the Freudian postulate on paranoia. In both studies, the records of patients who were primarily diagnosed as paranoid schizophrenic were examined. Klaf and Davis (1960) found the homosexual occupation during the illness significantly greater than a control group of nonpsychotic male and female patients. Klaf (1961) found that paranoid schizophrenic females did not show significant differences in homosexual preoccupation. Carr (1961) observed that no alternate theory has merited comparable attention, respect, and acceptance. The argument posited by Klein and Horowitz (1949) that there was little evidence of homosexual mentation in their paranoid patients as well as those reports that homosexuality can exist in paranoid patients, (Hastings, 1941) appear to contradict the stand that homosexuality as an unconscious conflict is at the core of all paranoia and that the paranoid sexual fantasy must belong strictly to the unconscious. Carr responded to that by noting the elusiveness of evidence of unconscious homosexuality and the problem of differences among observers. The latter, overt homosexuality, in paranoid patients was seen as plausible and no contradiction to Freud's position. The overt homosexuality may be acceptable and even comfortable to the individual patient. The psychotic defenses or paranoia may result as a reaction to the more primitive sadistic incorporative impulses (Carr, 1961).

In a paragraph on the syndrome under discusison, Bieber et al., (1961), who have studied scores of homosexual males through the psychoanalytic process and who assess homosexuality as a mental disorder evolving from pathogenic childhood experiences also noted that the idea of paranoia as a defense against homosexuality goes back to Freud's early analysis of the Schrebere case. In rebuttal, however, they added that anecdotal data from the Virgin Islands by public health psychiatrist E. A. Weinstein indicated that homosexual content was absent from the delusional systems of native Virgin Islanders during acute paranoid states. They concluded: 'We propose that schizophrenia and homosexuality represent two distinct types of personality maladaptation which may or may not coexist" (p. 306).

HOMOSEXUALITY AND PHOBIC REACTION

According to *Diagnostics and Statistics Manual of Mental Disorders III* (American Psychiatric Association, 1980) the essential feature of a phobic disorder is the irrational fear of a specific object activity or situation that "results in an compelling desire to avoid the dreaded object, activity, or situation (p. 225)." The list of items that can be involved in a phobic reaction is almost endless although English and English (1958) recorded more than 180 phobias bearing Greek and Latin designates.

Behaviorists stress the learned nature of phobias, and John Watson, often credited with being the first of that line of psychologists, demonstrated in his famous study with little Albert (Watson & Rayner, 1920) the acquisition of an irrational fear through classical conditioning. Before the experiment, the eleven-month old Albert showed no fear of a white rat, but when the rat was paired with a fear-eliciting loud noise, the rat soon acquired a fearsome character. The oversimplified view of phobic behavior is nowadays not acceptable without modification to most behavioral clinicians, and the changes in the model were brought about through the increased consideration of the role that cognitive proceses (thoughts, ideas, memories, etc.) play in the acquisition of phobias. Still, the basic premise that phobic behaviors can be attributed directly to the learning process remains central to the behaviorist view of that disorder. Besides the explanation of phobic behavior from paired stimuli in classical conditioning, behaviorists use observational learning (vicarious experience) and instrumental learning by punishment to explain the development of a phobic response.

Another major position, for the explanation of a phobic response is psychodynamic. In the psychoanalytic view the phobia may help the phobic person to conceal and deny conflicts as well as to hide guilt. The object of the phobia is never the specific cause but rather symbolic of the unconscious source of fear thus unlike the postulate used to explain Little Albert's phobic response to a rat, pairing a basic fear stimulus (noise) with the neutral stimulus (rat) to obtain a fear response to the rat (conditioned response). The psychodynamic psychologist views the phobic object as an external and symbolic displacement and projection of an instinctual sexual drive that has been brought into conflictual state. The phobic person thus has a tangible situation or object to deal with tension, anxiety and guilt by avoidance.

Although the development of some homosexuality has been viewed as a phobic reaction to heterosexuality, there is a dearth of discussion in the clinical literature. Despite the absence of attention to homosexuality as a phobia, the concept has a number of clinical advocates. The position is succinctly stated by James (1978).

> *From accounts of previous work it seemed that the prime target for treatment was heterophobia (heterosexual anxiety) which might not only prevent the conditioning of homosexual avoidance but also inhibit the arousal of heterosexual interest* (p. 29)

James approached homosexuality with desensitization and relaxation which had a considerable history of reported success as a treatment with phobic and anxiety disorders.

To define homosexuality as a phobic response the behaviorist must assume that traumatic events in the lives of homosexual men and women have come in the form of aversive reinforcement powerful enough to have created a phobic reaction to heterosexual goals but have left the individual free to pursue homosexual drives.

James reported a significantly greater improvement with regard to changing the degree of homosexuality measured by several measurements of heterosexual status in forty male subjects who were said to be more heterophobic than would have been expected by the aversive techniques used by Feldman and MacCulloch (1970) and these results are in part used to support a notion that there is a special kind of person who is heterophobic as opposed to those who are nonheterophobes.

Psychoanalysts have been less willing to find homosexuality a phobic reaction although Fenichel (1947, p. 195) has described a sexual phobia in women. Bieber et al. have emphasized a fear component in the development of male homosexuality. They investigated within a psychoanalytic framework the cause and cure of homosexuality of 106 male subjects and noted a relationship between homosexuality and the fear of genital injury relationship to castration in those subjects that had mothers labelled as Close Binding Intimate (CBI). Psychoanalytic theory allows that castration wishes and fears are unconscious and may be a factor in the development of both homosexuality and phobias. Bieber did not classify male homosexuality as a phobia.

Lamberd (1968) has been willing to describe a certain number of cases of male homosexuality as persons with phobic avoidance of women. He wrote:

> *If one could identify those patients in whom the phobic avoidance of women represented the greatest part of the problem and who were in other ways relatively intact, perhaps those persons could be treated as though they suffered from a monosymptomatic phobia* (p. 105)

After disqualifying the dependent and female identified patient, Lamberd stated that this could leave a relatively narrow group of patients with a fear of women leading to a homosexual adaptation that was based largely on Oedipal problems rather than pre-Oedipal conflicts. He offered the suggestion that in these cases an abbreviated form of therapy directed toward the removal of the phobic avoidance of women would lead to a redirection of sexuality without a marked change in personality. Lamberd emphasized the limited number of cases that could be approached in this way. Interestingly, he espoused a psychoanalytic explanation of the phobic reaction, one that has an etiology in the Oedipus conflict, and a treatment that is behavioral.

Wolpe (Gray, 1970) also viewed some homosexuality as heterosexual avoidance behavior. He stated that male homosexuality is a multifactorial possibility—a positive valence to men's general anxiety and anxiety responses to women. It seems a matter of theoretical sensitivity as to whether one would fully assert that some homosexuality can be determined a phobia in the psychoanalytic or the behavioral sense.

In conclusion, DSM-III, the way it is now written, must obviously tolerate a nonpathological male and female homosexuality and heterosexuality. It also, it appears, can tolerate, if not support, a view that homosexuality may be as other behaviors, enmeshed in a number of psychopathological states, thus permitting an examination of some enduring postulates relating homosexuality to a number of classified mental disorders. There is no intent here to make a statement that the discussion of these relationships depended on "permission from DSM-III," but it seemed more interesting to review them under that cover.

REFERENCES

Abraham, K. (1920). Manifestations of the female castration complex. In: *The selected papers of Karl Abraham*. New York: Basic Books. 1968.

American Psychiatric Assocition (1968, 1980). *Diagnostics and statistical manual of mental disorders*. Washington, D.C.

Bieber, I., Dain, H. J., Dince, P. R., Drelich, M. G., Brand, H. G., Gundlach, R. H., Kremer, M. W., Rifkin, A. H., Wilbur, C. B., & Bieber, T. B. (1962). *Homosexuality: A psychoanalytic study*. New York: Basic Books.

Carr, A. C. (1963). Observations on paranoia and their relationships to the Schreber case. *International Journal of Psychoanalysis, 44,* 195–200.

Clark, T. R. (1975). Homosexuality and psychopathology in nonpatient males. *American Journal of Psychoanalysis, 35*(2), 163–168.

English, H. B., & English, A. C. (1958). *A comprehensive dictionary of psychological and psychoanalytical terms: A guide to usage*. New York: Longmans Green.

Feldman, M. P. & MacCulloch, M. J. (1971). *Homosexual behavior: Therapy and assessment*. Oxford: Pergamon Press.

Fenichel, O. (1945). *The psychoanalytic theory of neurosis*. New York: W. W. Norton.

Freud, S. (1911). Psychoanalytic notes on a case of paranoia. In J. Strachey (Ed.). *The standard edition of the complete psychological works of Sigmund Freud,* (Vol. 12). London: Hogarth Press, 1958.

Freud, S. (1915). A cse of paranoia running counter to the psychoanalytic theory of the disease. In J. Strachey (Ed.). *The standard edition of the complete psychological works of Sigmund Freud,* (Vol. 14). London: Hogarth Press (1957).

Freud, S. (1922). Some neurotic mechanisms in jealousy, paranoia and homosexuality. In J. Strachey (Ed.). *The standard edition of the complete psychological works of Sigmund Freud* (Vol. 18). London: Hogarth Press, 1955. Frosch, J. (1981). The role of unconscious homosexuality in the paranoid constellation. *Psychoanalytic Quarterly, L,* 587–613.

Gonsiorek, J. C. (1982). An introduction to mental health issues and homosexuality. *American Behavioral Scientist, 25,* (4), 367–384.

Gonsiorek, J. C. (1982). Results of psychological testing on homosexual populations. *American Behavioral Scientist, 25,* (4), 385–396.

Gray, J. J. (1970). Case conference: Behavior therapy in a patient with homosexual fantasies and heterosexual anxiety. *Journal of Behavioral Therapy & Experimental Psychiatry, 1,* 225–232.

Hastings, D. (1941). A paranoid reaction with manifest homosexuality. *Archives of Neurology and Psychiatry, 45,* 379–381.

Heimann, P. (1957). A combination of defense mechanisms in paranoid states. In Klein, M., Heimann, P., and Money-Kyrle, R. E. (Eds.). *New directions in psychoanalysis*. New York: Basic Books.

Israelstam, S., & Lambert, S. (1983). Homosexuality as a cause of alcoholism: A historical review. *International Journal of Addiction, 18,* (8), 1085-1107.

James, S. (1978). Treatment of homosexuality. Superiority of densensitization/arousal as compared with anticipatory avoidance conditioning. Results of a controlled trial. *Behavior Therapy, 9,* 28-36.

Kinsey, A. C., Pomeroy, W. B., & Martin, C. E. (1948). *Sexual behavior in the human male.* Philadelphia: Saunders.

Kinsey, A. C., Pomeroy, W. B., Martin, C. E., & Gebhard, P. H. (1953). *Sexual behavior in the human female.* Philadelphia: Saunders.

Klaf, F. S. (1961). Female homosexuality and paranoid schizophrenia: A survey of seventy-five cases and controls. *Archives of General Psychiatry, 4,* 84-86.

Klaf, F. & Davis, C. (1950). Homosexuality and paranoid schizophrenia. A survey of 150 cases and controls. *American Journal of Psychiatry, 116,* 1070-1075.

Klein, H. R. & Horowitz, F. D. (1948). Psychosexual factors in the paranoid phenomena. *American Journal of Psychiatry, 105,* 697-705.

Lamberd, W. G. (1969). The treatment of homosexuality as a monosymptomatic phobia. *American Journal of Psychiatry, 126*(4), 512-518.

Lewis, C. E., Saghir, M. T., & Robins, E. (1982). Drinking patterns in homosexual and heterosexual women. *Journal of Clinical Psychiatry, 43,* (7), 277-279.

Lohrenz, L. J., Connelly, J. C., Coyne, L., et al. (1978). Alcohol problems in several Midwestern homosexual communities. *Journal of Studies on Alcohol, 39,* 1959-1963.

Meyers, M. F. (1980). Common psychiatric problems in homosexual men and women consulting family physicians. *Canadian Medical Association Journal, 123*(5), 359-363.

Nardi, P. M. (1982). Alcoholism and homosexuality: A theoretical perspective. *Journal of Homosexuality, 7*(4), 9-25.

National Council on Alcoholism/American Medical Society on Alcoholism Committee on Definitions (1976). *Annals of Internal Medicine, 85*(6), 764.

Saghir, M. T., & Robins, E. (1973). *Male and female homosexuality: A comprehensive investigation.* Baltimore: Williams and Wilkins.

Schacht, T. E. (1985). DSM-III and the politics of truth. *American Psychologist, 40,* 513-521.

Small, E. J., Jr., & Leach, B. (1977). Counseling homosexual alcoholics. *Journal or Studies on Alcohol, 38,,* 2077-2086.

Turner, W. J. (1981). Alcoholism, homosexuality, and bipolar affective disorder. *American Journal of Psychiatry, 138*(2), 262-263.

Watson, J. B., & Raynor, R. (1920). Conditioned emotional reactions. *Journal of Experimental Psychology, 3,* 1-14.

10

EGO–DYSTONIC HOMOSEXUALITY AND TREATMENT ALTERNATIVES

Faye E. Sultan
Denise M. Elsner
Jaime Smith

PSYCHIATRIC NOSOLOGY

Nosology is the study of disease. Taken from the Greek "nosos" (disease) and "logos" (study), nosology particularly refers to the classification of diseases. Psychiatric nosology is the study and classification of mental disorders according to patterns of behavior, thoughts, and emotions. The *Manual of the International Statistical Classification of Diseases, Injuries, and Causes of Death,* the ICD-9 (World Health Organization, 1977) is an internationally agreed upon system of medical nosology that facilitates communication among clinicians and researchers. The lack of clearly specified criteria for the diagnoses of mental disorders in the ICD-9 has produced an inconsistent usage of diagnostic terms, yet it remains the only international system of psychiatric nosology. The American Psychiatric Association published its own nosological system in 1952, the *Diagnostic and Statistical Manual of Mental Disorders* (DSM-I). The latest revision, the DSM-III (American Psychiatric Association, 1980), does specify diagnostic criteria for almost all of the disorders and has become the foundation of psychiatric diagnosis in this country.

The use of psychiatric classification systems is highly controversial. Physicians generally agree on what constitutes a physical disorder, such as lung cancer, but there may be no agreement on what constitutes a mental disorder, such as ego-dystonic homosexuality. Mental health professionals, theoreticians, and philosophers sharply disagree on definitions of mental disorder; in fact, no precise definition of "mental disorder" exists. The DSM-III (American Psychiatric Association, 1980) employs a series of concepts to facilitate psychiatric evaluations and research. A mental disorder is, according to the DSM-III, ". . . typically associated with either a painful symptom (distress) or impairment in one or more important areas of functioning (disability)," which is not limited to a conflict between society and the individual (DSM-III, American Psychiatric Association, 1980, p. 6). It must be noted that it is difficult to separate subjective distress due to social expectations and prejudices from distress stemming from other causes. Likewise, "important areas of functioning" are not operationally defined but rely on value judgments for the determination of a particular area as important or unimportant.

The concepts of "mental health" and "mental disorder" are man's creation and based on normative standards (Suppe, 1984). Thomas Szasz sees mental health as a vague, almost meaningless term. Probably it is only a new name for our age-old longing for security (Szasz, 1963, Introduction). The controversy concerning psychiatric diagnoses (whether they are medically and scientifically legitimate, or pseudo-scientific supports to social norms, mores, and prejudices) is plainly evident in the psychiatric nosological treatment of homosexuality.

EVOLUTION OF A DIAGNOSIS: THE DSM STORY

Prior to Freud, the Western societal pre-medical view of homosexuality placed it in legal and religious arenas. Freud and psychoanalytic theory situated it squarely in the medical arena by considering homosexuality to be a developmental problem. Freud's theory of psychosexual development provided the intial framework for the emergent diagnosis of homosexuality as a mental disorder. It would be many years until the diagnosis of homosexuality would be seriously reconsidered by the mainstream mental health community.

DSM-I

The DSM-I (American Psychiatric Association, 1952), in concurrence with the broad consensus of social opinion of the times, considered heterosexuality to be the behavioral norm, while homosexuality was seen as the mark of a mentally ill individual. The DSM-I classified homosexuality as the single diagnosis Sexual Deviation (52.2). It has been argued that the inclusion of homosexuality in the DSM-I is but another example of antiquated diagnoses that haunt psychiatric nosology (Silverstein, 1984). In fact, the DSM-I included diagnoses such as Vagabondage, Untruthfulness and Cruelty in its list of mental disorders; some of the diagnoses have been traced to originate with Benjamin Rush, a signer of the American Declaration of Independence (Silverstein, 1984).

DSM-II

When the DSM-II was published (American Psychiatric Association, 1968), afflictions such as Vagabondage had been downgraded from mental disorders to being symptoms of other disorders. Homosexuality retained its status as a mental disorder. It was now classified under the heading Other Non-Psychotic Mental Disorders, under the subheading Sexual Deviation (302), with the subdivision Homosexuality (302.0) distinguishing it from the DSM-I diagnostic category. There was no specific diagnostic criteria other than that outlined for Sexual Deviations. The mental health establishment continued to endorse heterosexual functioning as the norm, against which the statistical rarities of sexual deviations were compared.

Published twenty years prior to the DSM-II, *Sexual Behavior and the Human Male* (Kinsey, Pomeroy, & Martin, 1948) had made a strong case for homosexuality as a normal variant of sexual behavior. Although the Kinsey reports did much to shatter the consensus of opinion among mental health professionals regarding the psychopathology and prevalence of homosexuality, it was not until 1973 that the American Psychiatric Association seriously questioned its classification.

In the center of the 1973 controversy over the classification of homosexuality were those who viewed homosexuality as a mental disorder, and those who viewed it as a normal sexual variant. As a result of extensive lobbying by gay activists, ten research studies were presented to the American Psychiatric Association demonstrating little difference between homosexual individuals and heterosexual individuals in their levels of social functioning and psychopathology. Previous research supporting the psychopathology of homosexuality was challenged on the grounds that the majority of homosexual subjects studied were psychiatric patients, and that heterosexual or nonpatient controls were inadequate.

In light of the new research findings, the American Psychiatric Association removed homosexuality per se from the DSM-II listing of mental disorders. A group of psychiatrists led by Charles Socarides and Irving Bieber disagreed with this decision and forced a referendum vote of the American Psychiatric Association membership (Spitzer, 1981). Lobbying gay activists succeeded in defeating this referendum and abolishing homosexuality per se as a mental disorder from the DSM-II. Substituted in its place was the classification Sexual Orientation Disturbance (DSM-II, 1968, p. vi) "reserved for those homosexuals who are 'disturbed by, in conflict with, or wish to change their sexual orientation' " (DSM-III, 1980, p. 380).

The DSM-II reclassification was a compromise position between the two extremes, but the majority of the American Psychiatric Association membership only reluctantly went along with the new category of Sexual Orientation Disturbance. Those who had supported the removal of homosexuality from the DSM-II endorsed the new classification since it did not imply that the absence of heterosexual desire was equated with psychopathology in the homosexual individual. Those who opposed the 1973 decision saw it as a triumph of politics over sicence. They viewed the refutation of hundreds of resarch studies supporting the psychopathology of homosexuality as very bad science. The tenuous compromise agreement soon came under fire when work began in drafting the DSM-III in 1974 (Spitzer, 1981).

DSM-III

The controversy about the appropriate classification of homosexuality prompted the 1974 American Psychiatric Association Task Force on Nomenclature and Statistics, led by Robert Spitzer, to question the concept of "mental disorder" and its problematic definition. Spitzer, after an extensive review of the disorders in the DSM-II, concluded that all (with the exception of homosexuality and some of the other sexual deviations) caused subjective distress and/or were associated with an impairment in an important area of functioning (Spitzer, 1981). These ideas were worked into the introduction to the DSM-III as guiding concepts for psychiatric diagnosis.

Spitzer (1981) claimed that, in the final analysis, the determination of an area of functioning as "important" is always a value judgment. For him, the heart of the homosexuality issue revolved arround whether or not heterosexuality should be considered the norm for sexual functioning. The DSM-III takes the position that there is no consensus of opinion regarding heterosexuality as an important area of functioning. Spitzer (1981) suggested that the concept of "inherent disadvantage" might serve as a useful guideline for determining which areas of functioning are important. An individual who, relative to other people, is unable to satisfy basic biological and physiological needs due to certain constellations of behaviors, thoughts and emotions is at an inherent disadvantage (for example, an individual who cannot hold a job due to paranoid delusions). The concept of inherent disadvantage plays a large role in the rationale behind the Task Force's reformulation of Sexual Orientation Disturbance.

The DSM-II category, Sexual Orientation Disturbance, was vague and lacking in specificity. In efforts to improve upon it, the name was first changed to Homodysphilia, then to Dyshomophilia, later to Homosexual Conflict Disorder, and eventually to Ego-Dystonic Homosexuality. There was a lack of consensus about whether the inability to function heterosexually because of a homosexual orientation should be considered a mental disorder. The term Ego-Dystonic Homosexuality was accepted as a compromise solution, but with reservation (Spitzer, 1981).

A Glosary of Psychoanalytic Terms and Concepts (American Psychiatric Association, 1968) defines ego-dystonic as ". . . unacceptable mental contents are subjectively experienced by the observing ego as foreign to the self . . ." The DSM-III defines it as "a symptom or personality trait that is recognized by the individual as unacceptable and undesirable and is experienced as alien."

Criticism was presented to the Task Force that it was inconsistent to define Ego-Dystonic Homosexuality by distress alone, as Ego-Dystonic Heterosexuality also would have to be included to accommodate those individuals distressed by their heterosexuality (Suppe, 1984). In response to the criticism, the diagnostic criteria were altered to include that, along with reporting distress due to the homosexual orientation, the patient must desire sexual reorientation (DSM-III, American Psychiatric Association, 1980).

The decision to include Ego-Dystonic Homosexuality in the DSM-III was made by the Task Force and the Advisory Committee on Psychosexual Disorders, both having reached a majority vote. However, once gain, the American Psychiatric Association was embroiled in controversy. Charges were reiterated that this decision was the triumph of politics over science; this time the charges were voiced by those who viewed homosexuality as a normal variant of sexual behavior (Spitzer, 1981). The issue was that the new classification implied that the absence of heterosexual arousal may indicate psychopathology for some homosexual individuals. Others argued that an individual's motivation for treatment was not the typical criterion for determining whether that individual was mentally ill (Socarides & Volkan, 1981).

The inclusion of Ego-Dystonic Homosexuality into the DSM-III appears to have further weakened the consensus of opinion in the mental health community, splintering it into:

1. Those who maintain that defining any sort of homosexuality as a mental disorder is a moral judgment, not science, and that it is immoral to attempt sexual reorientation of homosexual people.
2. Those who do not consider homosexuality a mental disorder, yet do not find reorientation immoral for those people who find their homosexuality distressing.
3. Those who consider homosexuality to be a mental disorder, and consider it immoral to withhold reorientation treatment from those who desire it (Silverstein, 1984).

Because of this lack of consensus, the DSM-III adopts the compromise position that, in some cases, homosexuality is usefully conceptualized as a mental disorder. It considers it appropriate to help an individual develop a heterosexual arousal pattern, since the individual must admit to desiring heterosexual relationships (Spitzer, 1981). Spitzer (1981) defends the DSM-III position with the concept of inherent disadvantage; the homosexual individual is at a disadvantage because society's prejudices interfere with the attainment of psychological and biological needs. He notes that

> ... *inability to function heterosexually has built-in consequences of preventing, or at least interfering with, the ability to procreate—a matter*

that some (including some patients with Ego-Dystonic Homosexuality)
judge to be not inconsequential (Spitzer, 1981, p. 213).

The controversy over the place of homosexuality in psychiatric nosology
continues to rage, revealing larger issues in its wake (Schacht, 1985).
Questioning the validity of labeling homosexuality a mental disorder led to
questioning the notion of "mental disorder" itself. Until the larger issues are
settled, there can be no consensus of opinion on the psychiatric nosological
treatment of homosexuality.

THE DEVELOPMENT OF THE
EGO-DYSTONIC HOMOSEXUAL

The vast majority of homosexual men and women never consult with a
mental health professional of any sort. In studies of non-clinical homosexual
samples (Bell & Weinberg, 1978), most indicate satisfaction with their choice
of lifestyle. Since it is those individuals who are dissatisfied and unhappy with
their social orientation who are the source of discussion here, one must
hypothesize about those circumstances which separate the 'ego-dystonic' from
the 'ego-syntonic' homosexual.

Origins of Homosexuality

A review of the literature demonstrates no clear-cut or identifiable cause
of sexual object choice. To understand the development of Ego-dystonic
Homosexuality, to identify those homosexuals who are unhappy with their
sexuality, the psychosexual development of the homosexual individual must
be considered. Although there is still speculation about when and how a child
makes his/her sexual object choice, sex role behavior and gender identity are
thought to be largely determined by age three (Smith, 1980). The elementary
school years are crucial for the formation of the child's own belief system,
drawn from the particular familiar and societal values which dominate the
child's environment. In our society, the media, schools, churches, and family
units impress upon the child that heterosexual functioning is the expected
outcome of psychosexual development.

The conflict in the prehomosexual child becomes manifest during adolescence. The self-recognition of a homosexual orientation, along with the
knowledge of the negative social attitudes toward homosexuality, are coupled
with the normal adolescent identity crisis. This combination may lead to
disruptions in the behavioral, cognitive, and affective domains due to the
individual's anticipated rejection by parents and society.

Smith (1980) states that, at this point the dysphoric homosexual
adolescent either gets better or worse. Which direction the homosexual
adolescent takes depends upon both internal factors, such as basic sense of
self-esteem, level of need for homosexual gratification, and capacity for

bravery in the face of differences between the self and society, and external factors, such as peer support or regular sexual partners, and parental tolerance of the child's sexually deviant behavior.

Those who improve go through a gradual process of adjustment in restoring confidence and self-esteem, and to forming new social attachments. According to Smith, the other direction leads to deterioration or fixation. Those who deteriorate may demonstrate severe behavioral disturbances, psychosis, or even suicidal tendencies. Those who fixate have chronic low self-esteem because their sexual orientation conflicts with their internalized value system.

Figure 1 illustrates Smith's (1980) conceptualization of the psychosexual development of the homosexual.

Bell and Weinberg (1978) have formulated a very useful classification system to further describe the various levels of psychological and behavioral adjustment homosexual men and women may achieve. In their books, *Homosexualities* (1978), Bell and Weinberg descibe five types of homosexual adjustment among men and women. The typological variables included in their classification system include the individual's type of relationship with partner, regret over sexual orientation, presence of sexual problems such as an orgasmic or erectile difficulty, the number of different sexual partners, the amount of search for potential sex partners, and the level of sexual activity.

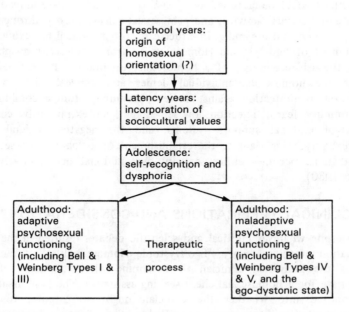

FIGURE 1. Developmental sequence leading to Ego-Dystonic Homosexuality, one form of maladaptive psychosexual functioning in the adult homosexual. (Smith, 1980)

They found that 71% of their samples could be classified according to one of the following five types:

- Type I "close coupled"—monogamous in a quasi-marriage.
- Type II "open coupled"—in a primary but nonmonogamous relationship.
- Type III "functional"—noncoupled, had many partners, high level of sexual activity, little regret.
- Type IV "dysfunctional"—noncoupled, had many partners, high level of sexual activity, high level of regret, more sexual problems.
- Type IV "asexual"—few partners, low sexual activity, high level of regret.

Those individuals who fulfill the diagnostic criteria for Ego-dystonic Homosexuality would probably be assigned to Types IV and V in the Bell Weinberg scheme (Smith, 1980). Such individuals might deal with their homosexual orientation by conscious denial and periodic anonymous homosexual gratification. These individuals may marry and attempt to include a heterosexual arousal pattern to their sexual response set, but this is often accompanied by chronic feelings of a lack of sexual fulfillment with their spouses, and guilt feelings over their homosexual impulses and periodic homosexual contacts. These individuals fit well into the Type IV classification.

Others could be classified as Type V or "asexual"; these individuals may renounce sociosexual activity, and gain sexual release mostly through masturbation, fantasy, and dreaming. In either case, the individual has evolved to the development of Ego-dystonic Homosexuality from adolescent dysphoria following the self-recognition of a homosexual orientation. It may be that the ego-dystonic homosexual individual denies and conceals the homosexual orientation as protection against anxiety, stemming from a combination of social timidity, fear of rejection, low self-esteem, and extrapunitive conscience, a lack of external support systems, and the negative societal view of homosexuality. This leads to the establishment of a "pathogenic secret" and the individual becomes either sexually dysfunctional or effectively asexual (Smith, 1980).

CLINICAL IMPLICATIONS AND CONSIDERATIONS

Despite whatever political and scientific debates resulted in the DSM III formulation of this category "Ego-Dystonic Homosexuality," it remains the task of the individual clinician to determine what treatment, if any, is appropriate for a homosexual client seeking assistance. The basic issue may be dichotomized into whether the clinician ought to attempt to promote heterosexuality in some way or whether the client is best treated by facilitating adjustment to the current sexual orientation. This treatment debate has raged for many years, well before the establishment of the DSM III diagnostic criteria. A vast diversity of treatment approaches have existed historically as well as those in current use.

The clinician's choice of treatment option in this case must clearly be viewed as a reflection of that particular individual's biases about homosexuality as a sexual choice. The clinician who views homosexuality as a sexual aberration will more easily prescribe treatment to increase heterosexual arousal and/or eliminate homosexual responsiveness. The clinician who firmly views homosexuality as a viable and legitimate lifestyle choice will be much more inclined to encourage the client to adjust to his/her homosexuality.

There are those who would argue most vigorously from each side of this treatment dichotomy. Perhaps, however, the motivation of the client and the specific sources of dissatisfaction of that particular individual ought to play a greater role in the choice of treatment offered to that client. The client who genuinely desires to develop heterosexual responsiveness in order that s/he might marry and produce biological children should be treated quite differently than the client who is suffering with poor self-esteem resulting from family and/or societal disapproval.

For those individuals who wish to increase their heterosexual responsiveness, two types of behavior therapies have generally been employed. One type focuses on existinguishing homosexual arousal and the other on *increasing* heterosexual arousal. The use of techniques designed to extinguish homosexual arousal can be criticized on a number of grounds. Such aversion techniques typically involve much physical suffering and have not been found to be successful over an extended period of time.

Techniques which seem more promising are those similar to the Masters and Johnson program (1979) which attempt to facilitate heterosexual responsiveness without specifically attempting to extinguish homosexuality. Sixty-seven ego-dystonic homosexuals in their study were treated by means of short-term couples sex therapy with opposite-gendered partners. While the success rate reported for this treatment method is not high if evaluated in terms of changes in basic sexual orientation, such techniques may be viewed as highly effective if increased ability to interact heterosexually is seen as the goal. Viewed in this light, heterosexual responsiveness was, in fact, increased (Smith, 1980).

In the case of the individual who is experiencing low self-esteem but who would like to adjust to a homosexual orientation, both internal and external resources must be mobilized to change this individual's self-perception. The mobilization of these resources would permit the individual to alter his/her lifestyle, to establish a more adaptive form of psychosexual adjustment. A shift in both self-regard and behavior is the anticipated goal (Smith, 1980).

The building of self-esteem is the basic internal factor to be addressed therapeutically. Positive self-regard msut be established. The client must explore the values relevant to his/her sexual behavior and develop pride in that sexuality. Whatever other psychological difficulties may exist for that individual may, of course, be treated simultaneously, with the overall goal remaining the establishment of positive self-regard (Smith, 1980).

The mobilization of external resources for the homosexual individual may be quite a complex process. The family of origin may, for example, be of considerable help to the troubled homosexual. Family therapy may alleviate the parents of any guilt they have harbored about producing a homosexual child and free the parents to be less rejecting of this child. In our clinical experience, this is sometimes an effective way of facilitating the re-establishment of supportive communication between homosexual clients and their parents.

It is sometimes helpful to recommend an increased involvement in the gay community to those homosexual clients who are socially isolated. The formation of new social and sexual attachments with the homosexual community may help to compensate for the rejections from family and former friends (Smith, 1980). There is often a variety of social, religious, political, and recreational activity within the gay communities in many cities. Clinicians have an obligation to be familiar with the resources available for homosexual clients in their community.

In our experience, short-term psychotherapy, along with increased social activity (the mobilization of external resources) is generally sufficient to increase the self-esteem and level of adjustment in homosexual clients. The mobilization of internal and external resources are both interdependent and mutually reinforcing. Progress in one area greatly facilitates progress in the other.

REFERENCES

A Glossary of Psychoanalytic Terms and Concepts. 2nd ed., New York: American Psychoanalytic Association, 1968.

American Psychiatric Association. *The Diagnostic and Statistical Manual of Mental Disorders.* Washington, D.C.: 1952.

American Psychiatric Association. *The Diagnostic and Statistical Manual of Mental Disorders.* 3rd ed., Washington, D.C.: 1980.

Bell, A. P., & Weinberg, M. S. *Homosexualities.* New York: Simon & Schuster, 1978.

Masters, W. H., & Johnson, V. E. *Homosexuality in perspective.* Boston: Little, Brown, 1979.

Kinsey, A., Pomeroy, W., & Martin, C. *Sexual behavior in the human male.* Philadelphia: W. B. Saunders, 1948.

Schacht, T. E., DSM-III and the politics of truth. *American Psychologist,* 1985, *40*(5), 513–521.

Silverstein, C. The ethical and moral implications of sexual classification: A commentary. *Journal of Homosexuality,* 1984, *9*(4), 29–38.

Smith, J. Ego-dystonic homosexuality. *Comprehensive Psychiatry,* 1980, *21*(2), 119–127.

Socarides, C. W., & Volkan, V. D. Challenging the diagnostic status of homosexuality. Letter, *American Journal of Psychiatry,* 1981, *138*(9), 1256–1257.

Spitzer, R. L. The diagnostic status of homosexuality in DSM-III: A reformulation of the issues. *American Journal of Psychiatry,* 1981, *138*(2), 210–215.

Suppe, F. Classifying sexual disorders: The Diagnostic and Statistical Manual of the American Psychiatric Association. *Journal of Homosexuality,* 1984, *9*(4), 9–27.

Szasz, T. *The myth of mental illness: Foundations of a theory of personal conduct.* New York: Hoeber-Harper, 1961.

Szasz, T. *Law, liberty, and psychiatry: An inquiry into the social uses of mental health practices.* New York: MacMillan, 1963.

World Health Organization. *Manual of the international statistical classification of diseases, injuries, and causes of death.* 9th rev., 2 vols., Geneva: Author, 1977.

11

THE THERAPIES

Louis Diamant

THE CLINICAL APPROACH: TRICK OR TREATMENT?

Kaplan and Stein (1984) may have said it all. "Homosexuality is one of the most difficult topics to approach" (p. 264). Yet approach we must.

A more poignant issue than a choice of theoretical approach may lie in the question of whether an anomalous behavior makes one an anomaly in the fuller context. It is an issue which dyes the whole cloth of scientific inquiry and in the long run may make the internecine squabbling among the behaviorally-oriented and the psychodynamic positionists appear like the growls of pet spaniels over a table scrap—full of harmless fury but resolving nothing. The treatment of homosexuality these days appears to leave no one really comfortable—neither clinicians nor clients nor social activists—and the discomfort is not totally to do with whether the treatment goes outside to change the anomaly behaviorally or inside to remediate at an internal source. The tensions have very much to do with the clinical perception of difference.

Preliminary to and yet intrinsic to a description of treatment is a clinically touchy and challenging issue. When does a condition of life or behavior qualify for action that is labeled a treatment or therapy? According to the *Diagnostic and Statistical Manual of Mental Disorders, Third Edition* (American Psychiatric Association, 1980) homosexuality itself cannot be considered a mental disorder. Homosexuality is a disorder only when it is accompanied by a marked condition of dissatisfaction and stress related to that behavior. Under those particular circumstances it would be classified as Ego-dystonic homosexuality (p. 281) and the person so affected might be considered a bona fide candidate for psychological or psychiatric treatment (Since DSM-III classifications are so widely used in establishing diagnoses for insurance, disability, legal, clinical and other circumstances, the importance of the DSM-III nomenclature cannot be underestimated). Earlier editions of the diagnostic and statistics manual (American Psychiatric Association 1952, 1968) did classify and codify homosexuality as a mental disorder. In 1973 the Board of Trustees of the American Psychiatric Association voted to expunge homosexuality from its classifications. The disorder-treatment relationship of homosexuality was in the "official" sense hereby interrupted making, oddly enough, the aspect of treatment something clinicians would approach with greater circumspection.

Books and journals published before the issuance of DSM-III were replete with descriptions of homosexualities in terms of a categorized disorder with prescribed cures in a number of treatment modalities. The post DSM-III era may reasonably be described as one with fewer papers concerned with the treatment and cure of homosexuality. But in fairness to those who have faced the criticism of being involved in a wand-waving approach to diagnosis and treatment, the tendency to judge homosexuality as a special classification of psychopathology was given persistent voice in the publications before the epic categorization change. It was, by then, common for authors to advocate psychotherapies and treatments oriented toward sex preference change and in the same journalistic breath suggest an approach that considered adjustment therapy for those patients whose well entrenched homosexual preference seemed too resistant for the primary psychotherapy to result in heterosexuality. This secondary goal for homosexual posture, when compared to outcome wishes for other disorders, indicates that by the time DSM-III was published, homosexuality was already an exception among the diagnostic categories. It is the only inclusion of the scores of classifications in DSM-III that bears that designation—ego-dystonic. The complexities related to this diagnosis have been discussed (Bayer, 1981; Bayer and Spitzer, 1982; Schacht, 1985). Ego-dystonic homosexuality is a classification considered at greater length in another chapter in this book and it is mentioned here only as it is related to the question of clinical treatments. Should, however, the history of clinicized homosexuality make it tempting to dismiss the concept as a chimera we note that phenomenologically it remains quite real.

Since the turn of the century adoption of homosexuality as a psychiatric concern, various methodological attacks have been made upon it in the name of that concern. These cures and deterrents have included moral themes, analytic therapies, behavioral therapies, primitive behavioral therapies, chemical therapies, surgery, and adjustment therapies, psychiatric incarceration and even relatively recent electrical brain stimulation (Moan and Heath, 1972). Currently we have been led to some observations and assumptions:

1. There has been a continual disagreement even among those who regard homosexuality as a pathological phenomenon as to the efficacy of psychotherapy or other palliative agent.

2. The description of homosexuality as a treatable behavior only when it is ego-dystonic makes it the only classified and specified nonpathological behavior that is normal until one is discomfited by it. Certainly one can think of other "normal" conditions not indexed in DSM-III that can cause concern and distress. The matter of common weight gains that are for large numbers of people acceptable (ego-syntonic) or unacceptable (ego-dystonic) comes very quickly to mind. English and English (1958) define ego-dystonic as ego-alien. DSM-III (American Psychiatric Association, p. 10) uses the term ego-dystonic in another connection not related to homosexuality and that is the description of symptoms which constitute a neurotic disorder. The lack of clarity in the diagnostic process tends to obfuscate motivation for treatment and to confuse therapeutic goals.

3. Homosexuality may be treated without major concern for psychiatric designation. Sex therapists Masters and Johnson did not concentrate on psychopathology when they accepted homosexual men and women for reversion, conversion or the treatment of sexual dysfunction. They treated those who wished to gain or regain heterosexual status because it would enhance their social or occupational opportunities; they were accepted by the institution as candidates for conversion without having to meet the distressful symptoms criterion that is involved in ego-dystonia. Thus, they qualified as patients only in the sense that one is a patient for a cosmetic nose change—a patient may improve his social and occupational opportunities with this decision but there is no illness involved.

4. The treatment of a sexual dysfunction involves an illness, and while homosexual dysfunction may not be what the committee had in mind when they created this classification of psychosexual disorder (American Psychiatric Association, 1980, p. 275), the manual does not specify sexual dysfunction as a psychopathology only when it involves heterosexual performance. Thus, as it presently stands, when psychiatric nomenclature is used as a reference point, therapy designed to change to heterosexuality a homosexual man or woman when no neurotic ego dystonic stress is involved is the treatment of a condition that is not diagnostically established, whereas the enhancement of homosexual performance represents the therapeutic approach to a mental disorder.

5. There is little question that there has been a change in Western and especially the American willingness to recognize homosexuality, that is, to acknowledge that it exists and to do this in a public and open manner. For example: homosexuality is now presentable along with

that other former taboo, heterosexuality, on network television. Masters and Johnson (1979) implied that there is now a more benign climate to publish a work dealing with sexual response in homosexuality than when they began research. They felt that as recently as the 1950s it was imprudent to do clinical investigation of cunnilingus and fellatio even with a heterosexual population.

THE MEDICAL BEGINNING

To review the literature on treatments and their efficacy is of necessity to review the concepts of causality and to note that what respected clinicians have postulated and what controversies have been aired historically do in most respects continue. Freud's psychology is perhaps the best starting place for reviewing homosexuality in terms of modern psychological dynamics and the principles of psychoanalysis (Freud, 1905) may be historically and conceptually the most logical point from which to study homosexuality in terms of a mental phenomenon explainable and treatable. Freud, while perhaps not always consistent, is the originator of a psychosexual model for explaining the development of heterosexuality and homosexuality. Freud did not, however, develop extensive case studies in homosexuality as did his contemporaries Krafft-Ebing (1958) and Havelock Ellis (1921) whose psychiatric celebrity grew from their reports. These two sexologists hold a similar view that homosexuality was an unavoidable constitutional condition and that little if anything could be done by way of treatment to change those who were afflicted. Krafft-Ebing, however, saw homosexuality as a degeneracy, an opinion that Ellis did not share. If Ellis advocated a therapy, it was the therapy of compassion and understanding for those who had the condition congenitally and therefore unalterably. Ellis had a different view of congenital homosexuality than that which he labeled pseudohomosexuality. Pseudohomosexuality developed from specific conducive conditioning situations, in a person who was not really homosexual. Prevention was the treatment for the pseudohomosexual. But for the congenital invert "prevention can have but small influence" (Ellis, 1921, p. 325). However, sound social hygiene would render difficult the acquisition of homosexual perversity. He denounced castration, a form of treatment which had its turn of the century medical advocacy. Ellis noted the failure of psychotherapy, psychoanalysis, and hypnosis, measures he found humane enough but means which were not equal to the task. He saw the British school system with its sexual segregation as a major factor in pseudohomosexuality and recommended a system of coeducation which would help to preserve the healthiness of sexual emotional attitudes. He admonished, however, that this would of course not prevent the development of congenital inversion, noting in this connection that in Sparta and Lesbos homosexuality was most ideally cultivated although the sexes mixed most frequently than in any other state. Ellis also recommended a regimen of physical and mental hygiene measures which could, in a favorable environment, if the patient were young and the perversion did not appear too deeply rooted in the organism, vitalize normal sexual impulses.

When the condition was truly organic and deep-rooted, Ellis recommended the use of the treatment of self-restraint and self-culture. To Ellis, chastity rather than a search for a normal sexuality or desexualization was the treatment answer. He apparently nurtured the notion that saintliness and humane good works could be the trade-off for homosexual activity, especially among those with what he called a finer nature which he found in considerable numbers of "inverts." He considered it outside of the province of the physician to recommend that his homosexual patients live according to their homosexual impulses even when these impulses seemed natural to the patient (in current terminology ego-syntonic). His conclusion as far as the physician was concerned: The most that he could do was to present the situation clearly and let him, the patient, decide for himself and accept the responsibility.

During his lifetime Ellis was a force in investigating and understanding human sexual behavior. A voice against many of the turn of the century medically supported treatments and therapies for homosexuality, i.e., castration, baths, hypnosis, medication, incarceration, and even lobotomy. Also, in contradistinction to most other professional voices was that of Magnus Hirschfeld, a physician and sexologist. His views were promulgated in his magnum opus, *Homosexuality in Men and Women* (Hirschfeld, 1914). Succinctly, Hirschfeld's basic treatment was a nondynamic adjustment therapy that went something like this: avoid denial, work hard, where possible continue your sexual behavior but do it safely and keep out of trouble. Change of orientation is virtually impossible.

PSYCHODYNAMIC TREATMENT, THEORY, RESEARCH, CASE STUDIES

The pursuit of heterosexuality (or the treatment of homosexuality) by psychotherapy is persistent and constant following Freud's formulation of psychoanalysis. The psychoanalytic theory of homosexuality elaborated upon elsewhere in this book, includes scores of postulates added by other psychoanalytic theorists (Fenichel, 1945). The position taken by the psychoanalytically oriented is that the foundation of both heterosexual behavior and homosexuality is in the Oedipus stage, between the ages of three to five when sexual identity is solidified and role models provide the stimuli toward same parent or opposite parent identification. Certain factors at that stage can change the aim and object of the sexual drive and result in homosexuality. Freud (1905) was not definite about psychological, social, or constitutional factors interfering with the progress from pregenital sexuality to adult heterosexuality. Neither was he constant in viewing homosexuality as a psychopathology. He deemed it a disorder but not an illness in the one case reported in which he undertook the psychoanalytic treatment of a lesbian (Freud, 1920).

When discussing psychoanalytic treatment it might be said at the outset that it is easier to describe procedures than to illustrate the dynamics that initiate change. If we accept Jones (1961), the motivation coming from important unconscious ideas and affect too painful for willing recall undergo regression which leads to certain memories being replaced by symptoms. So symptoms are the unwanted bitter fruit of repression. DSM-III states that the term "neurotic disorder" referred to a mental disorder in which the prominent disturbance is a symptom or group of symptoms that is distressing and is recognized by him or her as "ego-dystonic," that is, unacceptable and alien (American Psychiatric Association, 1980, p. 9). If that is the case, even now homosexuality could be thought of in terms of a phobia and thus treated as a neurotic disorder. Some instances of homosexuality have been considered among phobic disorders and even so-named, heterophobia (James, 1978).

Freud apparently never thought of homosexuality as a neurosis, and at least some time in his life, said that quite specifically in an often cited letter to an American mother who was concerned about her apparently homosexual son (Jones, 1961, p. 502). "Homosexuality is assuredly no advantage," he wrote, "but it is nothing to be ashamed of, no vice, no degradation; it cannot be classified as an illness." He added, however, that if he were neurotic and unhappy that psychoanalysis could bring him harmony and peace of mind whether or not he remained homosexual. It seems clear that Freud had in mind psychoanalysis as a method of treating the neurosis and not the homosexuality.

In his treatment of a lesbian, Freud (1920) had said that there were two stages in the psychoanalytic treatment, first sort of a preparatory stage, likened to going to the railroad station and buying a ticket and even sitting on the train, and the second stage would be the actual journey. Freud never did go into the second stage with his young patient. That is, he never made an analysis of the unconscious with her. The case noted as it is in psychoanalytic literature does not demonstrate the dynamics of psychoanalytic intervention if one were looking for the elucidation of the psychodynamics of treatment in terms of those deeper mental changes that would lead to a return or change to heterosexuality. Freud emphasized the difficulty of establishing a differential diagnosis between a congenital and an acquired homosexuality and deemed it inadvisable to pursue a conversion when the patient was satisfied, as she was, with the sexual preference. In this study he repeated earlier postulates about the causation of homosexuality and the role of the Oedipal conflict in determining a person's sexual aim and object. In the first state of analysis he saw many of the dynamics that affected her particular love choice duplicated in heterosexual relationships. In closing Freud tells us that it is not for psychoanalysis to solve the problems of homosexuality. "It must rest content," he stated, "with disclosing the psychical mechanisms that have resulted in determining the object choice (person to which one's libido is directed) and with tracing back the paths from them to the instinctual dispositions. There its work ends," he said, and he left the rest to biological research (Freud, 1920, p. 171).

Freud's less than enthusiastic view on changing sexual preference did not deter other psychoanalysts from attempting conversions or secondary adjustments through psychoanalytic procedures which bring fixated fantasies to the light of consciousness. It is possible that nowhere is the use of psychoanalysis and psychoanalytically oriented therapy given more emphasis as a treatment procedure than in the work of psychiatrist Irving Bieber (Bieber et al., 1962). Bieber (1969) is persistent in his view that homosexuality is a psychopathology, a view that he purported to support with hundreds of case studies on male homosexuality. Bieber is also constant in expressing the validity of treating male homosexuality as a disorder (Bieber, 1976), a point he argued with Davison (1976), a behavioral psychologist who was vehemently opposed to a treatment concept (Davison, 1978). Although Bieber et al. (1962) labeled homosexuality as a pathological regression, they did not classify diagnostically, in terms of homosexuality, the 106 cases presented in their major research project. However, the participating psychoanalysts did present diagnoses on the cases comprising their research group; and as it turned out, there is no single category of disorder to which all the patients were assigned. For example, twenty-six of the patients were labeled as schizophrenic, twenty-nine as psychoneurotic, forty-two as having character disorders, and two as "other." Only half of the patients were initially willing to reveal their homosexuality, and so it is possible that diagnostic designations would have been redistributed if the information about their homosexuality were known at the time of assessment.

Even though Bieber et al.'s investigation specified environmental conditions that could result in homosexuality, the obfuscation of classification could interfere with the formation of a mental illness model of homosexuality. The problem of reporting on treatment dynamics is not only complicated by the presence of a variety of disorders but also by the use of seventy-seven psychoanalysts. It is virtually impossible to get a homogeneity of diagnostic opinions, therapeutic techniques, insight, ego strength evaluations and treatment conclusions from seventy-seven individuals even though they may bear credentials from accredited psychoanalytic institutes. Bieber et al. lend some support to a concern about the difficulties involved in controlling these variables when it is noted, in another context, that psychoanalysts have different biases that affect their reporting (Bieber et al., 1962, p. 274). These observations, while they may provoke argument concerning the validity of treatment, are not made with argumentation specifically in mind. Judgements concerning clinical positions must in the final analysis rest with the reader.

In any case, Bieber et al. (1962, p. 276) reported that of the 106 homosexual men in the study that twenty-nine of the patients became totally heterosexual during the course of psychoanalytic treatment and that of these fourteen had been exclusively homosexual. Improvement in other personal areas was reported for ninety-seven of the patients. Heterosexuality appears in the study to be related to the total hours of treatment with those in psychoanalysis the longest the most likely to change to exclusive heterosexual behavior. Although his report does not include studies on psychoanalysis and female homosexuality, he expressed a belief that as in male homosexuality, lesbianism would result from a continuity of pathological parent child relationships; and also as in the case of male homosexuality, he believed that psychiatric intervention in the form of psychoanalysis or psychoanalytically oriented psychotherapy is the indicated treatment for the pathology (Bieber, 1969). In that respect Kay, (1967) reported a 50 percent conversion to exclusive heterosexuality through the psychoanalytic treatment of women and Albert Ellis' (1963) study indicated that in terms of achieving satisfactory sex love relationships with the other sex that 25 percent of the male patients were distinctly improved and 39 percent were considerably improved. Ellis reported that his female patients showed even more improvement with $33\frac{1}{3}$ percent distinctly improved and $66\frac{2}{3}$ considerably improved. Ellis concluded that there are some grounds to believe that homosexual patients who are seriously concerned about their condition and who are willing to work to improve it may with psychoanalytically oriented psychotherapy be helped to gain a more satisfactory heterosexual orientation. Although Ellis no longer treats patients with a psychoanalytic method, that fact alone cannot expunge the data collected in his study with twenty-eight male and twelve female patients (Ellis, 1963).

Psychoanalytic therapists express varying beliefs concerning the balancing of the therapeutic tasks involved in their treatment of homosexuality, and some in relatively recent years write about the need to turn to Freud's concept of bisexuality for the understanding of homosexuality and thus for creating a balance favorable to the establishment of heterosexuality. Socarides (1961) has reported on this aspect of sexual development. Edwardo Weiss has applied a concept of biologial bisexuality to the analytic treatment of female homosexuality. He stated that biological bisexuality is the precondition for both homosexuality and heterosexuality. According to Weiss the feeling of being complete comes from encompassing or egotizing the tendency of one's own sex. If a woman egotizes female sexual drives rather than masculine drives, her feminine drives can find direct satisfaction while the masculine ones, aroused by biological bisexuality, can be satisfied vicariously in her relation with a man. The psychoanalytic treatment, therefore, should establish a greater stability of distribution of male and female longing between ego and chosen sexual objects (Socarides, 1961).

In the psychotherapy of a male homosexual, Wallace (1969) based the treatment process on Gill's (1954) definition of psychoanalysis as a treatment which encourages the development of a regressive transference neurosis and the resolution of the neurosis by the analyst's interpretation. Using this notion of therapy, Wallace reported that a thirty-four year old homosexual male, after eighty-eight hours of therapy covering less than nine months, achieved a heterosexual image of himself and was married shortly thereafter. In addition to gaining heterosexuality, the patient was said to have attained insight into the basis of his fear of heterosexual activity and also appeared to become freer of the threat of ego boundary dissolution (pre-schizophrenic) in the relationship with his wife. In this case, the negative regression transference did not occur; but according to the author the transference did occur in such ways that the patient had a chance to see the transference figure of the psychoanalyst as a safe and helping parent substitute. The author stated that he had become a safe place for the transference of infantile distortions since he had established himself as a potential new object (mother was the original object stimulus) and he was thus able to use the therapeutic relationship to resume an interrupted growth toward a masculine identity.

Case studies and research involving psychodynamic principles have been presented in this section to illustrate the employment of those postulates in the treatment of homosexual patients. Those cited have been from the practices of noted clinicians. Psychoanalytic studies have been the mainstay in these illustrations although there are other established psychodynamic post-Freudian personality theories which are described in this book. It seems apparent that the psychoanalytically oriented have been more concerned with homosexuality its etiology and treatment than some other established schools of psychology with the possible, more recent exception of behavioral psychology.

BEHAVIORISTS AND THEIR TREATMENTS

The importance of psychoanalysis and behaviorism as the two competing theoretical colossi is supported by an introduction to Uhlman and Krasner's (1965) behavior modifications case study book in which they elaborate on the psychoanalytic and learning positions as competitive forces. They define the medical model in terms of symptoms caused by a central mental pathology, (conflict) that are curable or remediable by psychodynamic psychotherapy. Opposed to this model is the learning or behavioral model which is based on the conditioning and reinforcement principles of learning theory (Skinner, 1953, 1974). Feldman and MacCulloch (1971), who did pioneering work in the use of aversive conditioning techniques in converting male and female homosexuality into heterosexuality, also review prior psychoanalytic and behavioral therapies as an introduction to their major work.

The treatment method from which Feldman and MacCulloch (1971) processed the greatest change in sexual orientation was aversive therapy using anticipatory avoidance learning. Classical conditioning which was also used by these researchers was found to be effective but was less resistant to extinction than the instrumental learning method employed in the anticipatory avoidance technique. The authors, while conceding that a definite demarcation between instrumental learning and classical conditioning may not be possible, still emphasize a distinction. In classical aversion conditioning, a stimulus once not naturally inducing anxiety, preparatory to pain, may take on that attribute when presented with a disturbing electric shock to a patient who cannot control the situation. In anticipatory avoidance learning the painful shock can be avoided by some behavior on the part of the respondent. While in both conditions, the patients were discomforted by shocks during the presentation of homosexually provocative pictures, they were able to discontinue the shocks by removing the slide under the instrumental arrangement. The latter, anticipatory avoidance, was decided to be better than classical conditioning, far better than psychotherapy, and they put the data from their results up against Bieber et al. (1962) to support this contention. They had 60 percent heterosexual conversions against Bieber et al.'s 27 percent, and the expenditure of time in terms of hours with women patients was significantly lower.

The results of their investigation are limited. Of their forty-three patients, only two were women, and they were quite young, eighteen years old, and on the Kinsey scale might not have been considered lesbians. Davison and Wilson (1973) and Wilson and Davison (1974) have discussed the importance of different strategies when considering male and female homosexuality, and there is little evidence that Feldman and MacCulloch (1971) have made a distinction. Ellis (1963) conjectured on a number of factors that are different for gay men and lesbians to account for the significantly greater percentage of sex orientation change for females in his research employing psychotherapy as the treatment medium. Although the omission might be considered a serious one, Wilson and Davison (1974) saw Feldman and MacCulloch's research as the most systematic application of learning principle to the treatment of homosexuality at the time of its publication.

BEYOND AVERSIVE REINFORCEMENT

Aversive therapy for treating homosexuality has since come upon bad times and some of the criticism has centered on questions of not only its humaneness but of its failure with those who lacked prior heterosexual pleasurable experiences and those patients described by James (1978) as heterophobic. Criticism, further, included observations that aversive treatment might not only fail to stop homosexuality but it could add a phobic reaction to homosexual behavior on top of the existing heterosexual phobia. Such thinking among behavioral psychologists was to result in the search for a way to reduce heterosexual anxiety and increase heterosexual arousal without having aversive techniques shock out the last notion of even same sex behavior. In the armamentarium of behaviorally oriented clinicians, was, besides aversive techniques, a seemingly more benign method—desensitization (Blitch & Haynes 1972, Huff 1970, James 1978). Essentially desensitization is the removal of anxiety toward a feared or phobic object or situation through the induction of relaxation in the presence of, or with the image of, the high anxiety stimulus. Wolpe (1958, 1969) and Wolpe and Lazarus (1966) described the role of desensitization and assertiveness training. Briefly, a systematic desensitization pairs relaxation with anxiety producing stimulus in a hierarchy of approaches. The peak autonomic arousal is worked up step by step from the fringe of the feared stimulus to the center so that fear of flying could be approached in several steps of imagery or conditions that might go from the planning of the flight to buying the ticket to driving to the airport to being on the flight itself.

Huff's (1970) case was used to demonstrate that author's postulate that in some cases homosexuality was functionally related to a fear of the opposite sex and to illustrate that the reduction of the fear would lead to the initiation of heterosexual behavior. The patient, a nineteen year old male student, went through the desensitization process within a sixteen step hierarchy of anxiety producing images. The image at stage one was of a conversation with several girls. Mid-point at stage eight, it was kissing a girl on the lips and at age sixteen, the girl moved while he had his penis inserted. A six months' follow-up indicated that he had maintained and even furthered his interest in females. The experimenter pondered the question as to whether it was an innate or social variable that brought the subject toward heterosexuality once his fear of women had abated. Edwards (1972) has provided an illustration in which a homosexual pedophile of ten years' duration was rechanneled after thirteen sessions of assertiveness training. Five years prior to the assertiveness therapy the patient had spent a year in psychoanalysis. The psychoanalytic therapy did not change his sexual orientation but made him feel better about himself, even his pedophilia.

More recent use of assertiveness training in treating homosexual patients indicates that there is a reflection of a post-DSM-III spirit. Duehn and Mayadas (1976) described assertiveness training with a homosexual client which had for its objectives putting the sexual variant at ease with his life style rather than being used to direct the variance toward a different sexual behavior. Duehn and Mayadas pointed out that their work suits the time-honored clinical concept of self-determination and individual worth. They believed that their methodology and therapeutic procedures operationalize those values. Assertiveness training as a therapeutic vehicle has has some substantiation from a number of researchers. Basically, assertiveness training is the learning of social action-oriented skills designed to increase the social competency and self-affirmation. Assertiveness training involves modeling, role-playing, and social reinforcement. Duehn and Mayadas used as the focus for their assertiveness training stimulus modeling video tapes "Coming Out: Assertiveness Training for Living." Their case illustration is a male homosexual, but there is no indication that the video tape could not be used with females.

The enhancement of self-esteem, which they sought had been implied in all therapies. The newness of Duehn and Mayadas was the adjustive program for those who chose homosexuality as a way of life and was not a therapy designed to provide adjustment secondarily for those who failed to convert.

CONVERSION WITHOUT PATHOLOGY; SATISFACTION WITHOUT CHANGE

Kohlenberg's (1974) behavioral treatment resulting in a male pedophile converting to adult homosexuality drew considerable attention, but still it was implied or at least readily inferred that adult homosexuality was chosen because it was more attainable for the subject and certainly more acceptable than pedophilia. Duehn and Mayadas' research comes at that point in time when therapeutic aims were beginning to focus on the treatment of the homosexual person rather than just homosexuality. That change may be well exemplified in the research of Masters and Johnson (1979). These sex therapists divided their research and treatment in two main directions, treating homosexual dissatisfaction or homosexual dysfunction.

The treatment of a dysfunctional homosexual population really clinically is innovative in method and objective. Homosexual couples were seen together in therapy. The goal of treatment was the improvement of sexual competency in such areas as excitation, orgasm, and penile erection. According to the authors (Masters & Johnson, 1979, p. 255), their investigation demonstrated that heterosexual male and female sexual resonses were physiologically no different from male and female homosexual responses. Having learned this, they proceeded therapeutically by using the same treatment with homosexual men and women that they had used with their heterosexual subjects (Masters & Johnson, 1970). The outcome in terms of improved sexual functioning supported their assumption that the problems of impotence and inorgasmic states were similar in both the homosexual and the heterosexual populations. Although they referred to an earlier volume (Masters & Johnson, 1970) for the treatment methods for sexual dissatisfaction (p. 255) they did not deal with homosexual dissatisfaction in that volume; the subjects of the 1970 research were heterosexual. However, they maintained that they used the same treatment format although they had at first thought that they would have needed different procedures with homosexual men and women.

Although Masters and Johnson did not use the term, the process utilized what LoPicolo et al. (1972) called "in vivo desensitization" to reduce performance anxiety. According to their report (Masters & Johnson, 1979), treatment success depended largely on the motivation for change. The first condition for treatment was a strong wish to change the sex preference and the second was the availability of an understanding opposite sex partner who would be a major source of support during the transition. The authors found that partner support was a major requirement for treatment success and that the rapidity of treatment and continuing partner cooperation appeared related. Rapid treatment was seen as a technique rather than a time-saver. Treatment for homosexual dysfunction requires a committed or casual partner (a casual partner is one introduced for the purpose of the therapy). In their treatment of homosexual men and women, personal detailed histories were taken which were later to be related to the dysfunction or dissatisfaction. Physical examinations, designed to spot organic complicity, were given to dysfunctional clients, and opposite sex therapists were methodically assigned to both classifications of patients. The dual-sexed team approach was used in each therapeutic case. In working with dissatisfaction it appeared of some importance to establish the chronology of the developing homosexual dissatisfaction and an understanding of life style. They deemed it important also to mirror the influences that were etiologic in the development of the dysfunction or the dissatisfaction, to explain them, and attack them therapeutically. Although Masters and Johnson have been thought by some as behaviorally directed, they have never so categorized themselves; their treatment appears to employ the postulates of behavior therapy, desensitization, psychodynamic therapy, social learning and education.

The results of Masters and Johnson's (1979) treatment of the sexual problems of homosexual men and women are presented in terms of failure. The researchers believed that their results were better expressed in terms of failures than in what they considered the more vague concept of success. Results were as follows: for male homosexual dissatisfaction (54 subjects) after a ten-year follow-up 27.8 percent; for female conversion and reversion (13 subjects) 30.8 percent; for male homosexual dysfunction (57 subjects) 10.5 percent failure rate after ten year follow-up and for female (84 subjects) a 10.7 percent failure rate.

Masters and Johnson (1979) stated that the failure rates cannot be equated in terms of success rates but nevertheless it seems valid to compare the success that Masters and Johnson have had with those reported in other studies dealing with sex preference change.

TOWARD EGO-SYNTONIC HOMOSEXUALITY

In his widely read book, *The Homosexual Matrix*, C. A. Tripp (1975) deliberated on the cure and conversion issue. Succinctly, Tripp, whose arguments pre-date the Masters and Johnson (1979) report, positioned himself firmly against notions that there are treatments that can genuinely change homosexuality. Tripp was not ready to accept cure figures and not only did he eschew the term "cure" but reinterpreted the data provided by the reporters on high change rates. Personal communications from Waddell Pomeroy bolstered his antipathy to published treatment cures. According to the Kinsey research group, sexual propensities had changed little as the result of therapy with few instances worthy of mentioning and even those on closer examination failed to qualify. Tripp also noted from a personal communication from Waddell Pomeroy, that a psychiatrist who had developed an intensive research program on psychoanalytic therapy and male homosexuality could not muster any patients that would take the Kinsey research battery which Pomeroy had offered to administer for any therapist who wanted to validate a case of changed homosexuality (Tripp, 1965, p. 236). Tripp, unsympathetic to sex change therapy, commented favorably on therapists who focus on the homosexual patient's disturbances without trying to redirect his or her sexual preference. He felt that there were some excellent therapists who believed that sexual matters per se would take care of themselves if there were some improvement in the patient's social integration and ability to deal with interpersonal problems. He believed that this sort of therapy required an acceptance that would come across in ways that would give confidence and allow the patient's problem to be dealt with on its own merits.

Tripp's view of therapy seems appropriately capped by Silverberg's (1984) argument. In considering the homosexual as a patient, Silverberg commented

> *a small but growing number of therapists who view homosexuality not as an illness or other condition to be treated or tolerated but rather as an approach to life which is of as much inherent worth as heterosexuality* (p. 19).

Silverberg viewed the current body of clinical literature as inchoative in its development. He disagreed with clinical concern about the causes and cures of homosexuality. He noted that recent attitudinal changes made the issue of heterosexuality in treatment less conspicuous, but there was still an impetus among clinicians working with homosexual clients to change the client's sexual orientation, and thus homosexual feelings and ideas are minimized while heterosexual feelings, ideas, and relationships are given lengthy consideration. Silverberg suggested a number of things for therapists treating homosexual clients to consider regarding both clinical attitudes and methods. One, the therapist needs to be open to a multiplicity of sexual and nonsexual masculine and feminine roles. Two, the therapist must appreciate his own bisexual ideas, thoughts, and feelings and come to terms with his own homophobia. Three, should the therapist not accept the client's sexual preferences, he should be prepared to advise another therapist. Four, conversely, the clinician must avoid pushing a homosexual orientation and premature homosexual labeling on a client. Five, skill is required on the part of the therapist in helping with the decision and mechanisms of acceptance. In some cases a treatment plan is needed to aid a client to find an environment which has support groups, and physicians who are knowledgeable and nonjudgmental about gays and lesbians. He should also have a knowledge of attorneys who have some expertise in the special legal problems of gays and lesbians. Silverberg concluded that the therapeutic relationship should revolve around the client's self-actualization and the therapeutic program be reflected in the client's growing acceptance of self and not in a change of sexual orientation.

CONCLUSIONS

Treatment in this section is a clinical matter. Operationally, for the purpose of developing the chapter it is defined as a service performed by a mental health professional in any of a host of occupations in the psychological, social, medical and educational sciences. In modern times or at any rate since homosexuality became classified or seen as a mental or personality disorder it has been considered a condition, although a rather stubborn one, which most clinicians (mental health professionals) pursued with some treatment design. At first there were the physicians, perhaps simply because they were the first ones on the scene. They classified it, homosexuality, as a pathology (classification is still largely a psychiatric business) and treated it. There were a variety of explanations for male and female homosexuality with distinct etiological explanations for gay and lesbian development.

Among those now historical figures who concerned themselves with homosexuality were Havelock Ellis, Krafft-Ebing and Sigmund Freud, and they called it among other things a deviance or a perversion. Time had some effect on those labelings. Freud's ideas would be relevant if for no other reason that that he developed psychoanalysis through which certain of his practitioners have attempted to describe in terms of a psychoanalytic model the cause and cure of male and female homosexuality. Bieber went to Freud for some support for placing male and female homosexuality in the list of the pathologies, while others have used that first psychoanalyst's genius to the contrary. Bieber (1969) designated homosexuality as a serious psychiatric and social problem; while Freud in his response to the letter written by an American mother concerning her son's homosexuality, wrote that it could not be classified as an illness, and added "we consider it to be a variation of the sexual function by a certain arrest of sexual development." With regard to treatment he wrote, "by asking me if I can help, you mean, I suppose, if I can abolish homosexuality and make normal heterosexuality take its place. The answer is in a general way we cannot promise to achieve it" (Jones, 1961, p. 502).

Katz (1976) writing of himself in his scholarly volume *Gay American History* states:

> *I entered analysis voluntarily I thought with the idea that my "problem" was my homosexuality and my goal a heterosexual "cure.". . . By accident I found a therapist who helped people to find and be themselves who did not view my "problem" as I did myself. . . . After*

perhaps ten years of therapy and only as a result of the organized movement of gay people did I understand that I had earlier been socially pressured into feeling myself a psychological freak, in need of treatment. In entering therapy my goal had in truth, not been voluntarily chosen at all (p. 131).

Perhaps Katz's statement represents the essence of Davison's (1978) complaint concerning the treatment of homosexuality.

Social pressure, social desire, social acceptability may be valuable coercions. In cases of antisocial, delinquent, or criminal behavior, treatments often try to use those coercions as motivations. But in a world in which there is benign homosexuality, one must ask how much sex orientation change should be sought through behavioral treatment or psychodynamic therapy or even if there is a need for the classification "ego-dystonic homosexuality." Conjecture of course does not answer the question scientifically. We know that change in the aura surrounding homosexuality, whether or not politically instigated, has changed treatment emphasis. Halleck (1976) illustrates this point.

In the early years of my practice I was hesitant to treat those patients who sought help under duress but was quite willing to try to change the sexual orientation of those whose voluntarism was not complicated by obvious duress. I did this without too much inquiry as to the desirability of such change. In recent years I have become more skeptical as to the voluntary nature of any request to change homosexuality and far more sensitive to the political meaning of my intervention (p. 168)

Halleck believed that treatment specifically aimed at developing a heterosexual behavior should wait until a dialogue with the patient determines the patient's true motivation, i.e., social pressure versus internal value. Thus, to Halleck an informed patient must make the choice concerning sex orientation based on information and diagnosis (what is here diagnosis may elsewhere be considered as etiology). This done, the patient understands the causes of his difficulty and learns about the treatment available. The rules seem complicated and extracting "true motivation" from traditional values seems a complex task. Davison's (1978) message is clear: stop, change therapy, change society. Psychiatrist Jaime Smith (1980), while acknowledging some values in a Masters and Johnson sex orientation therapy for ego-dystonic homosexuality, observed that the therapist should make it clear to the patient that the increased heterosexuality does not mean the end of homosexual behavior and thinking. He, like Davison, concluded that the effective means of dealing with homosexually related ego dystonia is a shift in socioculture values so that all children may, regardless of their psychosexual orientation, be free from negative stereotyping and aggression.

In a summarizing and concluding statement it seems fair to say that there has been some change in publications on the treatment of homosexuality. Reports on aversive type conversion treatments are fewer, and counseling and psychotherapeutic efforts which disdain or minimize or forego emphasis on change to heterosexuality are more common. Psychodynamic psychiatrists like Halleck are less likely to seize opportunities to convert lesbian women and gay men because they are just that, gay or lesbian. A survey of the clinical scene reveals that while there has been no abandonment of the treatment of homosexuality, there are differences of emphasis. Psychoanalytic and psychodynamic theories still play a major part in clinical practice. Hypnosis, social learning, cognitive aversive treatment, existential treatment, assertiveness training along with other methods, are used to enhance heterosexual and homosexual responsiveness. In a personal communication (1985) a clinician of considerable experience, responsibility and reputation as a practitioner, teacher, and author complained that since DSM-III treating homosexuality clinically was socially and politically uncomfortable and that the situation was in a state of disarray. According to the same source, not many clinicians wish to do research or publish papers that are offensive to gay rights groups although they have not abandoned beliefs that homosexuality is a pathology nor refrained from treatments designed to promote heterosexuality. It would be a strange turn of events, then, that put the therapists in the closet and pulled their patients out and brought unity in one respect and disarray in another.

REFERENCES

American Psychiatric Association. (1952, 1968, 1980.) *Diagnostic and statistical manual of mental disorders.* Washington, DC: Author.

Bayer, G. (1981). *Homosexuality and American psychiatry: The politics of diagnosis.* New York: Basic Books.

Bayer, G., & Spitzer, R. L. (1982). Edited correspondence on the status of homosexuality in DSM III. *Journal of History of the Behavior Sciences, 18,* 32–52.

Bieber, I., Dain, H. J., Dince, P. R., Drelich, M. G., Brand, H. G., Gundlach, R. H., Kremer, M. W., Rifkin, A. H., Wilbur, C. B., & Bieber, T. B. (1962). *Homosexuality: A psychoanalytic study.* New York: Basic Books.

Bieber, I. (1969). Homosexuality. *American Journal of Nursing, 69,* 12, 2637–2641.

Bieber, I. (1976). A discussion of homosexuality: The ethical challenge. *Journal of Consulting and Clinical Psychology, 44,* 2, 163–166.

Blitch, J. W., & Haynes, S. N. (1972). Multiple behavioral techniques in a case of female homosexuality. *Journal of Behavior Therapy and Experimental Psychiatry, 3,* 319–322.

Davison, G. C., & Wilson, G. T. (1973). Attitude of behavior therapists toward homosexuality. *Behavior Research Therapy, 4,* 686–696.

Davison, G. C. (1976). Homosexuality: The ethical challenge. *Journal of Consulting and Clinical Psychology, 44,* 2, 157–162.

Davison, G. C. (1978). Not can, but ought: The treatment of homosexuality. *Journal of Consulting & Clinical Psychology, 46,* 1, 170–172.

Duehn, W. D., & Mayadas, N. S. (1976). The use of stimulus/modeling videotapes in assertive training for homosexuals. *Journal of Homosexuality,* Vol. 1, *4,* 373–381.

Edwards, N. B. (1972). Case conference: Assertive training in a case of homosexual pedophilia. *Journal of Behavior Therapy and Experimental Psychiatry, 3,* 55–63.

Ellis, A. The effectiveness of psychotherapy with individuals who have severe homosexual problems. (1965). In: Ruienbeek, H. M. (Ed.), *The problem of homosexuality in modern society.* (p. 175–182). C. P. Dutton.

Ellis, H. (1915). (3rd ed). *Studies in the psychology of sex* (Vol. II). *Sexual inversion.* Philadelphia: F. A. Davis.

English, H. B., & English, A. C. (1958). *A comprehensive dictionary of psychological and psychoanalytical terms: A guide to usage.* New York: Longmans Green.

Feldman, M. P. & MacCulloch, M. J. (1971). *Homosexual behavior: Therapy and assessment.* Oxford: Pergamon Press.

Fenechel, O. (1945). *The psychoanalytic theory of neuroses.* New York: W. W. Norton.

Freud, S. (1905). Three essays on sexuality and other works (1905). In J. Strachey, (Ed.). *The standard edition of the complete psychological works of Sigmund Freud (Vol. III).* London: Hogarth Press.

Freud, S. (1920). The psychogenesis of a case of homosexuality in a woman (1920). In *The standard edition of the complete psychological works of Sigmund Freud (Vol. 18).* London: Hogarth Press.

Gill, M. M. (1954). Psychoanalyses and exploratory behavior. *Journal of the American Psychoanalytic Association, 2,* 771–797.

Halleck, S. L. (1976). Another response to homosexuality. *Journal of Abnormal Psychology, 83,* 2, 192–195.

Hirschfeld, M. (1914). *Homosexuality in men and women.* Berlin: Lous Marcus.

Huff, F. W. (1970). The desensitization of a homosexual behavior. *Behavior and Therapy, 8,* 99–102.

James, S. (1978). Treatment of homosexuality II. Superiority of desensitization/arousal as compared with anticipatory avoidance conditioning. Result of a controlled treatment. *Behavior Therapy, 9,* 28–36.

Jones, E. (1961). *The life and work of Sigmund Freud.* Abridged and edited by Trilling, L., & Marcus, S. New York: Basic Books.

Kaplan, P., & Stein, J. (1984). *Psychology of adjustment* Belmont: Wadsworth.

Katz, I. (1976). *Gay American history: Lesbians and gay men in the U.S.A.* New York: Thomas Y. Rowell.

Kaye, Harvey E., Berl, S., Clare, J., Eleston, M. R., Gershwin, P., Kogan, L. S., Torda, C., Wilbur, C. B. (1967). Homosexuality in women. *Archives of General Psychiatry, 17,* 626–634.

Kohlenberg, R. J. (1974). Treatment of a homosexual pedophiliac using *in vivo* desensitization: A case study. *Journal of Abnormal Psychology, 83,* 192–195.

Krafft-Ebing, R. von. (1965). *Psychopathia-sexualis.* New York: Bell Publishing.

Lo Piccolo, J., Stewart, R., & Watkins, B. (1972). Treatment of erectile failure and ejaculatory incompetence of homosexual etiology. *Journal of Behavioral Therapy and Experimental Psychiatry, 3,* 233–236.

Masters, W. H., & Johnson, V. E. (1970). *Human sexual inadequacy.* Boston: Little, Brown.

Masters, W. H., & Johnson, V. E. (1979). *Homosexuality in perspective.* Boston: Little, Brown.

Moan, C. E., & Heath, R. G. (1972). Septal stimulation for the initiation of homosexual behavior in a homosexual male. *Journal of Behavioral Therapy and Experimental Psychiatry, 3,* 23–30.

Schacht, T. E. (1985). DSM III and the politics of truth. *American Psychologist, 40,* 513–521.

Silverberg, R. A. (1984). Gay. *Journal of Psychosocial Nursing, 22,* 2, 19–26.

Skinner, B. F. (1953). *Science and human behavior.* New York: MacMillan.

Skinner, B. F. (1974). *About behaviorism.* New York: Knopf.

Smith, Jaime (1980). Ego-dystonic homosexuality. *Comprehensive Psychiatry, 2,* 2, 119–127.

Socarides, C. W. (1961). Theoretical and clinical aspects of overt female homosexuality. Socarides, C. W. (Rep.) *Scientific proceedings, Fall Meeting of the American Psychoanalytic Association, 1,* 579–592.

Tripp, C. A. (1976). *The homosexual matrix.* New York: McGraw-Hill.

Uhllman, L. P., & Krasner, L. (1965). *Case studies in behavior modification.* New York: Holt, Rinehart and Winston.

Wallace, L. (1969). Psychotherapy of a male homosexual. *Psychoanalytic Review, 56,* 346–364.

Wilson, G. T., & Davison, G. C. (1974). Behavior therapy and homosexuality: A critical perspective. *Behavior Therapy, 5,* 16–28.

Wolpe, J. (1958). *Psychotherapy by reciprocal inhibition.* Stanford, CA: Stanford University Press.

Wolpe, J. (1969). *The practice of behavior therapy.* New York: Pergamon Press.

Wolpe, J., & Lazaras, A. A. (1966). *Behavior therapy techniques: A guide to the treatment of neuroses.* Oxford: Pergamon Press.

IV

SOCIETY
AND THE HOMOSEXUAL
INDIVIDUAL

12

CONTRIBUTIONS FROM SOCIAL PSYCHOLOGY

Gary T. Long
Faye E. Sultan

INTRODUCTION

There are several concepts and theoretical constructs in the field of Social Psychology which may be useful in understanding how society relates to the homosexual as well as how the homosexual relates to society and to him/herself. In this chapter we are going to discuss some theoretical issues and some practical issues that are related to the problematic relationship between the homosexual and society. The relationship is characterized as problematic because at this point in time there seem to be several difficulties resulting from being homosexual in our society and in the minds of many in the society there are difficulties for the social order as a result of the presence of homosexuality. Our discussion is intended to illuminate the nature of some of these problems with the hope that understanding them will make solutions or management of the problems more likely. Initially we will discuss how the phenomena of person perception includes several concepts that seem to make sense of how society views the homosexual and how she/he relates to society. Next we will discuss the effects and implications of the perceptual nature of many of the problems and then we will discuss some situational and individual variables that contribute to homosexual sexual preference. Finally we will describe some of the social problems of homosexual individuals caused by the prevailing attitudes of the society toward them.

SOCIAL PERCEPTION OF THE HOMOSEXUAL

In order to contribute to understanding how homosexuality is perceived, first we will briefly review some of the concepts of person perception that social psychologists have found to be useful in explaining how people describe other people. The implications of the process of "socially" defining others' characteristics will also be discussed. The process of perceiving others is preceded by the need to understand the social world. We all need to have some basic understanding of the nature of the people with whom we may come in contact. If we understand what the people around us are like we will be better able to predict what they will do and we can act accordingly. We will be much better able to achieve our ends as well as escape embarrassment or even danger if we understand the nature of the people who might help or harm us as well as those who will do neither. Given this need, the tendency of people to categorize and classify other people becomes understandable. The task of understanding the social world would be completely overwhelming if all people were unique. Once the biologist has classified a plant to beneficialness or toxicity he knows better how to deal with it in order to achieve a desired end. This is not to suggest that there is necessarily a basis of fear or aggression for the process of categorizing others but these motives may play an important role in shaping the nature of the perception of some types of groups. Groupings or categories of classification are economies for the perceiver. If there are groups with common characteristics then the perceiver can draw on past experiences of his own or of others who give him information to know how to interact or whether to avoid the classified other.

If each individual is perceived as unique the perceiver's job of knowing what to expect and how to interact would be very difficult to manage. For this reason people tend to categorize the individual in terms of their own set of categories developed somewhat from their own experiences but usually based more heavily on what they perceive to be social reality. Their social reality is created by the values and definitions they learn from others in society. Peers may be very influential in defining social reality as are family and others who are viewed as credible sources. Other credible sources may be admired public figures, such as Nancy Reagan, or abstract institutions in the society, such as the American Psychiatric Association.

Depending on our needs and fears we will value or devalue certain characteristics in others. We will be especially vigilant with respect to characteristics which may be related to important needs and fears we have. Obviously, the needs and fears of individuals vary and so there are individual differences in perceiving groups in general as well as differences in perceiving a given group.

There are two major implications of describing the person perception process as operating in this way. One result of this process is that the perceptions of others are based on subjective rather than objective matters.

The information from others is filtered by their needs and values as is the personal experience of the individual. This means that we often if not always do not see people as they are. In view of the proposed purpose of the person perception process we then behave toward people in a manner dictated by an inaccurate perception of their nature and of how they will affect us. A further implication is that these actions toward other people will affect the way they act toward us. We will discuss this in greater detail later.

With this general rationale for and description of the process of person perception in mind let's look at some of the concepts that explain specific aspects of the phenomena.

Probably the best known concept in the field of person perception is the concept of stereotyping. Stereotypes are widely held perceptions of the characteristics of people who are included in a particular classification. Usually resistant to change and always oversimplified, these perceptions are defined as inaccurate. They are inaccurate because all members of the group to which they apply do not possess all the characteristics of the stereotype. An individual who is classified as a member of a given group is perceived to have all the characteristics that are part of the group stereotype. The perceiver will then "know how to act" toward the individual and "know what to expect" from him or her. Because the stereotype is inaccurate in at least some aspects, the interactions will be based on false information. Of course if the information were entirely false and the stereotyped individual did not act in any way as expected the stereotyping process would not be reinforced and would reduce in frequency.

This does not tend to happen for two reasons. The first reason is usually ignored by social scientists most likely because of their own needs and values. The stereotype is probably never entirely incorrect and may even be a close approximation of the characteristics of many of the group members even though it is obvious that no group is so homogenous that all members are alike in every respect. Since most attributes that make up a stereotype are not objective the degree of accuracy of the stereotype is impossible to assess. It is difficult to assess the extent to which "all Americans are materialistic." Suppose this stereotyped characteristic of Americans could be operationally defined and found in 80% of Americans. Even though we would say that it is *not* true that all Americans are materialistic, we would be correct a vast majority of the time to assume that an American we meet would be materialistic. Since the kinds of attributes that make up stereotypes are not readily measured objectively it is difficult to determine whether many of the stereotypes have this degree of accuracy. It is the position of these authors that, while there is inaccuracy in stereotypes, they remain in existence because there is also a good deal of accuracy; especially from the point of view of the perceiver who is trying to understand and predict his world. What alternative to prejudging based on social stereotypes is there?

It is not the purpose of this discussion to show how accurate stereotypes are. The point relevant to the social perception of homosexuals is that because stereotypes are partly true they are highly resistant to change. Further, to argue that they are entirely untrue will be ineffective in changing the opinion of the holder of the stereotype. This is the first of the two reasons why stereotypes are very difficult to change, they are sometimes verified in part by the perceiver's experience and this reinforces the entire cluster of perceived characteristics. Those who wish to counter or eradicate certain stereotypes often are seen as saying that none of the group have the undesirable aspects of the stereotype and this lacks credibility to the perceiver who has seen "one like that" himself. A second and related reason stereotypes persist and are resistant to change is that those who are expected to have certain characteristics and are treated as if they do have them will often come to exhibit the characteristic to some degree (e.g., Rosenthal & Rubin, 1978). This further reinforces the stereotype and contributes to its continuation. This process may be described as a self-fulfilling prophecy. The behavior that is expected is more likely to be perceived and surprisingly, more likely to occur as a result of the expectation. Because stereotypes create expectations for certain behavior the perceiver is more likely to see that behavior when it occurs and the expectation may cause the target person to act in some ways consistently with the expectations. All of the person perception processes mentioned in this chapter are likely to contain an element of self-fulfilling prophecy.

Another process of person perception which is related to the social perception of homosexuality is stigmatization. While stereotypes almost always contain positive as well as negative characteristics those who are stigmatized are always viewed negatively. A "stigma," according to Goffman (1963), is a sign that indicates something uncommon and malevolent about the person possessing it. Physical deformities, character blemishes, and social flaws such as membership in an unfavored minority religion or race are types of stigmata. The stigma shapes the interaction between the stigmatized person and the "normal."

One interesting aspect of the interaction that is relevant to our purpose is that "normals" often pretend to accept the stigmatized individuals more than they really do. This leads to frequent attempts by the stigmatized to achieve friendly relations with the normals and frequent failure to do so as the normals tend to withdraw or reject the approaches. The stigmatization of others which leads to viewing them as inferior and rejecting them is not considered to be a socially desirable behavior. In the case of most stigmata there is likely some guilt on the part of the perceiver over unfairly devaluing the stigmatized. This guilt may lead to public denial of the negative view, but the negative feelings toward the bearer of the stigma remain and are brought out when there is close contact with him. The apparent indication of acceptance followed by rejection makes the plight of the stigmatized especially difficult.

It is interesting to note that stigma originally referred to a physical sign or brand which marked a slave. The role of visible identification in the process of stigmatization is related to this original connotation. The mark, whether physical or in the form of membership in some group, may often be hidden by the stigmatized person to escape the negative reactions of others. This is true of the homosexual who hides his/her sexual preference from social view.

The determination of a sign as a stigmata is based upon the values of the perceiver. The perceiver's values are determined by social influence and personal needs. Homosexuality represents in some way an antithesis of many individuals' needs and values with respect to an important and central feature of oneself. When one's social reality and self view are challenged by the characteristics of a group, strong rejection is likely to occur for protection of the perceiver's self image.

This reaction has been described as homophobia, a hostile attitude toward homosexuals that is based upon irrational fears. Homophobia, like other phobias, is seen as emotional, irrational, and excessive. It is this neurotic basis that distinguishes homophobia from the attitudinal component of the other processes of person perception. Although we agree with Herek (1984) that homophobia cannot explain all the negative attitudes toward homosexuals, it seems to be a significant and separable phenomena worth mentioning on its own. The phobia of homosexuals may be a result of the perceiver's discomfort about his/her own sexuality or gender identity. It has been found that those with negative attitudes toward homosexuals are more likely to feel sexual guilt and concern and to be sexually conservative (Dunbar, Brown, & Amoroso, 1973). Further, males have been found to show physiological reactions of increased tension when talking to a gay man (Heinemann, Pellander, Bogelbusch, & Wojtek, 1981). These signs of guilt and fear associated with the perception of homosexuals indicate that for at least some part of the population the attitude toward homosexuality has a very deep emotional basis. This indicates that the attitude will be resistant to change, especially by rational argument.

Probably the broadest of the theoretical approaches to person perception which is useful in understanding the perception of homosexuality is labeling theory. Labeling theory stresses the cultural and subcultural relativism of the labeling of deviant behavior. This means that deviance is created by those in society who have the power to label others. The powerful majority groups, such as major religions, have the power to designate certain behavior as deviant and to apply a label to those who engage in it. The particular behavior that a group chooses to label as deviant is a function of the values and needs of members of that group. Virtually every behavior a group labels as deviant, that is, as deviating from the norms for that group, is viewed negatively. However, each of us is a member of many groups and the behaviors that one group devalues may be tolerated or even valued by another group. The "redneck" of one portion of society is the "good ole boy" of another. This illustrates the complex implications of the theory.

There are two levels to the process of labeling. The first level consists of the labeling of behavior as deviant by various groups within the society. This labeling leads to a separation between those labeled and the group applying the label. The extent of the separation depends upon the importance of the norm that is violated. Many groups have rigid norms about sexual behavior. Violation of these norms is seen as a major deviation and leads to severe rejection of the norm violator. For this reason the label, homosexual, often leads to significant rejection by many groups.

The second level of the process of labeling involves the self-identification by the individual who has been labeled by the group. The labeled person may begin to apply the label to him/herself. According to the labeling theory approach this self-identification causes the individual to behave more like the label than would have occurred without it's application. In order to apply this to the labeling of homosexuality some further theorizing is necessary. It seems unlikely that homosexuals continue to choose same-sexed partners simply because they have been labeled homosexual, but the labeling may affect the lifestyle of the labeled individual. Labels carry with them a cluster of characteristics and expected behaviors beyond the central behavior which identifies the label. Labels carry with them a perception of general deviance beyond the specific deviation which led to the label. When the individual self-labels as a result of the central characteristic of the label, expectations for a whole cluster of characteristics and behaviors are developed. The homosexual person may begin to exhibit other expected behaviors as a result of the labeling.

In some cases the labeling group may be one the labeled individual respects and considers as a legitimate reference group for information. In this case the expectations communicated by the group and the beliefs that have led to the expectations by the group are the same expectations the individual has. The beliefs about what behaviors go with the label of homosexuality are often shared by the labeled individual and the group which applies the label to him/her. These beliefs create expectations which lead to self-fulfilling prophesies as discussed earlier.

In the case of homosexuality it is interesting to note that sometimes labels can have labels. The beliefs about the characteristics which go with a certain label constitute giving labels to labels. When the Diagnostic and Statistical Manual of the American Psychiatric Association (1968) classified homosexuality as a mental illness there was such a case. Homosexuality was labeled as a mental illness and was therefore considered to have the characteristics that go with mental illness. No doubt many homosexuals respected the authority and expertise of such an esteemed body and considered themselves to have characteristics of the mentally ill. This self view may have exacerbated any adjustment problems they were having. If you think of yourself as mentally ill you are more likely to behave as if you are mentally ill. Whatever your own beliefs about the set of behaviors that are expected of a person classified as mentally ill, the classification is unlikely to contribute to a positive adjustment to life.

From a labeling theory perspective the change in DSM III (American Psychological Association, 1980) which removed homosexuality from classification as a mental illness was a very positive one for the homosexual. This is a major change in the connotation of the label homosexual, at least from the perspective of one major label maker in our society.

There are numerous groups in society which have the social power to make labels, to define stereotypes, and to determine the signs which are stigmata. These groups shape the perceptions people have of others in the society. Each of the theoretical constructs of person perception which we have discussed so far have stressed the subjective nature of perceiving others. The values and needs of the groups with social power determine what will be perceived as good or bad, or threatening or harmless, in others. Initially we said people classify others because there is a need to know how to deal with the many types of people in the world and a lack of ability to perceive each individual as unique. The subjective classification of others determines how they will be dealt with. If others are perceived as threats to the values of the defining group they are viewed negatively and rejected. Homosexuals are seen by many as representing a threat to the traditional family and to one's personal sexual orientation. The family is valued highly by powerful religious groups as well as others. Personal sexual orientation and one's sexual identity are probably areas about which there is widespread insecurity, anxiety, and uncertainty. Whether or not homosexuals really challenge these values, they are perceived to represent a challenge. The perception is more powerful than the reality. The perceived threat to such basic values and areas of insecurity engenders a strong counterattack. The counterattack takes the form of negative characteristics associated with the label of homosexuality.

We are not talking here about what homosexuals are, but about what they are perceived to be. The concepts of person perception explain the cause of a common negative perception held by the members of some groups and how this perception may affect the self-perceptions of homosexuals. Given these conditions it would be very surprising if there were not some significant adjustment problems associated with being homosexual. The pressures from society and the resulting self perceptions would likely create a high level of stress which would take its toll. While avoiding the issue of whether homosexuals are less well adjusted than heterosexuals, we wish to suggest that many of the problems of adjustment that may be experienced by some homosexuals do not result directly from being homosexual, but are created by the way society views homosexuality; and further that the negative aspects of the social view are due to the fears and insecurities of influential groups within society.

If the major problems of homosexuality result from social prejudice, what is a solution? If the problem lies in society, should we treat society? Sturgis and Adams (1978) have an interesting comment on this proposition. They feel that, although treating society may be a legitimate course of action, the therapist must afford society the same ethical considerations that apply in the case of threatening an individual. That is, society must request the intervention, there must be adequate treatment procedures, and the therapist must know the effectiveness of the treatment program as well as the positive and negative side effects. They question whether it is ethical to change the behavior or values of society without the permission of or perhaps even against the wishes of society. Obviously since there is no monolithic society which can request and be given treatment to change any single set of values, this position leads nowhere. That is, it leads to no change or no treatment. Davison (1978) takes issue with the position of Adams and Sturgis on treatment. He proposes that ethical concerns demand an attempt to change the values of society. We suggest that an attempt to change major values of society is the hard way to achieve a greater general acceptance of homosexuality.

There is no one set of values of society. Society as we have pointed out, is best viewed as a complex of groups which each have their own values and needs. Each of the individuals in society belong to many of these groups simultaneously. To the extent that there are common values or similar ones shared by many of the groups, changing values might be an effective strategy if it could be done. It is much more likely that change in the perceived threat to values that homosexuality represents could be accomplished. It was mentioned earlier that the family, a basic value held by many groups, is perceived to be threatened by homosexuality. This value will not likely be changed even if some powerful group chooses to do so. The perception of homosexuality as a threat to this value could be changed through educational programs. The widespread insecurity of individuals about their sexuality is not likely to be changed in the near future, but the threat that individuals perceive homosexuality poses to their own security might be reduced to some extent. It seems likely that the education of society about the nature of homosexuality in such a way as to change the commonly held perception of homosexuals as a threat to basic and important values is the direction to a better relationship between homosexuals and the remainder of society. This situation would reduce the stress experienced by homosexuals resulting from rejection and the accompanying negative self view that may often occur.

We have been discussing variables that affect homosexuality at the level of society as a whole, now we will reduce our level of analysis from societal to that of situational influences on homosexuality.

HOMOSEXUALITY IN PRISON

Within the prison system, homosexual behavior among both men and women is quite common. Social scientists have devoted much attention to the study of such behavior (Giallombardo, 1966; Scacco, 1982). It is of particular interest to researchers that the prison environment itself seems to encourage and intensify homosexual behavior. Men and women, many of whom have had no homosexual contact prior to their incarceration, attempt to meet a variety of physical, social, and emotional needs through such contact. It appears that these needs greatly differ for men and women (Scacco, 1982; Ward & Kassebaum, 1964); and that homosexual contact is initiated and maintained by men and by women for different reasons. Because of these differences the discussion of male and female homosexuality in the prison context will be presented separately.

Females in Prison

In prison, as in our society as a whole, the sexuality of women is expressed quite differently from that of men. Women tolerate the absence of overt sexual behavior better than men (Buffum, 1982). They are far more disturbed by the loss of love and familial relationships than by the deprivation of sexual experience per se. The early incarceration period is a time of deep loneliness and isolation. The typical response of the female inmate to the depersonalization and alienation of incarceration might therefore be expected to differ from the adjustment of the male inmate.

In many female correctional institutions, it is the formation of "pseudo-families," with clearly defined familial roles, which characterize the female inmates coping strategy within prison (Giallombardo, 1966). The "pseudo-family," an extended family structure, is a system of interpersonal interaction and social roles which the inmates create. Such a "family" is frequently headed by a "mother-father" couple or by a solitary matriarchal figure who might serve as the "grandmother." Other inmates assume the roles of children, cousins, aunts, uncles, etc., each with a clearly defined pattern of interactions with other family members. "Children," for example, will ask the advice or comfort of their "parents" during stressful periods. Many such families exist within each prison, just as any small community is based upon the interaction and connection between family groups.

Often female inmates are the product of highly dysfunctional and disintegrated biological families. These women rarely have experienced a stable or nurturing home life. They are eager to find a source of security and comfort to help ease their sense of loneliness. The female inmate typically has very low self-esteem and feels powerless to control her destiny (Buffum, 1982). The "pseudo-family" operates to stablize relationships within the prison and to establish a hierarchy of dominance and submission (Giallombardo, 1966; Buffum, 1982).

It is within this "pseudo-family" context that most homosexual contacts take place in female prisons. Estimates of overt sexual contact between women range from 50 percent to 85 percent (Giallombardo, 1966; Ward & Kassebaum, 1965), although the precise nature of this contact varies a great deal. The primary motivation for homosexual contact between women is not sexual deprivation, but rather the deprivation of emotionally satisfying and stable relationships and the desire to create within prison a stable and predictable community. The homosexual relationship within this context offers security and protection from the stress and anxiety of prison life.

Since the opportunities for actual physical contact between women in prison are quite limited, it is often the illusion or fantasy of a "sexual" relationship which exists rather than the reality of explicit homosexual behavior. Hugging and kissing are the prevalent activities in which these couples engage. Such behavior between women is largely acceptable within heterosexual society. Even when genital contact occurs, the woman engaging in such activity will rarely label herself as a "lesbian" if she has not had homosexual experience prior to her incarceration.

Lesbians who are incarcerated may, naturally, continue to seek out sex partners within prison. Typically they will establish relationships with other "true" lesbians or bisexuals. It is the emotional bond between the female inmate and her partner that becomes important in prison rather than the specific nature of the activities in which they engage. Based on six years of clinical observation within a state women's prison, it is my opinion that women, because of their motivation in selecting partners and the general acceptability of physical affection between heterosexual women, often avoid labeling themselves as "homosexual." If they are successful in the avoidance of this "self-labeling," they are free to return to heterosexual relationships after their release from prison. This is quite different from the situation of the man who experiences homosexuality during his incarceration.

Males in Prison

Quite different from the initial homosexual encounters in which incarcerated women participate, male inmates are often introduced to homosexual behavior through rape (Scacco, 1982). Most male inmates have identified themselves as heterosexual until their incarceration.

Within the prison setting one man raping another is an assertion of dominance, of power, of control. As with heterosexual rape, the act itself has little connection with sexuality. Rather it is considered an act of . . . "violence, politics and ones acting out of power roles" (Rideau & Sinclair, 1982). Those inmates who become the victims of such assaults are then perceived by the other inmates to be "women." This "female" is now the property of his conquerer. He is treated as a "wife" and slave, and may be traded, gambled or sold to other "husbands." While this first sexual act within prison was non-sexual in its origin, it is the subsequent behavior of this victim which may cause him to re-define his own sense of masculinity, his own sexual identity. This rape victim will now be expected to perform sexually with one or any number of men. His security and safety within the prison depend upon his compliance and willingness to perform.

This repeated homosexual contact often produces within this individual the sense that he may in fact, be "homosexual." He is, after all, having repeated sexual contacts with men, and he is certainly being defined by others in this way. In fact, there is denial by his exploiters that he was ever really a victim of others. The mythology of prison is that a "real man" could not be forced to do anything, a "real man" cannot be exploited. This is quite similar to the myth in our culture that women who are raped by men in some way "asked for" or encouraged the assault. Within this powerful social context, therefore, this man is and always has been homosexual. His self-concept and self-perception now undergo tremendous change in a short period of time.

There are, of course, gay men, who have identified homosexual preference long before their incarceration. These men often find themselves to be the victims of discrimination, as in the free world (Rideau & Sinclair, 1982). In some institutions they may be segregated from the rest of the prison population. They may be denied prestigious job assignments and excluded from other privileges simply by having been labeled by the prison administration as "homosexual." Homosexual inmates have reported that they are considered by administrators to be mentally ill and dangerous to other inmates (Rideau & Sinclair, 1982).

SOCIAL PROBLEMS FOR THE HOMOSEXUAL INDIVIDUAL CAUSED BY SOCIAL ATTITUDES

The homosexual individual in our society is confronted by the pressures of living within a culture which largely views homosexuality as an aberation, a dangerous deviation from "normal" sexuality. The homosexual individual is still an outcast in our culture. Those who claim to have accepted homosexuality as an alternative lifestyle seem to have difficulty when it is their child being taught by a suspected or self-proclaimed gay person or their neighborhood into which a lesbian couple moves.

Some of the social bias homosexuals face is quite blatant (i.e., a school board of education demanding the resignation of a gay teacher). Other prejudices are more subtle (i.e., AIDS victims receiving little public attention while homosexuals were believed to be the primary victims). But, like racism, however blatant or subtle, these prejudices affect many aspects of the homosexual individual's life. The homosexual must confront the nonacceptability of his/her sexual choices within our culture (Ettore, 1980; Tripp, 1975). Many gay persons are so thwarted by the societal pressures that they lead a "double" existence, presenting a "straight," heterosexual image publicly to avoid discrimination and harassment and privately leading a homosexual lifestyle. A few of the areas in which societal attitudes have caused social and economic problems for the homosexual individual will be discussed here.

Security in Employment

Many homosexuals live with the constant fear that they will be fired from their jobs if their sexual orientation is revealed (Stivison, 1982). The homosexual individual, therefore, with the exception of those few gays who are openly accepted by their employers, is denied the right to security in employment. Legal battles challenging discrimination practices against homosexual public employees have been waged with some frequency in recent years (Rivera, 1982). These suits have met with some success on a local or statewide basis, preserving the right of homosexual public employees to keep their jobs unless their homosexual activity is shown to interfere with their jobs. In the 1969 landmark case of Morrison versus the State Board of Education, the California Supreme Court ordered a male homosexual's teaching credentials reinstated after they had been removed by the Board of Education. Utilizing both this decision as precedent and Title VII of the 1964 Civil Rights Act which prohibits discrimination on the basis of sex and race, employment rights have been obtained for some publicly employed homosexuals (Rivera, 1982).

Those statutes which protect the public employee do not restrict the behavior of the private employer. There is no federal or state legislation protecting the employment rights of homosexual persons who work for private employers. For such homosexual individuals job "security" depends on the good will of the employer or their ability to maintain secrecy about their sexual orientation.

Within the U.S. military homosexual individuals are still restricted from service. It is still the policy within the military to dismiss and dishonorably discharge those individuals found to be homosexual. These men and women must carry the stigma of "dishonorable discharge" (Rivera, 1982).

Thus, the homosexual faces a difficult choice with regard to employment. Deception and secrecy are often reluctantly chosen to avoid the possible consequences of discovery. There is still little legal protection for the job security of this group. Many gay people who wish to publicly acknowledge their sexual choice are forced to seek employment in large cities. Within large cities there is little integration of one's work and social lives. In such a setting with compartmentalized aspects of existence, an "anonymity" is created which produces greater freedom for the expression of one's homosexuality (Tripp, 1975).

The Homosexual Parent

Perhaps the aspect of life about which the homosexual is likely to face the greatest measure of societal criticism is the difficult arena of parenthood. A sizeable percentage of gay men are parents and estimates of the number of lesbian mothers range from 200,000 to 300,000 (Hoeffer, 1978). Many of these individuals have been married or have engaged in a long-term heterosexual relationships which produced a child. It is often in the context of an emotional or legal struggle with the child's other parent that the gay parent faces conflict.

In the vast majority of legal battles relating to this issue, a lesbian mother is fighting to attain or retain her rights as custodial parent of the child. In many situations in which "lesbianism" is raised as an issue in a custody dispute, it tends to be considered sufficient evidence that the mother is an unfit parent (Lewin & Lyons, 1982). This view of homosexuality has jeopardized the mother's claim to custody of her child, or even her right to regular visitation when custody is granted to the father. The major issue in such a dispute rests on the assumption that homosexuality cannot be combined successfully with the process and requirements of childrearing (Hunter & Polikoff, 1982).

Even a lesbian mother who does not lose her custody rights to her children may expect restrictions imposed by the judge. She may, for example, be told that she will be granted custody only if she terminates her relationship with her lover (Hunter & Polikoff, 1982). She may further be told that she is not permitted to associate with homosexuals in any social context. The judge might openly express concern that her children might in some way be damaged developmentally or become unsure of their gender identity.

Such a highly pressured atmosphere surrounding their relationship with their children imposes many hardships on homosexual parents. The lesbian mother, in particular, must make many financial and emotional sacrifices in an attempt to cope with her fear that her right to custody might be challenged at any time (Lewin & Lyons, 1982). She may forego child support payments from the father, for example. She may postpone or sacrifice the establishment of intimate relationships for fear of upsetting her children.

In fact, many homosexual parents choose to live the "double life" we have described earlier. They may choose to shield their children from the knowledge of their sexual orientation. For the gay parent whose child lives with him/her such a decision imposes large restrictions in the ability to establish and maintain relationships. For some homosexual parents, however, the risk of losing custody of their chidren is too great. They are willing to deny themselves much in order to insure their continued relationship with their children.

Homosexuality in our culture is considered to be a sexual choice, a preference for sexual and intimate social interaction with a person of one's own gender. In this chapter we have discussed several aspects of homosexuality which relate to the external influences on one's sexuality. Environmental changes, like imprisonment, which lead some individuals to engage in homosexual behavior which might not take place in other environments have been described as we have made observations on the way social pressures, like employment uncertainty and child custody serve to alter the behavior of some homosexual individuals. In this final section, we address yet another situational determinant of homosexuality: the political and social climate which might produce a "feminist-lesbian" alliance.

Political Lesbianism

For certain subgroups of women in our society during the last twenty or thirty years, the raising of political consciousness has resulted in the choice to form homosexual rather than heterosexual intimate liaisons (Ettorre, 1980; Faderman, 1985; Myron & Bunch, 1975). Thus social, political circumstance has affected sexual attitudes often considered psychological (Diamant, 1977). Such women have critically evaluated societal norms and the role of women in our culture. They have determined that they must make an "exclusive commitment" to women (Faderman, 1985) if women are to become free of the subservient and less powerful role they have played in relation to men. In an effort to eliminate "male supremacy" and build a non-sexist society, these women have shifted their relationships and dealings with the world to become reliant, almost exclusively, upon other women.

Such women may be said to have discovered lesbianism in the course of becoming feminists (Myron & Bunch, 1975; Ulmschneider, 1975). Their choice to intimately associate exclusively with women is based on their ideological belief that heterosexuality is deterimental to women's freedom. "Lesbian-feminism," as it has been labeled, is defined as a political choice more than a sexual preference (Faderman, 1985). Sexual activity is only one aspect of their commitment to a lesbian lifestyle. In fact, for many such women actual physical contact may not occur at all or may take place only occasionally. For many who enter into this subculture, homosexual contact begins after the choice to adopt such a lifestyle. These women may never have had a homosexual liaison prior to their political commitment.

By associating only with women, the lesbian-feminist alters the traditional organization of power. She is not dependent upon a man either emotionally or financially. She experiences a new flexibility in social and economic roles. Traditional sex-role stereotypes break down under this new system, allowing women a new consciousness and a new source of strength (Ettorre, 1980). Women grow to view themselves as sufficient for meeting all of their needs. This sexual/social/political choice redefines the traditional distribution of power within that subculture. It is one small group's way of eliminating sexism and elevating the status of women in our culture.

In this chapter we have described some of the ways that the principles and theories of social psychology contribute to understanding the relationship between homosexuals and society. The roles of interpersonal variables, situational variables, and individual variables have been discussed. We have discussed theories that deal with the perception of homosexuals as well as practical maters such as job security. We hope that application of the concepts discussed to the issues of homosexuality in society will further the understanding of the relationship in a beneficial way.

REFERENCES

American Psychiatric Association. (1968). *The diagnostic and statistical manual of mental disorders* (2nd. ed.). Washington, DC: Author.

American Psychiatric Association. (1980). *The diagnostic and statistical manual of mental disorders* (3rd. ed.). Washington, DC: Author.

Buffum, P. C. (1982). Racial factors in prison homosexuality. In A. M. Scacco, Jr. (Ed.). *Male rape: A casebook of sexual aggressions* (pp. 104–107). New York: AMS Press.

Davison, G. C. (1978). Not can but ought: The treatment of homosexuality. *Journal of Consulting and Clinical Psychology, 46,* 170–172.

Diamant, L. (1977). *An investigation of a relationship between liberalism and lesbianism.* Paper presented at the Meeting of the American Psychological Association, San Francisco.

Dunbar, J., Brown, M., & Amoroso, D. M. (1973). Some correlates of attitudes toward homosexuality. *Journal of Social Psychology, 89,* 271–279.

Ettorre, E. M. (1980). *Lesbians, women and society.* London: Routledge & Kegan Paul.

Faderman, L. (1985). The "new gay" lesbians. *Journal of Homosexuality, 10,* 85–95.

Giallombardo, R. (1966). *Society of women: A study of a women's prison.* New York: John Wiley & Sons.

Goffman, E. (1963). *Stigma: Notes on the management of spoiled identity.* Englewood Cliffs, NJ: Prentice-Hall.

Heinemann, W., Pellaner, F., Vogelbusch, A., & Wojtek, B. (1981). Meeting a deviant person: Subjective norms and affective reactions. *European Journal of Social Psychology, 11,* 1–25.

Herek, lG. M. (1984). Beyond "homophobia": A social psychological perspective on attitudes toward lesbians and gay men. *Journal of Homosexuality, 10,* 1–21.

Hoeffer, B. (1978). Single mothers and their children: Challenging traditional concepts of the American family. In P. Brandt, et al. (Eds.). *Current Practice in Pediatric Nursing.* St. Louis: C. V. Mosby.

Hunter, N. D., & Polikoff, N. D. (1976). Custody rights of lesbian mothers: Legal theory and litigation strategy. *Buffalo Law Review, 25,* 691–733.

Lewin, E., & Lyons, T. A. (1982). Everything in its place: The coexistence of lesbianism and motherhood. In W. Paul, J. D. Weinrich, J. C. Gonsiovek, & M. E. Hotvedt (Eds.). *Homosexuality: Social, psychological, and biological issues.* Beverly Hills: Sage Publications.

Myron, N., & Bunch, C. (1975). Introductions. *Lesbianism and the women's movement.* Baltimore: Diana Press.

Rideau, W., & Sinclair, B. (1982). Prison: The sexual jungle. In A. M. Scacco, Jr. (Ed.). *Male rape: A casebook of sexual aggression* (pp. 3–30). New York: AMS Press.

Rivera, R. (1982). Homosexuality and the law. In W. Paul, J. D. Weinrich, J. C. Gonsiorek, & M. E. Hotvedt, (Eds.), *Homosexuality: Social, psychological, and biological issues.* Beverly Hills: Sage Publications.

Rosenthal, R., & Rubin, D. B. (1978). Interpersonal expectancy effects: The first 345 studies. *The Behavioral and Brain Sciences, 3,* 377–415.

Scacco, A. M., Jr. (1982). The scapegoat is almost always white. In A. M. Scacco, Jr. *Male rape: A casebook of sexual aggressions* (pp. 91–104). New York: AMS Press.

Stivison, D. (1982). Homosexuals and the constitution. In W. Paul, J. D. Weinrich, J. C. Gonsiorek, & M. E. Hotvedt, (Eds.). *Homosexuality: Social, psychological, and biological issue.* Beverly Hills: Sage Publications.

Sturgis, E. T., & Adams, H. E. (1978). The right to treatment: Issues in the treatment of homosexuality. *Journal of Consulting and Clinical Psychology, 46,* 165–169.

Tripp, C. A. (1975). *The homosexual matrix.* New York: McGraw-Hill.

Ulmschneider, L. (1975). Bisexuality. In N. Myron & C. Bunch, (Eds.). *Lesbianism in the women's movement* (pp. 85–88). Baltimore: Diana Press.

Ward, D., and Kassebaum, G. (1964). Homosexuality: A mode of adaptation in a prison for women. *Social Problems, 12,* 2, pp. 159–177.

Ward, D., and Kassebaum, G. (1965). *Women's prison: Sex and social structure.* London: Weidenfeld & Nicholson.

13

A THEORY OF NORMAL HOMOSEXUALITY

Michael W. Ross

INTRODUCTION

Theories of homosexuality have in the past been heavily weighted toward particular models or paradigms of sexual behavior, and toward western societies. These two biases make it difficult to provide a comprehensive psychological theory of homosexuality. First, any psychological theory must take into account all homosexual behavior, not just in a particular group of societies, if it is to be other than a sociological theory. Second, the designation of a behavior or identity as "normal" or "abnormal" is clearly culturally bound as well as being bound to particular models of sexual behavior and moral values. Third, current theories in many cases do not distinguish between homosexual behavior and a homosexual identity, or ascribe different degrees of normality to the two.

The task facing any theorist who wishes to describe a theory of normal homosexuality is thus complicated by the need to provide a model which applies equally to homosexual behaviors as well as identities, and equally well in all cultures. It also needs to take account of prevailing moral values to explain current theories and differences between homosexual behavior and a homosexual identity ("homosexuality" as an essentialized condition). The term "normal," however, is taken here to mean independence of mental illness (normality in terms of mental health rather than normative social or moral values). In order to achieve these aims, it is necessary first to examine the models in which we currently categorize homosexual behavior and a homosexual condition. This will be done in the context of male homosexual behaviors and identities only.

DeCecco and Shively (1983–1984) have noted that discourse on homosexual identity for the past hundred years has conceptualized homosexuality in a biological form: that is, the biological sex of partners in sexual relationships is the crucial distinction. They also note that, along with the emphasis on sex of partner, uncritical use of popular concepts and explanations of sexual identity and unacknowledged moral judgments are often incorporated into scientific thinking in the area. Similarly, Ross, Rogers, and McCulloch (1978) have argued that many of the theories of the etiology of homosexuality have started from the assumption that the only acceptable "normal" relationships are male-female ones, so that individuals who prefer same-sex partners are thus assumed to have opposite-sex gender identity (since males *prefer* males, they must be *like* females) or inappropriate parent identification (since they prefer males, they must have identified with mother and not father). Biological theorists simply take the supposed cross-gender behavior belief one step further and postulate a biological mechanism for the postulated cross-gender identification.

Any normal theory of homosexuality must thus question whether gender is the critical determining variable in a sexual relationship, and also explain why homosexuality is seen as an essential condition in some cultures and simply as a behavior in others.

More important, however, is the fact that while the assumptions behind most current research into sexual orientation are illuminated, there is much less illumination of where to go once we have recognized that we are testing within a paradigm rather than between, or within, alternate paradigms. In the sense that our model of sexual relationships determines *how* we investigate them and what variables we choose to consider, it is of central importance for us to start to test alternative models of sexuality: the very terms homosexual, bisexual, and heterosexual are themselves paradigm-bound. As a consequence, it is important to suggest directions in which, and models to which, sexual relationship research may move in order to avoid continually researching around in circles. Several such directions are suggested here, after an analysis and explication of the present biologically and reproductively-based paradigm which sees, and essentializes, partner gender as the defining factor in sexual relationships.

THE ESSENTIALIST-GENDER BASED PARADIGM

Categorizing of sexual orientation, as Boswell (1982/1983) has done, into polymorphous perversity throughout life (the nominalist theory) or into either heterosexual, bisexual, or homosexual (the realist theory), ignores the influence of social mores. The "realist" theory is realistic only in terms of its unquestioning acceptance of current popular theory of sexual orientation, as DeCecco and Shively (1983-1984) point out, and then realistic only in the sense of current western, Judeo-Christian sexuality. The inherent biological basis in this, as DeCecco and Shively also point out, rests on the emphasis on the biological sex of the partner in a relationship, and as such is simply an extension of the binary classification of individuals by gender. As has previously been noted (Ross, 1983a), the fact that gender is a useful and universal classification system (despite discrepancies in what is classified as male or female) does not mean that the metaphor need be stretched to the point where behaviors or objects so classified actually become synonymous with masculinity and maleness, or femininity and femaleness.

Perhaps the ultimate illustration of how biological "realism" has influenced research into sexual orientation is the fact that the two metaphors of preference for male or female partner (homosexual or heterosexual) have consistently been contrasted. No research to date has looked at heterosexual and homosexual men as one group which has succumbed to social pressure to adopt a consistent and stable sexual orientation, as opposed to bisexual men who are able to make choices of partner sex (or for whom partner sex is secondary to other characteristics). The fact that partner sex is the critical variable in most research into sexual orientation yet again points to our continuing to test within the biological model, often while concurrently examining correlates which are explicitly nonbiological. It has already been pointed out that homosexuality has been structured in terms of biological models by the assumption that because one male prefers another male as an erotic object, then one or both must therefore contain attributes of, or think of themselves as being like, females (Ross, Rogers & McCulloch, 1978). This occurs simply because relationships are seen as being acceptable only between males and females. Direct evidence to support this assumption is provided by Ross (1983b,c) who found that degree of femininity and masculinity in homosexual men differs significantly in societies which differ in both their acceptance of homosexuality and their sex-role rigidity. Thus, the less antihomosexual and less sex-role rigid the culture, the less homosexual men in it felt that they needed to fit into the complementary two-sex model with regard to opposite-sex characteristics.

Preliminary data looking at preference for partner characteristics (not including gender of partner) in these countries show that there has developed in the less antihomosexual and less sex-role rigid of those societies looked at, a preference for partners with significantly different characteristics to one's own, and that this is not related to masculinity or femininity (Ross, 1987). As the four societies became more antihomosexual and sex-role rigid, relationship of preferred partner characteristics to femininity or masculinity increased, as did preferred similarity of partner characteristics. These preliminary data do suggest that relationship of gender characteristics to homosexuality is imposed by societal beliefs about maleness, femaleness and sexuality, and thus based on biological metaphors rather than the biological "reality" which is assumed by the "realist" theory of sexual orientation.

The point has been well made by DeCecco and Shively (1983/1984) that homosexuality, heterosexuality, and bisexuality have been distinguished by the biological sex of partners in sexual relationships. This definition in terms of gender or partner strikes at the root of the problem of how *else* one may see homosexuality, however. The very term used to portray the entity, and its very existence, is defined in terms of the biological model by callilng it *homosexuality:* homo, same; sexual, sexual relations with. Like the parallel issue of sexist language in science, we must avoid having our language define our position: While alternatives, such as the term homophile, have been suggested, the issue is still one of defining the research question in terms of biological sex of partner in erotic encounters. It would be foolish to imagine that the term homosexual could be supplanted, so wide is its currency. But it may be possible to explore human sexuality without the tunnel vision that is usually so apparent with regard to research on homosexual individuals. The term "homosexual" does channel research into focusing on the gender of the partner, on the definition as involving sexual contact with same-sex partners (despite the well-established distinctions between a homosexual erotic preference and homosexual behavior), and on the essentiality and stability of the definition as involving homosexual persons who retain such an identity or condition throughout their life. Homosexuality as so defined similarly colors the beliefs of those so defined in what may become a form of self-fulfilling prophecy: It has already been demonstrated (Ross, 1980) that homosexual men distort their perceptions of their childhood and upbringing in line with popularly accepted theories held in their society about the nature of homosexuality. As DeCecco and Shively correctly note, this has meant avoidance of such issues as age discrepancies in relationships, which may define the situation to the participants more centrally than partner gender. Similarly, Shively, Jones, and DeCecco (1983/1984) note that sample selection in homosexual research has made a number of assumptions, chief among which are those of partner gender and essentiality of the condition. While the term homosexual is too well entrenched to do away with, it is essential that we understand how this term shapes our social and scientific thinking about sexual relationships and stability of erotic preference among other things. Choice of samples and their definition in terms of same-sex activity can only reify partner gender to the extent where all other variables influencing partner choice are ignored. Perhaps, in this context, it is important for future theory on and research into homosexuality to look at erotic encounters in terms of person-situation interactions rather than take it for granted that all that is involved is sex and gender.

With regard to the homosexual content of sexual relationships, DeCecco and Shively note that the gay identity is a socio-cultural identity because of the requirement of disclosure to heterosexuals, and because of implicit moral assumptions about a gay identity. In making these moral assumptions explicit, they also raise implicitly a question beyond that of morality: What is the *meaning* of sexuality? Unless we can trace moral assumptions this further step back, we cannot understand in much greater depth the meaning of sexual relationships to those involved. By making such meanings explicit, we may be able to look at gender of partner choice as a function of meaning rather than of gender as such: As DeCecco and Shively put it, go beyond the belief that "people's biological sex is the brute reality before which all human relationships must bow" (1983/1984, p. 10).

MEANING OF SEXUALITY AS A DETERMINANT OF PARTNER CHOICE

Perhaps the major meaning of sex, and one which has led to the biological categorization of sexual relationships to the exclusion of almost all other meanings, is tied up with reproduction: The use of biological metaphors to explain sexual relationships assumes that sex and reproduction are indissolubly linked and that sex is *for* reproduction. While the advent of the anovulent pill has threatened this meaning of sexual behavior, the assumption still remains. As Richardson (1983/1984) suggests, what is crucial is the *meaning* that individuals ascribe to their sexual feelings, activity, and relationships (italics added). Thus the meaning of the sexual encounter must be our first choice of investigation in order to determine whether a partner may have particular characteristics, including gender. What meanings may sexual encounters have? What distinguishes a relationship that is sexual from one which is nonsexual? Perhaps the problem is better expressed by asking what the meanings of a relationship, either sexual or homosexual, may be. Crossculturally, a number of different meanings can be derived (none of which are necessarily mutually exclusive).

If we examine such meanings, we arrive at a list (not mutually exclusive) of motivations for sexual relationships (see Table 1).

Elaboration of the sexual meanings in Table 1 reveals that sexual encounters may have religious meanings, as when marriages represent God's plan for social order; emotional meanings, as when they represent part of an emotional attachment or love between individuals; libidinal meanings, as release of sexual urge; financial meanings, as in prostitution, being provided for, or economic security; meanings of duty, as when sex occurs as an expected activity as in the context of marriage; and antisocial meanings, as when individuals have sex as an expression of rejection of sex-negative values of parents or society, and as part of a rebellion against the prevailing mores. Similarly, sexual encounters may have ritual meanings, as when oral sex conveys the essence of masculinity in some tribal groups; hedonistic meanings, as when sex is seen as an enjoyable recreation; experimental meanings, as

TABLE 1   Theoretical Aspects and Meanings of Sexual Relationships

Aspects	Meanings
Reproduction	Continuation of species
Religious	Symbolic of union
Emotional	Extension of love for partner
Release of sexual urge	Release of frustration or libido
Financial	Prostitution
Duty	Socially expected, as in some marriages
Antisocial statement	Rejection of parental/social values
Ritual	During particular ceremonies; symbolic
Hedonistic (Recreational)	Enjoyment
Experimental	Exploration of sexual feelings and behaviors
Relational	As part of wider social and attitudinal affinities
Dominance	Rape; expression of difference in relative power
Peer-sanctioned	Normative; status-associated
Forbidden or Taboo	Associated with guilt or punishment
Dynastic	Cementing relations between families or groups
Mentor	Teaching sexuality to younger individuals

when adolescents explore their genitals with peers; relational meanings, as when sex may express affinities in attitudes and other areas of common ground but without strong emotional commitment; dominance meanings, as in rape or where one partner is seen as the "property" of another; peer-sanctioned meanings, as when the status of some adolescents is enhanced by sexual experience; and meanings of being forbidden or taboo, such as sex with particular individuals, classes of individuals, or objects. Finally, sex may have dynastic meanings, when it may serve to link clans or families into a wider group, and meanings of mentorship, as when an older individual tutors a younger one, including sexually. With the exception of reproduction, all these may apply to homosexual sex, and *without* any gender-linked implications.

However, two cautions must also be expressed: first, the term, and concept of, homosexuality may be so gender-based (that is, paradigm-specific) that it has no meaning outside that paradigm. Secondly, as Kuhn has noted, paradigms are socially based, in that they reflect social constructions during their period of influence. In the case of homosexual research, it is clear (Ross, 1980) that social constructions of homosexuality significantly influence homosexual's recall and attribution of previous events. It is questionable whether it is possible to remove the influence of the previous paradigm on the thinking of possible resarch respondents without extremely careful research design. In the context of paradigms, perspective is also lent to this conceptualization of dominant models of sexual behavior by McIntosh's (1968) paper in which she identified the previous paradigm in western society, in which up to about the middle of the eighteenth century homosexuality was seen as neither exclusive nor gender-related: It is possible that what we are arguing to be a new paradigm is in fact a reversion to a previous one.

On the other hand, the prebiological western paradigm which McIntosh describes, while not essentializing homosexuality or heterosexuality, is radically different in its view of the meanings of sexuality, particularly with regard to religious, dynastic, and reproductive aspects of sexuality.

So far, predominantly western paradigms have been considered: However, a number of other sexual models are also evident. These include those in which homosexual relations have a *masculinizing* effect via the transmission of semen, and where homosexual liaisons are seen as an important step in the development of maturity in a younger individual as an integral part of a relationship with a mentor. It could be argued that any one of the meanings of sexual encounters listed in Table 1 could become the basis for a paradigm for viewing homosexual behavior: Some of these cross-cultural paradigms ar considered later in this chapter.

The belief that reproduction and sexuality are indissolubly linked has probably led to the emphasis of gender as the principal criterion of sexual relationships and partner preference. Other meanings of sexual encounters, apart perhaps from dominance, which may in a society of unequal power distribution between men and women be gender-based, are *unrelated to gender*. This fact alone more than any other emphasizes that the gender paradigm may have little if any explanatory power in the area of sexual relationships.

POSSIBLE ALTERNATIVE PARADIGMS

It has been argued previously (Ross, 1983a) that biological sex has become a metaphor for classification of relationships and objects, and it is probably as a consequence of the overemphasis on classification that we still talk of homosexual and heterosexual individuals. The emphasis on the binary classification, which mirrors male-female categories, in the term "homosexual" divides it into two further but binary classifications: same or opposite sex preference (prefering a male or a female), and sexual vesus non-sexual (genital relations as occur between males and females). Research has been trapped within this binary categorization for over 100 years, and the real difficulty is to escape from this model and to stop conceptualizing homosexuality as being necessarily gender-related. Until this happens, research on sexual orientation will probably remain at an impasse. In this regard, it is instructive to look at the history of research into homosexuality. Initially, research concentrated on the etiology and correlates of what was essentially considered a pathology. From the mid-1950s, research concentrated on disproving the myths which had grown up around homosexuality: child molestation, deviant social sex-role or gender identity, inherent psychopathology, a relationship between parental rearing patterns and partner preference, and the presence of neuroanatomical, physiological, and endocrinological concommitants or precursors to homosexuality. Now that most of these myths have been exploded, research on homosexuality has reached a hiatus with no direction or theory to guide it. It could be argued that this is precisely because we have been arguing within a dual-gender model rather than between models. As Kuhn (1970) has already forcibly argued, such approaches test only the currently socially accepted paradigm and demonstrate nothing. What is needed is another model to test *against* the old gender-based model.

Kuhn's thesis is that science proceeds in terms of models or "paradigms" which define the domain of what may be considered a "problem" and provide a relatively inflexible box to force nature within the conceptual framework of the paradigm. As Charlesworth (1982) notes, Kuhn developed his notion of the paradigmatic nature of science from his appreciation of the fact that the meaning of motion for Aristotle was quite different to the meaning of motion for Newton, and that both systems were based on totally different assumptions. In the field of sexual orientation, DeCecco and Shively (1983/1984) have elegantly illustrated that the current paradigm assumes that the meaning of sexual relationships is equivalent to the meaning of gender, and that they covary. However, from Table 1 it can be argued that many of the meanings of sexuality (and this list is neither representative, exclusive, nor exhaustive) do not fit this paradigm. In the sense that Kuhn uses the term paradigm, the study of sexual relationships is redefining its model.

Having identified that the previous paradigm conceptualizes all sexual encounters within the rubric of gender, it is equally necessary to identify a new paradigm to guide research on homosexuality. While it would be unjustified to give this the status of a theory, we can probably advance the following preliminary proposition for empirical test:

> *that homosexual relationships may occur for reasons unrelated or indirectly related to the gender of the participants; and that included in such reasons is the meanings given to sexual encounters by the participants.*

Clearly, depending on the culture in which these occur and its norms, these will be considered normal or abnormal to some degree.

In looking at sexual orientation, it is therefore important not to look at homosexuals and heterosexuals contrasted: such a comparison tells us only about sex of preferred partner and litle about etiology of partner choices. If we are to really understand sexual relationships, and not just sex of partner, we need to look at what, *apart* from sex of partner, is important in choice. It may be that partner gender is a variable which is commonly noted because of our preoccupation with classifying everything according to gender, but which is a covariant of a choice according to personality variables which commonly occur in males rather than females (Ross, Rogers & McCulloch, 1978). In such a circumstance, we can only begin to understand the meaning of choosing a same-sex partner by looking at bisexual individuals (Kinsey Scale levels two through four), and partner gender as one of a number of variables in partner choice along with psychological and physical attributes. Thus the reasons why a bisexual individual chooses a male as opposed to a female may be related to personality, temporal and situational needs, reasons for the relationship being entered into, and anticipated duration, physical characteristics, age, and any one of a number of variables of which gender may be a secondary correlate. Such combinations and interactions cannot be ascertained when looking at individuals who are homogeneous for preferred sex of partner, and as a consequence almost all of the research on the etiology of homosexuality (and heterosexuality) has probably asked the wrong questions. Only in studying bisexual individuals and determining the similarities and differences between their choice of male and female partners can the etiology of sexual orientation, and the meanings of partner preference, be elucidated.

The unfortunate definition of the bisexual in terms of homosexual or heterosexual degree of preference probably obscures the central importance of such a category. The very fact that gender of partner *may not be important* for the bisexual strikes at the heart of the issue of defining sexual encounters in terms of gender. This fact has been all but ignored previously (Blumstein & Schwartz, 1977), and may also be the reason why bisexual individuals have been regarded with disapproval by both homosexual and heterosexual groups. Previously, it has been suggested that this rejection of the bisexual individual has been because they threaten the stability of the self-definition of individuals as being in one category or the other, and as such may threaten the stability of the established roles. Such an analysis is still within the framework of the essentiality of partner gender: It can be argued, however, that the rejection of the bisexual orientation is because it challenges whether gender of partner is an issue *at all.*

From this, it is a small step to the proposition that partner characteristics other than gender may be of more importance than, or interact significantly with, gender. No amount of research comparing exclusive homosexuals with exclusive heterosexuals can demonstrate this, and thus research on bisexuality may hold the key to the meaning of gender along with other variables in partner selection. As previously noted, at least two other key variables may also be involved: meaning of sexuality, and the situation in which it occurs.

There are in addition a number of other variables which may be of equal or greater importance to analysis of sexual relationships, particularly in terms of social analysis: class, race, income, personality, religion, and so on. Any one of these may be of greater importance in partner choice than gender, but as yet have not been adequately looked at even in conjunction with gender of partner.

What is thus being suggested as an alternative paradigm is a model in which gender of partner is conceptualized as one of a number of independent variables along with physical and psychological aspects of partner, demographic and social factors, situation, and particularly meaning of sexual encounters.

Particularly by looking at such research designs in cultures which themselves have clearly differing views of sexuality, the relative importance of gender as one among many variables, rather than as the only defining variable, may be ascertained. What we are suggesting is that future research looks at necessary and sufficient conditions for sexual relationships in a multivariate mode and at the interactions between these conditions depending on culture and context.

It must be concluded that, as Richardson (1983/1984) has commented, what is crucial is the meaning that individuals ascribe to their sexual feelings, activity, and relationships. Homosexuality, in the final analysis, is a series of behaviors which may be unrelated apart from the gender of the participants. The task of the researcher in this area is to move beyond the biologically-based assumptions constructed around sex and gender and to look at the factors other than gender (although perhaps gender-linked, such as personality variables which may be more common among males than females) which determine partner choice. Other variables such as situation, and partner-situation interactions, must also be investigated. Illustrating this latter point, Laner (1979) and Bell (1974) both provide some indication of desired characteristics in same-sex partners for permanent partners (Laner) and, presumably, short-term encounters (Bell). The difference between these two sets suggests strongly that very different sets of characteristics are involved depending on situation.

However, the alternative research emphasis which this paper has proposed can really only provide initial hypotheses and theories by examining bisexuals. Bisexuals could be contrasted with exclusive homosexual or heterosexual individuals in an attempt to elucidate the mechanisms of exclusive choice (the underlying assumption being one of polymorphous perversity). More critically, however, bisexuals should be looked at to determine what variables in partner choice are significant *when the preferred partner could be either male or female.* In this context, choice of gender-reassigned partner, or preoperative transsexual, should also reveal the critical variables involved while minimizing or controlling for partner gender.

It is time that researchers in the field of sexuality realized the assumptions inherent in current essentialistic, biologically-determined models of homosexuality and commenced testing between paradigms rather than within them. This can only be done by ignoring or devaluing gender or preferred partner and concentrating on other variables influencing partner preferences and particularly on the meanings of sexual encounters to the participants. Such approaches are one of the only ways we can avoid reinforcing essentialistic and gender-based theories of sexual orientation by unquestioning testing of hypotheses based solely on such a paradigm. One of the other ways is to examine homosexuality in cross-cultural context: Any general theory of homosexuality must take into account nonwestern cultures as well as nongendered paradigms.

HOMOSEXUALITY AND NORMALITY:
CROSS-CULTURAL ISSUES

Inclusion of homosexuality in any international classification of disease or abnormality is problematic, and raises a number of nosologic and value-related issues as well as cultural ones. It can be argued that the definition of homosexuality as abnormal is both culturally and temporally bound in western society, and thus cannot be used to describe or ascribe characteristics to individuals in other societies. As such, it is inappropriate to even attempt to introduce as abnormal a behavior which may have been essentialized into an identity in only part of the world, and which may have multiple meanings in different cultures. Even where homosexuality is essentialized as a condition or identity rather than as a behavior, no relationship can be demonstrated between mental health and homosexual identification (Gonsiorek, 1982a,b,c). While there may be a causal association between stigmatization and mental health, however, this is not linkable to any particular minority or ethnic status as such but to the stigmatization. Indeed, Cass (1979) has suggested that homosexual identification as an exclusive or central definition of one's identity is only one stage of a developmental process in which the end point is integration of sexual object preference into other core identities.

Definition and Prevalence

In western societies, homosexuality is commonly separated into primary and secondary homosexuality: homosexual acts and homosexual feelings respectively. Primary homosexuality involves sexual acts between members of the same sex. It may occur transiently in adolescence, all male or all female environments, and may even occur in heterosexual men who desire an outlet less lonely than masturbation (Humphreys, 1970). Homosexual orientation, on the other hand, may occur without homosexual acts, in situations where there is an emotional attraction or desire to interact at a physical level between two people of the same sex. It is, basically, an affective relationship between members of the same sex.

Thus individuals may indulge in homosexual acts without defining themselves as homosexual, and similarly, individuals may be predominantly attracted to members of their own sex yet never have a physical relationship that is homosexual. Generally, though in most individuals, the feelings and actions are congruent.

From the point of view of classification, it is necessary to point out that there are major differences between homosexual *identity* and homosexual *behavior*. If one is to classify homosexual identity, then one is looking at a process by which individuals come to see gender of preferred partner as a variable which defines other aspects of their lifestyle. If one is to classify homosexual identity, then one is looking at a process by which individuals come to see gender of preferred partner as a variable which defines other aspects of their lifestyle. If one is to classify homosexual behavior, then one is looking at behavior which may have multiple meanings between and within societies which are too broad to be classified. Weinberg (1983) notes that many men who have had sex with other males neither suspect themselves of, or adopt, a homosexual identity. Such people who do identify, at some stage, as homosexuals, are those who are able to conceive a special relationship between *being* and *doing*. It seems nosologically rather arbitrary to classify those who can conceive of this relationship as "homosexual," and to ignore those who cannot or do not make this link. In looking at mental health and homosexual *identity*, it is also important to realize that this category occurs in only some societies, and may have very differnt meanings and social sanctions attached to it. It is impossible to classify homosexual behavior as having any necessary mental health implications ("normal" or "abnormal") cross culturally, and exceedingly difficult and culturally-bound to classify homosexual identity as having any mental health implications particularly as a homosexual *identity* appears only in societies where it is stigmatized. Any such implications will be primarily relatable to stigmatization, not to identity: As a consequence, the "condition" of homosexuality as such is probably a *function* of stigmatization and even where definable, the definition may be cross-culturally variable.

Homosexuality cannot be described as a simple or single behavior any more than heterosexuality can: The homosexual orientation comprises as wide a range of attitudes, practices, and behaviors as the heterosexual one. The very definition of an individual as homosexual *or* heterosexual is misleading, because not only may individuals be both to a greater or lesser degree, but homosexual acts may be performed by people with heterosexual orientation, and vice versa. Were it not stigmatized, it is doubtful whether it would need to be emphasized to the point where individuals needed to explain homosexual behavior and thus adopt as part of a self-affirmation, a homosexual identity.

Richardson (1983/1984) reviews the literature on what if anything can be considered essential to the homosexual category, and concludes that not only is the term "homosexual" to designate a particular category of person a recent one, but that in the last century psychiatry has essentialized homosexuality as part of an attempt to explain behavior predefined as immoral or unnatural. In some cases, this was the price to pay for removing such behavior from the realm of the criminal to the medical. She concludes that the definition of homosexuality as an inherent aspect of the structure of society and of individual personality is a history of definitional crises. These crises have arisen in attempting to decide what is essential to the homosexual category: behavior? personal identification? underlying orientation? Maghan and Sagarin (1983) raise additional questions as to whether homosexuality can be seen as a "master status" which colors all other statuses: they note that in many situations, whether individuals indulge in same-gender sexual activity or define themselves as "homosexual" has no implications for their behavior or the consequences of that behavior. As noted earlier, Cass (1979) has suggested that a homosexual identity (in which individuals do see homosexuality as a superordinate defining status) may simply be one stage of accepting one's same-gender sexual behavior. Her stage 6 of homosexual adjustment is defined as the point where having a homosexual sex-object preference is only one facet of, and has few implications for, personality and lifestyle.

We would go further, and argue that the homosexual "condition" is a product of a particular society which stigmatizes homosexual behavior (western european) and of a particular period (since the eighteenth century: McIntosh, 1968). Such essentialization, incorporated into western psychiatric thinking in the past hundred years, bears little relationship to same-sex interactions in other cultures, and must either be seen as a culture-bound classification or rejected as having little meaning in or for mental health in an international context. Prevalence studies dating from the time of some of the most rigid homosexual/heterosexual classifications and punishment of homosexual behavior show that even in western society, homosexuality cannot easily be essentialized.

Perhaps the best-known and largest study to look at the prevalence of homosexuality in western society was that of Kinsey and his colleagues in the United States (Kinsey, Pomeroy, & Martin, 1948). They found that male and female homosexuality could best be described as a continuum of degrees of attraction to members of one's own sex, and categorized individuals in terms of this Kinsey Scale. Thus Kinsey and his colleagues found that 37 percent of the male population had had sex with another male to orgasm between the ages of 16 and 55: over one-third of the population. Of these, only about 4 percent would be exclusively homosexual all their lives. Nevertheless, their data showed that about 18 percent of the male population would have as much homosexual as heterosexual experience between the ages of 16 and 55, nearly one in five of the population. The later Kinsey Report on women (Kinsey, Pomeroy, Martin, & Gebhard, 1953) noted somewhat lower figures for female homosexual experiences, 26 percent of women having been erotically aroused in homosexual situations and half that number reaching orgasm with another woman by the age of 45. As women have become more sexually active since Kinsey collected his data in the 1940s, the female prevalence is probably somewhat higher now.

What is important to note is that homosexuality cannot be described as uncommon or statistically abnormal on this evidence. It is clear that a large proportion of the population have engaged in homosexual activity, and recent studies (McConaghy, Armstrong, Birrell, & Buhrich, 1979) have shown that around 40 percent of men and a higher proportion of women have been erotically attracted to members of their own sex at some time. Thus homosexual attraction, as well, appears to be fairly common. It must be concluded, then, that popular definitions of two classes of people, "homosexual" and "heterosexual," are inaccurate and only serve to draw attention away from the actual proportion of homosexual behavior in the population. What is meant by "homosexual" in the western scientific literature is usually those individuals who are predominantly homosexual and who acknowledge this fact to themselves or to others. It will be used in the same context here.

It must be recognized, however, that dividing individuals up into classes such as homosexual or heterosexual not only ignores evidence suggesting a continuum but also serves a social function of anxiety reduction. It enables individuals to be typecast as either one identity or the other, thus preventing heterosexuals from recognizing their homosocial, homoerotic, and homosexual feelings or behaviors as threatening, and the converse for the persons who have identified themselves as being homosexual. The security derived from such a categorization, while decreasing the individuals' examination of their sexual feelings on the basis of gender, does serve to perpetuate the idea of examination of sexual feelings on the basis of gender. It also serves to perpetuate the binary classification of sex object preference and aids in the definition of homosexual interest as a "condition." This is somewhat analogous to the popular concept of mental health in which individuals are branded by society as either "mentally ill" or "normal," essentializing mental illness and ignoring the presence of continua of psychosocial adjustment.

While most data on homosexuals are derived from western societies, there is considerable agreement that the figures of Kinsey are reasonably accurate. For example, proportions of Kinsey Scale levels 5 and 6 males could be accounted for by number of homosexual acts in a population: In a recent survey in Finland, Talikka (1975) found that in the past two years, 11 percent of all adult males surveyed had had a homosexual sexual encounter. This survey was based on a random sample of the population.

Cross-Cultural Aspects of Homosexuality

The question of whether there is any general consensus on homosexuality as a mental illness is effectively answered by Ford and Beach (1952), who analyzed the human relations area files for 77 societies, and found that in 64 percent of these societies, homosexual behavior is considered normal or socially acceptable for some or all members of the community. There can be no doubt from these data that homosexuality is present in the vast majority of cultures, and is generally stigmatized in only about one-third of them. Consensus about the deviant status of homosexuality is not present, and would appear in fact to be in the direction of acceptance of same-sex contacts. It is interesting to note that Whitehead (1981) among others reported that the rate of homosexuality in the world appears to vary independently of the official cultural "attitude" toward it. The rate may be high where it is condemned (twentieth century North America) or low (Trobriands); low where it is permitted (Nambikwara) or high (Desana). She also notes that acceptance of heterosexual expression might appear equally elusive were it not, in some form, universally "institutionalized."

Before looking at institutionalization of homosexuality and exclusive homosexuality, it is necessary to look at homosexual behavior in various societies in order to ascertain whether homosexual behavior is universally considered normal or abnormal, and whether homosexual behavior can be considered a unitary behavior.

Bullough (1976), reviewing sexual variance in history across cultures, made the point that homosexuality may be seen as being contrary to a number of perceived purposes. Five major aspects of homosexuality, then, can probably be noted in this context: homosexuality as it is concerned with the procreational aspects of sex, homosexuality as an indicator of social status (dominance-submission), homosexuality as recreation (hedonistic sexuality), homosexuality as an educational activity (mentoring), and homosexuality as an emotional preference (affectional sexuality). There are also numerous other meanings that sexual (and specifically homosexual as well as heterosexual) interactions may have to the participants as has already been noted (Table 1): examples may be provided for all of these in various cultures. Clearly, in the course of history, some aspects of homosexuality have been acceptable while others have not. As examples, homosexuality in pre-Christian Jewish society was unacceptable because it did not lead to procreation, which was regarded as the leading imperative for survival of the race. In Egyptian society, homosexuality was regarded as an index of submission if an individual took the so-called passive role in anal intercourse, but as an acceptable behavior for the active partner. After defeat in battle, the soldiers in a defeated army could expect to be sodomized by the Egyptian victors, with stigma attached only to the passive role. This, however, appears only to have been attached to anal intercourse, and not to other forms of homosexual behavior. Hedonistic sexuality in which sexual relations between males was for sexual release was and is unstigmatized in many societies, including Roman society and in some middle Eastern cultures, as long as a passive role is not taken. Similarly, in some Polynesian societies such as Samoa (Shore, 1981) and Mexico (Carrier, 1980), it is acceptable for males to engage in homosexual activity as long as there is no deviation in social sex role or the insertee role is not taken in anal intercourse.

As a subset of hedonistic homosexuality, homosexual behavior as substitution may also be considered in some societies. In some cases, where strict segregation of the sexes between adolescents or adults is practiced, it may be acceptable for homosexual behavior to occur because heterosexual activity is forbidden or impossible. Generally, however, this is referred to as institutionalized homosexuality. It may also become part of educational homosexuality if there is an age or status gap between the partners. Educational homosexuality describes the form of homosexual behavior typical of classical Greece and of several New Guinean societies, in which a youth is adopted by an older man who acts as his mentor. While such homosexual unions serve other purposes as well, including emotional ones, they are recognized as having educational and social importance and accepted as both homosexual and homosocial in nature. Herdt (1981) describes the Sambia of New Guinea, in which passive homosexual fellation is universally practiced as a means of developing *masculinity* (directly *opposite* to western conceptions of associated sex roles), as well as having educational and affective functions. Finally, affectional homosexual behavior, which may be subdivided into homosocial and homosexual (although both usually occur together), may be accepted if there is no overt sexual component in some societies (for example, con-temporary western society) or accepted without reservation (as in the Siwans of North Africa). While these classifications cover the general spectrum of male homosexual relations, they are not exclusive, and one or more categories may co-exist. What is demonstrated by these categories is, however, that homosexuality cannot be regarded as a single, coherent behavior cross-culturally, and nor can stigmatization of homosexuality be linked to homosexuality as such, but to homosexuality as it is seen to conflict with various societal values. Thus it is more correct, as Bell and Weinberg (1978) do, to speak of "homosexualities," than to see it as a unitary behavior. It is equally important to recognize, given that homosexuality is a behavior which reflects a multiplicity of motivations, that the behavioral manifestation of these motiva-tions cannot be considered a distinct condition or to have consistent etiology. Belief in a homosexual identity as it has been essentialized by western society is culture-bound and socially determined, and thus should not be used to define a behavior and its associated meanings in other cultures.

The wide variation of diagnosis (or labelling) of homosexuality cross-culturally further complicates matters. Behavior that is labelled homosexual, and thus subject in some societies to stigma as being "abnormal" or to the assumption of mental illness is not consistent. In western societies, homosexual behavior is so labelled if it involves genital contact between two members of the same sex, whether manual, oral, anal, or somatic. In contrast, in Mediterranean cultures and their derivatives, the homosexual is regarded as the passive partner in intercourse, and the active partner is neither labelled, stigmatized, nor assumed to be abnormal (Carrier, 1980). In some cultures, particularly in the New Guinea Highlands and in ancient Greece, there is no stigma attached to either partner, regardless of role (Bullough, 1976; Herdt, 1981): in fact, *failure* to act homosexually would be stigmatized, as Herdt makes clear. In yet others, passive homosexuals are considered to be a third sex, functioning as women yet having the soma of a male, and are institutionalized as such (Wikan, 1977). This latter situation can probably be considered an exaggeration of the Mediterranean definition of homosexuality to an extreme position.

Similarly, the cross-cultural literature has abounded with assumptions of what constitutes homosexual behavior, many of which may on examination be shown to be inaccurate. Whitehead (1981), in particular, has analyzed the situation of the homosexual in native North America, and found that descriptions of the Berdache phenomenon as institutionalized homosexuality do not fit the data. She argues that the interpretation of homosexuality in other cultures is invariably interpreted in terms of western notions of homosexuality, and that processes may be quite different in a culture in which they are formally instituted as opposed to those where they are spontaneously expressed. In native North America it was permissible in certain social respects for a man to become a woman (and, more infrequently, vice-versa). Homosexual practice was a common accompaniment to this but, as she forcefully points out, sexual object choice was outside the realm of what was publically and officially important about the role of the two sexes: cross-sex occupational choice and cross-dressing were the two definitive aspects. Sexual object choice variation did not provoke reclassification of the individual, and in fact Berdaches could have sex with either males or females without compromizing their status. Conversely, homosexual behavior in males and females was well known and had specific appellations, but was not considered objectionable or evidence of Berdache status. It is thus clear, as Whitehead argues, that the Berdache was a case of institutionalized cross-sex status rather than homosexuality, and that analyses of homosexual behavior in other cultures are invariably tainted with western assumptions about sexual behavior and gender roles. It could be argued that the homosexual "role" in western society (McIntosh, 1968) is equally an institutionalization, as a function of the need of medical science and the general population to essentialize sexual preference as an "either/or" phenomenon. As a consequence of the conceptualization of sexual preference as either homosexual *or* heterosexual, individuals are forced into socially-prescribed categories and the continual nature of sexual preference as demonstrated by Kinsey et al. (1948) not recognized.

Implicit in Whitehead's argument that the definition of homosexuality cross-culturally has been dependent upon imposing western values and interpretations is the suggestion that homosexuality and deviant gender identity and social sex role are linked. Despite research evidence which illustrates that inappropriate social sex role is not necessarily associated with homosexuality (Heilbrun & Thompson, 1977), the argument that feminine indentification is linked with male homosexuality and masculine identification is linked with female homosexuality has continued in psychiatry. This is probably due to the assumption that in a society where homosexuality is the accepted relational model, any individual who prefers a same-sex partner must therefore contain attributes of, or consider themselves a member of, the opposite sex (Ross, Rogers & McCulloch, 1978). This may be a legitimating ploy on the part of a heterosexually-based society, but psychiatry has to some degree accepted this societal reasoning in its formulation of homosexuality as psychopathology, by arguing that it is a psychopathology because of the opposite-sex identification. However, several points must be noted in this regard. First, studies such as those by Siegelman (1972) have shown that femininity in male homosexuals is related not to homosexuality as such but to the degree of neurosis in homosexuals: Similarly, Dickey (1961) noted that those male homosexuals who had a traditional masculine role were better psychologically adjusted. The lack of any consistent relationship between homosexuality and social sex role has also been shown by Ross (1983a,b). Ross demonstrated that degree of masculinity or femininity in homosexuals was not dependent on degree of homosexuality, but was in fact dependent on the attitudes to homosexuality and rigidity of sex roles in the society in which the homosexual lives. Thus there is now clear evidence that deviant masculinity and femininity in homosexuals may be dependent on societal factors, and are not necessarily inherent in homosexual behavior. Evidence that in some contexts, homosexual behavior may *masculinize* the actor (Herdt, 1981; Carrier, 1980) emphasizes this point.

Psychiatry has nevertheless developed the assumption that homosexuality is a function of disturbance of parental rearing patterns, particularly identification with parental models. While again this has been demonstrated by Siegelman (1974) to be correct only for some homosexuals, by Ross (1980) to be dependent on homosexuals recalling parent-child relations in terms of current theorizing on the etiology purported by psychoanalysts, and by Freund and Blanchard (1983) to be based on increased father-son distance where it does exist in male homosexuals being a *result* of the son's sexual preference rather than a *cause* of it, psychiatric theorizing nevertheless has accepted this as the main basis of abnormality. The logical fallacy of this has been pointed out by Davison (1982), who states that:

> one cannot attach a pathogenic label to a particular pattern of child-rearing unless one a priori labels the adult behavior pattern as pathological. For example, Bieber et al. found that what they called a "close-binding intimate mother" was present much more often in the life histories of the analytic male homosexual patients than among the heterosexual controls. But what is wrong with such a mother unless you happen to find her in the background of people whose current behavior you judge beforehand to be pathological?

As Davison so cogently argues, to be consistent one must judge a heterosexual with such a parental constellation pathological, as well as all such parents, if homosexuality is to be considered pathological on these grounds. There is of course another argument which illustrates the arbitrary nature of the association between social sex roles and homosexuality as well as the cultural variation involved. In the New Guinea Highlands, semen which enters the body via homosexual intercourse is regarded as *masculinizing* the individual, whereas in Mediterranean society the same act would be regarded as *feminizing*. Both, it could be argued, involve homosexual behavior: in New Guinea, ritually, and in Mediterranean areas, a socially prescribed institutionalization via the recognized homosexual role for the passive partner only.

Nevertheless, Gadpaille (1980) argues that *preferential* homosexual behavior seems to be regarded universally as deviant. While he notes that much of the anthropological data on cultures accepting some homosexual activity are too vague to permit conclusions about degree of "approval," he fails to distinguish between the bases for homosexual behavior (educational, affectional, etc.) and to distinguish between the different meanings of homosexuality in different cultures and different degrees of institutionalization. It is probably a mistake to assume that preferential homosexuality is not a form of institutionalization in western society given the emergency of a clear homosexual "role" (or stereotype) and the tendency of society to classify individuals as either *heterosexual* or *homosexual.* Certainly Saghir and Robins (1973) indicate that some 48 percent of their homosexual subjects had had heterosexual experience, despite the fact that they were preferentially homosexual at the point in time they were interviewed.

A second difficulty with Gadpaille's assertion about preferential homosexuality is the question as to when it becomes preferential. Is it preferential just on the homosexual side of bisexual, or only when it is totally exclusive? Is the label of preferential homosexuality one which ignores the data of Kinsey et al. (1948), which indicate that 13 percent of males will be more homosexual than heterosexual for a three year period in their lives, but not throughout their lives? Given the extreme difficulty of deciding what is preferential homosexuality, and the point at which it becomes preferential, there is little point in making definition of normality or abnormality dependent on this, particularly as preferential homosexuality may also be seen simply as the western form of institutionalized, socially imposed homosexuality. For what it is worth, animal studies involving infrahuman primates have also reported preferential homosexuality in some situations, suggesting that it may simply be one end of the continuum of plasticity with regard to sex of partner (Erwin & Maple, 1976).

Evidence presented here indicates that homosexuality, either within or across cultures, does not meet the criteria of universal abnormality. There is no cross-cultural consensus as to the acceptability of homosexuality, and what data exist suggest that the consensus is toward acceptance. Cross-culturally, homosexual behavior may have different meanings or be institutionalized to different degrees, and the reaction of societies to such behavior may range from rejection to acceptance of an identical behavior in different societies. Similarly, different bases for stigmatization of homosexual behavior as abnormal may be identified (including procreation, status, recreation, education and affection), and stigmatization as abnormal may be directed not so much at the homosexuality but at the societal values each of these may transgress. Given these data, it is impossible to state that homosexuality is either evidence of abnormality or that there is a common reaction to it cross-culturally which may lead to stigmatization of homosexual behavior. In each society, any stigmatization of homosexuality as psychopathological or deviant is based upon that society supporting the value judgments made rather than on any empirical evidence of psychopathology. The very fact that what is stigmatized in one culture is acceptable in another is evidence of this.

We can only conclude, as did Freud (1920), that "(Homosexuality) is found in peoples who exhibit no other serious deviations from the normal. It is similarly found in people whose efficiency is unimpaired. . . ." Nor can we conclude cross-culturally that homosexual behaviors are essentialized as a condition or identity in other than societies which create such an identity by stigmatizing homosexual behavior.

Where, then, does that leave theory of homosexual behavior and identity? First, seeing homosexual behavior or identity depends on the cultural and temporal context, and thus it is impossible to erect a universal theory of abnormal homosexuality. Any theory which is culture-bound cannot claim to explain homosexual behavior or identity as such, only the imposition of labels on deviant behaviors. The juxtaposition of the adjectives "normal" or "abnormal" with homosexual behavior or identity cannot be justified since the adjective describes a societal reaction and the phrase homosexual behavior or identity an act or self-classification. Where there is variation in labeling of behavior as "normal" or "abnormal," it is impossible to erect a universal theory to explain the etiology of homosexual behavior/identity in terms of an inherent state of deviance or normality.

Second, any universal theory of homosexual identity must also explain homosexual behavior and identity. Are they points on the same continuum or do they require separate etiological theories? The answer must be that they are the same entity which has been moulded by different environments. How, then, does one explain homosexual behavior (the baseline which may be elaborated into an identity)? The only theory which takes into account these distinctions is Freud's original theory that humans are polymorphous perverse: born with an undifferentiated sex drive which is then directed, through socialization, into particular directions in line with societal beliefs. Psychological theories of homosexual behavior and identity must therefore describe not the etiology of same-sex erotic contacts but the etiology of its expression, of the multiple meanings that may be ascribed to it, and of its institutionalization from a behavior to an identity in some individuals. This requires not a theory of homosexuality, or even of sexuality, but a general theory of how social realities color the meanings of interpersonal social and sexual interactions.

What has been presented here argues that any new theory of homosexual behavior must explain not the etiology of same-gender sexual interactions but the development of the multiple meanings such behaviors may have, when a relationship is defined as sexual, how in some cultures such meanings have greater strength than societal proscriptions, and how a homosexual identity develops from homosexual behavior. Attempts to define a uniform etiology from an essentialized condition, as old theories of "homosexuality" have, so far have provided little information that is not culturally and behaviorally ungeneralizable, and are probably limited to a particular gender-based paradigm. As such, they cannot contribute much to our understanding of homosexual behavior in man.

REFERENCES

Bell, A. P. Homosexualities: Their range and character. In: Cole, J. K. and Dienstbier, R. (Eds.), *1973 Nebraska symposium on motivation.* Lincoln, NE: University of Nebraska Press, 1974.

Bell, A. P. and Weinberg, M. S. *Homosexualities, a study of diversity among men and women.* New York: Simon and Schuster, 1978.

Blumstein, P. W. and Schwartz, P. Bisexuality: Some social psychological issues. *Journal of Social Issues,* 1977, *33*(2), 30–45.

Boswell, J. Revolutions, universals, and sexual categories. *Salmagundi,* 1982/1983, *58–59,* 89–113.

Bullough, V. L. *Sexual variance in society and history.* Chicago: University of Chicago Press, 1976.

Carrier, J. M. Homosexual behavior in cross-cultural perspective. In: J. Marmor (Ed.), *Homosexual behavior: A modern reappraisal.* New York: Basic Books, 1980.

Cass, V. C. Homosexual identity formation: A theoretical model. *Journal of Homosexuality,* 1979, *4,* 219–235.

Charlesworth, M. *Science, non-science and pseudo-science.* Victoria: Deakin University Press, 1982.

Davison, G. C. Politics, ethics and treatment for homosexuality. *American Behavioral Scientist,* 1982, *24,* 423–434.

DeCecco, J. P. and Shively, M. G. From sexual identity to sexual relationships: A contextual shift. *Journal of Homosexuality,* 1983/1984, *9*(2&3), 1–26.

Dickey, B. A. Attitudes toward sex roles and feeling of adequacy in homosexual males. *Journal of Consulting Psychology,* 1961, *25,* 116–122.

Erwin, J. and Maple, T. Ambisexual behavior with male-male anal penetration in male rhesus monkeys. *Archives of Sexual Behavior,* 1976, *5,* 9–14.

Ford, C. S. and Beach, F. A. *Patterns of sexual behavior.* London: Eyre and Spottiswoode, 1952.

Freud, S. *A general introduction to psychoanalysis.* New York: Boni and Liveright, 1920.

Freund, K. and Blanchard, R. Is the distant relationship of fathers and sons related to the son's erotic preference for male partners, or to the son's atypical gender identity, or both? *Journal of Homosexuality,* 1983, *9*(1), 7–25.

Gadpaille, W. J. Cross-species and cross-cultural contributions to understanding homosexual activity. *Archives of General Psychiatry,* 1980, *37,* 349–357.

Gonsiorek, J. C. Introduction to mental health issues and homosexuality. *American Behavioral Scientist*, 1982, *25*, 267–384.

Gonsiorek, J. C. Results of psychological testing on homosexual populations. *American Behavioral Scientist*, 1982, *25*, 385–396.

Gonsiorek, J. C. Social psychological concepts in the understanding of homosexuality. *American Behavioral Scientist*, 1982, *25*, 438–492.

Heilbrun, A. B. and Thompson, M. L. Sex-role identity and male and female homosexuality. *Sex Roles*, 1977, *3*, 65–79.

Herdt, G. H. *Guardians of the flutes: Idioms of masculinity*. New York: McGraw-Hill, 1981.

Humphreys, R. A. L. *Tearoom trade: A study of homosexual encounters in public places*. London: Duckworth, 1970.

Kinsey, A. C., Pomeroy, W. B. and Martin, C. E. *Sexual behavior in the human male*. Philadelphia: W. B. Saunders, 1948.

Kinsey, A. C., Pomeroy, W. B., Martin, C. E. and Gebhard, P. H. *Sexual behavior in the human female*. Philadelphia: W. B. Saunders, 1953.

Kuhn, T. S. *The structure of scientific revolutions* (2nd. ed.). Chicago: University of Chicago Press, 1970.

Laner, M. R. Permanent partner priorities: Gay and straight. *Journal of Homosexuality*, 1977, *3*, 21–39.

McConaghy, N., Armstrong, M. S., Birrell, P. C. and Buhrich, N. The incidence of bisexual feelings and opposite sex behaviour in medical students. *Journal of Nervous and Mental Disease*, 1979, *167*, 685–688.

McIntosh, M. The homosexual role. *Social Problems*, 1968, *16*, 182–192.

Maghan, J. and Sagarin, E. Homosexuals as victimizers and victims. In McNamara, D. E. J. and Karmen, A. (Eds.). *Deviants: Victims or victimizers?* Beverly Hills: Sage, 1983.

Richardson, D. The dilemma of essentiality in homosexual theory. *Journal of Homosexuality*, 1983/1984, *9*(2&3), 79–90.

Ross, M. W., Rogers, L. J. and McCulloch, H. Stigma, sex and society: A new look at gender differentiation and sexual variation. *Journal of Homosexuality*, 1978, *3*, 315–330.

Ross, M. W. Retrospective distortion in homosexual research. *Archives of Sexual Behavior*, 1980, *9*, 523–531.

Ross, M. W. Homosexuality and social sex roles: A re-evaluation. *Journal of Homosexuality*, 1983, *9*(1), 1–6.

Ross, M. W. Femininity, masculinity, and sexual orientation: Some cross-cultural comparisons. *Journal of Homosexuality*, 1983, *9*(1), 27–36.

Ross, M. W. Societal relationships and gender role in homosexuals: A cross-cultural comparison. *Journal of Sex Research*, 1983, *19*, 273–288.

Ross, M. W. Partner preference in homosexual men: A comparison of four societies. *Journal of Sex Research*, 1987, *23*, in press.

Shively, M. G., Jones, C. and DeCecco, J. P. Research on sexual orientation: Definitions and methods. *Journal of Homosexuality*, 1983/1984, *9*(2&3), 127–136.

Shore, B. Sexuality and gender in Samoa: Conceptions and missed conceptions. In Ortner, S. B. and Whitehead, H. (Eds.). *Sexual meanings: The cultural constuction of gender and sexuality.* Cambridge: Cambridge University Press, 1981.

Siegelman, M. Adjustment of male homosexuals and heterosexuals. *Archives of Sexual Behavior,* 1972, *2,* 9–25.

Siegelman, M. Parental background of male homosexuals and heterosexuals. *Archives of Sexual Behavior,* 1974, *3,* 3–18.

Talikka, A. Uusia tutkimustuloksia. *SETA,* 1975, *3,* 13–15.

Weinberg, T. S. *Gay men, gay selves: The social construction of homosexual identities.* New York: Irvington, 1983.

Whitehead, H. The bow and the burden strap: A new look at institutionalized homosexuality in native North America. In Ortner, S. B. and Whitehead, H. (Eds.). *Sexual meanings: The cultural construction of gender and sexuality.* Cambridge: Cambridge University Press, 1981.

Wikan, U. Man becomes woman: Transsexualism in Oman as a key to gender roles. *Man,* 1977, *12,* 304–319.

14

THE HUMANISTIC OUTLOOK

Josef E. Garai

Dennis Altman (1983) has described the problems of definition related to homosexuality and homosexuals as follows:

> If the thrust of most of the changes that took place over the past decade has been toward the construction and recognition of a homosexual minority, it is important to realize that this thrust is double-edged. On the one hand, the recent changes have undoubtedly been important in developing a sense of self-confidence and acceptance among those who conceive of themselves as homosexuals; "gay pride" and "glad to be gay" were slogans that expressed this feeling very well. On the other hand, the more stress that is placed on the idea of a homosexual minority, the more difficult it is to recognize that homosexuality, whether acted out or repressed, is part of everyone's sexuality and has implications for many people other than those who conceptualize themselves as part of the gay minority.

This view of homosexuality is derived from Freud, who differed from most of his contemporaries insisting that homosexual desire was part of the infant's "polymorphous perversity"; that is, we are all born with an undifferentiated sexuality, in terms of both sexual object (the sought-after partner) and sexual aim (the sought-after act). Certain variations from the "normal" pattern of sexual development, somewhat different depending on one's gender, were advanced by Freud to explain why some people become largely or exclusively homosexual in terms of the sexual object, but Freud never regarded homosexuals as a discrete category and stressed the existence of repressed and/or sublimated homosexuality in everyone.

> *By studying sexual excitations other than those that are manifestly displayed, it (psychoanalysis) has found that all human beings are capable of making a homosexual object choice and have in fact made one in their unconscious.* (Freud, 1962, p. 11).

Consequently, Freud denied that there was such a thing as "innate inversion" (p. 6) and rejected the ideas of those earlier writers such as Ulrichs and Krafft-Ebing who had argued for it. Ulrichs had seen homosexuals as men with "a feminine brain in a masculine body," constituting a "third sex," a term already used by Gautier in 1935 of women, and by Balzac in 1844 of men. The idea of "urnings" (Ulrich's term) who are innately quite different from heterosexuals in some unspecified way was strongly rejected by Freud. Ulrichs paid virtually no attention to lesbians.

Freud's view of homosexuality was both complex and changing, for he discussed it in a number of both clinical and theoretical works written over a long period of time. But the essential point is that Freud consistently rejected the notion of a defined group of people who were in some innate and unchangeable way homosexual, and it was probably the influence of Freud that ended the tendency of late nineteenth century apologists to so define homosexuals. It was also a major reason for Havelock Ellis' disagreements with Freud, with Ellis clinging to the congenital theory of homosexuality.

Freud remains a figure of considerable controversy, and even many people who employ his concepts remain unwilling to acknowledge his influence. Yet in certain key areas—the fluidity of sexual desire, the existence of the unconscious, the importance of sexuality and the concepts of repression and sublimation—Freud's insights seem to me to have withstood attempts over the past half-century to discredit him. We may doubt (as I do) much of what he had to say about female sexuality, about the mechanism of sexual development, about the workings of dreams, and especially about the therapeutic value of psychoanalysis, while recognizing that his remains overall the most satisfactory framework for understanding human sexuality.

Much gay hostility to Freud stems from a perception that he saw homosexuality as immature and a perversion. Yet it is important to stress that Freud was far less homophobic than the bulk of psychoanalysts who have followed him, particularly in the United States where psychoanalysis has become associated with considerable antipathy to homosexuality. American psychoanalysts like Irving Bieber whose insistence on pathology of homosexuality influenced a whole generation of analysts and psychiatrists, quite consciously rejected Freud's belief in innate bisexuality. Freud, however, saw homosexuals as neither sick nor criminal, was careful to spell out that "inverts cannot be regarded as degenerate," and he supported the early German and Austrian campaigns to decriminalize homosexuality (Spiers and Lynch, 1977). In some ways he wrote about homosexuality with a degree of acceptance not found again among psychiatrists until the early seventies. For Freud, of course, sublimation of homosexuality was a crucial part of both social and cultulral life, as he argued in his study of Leonardo da Vinci. Was not this, indeed, reflected in his own life, in which there is evidence of very strong repressed homosexuality—his idealized relationship with his wife, his strong attachment to men friends (Freud actually fainted after his break with Jung), his paternalistic yet passionless relationships with women? Samuel Rosenberg has seen evidence for this claim in Freud's passionate friendship with Wilhelm Fliess, who suggested to him the idea of inherent bisexuality and whose wife became increasingly jealous of the friendship (Rosenberg, 1978, pp. 189-203).

Any discussion of sexuality must balance the contribution to our behavior and emotions of inborn desire and of social constructs. This balance is often posed as a simple conflict between two discrete alternatives: that of ethology and sociobiology, which seems to claim that our sexual behavior is genetically programmed, and that of cultural anthropology, which sees societies as regulating sexuality in very diverse ways. Thus the sociologists Gagnon and Simon have argued that "the sexual area may be precisely that realm wherein the superordinate position of the sociocultural over the biological level is most complete" (Gagnon and Simon, 1973, p. 15).

But this is something of a false polarization: Biology and culture are not alternatives, but rather dual factors that interact with each other to produce particular expressions of sexuality. Such sexual expressions can take many and varied forms (including abstinence), but ultimately they involve a universal need for body contact, erotic stimulation, and orgasmic release. While it is true that our sexuality is shaped and influenced to a large extent by social pressures, this can only occur within the real limits imposed by biology. Thus, however far one tries to get away from Freud's concept of natural drives that need be distorted in the interests of civilization, in almost any discussion of sexuality one is forced to fall back ultimately on some idea of a basic instinctual desire, even if such desire is not necessarily translated into what would commonly be regarded as sexual acts.

The most controversial part of Freud's analysis of homosexuality involves the concept of repression and the idea that everyone has experienced homosexual desire that, in most cases, is more or less successfully repressed. To argue that homosexuals are genetically determined would seem to reject this view, but Edward O. Wilson, the best-known exponent of sociobiology, has written that "there is a potential for bisexuality in the brain, and it is sometimes expressed fully by persons who switch back and forth in their sexual preference" (Wilson, 1979, p. 149). What happens to such potential in those people who do not switch is not clear.

There is considerable evidence that people are capable of very fluid sexual response; in the Kinsey surveys 37 percent of the men and 19 percent of the women acknowledged at least one orgasm with a partner of the same sex, though this says nothing about emotional responses. Masters and Johnson's study *Homosexuality in Perspective* provides considerable support for the thesis that we all possess the potential for bisexual desire; among the group studied, sexual fantasies almost invariably included persons of both sexes (Masters and Johnson, 1979, pp. 186–188). As poets have always known, our sexual desires are foreshadowed in fantasies, dreams, and poetry, however unamenable these may be to empirical research (Altman, pp. 39–42).

We may state that Freud's early views on bisexuality and homosexuality reflect a basically humanistic orientation which unfortunately failed to affect his followers, particularly in the United States. From the confluence of ideas expressed by Ferguson (1980), Garai (1979), and Roszak (1979), Garai formulated the following five principles of the humanistic-holistic approach as follows:

1. Each individual has the inalienable right to the fullest development of unique personhood, identity, and lifestyle.
2. Each individual has the right to expect respect for unique personhood, identity, and integrity or wholeness from all other people.
3. Each individual is encouraged to associate with other individuals on the basis of sharing common goals, ideas, interests, handicaps, or lifestyles.
4. Each individual has the right to challenge any authority or institution to respond positively to one's own need for recognition of unique identity and personhood.
5. Each individual is encouraged to seek internal wholeness, that is, a harmonioius balance between body, mind, and spirit as well as external wholeness, that is, a wholesome connectedness with other people and a profound respect for the inviolability of the ecological environment as our common human habitat. (Garai, 1984, pp. 77–78).

We will attempt to apply these principles as basic guidelines for a humanistic-holistic approach to bisexuality and homosexuality. As we can easily see, the first principle guarantees each individual the inalienable right to the fullest development of unique personhood, identity, and lifestyle. Sexual preference depends on the choice of lifestyle made by a person and falls therefore within the limits of the range determined by the first principle. The third principle states that each individual is encouraged to associate with other individuals on the basis of sharing common goals, ideas, interests, handicaps, or lifestyles. This forms the basis for the creation of gay liberation movements and the open assertion of a gay identity as well as a bisexual identity. While gays may regard the gay lifestyle and bisexuals the bisexual lifestyle as normal, other people may consider it a "handicap." But they must insist on the rights of "handicapped" persons to seek full equality and acceptance as real people. The other principles seek to establish the homosexual's and the bisexual's right to seek internal and external wholeness like all other persons.

The humanistic approach to homosexuality and bisexuality is deeply concerned with the moral and ethical quality of any type of sexual behavior. We might state that it is not so much the sexual object or the sexual aim, that is the partner and the type of sexual behavior, whether homosexual, bisexual, or heterosexual but rather the *meaningfulness* and quality of sexual interaction that must be considered. Any sexual interaction that leads to intimacy and personal closeness is morally right and ethically responsible. Any sexual interaction which is engaged in for the purpose of exploitation of the sexual partner to gain dominance or submissiveness such as sado-masochistic interaction is morally wrong and ethically irresponsible. The humanist places these basic human values of cooperation, intimacy, closeness, and willingness to satisfy the partner higher than any other considerations. Excessive competition, aloofness, coldness, and a desire to please oneself exclusively are attitudes of exploitation which distort and degrade the meaning of sexual activity.

The humanistic approach is aware of the fact that homosexuality is frequently a stimulus for creative expression and artistic achievements. In their book: *Higher Creativity: Liberating the Unconscious for Breakthrough Insights* Harman and Rheingold describe the basic attitudes which help a person to become more creative, while using the imagination to free the person. They are: I am not separate; I can trust; I can know; I am responsible; and I am single-minded. Homosexuals and bisexuals who are able to express their creativity positively feel that they are not separate but profoundly related to other human beings whom they can trust as being sympathetic and intuitive. They are imbued with a thirst for knowledge which they must satisfy, and they feel that they wish to act responsibly so as not to betray their own trust and the trust others place in them. They are single-minded in their attempts to create unique works of art and trying to achieve perfection. The contributions made by homosexuals to civilization throughout the ages are far higher than the numerical proportions of homosexuals in the population. One of the factors we must take into account to help explain this high level of creativity consists in the need for the homosexual or bisexual to utilize his or her imagination to create a lifestyle which is certain to meet with the disapproval of his or her immediate environment.

From my own work as a therapist with homosexual and bisexual artists, I have come to the conclusion that they are more closely in touch with their deepest layers of the unconscious which they are able to bring into conscious awareness to promote artistic productivity. They remember more dreams and they seem to be able to transform these dreams into their paintings, sculptures, poems, dramas, music, and other creative expressions during their waking hours. They frequently have "lucid" dreams similar to those described by Garai (1973, 1976).

For the research-oriented individual who might wish to further explore the issues of bisexuality and homosexuality Fritz Klein and Timothy J. Wolf edited a double issue of the *Journal of Homosexuality* entitled: Bisexualism, Theory and Research (Fritz & Wolf, 1985).

Lonnie Barbach (1982) deals with the subject of sexuality in the spirit of a sensible and enlightened humanistic approach. Another excellent source for clarification of the subject of bisexuality and homosexuality is *Controversy over the Bisexual and Homosexual Identities: Commentaries and Reactions,* by John P. DeCecco (1984). A specially sharply analytical analysis of bisexuality was contributed in the same issue by Gilbert H. Herdt (Herdt, 1984). Critical theoretical isues of the idea of bisexual identity are examined from the standpoint of their cross-cultural significance. Examples from recent studies in Melanesia are used to highlight possible areas of exploration for future research in homosexuality and bisexuality. The idea of *fluidity* of sexual identity is examined, including the notion of sexual desire (Herdt, p. 53). In the article *Breaking Out of the Dominant Paradigm: A New Look at Sexual Attraction,* Gisela T. Kaplan and Lesley J. Rogers, in their asbstract, state the following conclusions:

> *Concepts of sexuality based on the physical sex of partners limit the way in which human sexuality is conceived and investigated. The shift in focus of inquiry from the sexual identity of individuals to the structure of their sexual relationships is an important step toward exploding concepts that, for the most part, have been severely restricted to male-female genital distinctions. This article argues that the genital organs are not the prime focus of sexual attraction. Careful studies may reveal that sexual arousal is based on criteria that transcend genital categories. To determine the basis of sexual attraction it is important to investigate an amalgam of characteristics—those related and unrelated to the partners' physical sex. There are indications that individuals with a greater mix of feminine and masculine characteristics (both mental and physical) are actually more arousing than those who fall closer to the stereotypes. The arts, it is suggested, have explored this phenomenon.* (Kaplan & Rogers, p. 71).

It is quite interesting to observe how the conclusions of these internationally renowned research scientists corroborate the statements which we have made in our analysis of homosexual and bisexual behavior as viewed from the humanistic perspective.

We have not yet adequately described the humanistic approach to interactions between mature couples who engage in sexual activities by expressed mutual consent and planning. For instance, any couple who wish to engage in homosexual acts or sexual acts which are misdefined by society as "sexual perversions" including cunnilingus, fellatio, and sadistic-masochistic, or sado-masochistic practices, and who decide to do so after discussion achieving mutual consent are permitted to do so in their privacy as a couple. Since they do not exploit anybody but engage in these practices for their own personal enjoyment exclusively, society must place the right of couples and their own privacy above considerations of denouncing such activities as perversions. It is quite difficult to understand that "sodomy, and other sexual perversions such as cunnilingus, fellatio, mutual masturbation, or nudist exhibitionism are still officially designated as 'criminal' offenses" in seventeen of the states of the United States. One shudders if one tries to imagine how private citizens might sneak into the bedrooms of their friends and neighbors to discover such heinous sexual preoccupations. In the well-known case of following a spouse who is suspected by the other spouse with private detectives to motels, hotels, or private residences with photographers suddenly breaking in and taking photographs of the sexual act as potential "evidence" to convict the "unfaithful" spouse as a criminal offender, we have already come very close to establishing George Orwell's "1984" society as early as 1952 when the first such case was argued in California.

The following statement made by Altman (1983) clarifies the changing role of homosexuality in society during the past decades in the main as:

> Under existing social conditions, to say someone is homosexual is to describe far more about a person than what he or she does in bed, which, as one wit suggested, may be the one place where homosexuals and heterosexuals do not much differ. An awareness of homosexuality affects us socially, in relationships with family, friends, and coworkers, and indeed on the most intimate levels of everyday life. The burgeoning gay culture is beginning both to delineate—and itself to shape—the ways in which we are not just like everyone else. (p. 214).

Further insightful discussions of the roles played by homosexuality and bisexuality were made by Ruitenbek (1963), Simonton (1980), Singer and Pope (1978), Tannahill (1982), and Wolman and Money (1980).

Summarizing the basic statements related to the humanistic-holistic approach to homosexuality, we may state that it assumes that the choice of sexual preference must be permitted to each individual person as the result of his or her own sexual desires, needs, and ways of seeking closeness and intimacy. The humanist is not so much concerned with the choice of the sexual partner or the preference for certain sexual acts than with the question, whether the sexual behavior is mainly concerned with the creation of mutual intimacy and closeness and mutual acceptance in a climate of playful spontaneity or whether it is conducted for the main purpose of selfish exploitation of each partner to enhance his or her personal satisfaction regardless of the consequences for the partner. The former attitude is regarded as morally right and ethically responsible. The latter attitude is morally wrong and ethically irresponsible. Furthermore, the humanist regards the relationship between the two sexual partners as inviolable and finds that whatever the two partners decide to do in the privacy of their sexual encounters by express mutual consent and joint planning is morally right and ethically responsible.

REFERENCES

Altman, D. The homosexualization of America. Boston: Beacon Press, 1983.

Barbach, L. For each other: Sharing sexual intimacy. New York: New American Library Signet, 1982.

DeCecco J. P. (Ed.). Controversy over the bisexual and homosexual identities. Journal of Homosexuality, 10(3, 4), Winter 1984.

Ellis, Havelock. Psychology of sex: A manual for students. New York: Bucanan Paperback, 1972.

Ferguson, M. The Aquarian conspiracy: Personal and Social Transformation in the 1980s. Los Angeles: J. P. Tarcher, 1980.

Freud, S. Three essays on sexuality. London: Hogarth, 1962.

Garai, J. E. New horizons of holistic healing through creative expression. Art Therapy, 1(2), May 1984, pp. 76–82.

Garai, J. E. New horizons of the humanistic approach to expressive therapies and creativity development. Art Psychotherapy, 6, 1979, pp. 177–183.

Garai, J. E. New vistas in the exploration of inner and outer space through art therapy. Art Psychotherapy, 3, 1976, pp. 157–167.

Garai, J. E. Reflections of the struggle for identity in art therapy. Art Psychotherapy, 1, 1973, pp. 261–275.

Garai, J. E. The humanistic approach to art therapy and creativity development. New-ways, 1(2), pp. 2, 8, 19.

Gsgnon, J. H. & Simon, W. Sexual conduct. Chicago: Aldine, 1973.

Harman, W. & Rheingold, H. Higher creativity: Liberating the unconscious for breakthrough insights. Los Angeles: CA: Jeremy P. Tarcher, 1984.

Herdt, G. A comment on cultural attributes and fluidity of bisexuality. In J. P. DeCecco (Ed.), Journal of Homosexuality, Winter 1984, 10(3, 4) (Bisexual context section).

Kaplan, G. T. & Rogers, L. J. Breaking out of the dominant paradigm: A new look at sexual attraction. In J. P. DeCecco (Ed.), Journal of Homosexuality, Winter 1984, 10(3, 4).

Klein, F., M.D., and Wolf, T. J., Ph.D. Bisexualities: Theory and research. Journal of Homosexuality, 11(1/2), Spring 1985.

Krafft-Ebing, R. Psychopathia sexualis, 1886. New York, 1965, and 1978 paperback.

Masters, W. & Johnson, V. Homosexuality in perspective. Boston: Little, Brown, 1979.

Rosenberg, S. *Why Freud fainted.* Indianapolis: Bobbs-Merrill, 1978.

Roszak, T. *Person/planet: The creative disintegration of industrial society.* New York: Doubleday Anchor, 1979.

Ruitenbek, H. M. The problem of homosexuality in modern society. New York: Dutton, 1963.

Simonton, C. *Getting well again.* New York: Bantam, 1980.

Singer, J. L. & Pope, K. *The power of human imagination: New methods in psychotherapy.* New York & London: Plenum Press, 1978.

Spiers, H. & Lynch, M. *The gay rights Freud, body politic, 1977.*

Tannahill, R. *Sex in history.* New York: Stein & Day, 1982.

Wolman, B. & Money, J. (Eds.). *Handbook of human sexuality.* Englewood Cliffs, NJ: Prentice-Hall, 1980.

Wilson, E. O. *On human nature.* New York: Bantam, 1979.

15

ON MORALS AND ETHICS

C. A. Tripp

Every modern dictionary lists morals and ethics as synonyms. The word morals is from the latin *mores,* meaning customs, while ethics is from the Greek *ethike,* also meaning customs. But their synonymy is less true in practice, where the words and meanings are far from identical. The Catholic Church comes closer to the mark by considering moral behavior as what one owes to God, and ethics as what is owed to man—though with certain obvious overlaps. By any definition, stealing and forced sexual relaions, for instance, are clearly violations of both morals and ethics.

But for once, common usage is more discriminating. Ethics and ethical standards reflect the concerns and the language of professionals—doctors, lawyers, and scientists. (It is unethical for a doctor to have sex with a patient, or for a lawyer to break a client's confidence, or for a scientist to falsify data.) Morals and morality on the other hand, are what guide the words and judgments of preachers, of rabbis, and of most laymen who, in turn, seldom use the word ethics. (It is immoral for Jews to eat certain foods, for Catholics to use artificial birth control, for Muslims to have five wives, or for any Jews or Christians ever to fornicate or to masturbate anywhere, anyplace, anytime.) In short, morals and moralistic attitudes are the stuff of religion, tradition, and social expectation, while ethics and ethical concerns focus on fair play and the rights of others.

A far-reaching consequence of this difference is that morals tend to be provincial, while ethics are largely universal. Morals vary noticeably from one community to the next. Even within a single society or small town, people at different social levels may hold sharply different attitudes toward such things as how much nudity is permissible, which sexual practices are found acceptable or unacceptable, and what is to be thought of violators.* Ethicists, on the other hand, tend to sweep over such details, being concerned instead with violations of fair play and with questions of what is materially harmful to others—standards that are largely the same the world over.

Thus in reacting to disapproved sexual practices, moralists tend to use religious and traditional values as their judgment-base. For them, rules and regulations, social standards, and "natural law" come ahead of personal rights, and far ahead of any individual's particular needs and motives.

As if embarrassed by this emphasis on religious and philosophical values at the expense of individual rights, moralists have frequently rationalized their demands as reasonable by citing worldly and practical considerations—insisting that moral rules are necessary for safety, or for some larger social good. But it is hard to find a single sexual example in which moralistic warnings have proved valid.

Moralists long warned, for instance, that masturbation could lead to blindness, to early impotence, and to other dire consequences. But such predictions proved either completely groundless, or precisely incorrect. As Kinsey found, not only are early and extensive masturbation harmless and not at all weakening, both happen to be correlated with an especially vigorous and longlasting sex life (more early, more late—long lasting sex life. Kinsey, Pomeroy & Martin, p. 307). And of the numerous psychological disturbances attributed to sex, far more have been linked to abstinence and to other forms of *resisting* sexual temptations than to their practice (conscientious objectors. Kinsey et al. p. 211).

Some of morality's standard charges against homosexuality have proved equally ironic. For whatever might be said against it, homosexuality certainly does not "threaten the species." Its effects are too trivial for that—and anyway, for reasons which probably stem from the effects of morality itself, homosexuality has long tended to be highest precisely in societies in which birthrates and problems of overpopulation are at their most extreme—for instance in Arabic and Moslem societies** (Tripp, 1975; Westermarck, 1908).

---

*It is widely assumed that lower social level individuals are free and unrestrained in sex compared with the better educated and "more inhibited" higher social levels. Indeed, as group data from the Kinsey research show, lower level individuals tend to have earlier sex-with-a-partner, and far more partners, than do middle and upper levels. But in every other parameter just the reverse is the case: upper level individuals much more frequently accept nudity, masturbation, mouth-genital contacts, role inversions and numerous other variations, all of which tend to be seen as perversions by the actually *more* inhibited lower social levels.

**It is not that homosexuality itself has any relevance to low or high birthrates. Rather, the same antisexual mores which tightly restrict homosexuality also tend to restrict heterosexuality, and thus birthrates. Conversely, "loose" attitudes toward sex tend to facilitate both heterosexual and homosexual expressions. Thus high birthrates and high homosexuality are inclined to move together, without being directly connected.

Not that moralistic judgments are limited to laymen and to untrained minds. They are a constant hazard to logic that even unwary ethicists can fall victim to. Lawyers and courts of law regularly claim ethics and ethical standards as their special province, a posture that makes much of human and individual rights. Yet under the stress of social conflict it is not unusual for the legal profession's ethics to give way to moralistic biases, so much so that not even our separation of church and state can be taken for granted; it requires constant vigilance.

Nowhere is this more apparent than in sexuality, where courts of law are especially prone to regress into moral judgments at the expense of individual rights. A lesbian mother, for instance, may find her own rights and those of her child put aside in favor of stereotype moral judgments that ignore both her qualities as a mother, and the desires of the child.

With equally blind eyes, laws against "sodomy" and "unnatural practices" remain on the books in many states, and are sometimes still enforced. In practice, arrest and various forms of harrassment are mainly reserved for morally disapproved minority practices, homosexuality in particular. But this is just the point, that in the case of both individuals and courts of law, any failure to differentiate morals and ethics and keep them separate, leaves individual rights unprotected from a backslide toward the often hostile judgments of religious morality.

And yet, for reasons too complex for perhaps anyone to fully understand, entire sets of morals and sexual standards are occasionally subject to a quite sudden, even revolutionary change. Our own "sexual revolution" of the 1960s is an example, as was an earlier shift toward sexual liberality in the 1920s. In both cases, morals but not ethics came under attack. Throughout a veritable orgy of recent liberation—coed dormitories, nude beaches, open marriage, pornographic films, gay parades—ethics were never jeopardized. In fact, as morality weakened, ethical standards often gained authority, as in our society's increased readiness to recognize and oppose unfair discrimination against women, sexual harassment, forced sex relations, any flagrant disregard for other people's desires, and the like.

But sexual revolutions tend to be self-limiting. They go just so far in a period of ten or fifteen years, and then backlash toward a more conservative position. But the backlash is uneven. It withdraws little if any recent liberalness from such items as masturbation, oral sex, and a tolerance for more nudity; it even comes to terms with easier and more frequent sex contacts, and at younger ages, too.

Moralists, for their part, usually revel in any new conservatism, stay silent on their numerous unretrieved losses and champion the resurrection of older standards as a return to God's will, or to some so-called "wisdom of the ages." Less biased observers might see the targets of backlash as merely those items which, by the very fact of their being and remaining minority choices, are especially vulnerable to a reestablished conservatism, a move toward the right that simply gets them voted down again. Their point is well taken.

But there is more to it than that. Some combination of an increased knowledge about sex, and the sheer popularity of a sexual practice may be enough to ward off any new conservatism., Once it is realized, for instance, that masturbation is harmless and virtually universal, no mere shift in liberal/conservative attitudes is enough to reignite fears about it. Likewise, when an increased tolerance for nudity and freer sexual contacts catch on and prove to be fun and harmless, they are hard to take back. Not so in the case of homosexuality. Where it is concerned, a conservative backlash quickly begins to "take back" much previous liberality. Homosexual motivations are not broadly understood in the first place and where they are pronounced enough to constitute a sexual alternaive they hold a decidedly minority status. Moreover, liberal attitudes toward homosexuality have hardly any effect on its frequency and add little to understanding it.*

Yet a wave of liberalness can mimic understanding, at least for a while. During the 1960s and early 1970s sex researchers were repeatedly astonished at the extent and breadth of what appeared to be a sudden and easy social acceptance of homosexuality. Indeed, the new acceptance comprised the very kinds of liberal attitudes which were, in fact, supported by an extensive knowledge of the subject. So much so that for a while it began to look as if the findings of sex research and many of its conclusions had somhow gotten across to large sections of the general public, and thus into the body politic. But it is now evident that many of the recently liberal attitudes toward homosexuality were quite shallow—based more on fashion, and on a spirit of revolt and of new-freedoms than on any increased knowledge.

Thus when fashion had run its course and the forces of a conservative backlash took over, what survived the onslaught were those items which had gained either in understanding, or in actual frequency—everything from masturbation and premarital intercourse, to the Beatles' long hair. Recent liberal attitudes toward homosexuality simply vanished, or were reversed into reborn taboos. The crux of the matter, as before, is that when liberal attitudes fail to be consolidated (are not nailed down by new knowledge or by numbers), they are left to winds of fashion that can blow them right back into the arms of morality, where they are soon measured against the mores and crushed.

Persons holding ethical positions frequently argue the case for minority rights and practices (just as throughout history ethicists have argued for the individual's right to hold contrary opinions), but the effort is seldom

---

*The 1920s brought a startling increase in the awareness of homosexuality and much talk about it, but when the Kinsey researchers later checked its frequency over a span of five generations and graphed the results, the effects of the 1920s liberalness merely looked like a bump in an otherwise smooth curve. Likewise, a more recent study by the Institute for Sex Research (their unpublished "Youth Study," c. 1967), found no detectable increase in the frequency of homosexuality following more liberal attitudes toward it during the 1960s.

successful. It is not so much that people are ungenerous or fundamentally incapable of assimilating new ideas. On the contrary, much in the human spirit supports a policy of live-and-let-live, and much else is quick to accept new attitudes—unless and until these run head-on into conflict with morality.

But such observations raise central questions. What, exactly, is morality? What holds it in place and in power, and what gives it such appeal? As for what morality is, it is largely an agreed-upon set of values based on a belief-system—beliefs which, in turn, rest on a composite of stories and tenets usually held in place by magical and religious expectations. But it is more than that. Morality, like much else related to religion, gains part of its certainty and wide appeal from its very structure: the traditional and often formal set of rules and expectancies with which it is obsessed, as well as the fixed ideas and fixed regimens of thought it uses to measure and judge behavior. Behavior that contradicts expectancy is perhaps always a shock and a surprise; but in the eyes of the moralist it spells a kind of social disloyalty, heresy against common belief. And since most societies codify their beliefs into civil and religious law, violators become offenders and sinners almost by definition, immediate targets of both church and state.

Does this mean religion is always implicated in the basic attitudes morality tries to defend? Not necessarily. For while every society holds whole sets of traditions and sex taboos, these are sometimes based on social custom alone, with little or no help from religion. (Buddhist societies, for instance, rate various sex acts as serious offenses, but do not see them as religious violations, let alone as offenses against Buddha.) But whenever religion raises its voice in such matters as it usually does, morality is inclined to take on religion's dogmatic certainty, along with more than a few of its demands and fears. Behavior that deviates from religious expectations can land someone in hell.*

But to what extent is religion actually involved in present-day morality? A relevant question, since the world is filled with moralists, but is much less filled with people who take their religion all that seriously. Moreover, some of the fiercest moralists are at the opposite extreme from religious types. These include members of numerous kinds of gangs—from organized teen-agers in big

---

*But morality even in an entirely nonreligious context represents a considerable danger for everyone, a social hell sufficiently threatening to make nearly everyone keep up a guard. As Alfred Kinsey observed after taking the sex histories of more than twelve-thousand men and women:

> Our laws and customs are so far removed from the actual behavior of the human animal that there are few persons who can afford to let their full histories be known to the courts or even to their neighbors and their best friends (Mead, 1961).

Thus each individual gains the double illusion of his or her own regularness, and of considerably more uniformity among the social majority than, in fact, exists.

cities, to the Mafia, to the many cliques and gang-like affiliations that prevail in prisons—all have their own morality and readily mete out a crude "justice" not only for group disloyalty, but for various sex offenses as well. (For an arrested child-molester to be thrown in among regular prisoners is to sentence him to immediate and serious harassment, if not death.)

But exactly what does the morality of such criminal types try to defend through its fierce verdicts? Basically, it aims to dispense justice quite as do other moralities: by rewarding behavior it admires, and punishing whatever in any way threatens its own social order. Likewise, in both brands of morality the disloyalty of a member is viewed not only as an insult and a breach of confidence, but as damage to their shared social order. (However, behavior that would be punished or ridiculed in one's own group is easy to ignore or to laugh at when seen from afar—say, in a foreign land, or even in persons of the same town if they live on different sides of the tracks.)

The same rules apply in religious moralities which, in addition, tend to place artificial restraints on many easy and natural pleasures—tempering them with fear and with superstitious rules and regulations. Ascetic religions in particular are inclined to raise the price of joy and comfort by demanding equal "payment" in the form of privations and sacrifice. But the ascetics are not alone; anthropologists have yet to find a single tribe or civilization that does not constrict itself with numerous arbitrary and "unnecessary" restrictions and restraints. These have included painful circumcision ceremonies and clitoridectomies along with countless moralistic taboos on what must not be touched, or eaten, or treated casually, everything from holy cows, sacred monkeys and the flesh of countless other animals, to menstruating women, holy objects, burnt offerings and nearly all sexual variations—paraphernalia left over from the childhood of man.

That such self-imposed pains and sacrifices continue to be practiced in numerous real and symbolic forms far beyond religion certainly attests to their utility. But utility for what? Mainly to control anxiety—either to assuage God, or to bias fate toward better results than might otherwise be expected.

Just why the human species should be as anxiety-prone and guilt-ridden as it is, is a not yet fully answered (or even answerable) question. Undoubtedly human anxiety and a need for solace are increased by man's unique capacity to anticipate the future, including his own death; no doubt this awareness of vulnerability in the face of uncontrollable events sharply increases an urge to strike a bargain with the fates. Perhaps too, human anxiety and guilt-feelings are increased, as Freud (1942) suggested, by a brand of close family living which inevitably tends to generate more hostility and frustration than can safely be expressed. Certainly inhibited hostility and aggression can undermine self-confidence and sponsor guilt-like feelings.

These and other explanations may well apply; although just as important as "explaining" the guiltiness and penance-proneness of humans is to remember that it is pervasive, and that it is not to be attributed to such commonplace local factors as a failure to live up to personal or social expectations. Religiously devout individuals, both by their beliefs and their failure to satisfy idealistic demands, are constantly reminded of their shortcomings and seem particularly inclined to feel that their sins and failures can and ought to be paid for by suffering and reparations. But cross-cultural studies suggest that something in the very nature of religion itself (possibly in human nature, as well) needs and welcomes guilt-feelings. So much so that a sense of guilt and remorse is regularly evidenced in *advance* of the sins to which they are later attached—thus the Bible's scores of references to burnt offerings and sin offerings, most of which come before any offense, as is also true in Christian notions of Original Sin and of Jesus "dying for our sins."

Other societies stir up the same or even more intense feelings of sin and guilt by levying social demands that cannot posibly be met. The Mundugumor of the South Pacific, for instance, hold the demand that every man should marry his mother's father's mother's father's sister's son's daughter's son's daughter—and that he give his sister in exchange for this man's daughter. As Margaret Mead has recalled, "This requirement was so impossible to meet that everybody in the community was married incorrectly, with correlated feelings of shame and delinquency. . ." (Mead, 1961). Here, as in Jewish and Christian examples, the basic motivation is undoubtedly an urge and a readiness to feel shame and contrition, and to earn moral credits through suffering and feeling guilty.

Not that the high prices people are ready to pay for moral and religious consolation are entirely attributable to their guilt and anxiety, or to various god-theories. The whole moral system is the prize, one that offers quite a number of benefits. These include the fraternal comforts of social living as well as the pleasure of giving and receiving the kinds of love and respect that every society grants to its conformists and lavishes on its models of good behavior. The rewards also include the pleasure and catharsis of projecting blame, that is, of finding and targeting the faults of others, of expressing hostility and righteous indignation and through it all, consolidating the unity and togetherness of the social group. Thus it is no surprise that every known religion supports a rigorous morality—and conversely, that all moralities seek to please and to align themselves with the words and wishes of some god or worldly teacher. Their pleasant side, their fellowship and their in-group kindnesses are real enough—but the fact remains that every morality, by its very nature, is best and most sharply defined by its negative expressions: the sins and thoughts and persons it is most inclined to hate, to reject, and to war against.

Is this the same brand of aggressive hostility, marching under a flag of righteousness, that so often expresses itself in morality's fierce targeting of sexual variations? Yes it is, but our society has more than a few reasons, even specific edicts, for rejecting easy heterosexual consummations and all homosexuality. The Bible's marked asceticism and antisexuality, as well as its blanket opposition to "the ways of the pagans," have long been grounds enough for excoriating homosexuality—a sin made worse, of course, by specific Old and New Testament proscriptions against it.* Probably few evangelists and fewer laymen are aware of the many questionable points that arise in applying biblical texts to everyday life—for instance, that most of the antisexual taboos listed in Leviticus were written for rabbinical candidates and were never intended for the laity.

Not that such technical details necessarily count for much at this late date. Centuries of religious and ascetic bias have so firmly set our society's sexual attitudes that even completely unreligious persons tend to take conventional mores at face value, with little thought of their specific origins. Such a person may have no truck with persecutory attitudes but may still be disturbed by what is seen as the homosexual's rejection of conventional values. It is just such a measuring of actions and individuals against conventional norms that epitomize moralistic judgments in most of their forms.

Ethicists approach these same problems very differently. Since every ethical concern places its main focus on the rights of individuals and on fair play, it can operate quite apart from religion—and from a host of other conventionalisms. But if there is "something basic" in the human proclivity to feel guilty, how does the ethicist avoid feeling the same guilt with which moralists seem obsessed? He may half-proudly point out that he is simply "not religious" and perhaps insist that his actions and judgments are closer to the spirit of religion ("more Christian") than are those of the moralist.

And yet careful analysis suggests that the ethicist's "guilt level" is not appreciably less than that of the moralist, although it is discharged differently. For while the ethicist places individuals and even community concerns ahead of group conformity, any failure to act according to these lights fills him with a brand of discomfort and foreboding quite akin to that of the moralist. Thus the two approaches are much alike in two respects: the disquietude of each in the face of whatever is felt to be wrong, and a dependence in both cases on what is seen as appropriate action—the action each takes for comfort and for self-justification. And yet across the board, the ethicist's standards and practices unquestionably hold up as more reasonable—and by and large, as

---

Genesis 19 (the classical story of Sodom and Gomorrah, a rewrite of the older *Judges 19* version); *Leviticus 18:22, 20:13;* Deuteronomy 23:17;* I Kings 14:24,* 15:12,* 22:46;* II Kings 23:7;* *Romans 1:27; I Corinthians 6:9;* I Timothy 1:10.* Italicized references are those expressing opposition against ordinary forms of homosexuality. Asterisked items oppose the "cult prostitutes" mentioned in the Revised Standard Version and the New International Version of the Bible. The King James Version deletes or obscures all references to such Temple Prostitution, the previously approved First Temple tradition of having male and female prostitutes offer homosexual and heterosexual sex within the temple, and/or ceremonially accepting monies collected for these acts as part of the worship.

more humanitarian—than do the often arbitrary, tradition-bound judgments of the moralist.*

HISTORICAL PERSPECTIVES

Morals and morality have a long history reflected in the needs and tendencies of human societies everywhere to live in groups, to standardize the particular behavior they expect, and to thrust out deviants. In part, these social mores are based on fundamental biological (not merely cultural) grounds. For instance, nearly all living creatures are inclined to live in groups, as is evident in the tendency of single-cell animals to cluster, of range animals to herd, of birds to flock, and fish to school. The reasons probably have as much to do with "species comfort" and communication between members as with the often cited safety that group-living is supposed to afford.

In any case, an individual is instantly in jeopardy when and if his or her behavior noticeably deviates from that of others. Odd behavior of whatever kind not only catches the attention of predators (who tend to pick off such individuals), but in quite a few species including man, oddness of any sort is likely to bring an individual under attack, even within its own group. Or to put it the other way around, the group-acceptability or an individual depends on the smoothness with which his or her actions jibe and fit-in with those of others.

Thus over eons of phylogenetic history, natural selection has continually favored the kinds of social behavior that have reinforced deviance-elimination. Human societies in particular have felt an urgent need to establish norms and eliminate deviance (often at the price of wiping out their innovators and bringers of new ideas). Perhaps this conservative trend has been helped along still further in humans by their close-knit family life, protracted as it is over the years it takes their young to mature, years that consistently cry out for a degree of social accord that only specific sets of rules and values can achieve.

Of course there is more to it than that. The human brain has developed many new capacities unprecedented in lower animals—capacities which add variety to human behavior and greatly increase the urge and the need to regulate it. These new sources of variation include the ability to contemplate one's past and future, to love and care for others, to value justice, to abhor

---

*These differentiations of morals and ethics are meant to highlight and contrast their basic, underlying philosophies. But like other philosophic tenets, they do not always dominate and predict a person's specific behavior. (Individual human psychology is far too complex and too varied in its resources for that.) In practice, even a strict moralist may be inclined to lay aside his or her traditional group-identity or even suspend religious conviction in favor of consistently generous expressions of kindness toward others. Conversely, some ethicist may have all his knowledge and philosophy in perfect order, and yet so fail in empathy as to sit unmoved in the presence of someone else's plight.

domination by brute force, along with a strong urge to protect the weak from the strong and to identify with the underdog. Not that such motives are all sweetness and light. Humans also far exceed every other species in a brand of aggressiveness that supports a frequent urge to act with hate or hostility, even vindictiveness. Humans are the only moral creatures, true, but a goodly part of this new, high-order capacity is spent in fierce pursuits of "justice" and of deviance-elimination, so often exercised ruthlessly with amplifications of moral outrage.

Ethics, too, has a long history. Throughout the human species at least, ethical motives and actions are clearly evident. The most prominent of these is a tit-for-tat sense of justice and fair play. Even the most primitive tribal peoples show a remarkable tendency to extend themselves to others, to return favors they receive with ones of equal or higher values, and to otherwise play fair. Such impulses extend from ordinary expressions of kindness and gratitude to such extraordinary examples as the *potlatch* of the Northwest Indians (who from time to time scrimp and save and deprive themselves in order to carry out this social rite by pouring their all into a veritable orgy of giving valuable presents during elaborate feasts).* More commonplace forms of fairness as well as a certain generosity are evident in a basic, powerful human tendency that urges people not to strike out at others, not even total strangers, without the excuse of a real or imagined provocation of some kind.

The obvious question, of course, is that if all this kindness and fairness are so prevalent, why are they not more evident? Because fairness is in conflict with two other major motives. One of these is a certain selfishness; often enough a basic kindness and fairness are drowned out by urgent, self-seeking desires that range from ambition, envy, and hunger to greed and avarice, and that so easily support motives of me-first and we-first. In this mode, excuses and imagined provocations are easily invented, as is evident all the way from instances of early Americans taking land from the Indians, down to the level of a common thief who readily finds excuses for taking what he wants. (Although the very fact that people *need* to find excuses for trampling the rights of others attests again to the pervasive appeal of justice and fair play.)**

---

*Extreme examples of human generosity seem always to invite debunking interpretations. Arranging a *Potlatch* has been attributed to the giver's attempt to gain higher social status, and/or to place other members of the tribe under obligation to him—just as "objective" analyses of altrusim have usually sought and found elements of selfishness and ambition in its motives. But the fact remains that kindness and generosity clearly contain and express something more than self-serving motives.

**In the early 1950s a study privately conducted by the New York City Police Department found to its own surprise that pickpockets seldom ply their trade randomly by opportunity alone. Rather, they tend to select a victim and in a preliminary moment, run through some kind of justification fantasy, such as "That bastard is probably cheating on his wife and at this moment may be on his way to see the other woman"—thus imbuing the victim with guilt, and their own action with a Robin-Hood-like ethic.

The second major motive is destructive aggression. Often, disastrously, aggression is carried out in the name of fairness. Wars and warfare, for instance, have much more often been predicated on revenge (the fair play of "getting even") than on any other complaint or motive (Metraux, 1963). And in countless small events in everyday life, one sees at least as many hostile as generous examples of a kind of turnabout fair play. An urge for justice certainly can incite extreme anger and fierce retaliatory attacks.

Faced with these conflicting motives, the ethicist has no choice but to remain true to his guiding principle of fairness. Anything else would be unethical. He cannot hide.

But the moralist—who may also start out with motives of kindness and fairness, can drop these quite entirely in some intense loyalty to church and state. But how can he?—How can and how does the moralist entertain these fierce emotions without in the same breath contradicting quite opposite ideals he may also hold dear, such as striving toward a reasonable, gentle, or "loving" disposition? Mainly by embracing various rationalizations. For instance, he may convince himself that friendship is less important than the nation and the law—like some Nazi functionary who honestly feels and knows he hates what he is doing but also believes he must do it to stay loyal to the Reich and the Füher. When people were once burned at the stake for being heretics, the Church held the position (as many Christians still do) of hating sin while "loving" the sinner. Under this claim, even the punishment and suffering of some victim screaming in anguish may bring minimal sympathy, his pain being neatly rationalized as justly deserved or "for his own good"—either to purify his soul or to teach him the folly of his ways.

In further accounting for their own moralistic motives, religious people are quick to say their intent is to serve God, as they police and enforce His laws. And indeed, religious zeal behind various moralistic campaigns has been the source of moral indignation in some of its worst forms. Yet these religious extremes evidently owe as much to some human urge to make a full commitment to some supreme authority as they do to the attractions of God, since communist ideologies with no god are also fiercely moralistic in smashing competition and in smothering individual rights as they rigorously police any and all behavior that conflicts (or that even might conflict) with the party line. Here, as in religion, one sees authoritarianism at work, along with a hand-in-glove affiliation between morality and deviance-elimination. Both express a fierce and dangerous demand for group uniformity—like a school of sharks ready to zero-in on any irregular swimmer.

Most certainly it is morality's unholy alliance with power and its penchant for arbitrary rules that have so regularly led to it inhumane corruptions. Thus the Church, when it had the power, held its Inquisition and savaged its victims—just as many another regime has set up its own arbitrary rules and new moralities, demanded total adherence and enforced its laws to banish real or imagined non-believers. Jews, gypsies, and homosexuals have been among the more recent heretics, but if history teaches us anything it is that everyone, at some private level of reality belongs to some minority, and ultimately, that no member of any minority is ever permanently safe from the iron teeth of an enforceable morality.

REFERENCES

Freud, S. *The ego and the id.* London: The Hogarth Press, 1942, p. 73.

Kinsey, A. C., Pomeroy, W. B., and Martin, C. E., *Sexual behavior in the human male.* Philadelphia: Saunders, 1948.

Mead, M. Clinical determinants of sexual behavior. In W. C. Young (Ed.), *Sex and internal secretions.* Baltimore: Williams & Wilkins, 1961, Vol. II, p. 1459.

Metraux, A. Warfare, Cannibalism, and human trophies. In J. H. Steward (Ed.), *Handbook of South American Indians.* New York: Cooper Square, 1963, Vol. V, p. 383–409.

Tripp, C. A. *The homosexual matrix.* New York: McGraw-Hill, 1975, p. 38n.

Westermarck, E. *The origin and development of the moral ideas.* London: Macmillan, 1908, Vol. II, p. 456f.

INDEX

Abraham, K., 173
Adjustive value, 8
Adjustment, 14, 15–16, 34, 48, 60–61, 193, 227
  homosexual vs heterosexual, 64
    age, 14
    anxiety, 14
    depression, 14
    education, 14
    ego development, 48
    IQ, 14
    neuroticism, 14
    self-confidence, 45
    submission, 14
    tender-mindedness, 14
  research on: age, 63
    females, 49–51
    males, 44–49
    parents-child, 51–59
    socioeconomic factors, 63
Adler, A., 8, 28, 34, 98–100
Adolescent homosexuality:
  behavioral disturbances, 193
  deterioration, 193
  fixation, 193
  internalized value system, 193
  psychosis, 193

self-esteem, 192, 193
suicidal tendencies, 193
Adolescents, 87, 177–178, 192
  and identity crisis, 192
Aggression:
  and fairness, 281
  and homosexual behavior, males, 161
Alcohol:
  abuse, 15, 174–178
    and anxiety disorder, 178
  homosexuality, 174–178
  jealousy, 175, 179
  organic mental disorders, 175
  pathological organ changes, 174
  psychoanalytic theory, 175
  psychological problems, 175
  as substance abuse, 174
  tolerance, 174
  use by females, 165
Alcoholism and homosexuality, 174–178
  adolescent drinking, 177–178
  bars, 177, 179
  biological genetic theory, 176
  bipolar affective disorder, 176
  chronic and progressive, 174
  dependency, 174
  drinking histories of women, 176

Alcoholism and homosexuality (*Cont.*):
   family, 177
   latent homosexuality, 176
   learning theory, 176
   MMPI responses, 41
   parental drinking, 177
   psychoanalytic theory of, 176
   socio-cultural approach to, 176
   social support system, 177
5-alpha-reductase deficiency, 140
American Psychiatric Association, 12, 13,
      87, 109, 172–173, 187, 188, 189,
      190–191, 199
   Task Force on Nomenclature and
      Statistics, 190
American Psychological Association, 13,
      181
Anal intercourse, 251
Anal sadomasochistic attachment, 180
Anality, 89, 92
Analytic ideal, 83, 86
Androgeny, 24
   and parental relationship, 56
Anomic Pressure Rating Schedule, 50
Anxiety, 98, 164–165
   over homosexual orientation, 194
Archetypes, 8
Artistic expression and creativity, 265–266
Ascendancy:
   struggle for, 104
Assertiveness, 103
Assessment, 34
   pre-Kinsey, 34
   psychometric, 37–44
Attitude of homosexual males, 53
   toward father, mother, 53
Attribution theory, 16
Augustine, 5
Australia, 47
Austria, 6
Autoeroticism, 180

Bars, 171, 177
Behavioral theory, 16
Behaviorism, 10
   and change of sexual orientation, 111,
      112
   radical and orientation, 110, 112
      and treatment, 111–112
   view on sexual arousal, 119

Bell, A. P., 48, 49, 62, 63, 64, 89, 135, 146,
      182, 193–194, 246, 252
Bellak, L., 83
Bem Sex Role Inventory, 43, 48, 157
Bene-Anthony Family Relations Test, 53
Benkert, K. M., 23
Berdache, 6, 161, 253
Bergler, E., 28, 34
Bible, 5, 277, 278
Bieber, I., 7, 16, 17, 28, 47, 52, 53, 54, 55,
      57, 58, 84, 98, 104, 115, 162–163,
      182, 183–184, 189, 204, 205–206,
      213, 254, 262
   lack of empirical support of, 55
   treatment on, 204
Binary classification, 243
Binet, A., 25
Biographical data, 56
Biographical questionnaire, 58–59
Biological determinants of homosexuality,
      27, 35
   as dual factors, 263
   Hirschfeld on, 27
   origin of homosexuality 100, 103
   Thompson on, 9
   (*See also* Hormones; Heredity)
Biological realism, 239
Birthrate and homosexuality, 272n
Bisexuality, 81, 84, 102, 118, 206, 212,
      245, 246, 255, 264
   in the brain, 263
   and challenge to gender concept, 245
   Freud on, 9, 262, 263
   Horney on, 104
   importance of research on, 245–246
   inherent, 263
Bodily equation in homosexuality, 101
Borderline personality, 93
Brazil vs. United States, 54
   hostile father/strong mother, 54
Brill, A. A. 28, 34
British school system, 202
Brothers of homosexual males, 56
Butch and femme, 158–160

California Personality Inventory, 47
Castration, 203
   anxiety, 104
   and hormones, 138
   in animals, 131
   suggestion of, 104

Cattell 16 PF (*see* Sixteen Personality Factor Questionnaire)
Character disorders, 204
Character structure, 82
Chastity, 203
Childhood peers of homosexual males:
as rejecting 56–57
Christianity, 21
Christians, 271
Chumming, 102
Church:
Catholic, 12, 271
and homosexuality, 5–6
and morality, 281
Circumcision, 277
Clitoridectomy, 276
Close-binding, 57
Close Binding Intimate (CBI), 184, 254
Compensation, 8, 65, 100
Compulsion, 103
Compulsive homosexuality, 82, 90
Conditioning (classical):
and homosexuality, 101–102
and phobia, 182, 183
Conflict:
unconscious homosexual, 179
Congenital adrenal hyperplasia, 139–140, 142–143
cause of, 139
treatment of, 139–140
Congenital theory, 7, 23, 25, 26, 35
Contrary feeling, 23, 25
Conversion to heterosexuality, 201, 204, 206
Cornell Medical Index, 50
Crime, 6
Critical period, 65
Cross-cultural issues, 247–257
and religion, 277
Culture, 13, 160
as a contributor to homosexuality, 65
and diagnosis of homosexuality, 13
and gender role, 156
and human sexuality, 145
and sex roles, 239–240
Cultures, homosexuality in, 6, 92, 161, 182, 250–254
Cunnilingus, 202, 267

Darwinism, 87
Decriminalization of homosexuality, 109

Definition of homosexuality:
behavioral, 115
primary, 247
problems of, 261
secondary, 247
by West, 4
in Western scientific literature, 250
Degeneracy, 7, 24, 97, 202
challenge to, 25, 263
Delinquent boys:
father closeness and homosexuality, 55
Delusional jealousy, 180
Denial, 91
of homosexual orientation, 194
Denmark, 47
Dependency, 103, 104
Depression:
in black males, 42
in homosexuals, 164
MMPI responses, 41
Desensitization, 183
Deutsch, H., 34
Diagnostic and Statistical Manual of Mental Disorders:
DSM I, 11, 187, 188, 189
DSM II, 11, 87, 189–190, 226
DSM III, 13, 88, 172–173, 174–175, 181, 182, 184, 187, 190–192, 194, 195, 199–200, 201, 204, 215, 227
Diagnostic Classification, 172–174
Dignity, 11
Dildo, 92, 158
Dissatisfaction with homosexuality, 210, 211
Don Juanism, 173
Draw a Person Test, 51
Dynamic Personality Inventory, 43
Dysfunction, homosexual, 210, 211
Dyshomophilia, 190

Ego, 47, 83, 187
Ego boundary, 207
Ego-dysthonic, 13, 87, 172–173, 187, 201, 214
Ego-Dysthonic Homosexuality, 172, 190, 191, 194, 195, 200
and division of clinical opinion, 191
etiology of, 192–194
Ego synthonic, 201, 203
Egypt, ancient, 160

Elias Family Adjustment Test, 58
Ellis, H., 3, 7, 11, 25, 28, 34, 35, 202, 213,
    262
Encephalization, 98
Endocrine system, 131
England, 6, 50–51, 59
Environmental factors and homosexuality,
    114–115
Erotic encounter in homosexual research,
    240
Erotic materials, 123
Ethical issues:
    and behavioral therapy, 109–113
    historical perspectives of, 279–281
Ethics:
    and fairness, 281
    as universal, 271–272
Existential psychology, 175
Eysenck Personality Inventory, 47, 50–51
    Neuroticism Scale, 51

Fantasies of homosexuality, 65
Fathers of homosexual females, 57–59
    absent, 58
    aggressive, 57
    and attitude toward sex, 163
    close-binding, 58
    cold, 58
    detached, 58
    disappointing, 58
    distant, 58
    dominant, 58
    domineering, 57
    exploitative, 58
    hostile, 58
    inadequate, 57
    intimate, 57
    loving, 58, 59
    as models, 57
    moody, 58
    neglecting, 58
    protecting, 59
    rejecting, 57, 58, 59
    selfish, 58
    untrustworthy, 58
    weak, 57, 58
Fathers of homosexual males, 51
    absence of, 51
    and affection, 54
    alienation, 55
    attitude toward sex, 163

close, 56
constructive, 52
distant, 163
encouragement of masculine behavior,
    163
fearful, 55
hostility, 54, 163
incompetence, 54
insecure, 55
loving, 56
low on nurturance, 52
and masculine behavior of sons, 55
and nurturance, 56
permissive, 56
and positive involvement, 56
reaction to cross-gendered behavior,
    53–54
rejecting, 52, 55, 56
rigid, 55
son coalition, 53
son's fear of, 52
strict, 55, 56
supportive, 52
weakness of, 51
Fellatio, 92, 202, 252, 267
Femininity:
    and attitude toward father and mother,
        56
    in females, 59
    in males, 59, 89, 253–254
    and masculinity, 156–157, 254
Feminized brain, 136, 137
Fenichel, O., 7, 103, 183, 203
Ferenczi, S., 82, 88
Fetal state, 64
Fixation, 101
Franck Drawing Completion Test, 44
Freud, A., 83, 91
Freud, S., 3, 6–7, 9, 11, 28, 34, 51, 60, 81,
        82, 87, 93, 97, 99, 103, 178–180,
        181, 182 188, 202–204, 206, 207,
        208, 213, 255, 261–262, 263, 276
    on biological research, 204
Freud's letter to an American mother, 204,
    213

Gay Activist, 4, 189
Gay and lesbian, distinction, 4
Gay identity, 240–241
    and moral assumptions, 241
Gay Liberation, 4, 12–13

Gender:
    cross-gender behavior, 64
    differentiation, 9
    identity, 9, 51, 139, 141, 192, 225, 243,
        252
        disorder, 155
        masculine, feminine, and psychiatry,
            253
        as a neo-Freudian focus, 98
        and testosterone, 140
    link and homosexuality, 242–243, 244
    role, 9, 60, 61, 155, 253
        dominance, 159
        identity, definition, 155
        lesbian relationship, 158
        as related to pragmatic condition,
            159
        parent-child relationship, 162–164
        passive and active behavior, 158–160
        reversal and attitude toward homo-
            sexuality, 160–162
        reversal and homosexual relationship,
            157–160
        reversal in homosexuality, 156–157
        reversal and psychopathology,
            164–165
Genetic (see Heredity)
Genital phobia, 102
Goodenough Draw a Man Test, 34, 37
Gough-Heilbrun Adjective Check List, 51,
    156
Gough Masculinity-Femininity Scale, 44
Greece and homosexuality, 4–5, 83, 152,
    160
Greenwich Village riots, 13
Group stereotype, 223
Groupings, 222
Guatemala vs. United States, 54
    on hostile father/strong mother, 54
Guilt, 106, 224, 225
    over homosexual impulses, 194
Gypsies, 281

Hallucinations in schizophrenia, 181
Heilbrun Adjective Check List, 44
Heredity, 35, 64, 81, 91, 99, 101, 143
Hermaphroditism, 24
Heterophobia, 183, 204
Hirschfeld, M., 27, 34, 203
Homodysphilia, 190
Homophobia, 133, 183, 212, 225,
    262

Homosexual couples and traditional gender
    roles, 158–159
Homosexualities, 193–194, 252
Homosexuals as heretics, 281
Hooker, E., 14, 34, 35, 38, 39, 40, 44, 60,
    62, 65, 88–89, 101, 157, 164
Hormone-brain interaction, 134–143
    and "critical period," 134, 137
Hormone theory, 104–106, 131–143
Hormone-treated pregnancies, 136
Hormones, 9, 16, 64, 145
    androgen, 132, 133, 135, 136, 137, 141,
        142n
    androstenedione, 133, 134
    brain response and life style, 138
    cortisol, 133
    differentiation, 135
    dihydrotestosterone (DHT), 140, 141
    estradiol, 133, 141, 142n
    estrogen, 131, 132, 133, 134, 136, 137,
        140, 141
    estrogen diethylstilbestrol (DES), 141,
        142, 145
    estrone, 141
    gonadal, 135, 138, 145
    gonadotropin, 131, 132, 136n
    luteinizing (LH), 136, 137, 138
    neuroendocrins, 135
    pituitary, 138
    progestins, 140, 141
    sensitivity differences, 138
    sexual orientation, 133–134
    testosterone, 9, 131, 132, 133, 134, 137,
        138, 140, 141–142
Horney, K., 104
Hostility, 82, 86, 91
Humanistic-holistic approach to bisexuality
    and homosexuality, 264–268
Humanistic-holistic principles, 265
Humanistic psychology, 175
Humm-Wadsworth Temperament Scale, 47
Hypnosis, 25, 203
    failure of, 202

Id, 83
Identification, 104
    with aggressor, 91
    feminine, 38
    and homosexuality, 59–60
    males with fathers and mothers, 54, 55,
        62
    and traditional gender roles, 159

Identification (*Cont.*):
  with parents, 101, 254
  sexual, 37, 38, 180
Identity, 48, 83, 237–238, 247–248, 250,
    266
  anxiety, 98
  theory, 256
Immaturity, 93
Imitation, 99
Incarceration, 203
Incest, 27, 28
Incestual feelings, 106
Incidence of homosexuality, 13, 249–250,
    255
Inferiority, 8, 100, 159
Inquisition, 12
Instinctual drive, 27
Institutionalization of homosexuality, 251,
    253, 255, 256
Instrumental learning, 183
Inversion, 3, 24, 37

Jealousy, 180
Jesus, 277
Jews, 6, 271, 281
Johnson, V. E., 81, 85, 111, 112, 195, 201,
    202, 264
Jones, E., 101, 204, 213
Judeo-Christian, 239
  ethics, 6
Jung, C. G., 8

Kallman, F. J., 100–101, 143
Kinsey, A. C., 3, 10, 12, 13, 33, 34, 35–36,
    46, 49, 60, 63, 87, 101, 144–145,
    146, 171, 189, 208, 212, 249, 250,
    253, 255, 264, 272, 274*n*
  Rating Scale, 3–4, 63, 101, 244–245,
    249, 250
Klein, M., 91, 101, 104
Krafft-Ebing, R. V., 7, 24, 25, 34, 202, 213,
    262

Labeling, 16, 212, 213, 225–227, 256
  and cultural relativism, 225
  expected behaviors, 226
  mental illness, 226
  self-identification, 226
  self-labeling, 226

Latent homosexuality, 180
Law and homosexuality, 4, 161
  Carolingian, 6
  Ecclesiastical, 6
  ethics and morals, 273
  in European countries, 6
  Roman, 6
  sodomy, 273
  in United States, 6, 12
Learning, 10
Leonardo da Vinci, Freud on, 263
Lesbian couple:
  mother-daughter roles, 158
Lesbianism in literature, 162
Lesbos, 202
Libido, 97
Little Albert, 182, 183
Lobotomy, 203
Love, 83
Lust, 102
Luther, M., 5

Machover Human Figure Drawing Test, 37
Make a Picture Story, 14, 45, 89
Maladjustment, 83
Masculilne protest, 8, 100
Masculinity/femininity, 59–60, 99, 156–157
  sexual arousal, 266
Masculinization of females and DES, 142
Masculinized brain, 137, 140, 141–142
Masochistic practices, 267
Masters, W. H., 81, 85, 111, 112, 195, 201,
    202, 264
Masturbation, 22, 24, 25
  homosexuality and, 22
  insanity and, 22
  Kinsey on, 272
  orgasm and, 65
Mattachine Society, 12–13, 88
Maturational retardation, 102
Maudsley Personality Inventory, 15
Measurement of homosexual behavior, 114
Meninger Word Association Test, 46
Mental defectiveness of homosexuals vs.
    heterosexuals, 38
Mental disorders, medical model, 11
Mexico and gender role dichotomization,
    160
Minnesota Multiphasic Personality Inven-
    tory (MMPI), 14, 34, 40–42, 45, 50,
    59, 88

Minnesota Multiphasic Personality Inventory (MMPI) (*Cont.*):
    Masculinity-femininity (MF) Scales, 40–42, 59
Money, J., 9–10, 34, 35, 64, 65, 135, 139, 140
Monosymptomatic phobia, 184
Monozygotic studies (*see* Kallman)
Mooney Problem Check List, 45
Moral insanity, 24
Morality:
    deviants, 281
    liberal attitude, 274
    religion, 275–276
    structure of, 275
Morals:
    and deviants, 279, 280
    historical perspectives of, 279–281
    as provincial, 271–272
Morrison vs. State Board of Education, 232
Moscher Forced-Choice Guilt Inventory, 45
Moslems, 271
Mothers of homosexual females, 57–59
    affiliative, 59
    aggressive-dominant, 59
    attitude toward sex, 163
    dominant, 58
    fearful, 58
    inadequate, 58
    independent, 59
    indifference to, 57
    loving, 57, 58–59
    as models, 57
    over burdened, 58
    preoccupied, 58
    rejecting, 57, 58–59
Mothers of homosexual males, 51
    affection, 54, 55
    attitude toward fathers, 54
    attitude toward sex, 163
    as close-binding, 52, 53, 55, 56
    controlling, 52, 54
    devotion to sons, 52
    distant, 59
    dominant, 51, 53–55, 163
    encouraging femininity, 163
    excessive love, hostility, intimacy of, 51, 52
    loving, 56
    and masculine behavior of sons, 55
    nurturant, 54
    and punishment, 54
    rejecting, 56
    and son coalition, 53
    strong, 54
Myths of homosexuality, 243

Narcissistic personality, 93
National Council on Alcoholism, 174
Natural selection, 279
Needs, 223, 227, 228
Netherlands, 48
Neuroendocrine function, 135
    studies, 136–139
Neurosis, 82, 83, 85, 86, 90, 100, 201, 204
    obsessional, 92–93
Neurotic pride and homosexuality, 104
Neuroticism and homosexuality, 60–61
Neuroticism Scale Questionnaire, 45–46
New Testament, 278
Nominalist theory of sexuality, 238–239
Nonpsychopathological homosexuality, 173
Norms, 226
Nosology, 187–188

Object love, 181, 207
Object relation in homosexuality, 90–91
Observational learning, 183
Oedipal fantasies, 180
Oedipus complex, 7–8, 103, 104, 106, 184, 203, 204–205
Old Testament, 278
Orality, 92
Original Sin, 277

Paranoia and homosexuality, 178–182
    and alcohol, 179
    in bars, 179
    delusional thinking, 178, 179
    Freudian clinical syndrome, 179–180
    Freudian theory of, 39, 178–180, 181–182
    humiliation, 180
    jealousy, 179, 180
    megalomania, 178
    and persecutor, 179
    and projection, 179, 181
    and transference, 179
Paranoid disorder, 179, 180
Paranoid reaction, 38

Paranoid schizophrenia, 180–181
  Rorschach responses by males, 39
Parent behavior, 58–59
Parent Behavior Inventory, 55
Parent Characteristics Questionnaire, 57, 59
Parent-child relationship, 48, 51–59, 61–62,
    64, 243
  adjustment of lesbians to, 163–164
  alienation of homosexual females to,
    58, 164
  degree of overt homosexual experience
    in, 56
  and effeminancy in males, 56
  and emotional stability, 163
  and female homosexuals, 57–59
  and homosexuality of delinquent boys,
    55
  and identification of homosexual
    females, 58
  and indifference of females to parents,
    57
  and male homosexuals, 51–57
  and psychiatric position, 254
  and punishment, 116
  and radical behavioral position, 115–116
Parent-Child Relationship Questionnaire,
    56, 57, 58–59
Parental background, 36, 62
Parental guilt, 195
Passive position in homosexual behavior,
    males, 160–161, 251
Pederast, 25
Pedophiles, 37–38, 123
  conversion to heterosexuality, 209
Penile plethysmograph, 123
Perception of homosexuality as threatening,
    227
  education of society, 228
Perception of Parent Behavior Scale, 55
Person perception, 222, 223, 227
Personal Attributes Questionnaire, 55
Personality, 90
  and sexual choice, 244–245
  structure, 92–93
Phallic elements, 92
Phobia, 225
Phobic disorders, 164–165, 182, 204
  psychodynamic explanation of,
    183
Phobic reaction and homosexuality,
    182–184
Physical appearance and sexual preference,
    157

Pituitary glands, 131
Political lesbianism, 234
  feminists and political consciousness,
    234
Polymorphous perversity, 103, 238, 256,
    261
Polysexuality, 103
Power, strivings for, 100
Preadolescent experience, 102
Preferential homosexuality, 255
  primate research on, 255
Pregenital fixation, 8
  sexuality, 203
Pregnancy, 140–142
  diethylstilbestrol (DES) effects on, 141
  and progesterone compounds, 141
  and progestin, 141
Prenatal endocrine disorders, 139–140
  and androgen insensitivity and effects,
    139
  gender identity, 139, 140
Prince, M., 81
Prison, 228–231
  as reinforcing environment, 118–119
Prisoners:
  female, 41, 229–230
  gay, 231
  male, 40, 43, 46, 47, 51, 53, 63,
    230–231
    power roles, 230
    rape, 230
    self-perception, 231
Profile Mood State, 55
Projection and phobia, 183
Promiscuity, 165
Pseudo-homosexuality, 202
Pseudo-love in homosexuality, 91
Psychiatric nosology, 187–188
Psychoanalysis, 28, 47, 82, 83, 90, 93, 125,
    203, 254
  failure of, 202
  as a research tool, 89
Psychodynamics of homosexuality, 90–93
Psychoendocrinology, 132
Psychopathic personality, 100
Psychopathology, 15, 173, 243, 253
  of opposite sex indentification, 253
  of parental relationship 55–56, 254
Psychosis, 100
Puberty and sexual identity, 143–144
Punishment:
  and behavior, 119
  instrumental learning, 183

Rado, S., 98
Rape and childhood, 10
Realist theory of sexuality, 238–239
Regression, 100
Reinforcement:
    effect on behavior, 116–118
    and homosexuality, 118–119
Rejection:
    and compensation in Gay community,
        196
    by family, 196
    fear of, 194
Repression, 263
Research methodology, Siegelman's, 62–67
Reversion, 201
Rogers, C., 65, 67
Rorschach Inkblot Test, 36, 45, 87
    responses to, 40–42
    Wheeler signs, 39–40, 89
Rush, B., 188

Sadistic incorporative impulses, 182
Sadistic practices, 267
Sappho, 4
Schaefer Child Report of Parental
        Behavior Inventory, 58
Schizophrenia, 181, 182, 204
    MMPI responses in, 41
Schreber, case of, 178–179
Self-concept, 15, 48, 50, 62
Self-esteem, 194, 195–196, 210
Self-fulfilling prophecy, 224, 240
Self-perception, 227
Self-restraint, 203
Sex-dimorphic pattern, 137, 156
Sexual development, 8
Sexual deviation, 188, 189
Sexual dysfunction, 201
Sexual encounters, meaning of, 241–243
Sexual orientation disturbance, 189, 190
Sexual parastesia, 81
Sexual patterns, 92
Sexual preference, 62
Sexual revolution, 97, 273
Sexuality and procreation, 98, 241, 251
Short-term psychotherapy, 196
Siegelman-Roe Parent-Child Relationship
        Questionnaire II, 55, 56
Sin and homosexuality, 11, 21
Situation and sexual choice, 245

Sixteen Personality Factor Questionnaire,
        14–15, 43, 45, 48
Skinner, B. F., 10, 123
Socarides, C. W., 51, 87, 88, 91, 189, 206
Social factors, lesbianism, 15
Social perception, 224
Social prejudice, 227
Social problems, 231–234
    child custody, 233
    in employment, 231–232
    of homosexual parent, 232–233
    of lesbian mothers, 233
    in the military, 232
    prejudices, 231
Social development process, 99–100
Social reality, 222, 225
Social skills training, 126
Society and heterosexual expectations, 192
Societies and homosexuality (see Cultures)
Socio-economic class, 15
Socio-economic factors, 63
Sodomy and law, 273
South Africa, 45, 54
Sparta, 202
Stability of homosexual relationships, 48,
        165
Steroid:
    insensitivity, 139
    level, 138
Stereotyping, 223–224, 227, 255
Stigmatization, 224, 247–249, 252, 255,
        256
    and sodomy, Ancient Egypt, 251
Suicide, 15, 165
Sullivan, H. S., 8–9, 102, 103
Superego, 47, 83
Superiority, 8, 100, 159
Symptoms, 82
Szasz, T., 5, 12, 188

Taylor Manifest Anxiety Scale, 46
Teachers Characteristic Schedule, 50
Tennessee Self-Concept Scale, 15, 48, 50
Testicular function, 137–138
Testosterone, 9
Thematic Apperception Test (TAT), 14, 43,
        45, 88, 89
Theories of homosexual etiology:
    criticism of, 256–257
    neo-Freudian, 8, 97–106

Theories of homosexual etiology (*Cont.*):
   psychoanalytic, 7, 90–93, 103, 106, 162, 184, 256, 261–262, 263
   radical behaviorism, 113–120
   Siegelman, 59–62
   Siegelman's bipolar-orthogonal model, 66
   Smith's developmental model, 193–194
Therapists, 86
Therapy (*see* Treatment of homosexuality)
Thompson, C., 9, 102–103, 104
Transference, 179, 207
Transsexualism, 24
Transvesticism, 155
Treatment of homosexuality, 28, 47, 62, 84–86, 120–127, 157
   adjustment therapy, 203
   anticipatory avoidance learning, 207
   assertiveness training in, 209
   and arousal hierarchy and responses, 123–124
   aversive consequences, 123
   avoidance responses, 123
   baseline of, 121, 123–124, 126
   behavioral, 16, 85, 120–127, 184, 207–208
   behavioral techniques, 123–126, 207–208
   by family therapy, 195
   client's choice, 120–121, 195
   client's self-report data, 126
   clinician's choice of, 195
   concept of, 199–202
   conditioning in, 16
   control of reinforcers, 121–122
   critical determinants, 110
   difficulty of change, 121
   discriminative stimulus, 120, 121
   errorless discrimination, 124–125
   ethics, 227–228
   extinction, 122, 208
   fading procedure, 124–125
   generalization, 124, 125
   humanistic-existential, 10–11
   identification of reinforcers, 121
   instrumental learning, 208
   Masters and Johnson position on, 210–211
   modeling, 209
   pedophile, 209, 210
   phobic reaction, 208–209
      prognostic indicators of, 84–85
      psychoanalysis, 84, 209
      psychodynamic approach, 84, 203–207
      psychotherapy in, 85, 86, 93, 202
      punishment, 122
      results of, 85
      role playing in, 209
      self-esteem, 210
      sex partner, 125–126
      social pressure, 214
      social reinforcement in, 209
      string gauge, 123, 125
      systematic desensitization in, 209
      treatability, 84–86
      Tripps's view of, 212
      vs. internal value, 214
      with classical conditioning, 207–208
      with desensitization, 209
      with electric shock, 123
      with hypnosis, 85
      with in vivo approach, 122
Triangular System Hypothesis, 61
Tribadism, 158
Tripp, C. A., 10–11, 60, 65, 211–212
Twin studies, 100–101, 143
Typecasting and security, 250

Ulrichs, K. H., 23
Unconscious conflict, 179
Unconscious homosexuality, 180
Unconscious paranoid sexual fantasy, 182
Urning, 23, 262
U.S. Supreme Court, 12

Values, 222–223, 225, 227, 228

Washington University Sentence Completion Test, 50
Weinberg, M. S., 48, 49, 62–64, 89, 135, 146, 182, 193–194, 248, 252
Western paradigms of homosexuality, 242–243
Western psychiatric thinking, 249
Westphal, C., 23, 25
Wolpe, J., 85
Women's genitals, perception of as castrating, 104